Urbanism and Globalization

The European City in Transition

Edited by Frank Eckardt
and Dieter Hassenpflug

Band 2

PETER LANG

Frankfurt am Main · Berlin · Bern · Bruxelles · New York · Oxford · Wien

Frank Eckardt/Dieter Hassenpflug (eds.)

Urbanism and Globalization

PETER LANG
Europäischer Verlag der Wissenschaften

Bibliographic Information published by Die Deutsche Bibliothek
Die Deutsche Bibliothek lists this publication in the Deutsche Nationalbibliografie; detailed bibliographic data is available in the internet at <http://dnb.ddb.de>.

This book has been realized with the support of the
European Commission
and the Deutsche Forschungsgemeinschaft.

ISSN 1619-375X
ISBN 3-631-50744-5
US-ISBN 0-8204-7363-4

© Peter Lang GmbH
Europäischer Verlag der Wissenschaften
Frankfurt am Main 2004
All rights reserved.

All parts of this publication are protected by copyright. Any utilisation outside the strict limits of the copyright law, without the permission of the publisher, is forbidden and liable to prosecution. This applies in particular to reproductions, translations, microfilming, and storage and processing in electronic retrieval systems.

Printed in Germany 1 2 3 4 6 7

www.peterlang.de

The European Cities in Transition Series

Cities are a mirror of society and a motor of change. Especially the challenges produced by the growing interconnection of people and places find their spatial organisation in the world's metropolis. Globalization shapes new forms of economy, culture and social life and it comes all together in the historically grown European city. The increasing of mobility and communication brings forward the key questions of urban life again: How can the heritages of a European city been transmitted to a city in times of profound changes? What does it mean for political, cultural, social and architectural decision makers to act in an urban setting transformed by major societal trends?

The "European Cities in Transition Series" aims at publishing answers from all disciplines that are dedicated to find theoretical and practical solutions for the European City under the circumstances of the globalization and the unification of Europe. Edited by Dieter Hassenpflug and Frank Eckardt who both work at the Bauhaus-Universität Weimar, the tradition of the first Bauhaus is remembered: The Bauhaus architects like Mies van der Rohe and Walter Gropius have been searching for adequate solutions for the city of modernity. Today, this spirit has to be brought in, again. The post-national age requires new approaches for understanding the European city. Bringing together the findings of research of scientists, city planers and architectures, the series will focus on different aspects of the current transition of urban life.

First volume: Consumption and the Post-Industrial City
Second volume: Urbanism and Globalization
Third volume: City Images and Urban Regeneration

Forthcoming:

The City and the Region

Paths of Urban Transformation

Contents

Germany, Weimar and the Bauhaus:
A Micro-Analysis of Globalization
DieterHassenpflug   15

Urbanism and Globalization: Introduction
Frank Eckardt   23

1. Cities and global hierarchies

European cities in a global world
Peter Hall   31

Ukrainian Cities as a Gateway to the Global Innovative Economy
Olga Mrinska   47

Globalization and third-tier cities: the European experience
Mark Jayne   65

2. Global Cities from the Inside

The Dark Side of Really Existing Globalization
Peter Marcuse   87

Welfare and Immigrants' Inclusion in a Context of Weak Civil Society:
Associations and local politics in Oeiras (Lisbon)
Margarida Marques and Rui Santos   107

Shaping the identity and mobilising the "ethnic capital"
in three European cities
Lionel Arnaud and Gilles Pinson   131

Baby Bronks: Place and Identity in a Parisian Banlieue
Leeke Reinders   151

The houses of foreign gods
Tuomas Martikainen   175

3. Middle Ground and actors of global urbanism

Living the globalising city: globalisation in the context of
European urban development.
John Eade   191

Globalisation, Eyes and Urban Space: Visual Perception
of Globalising Prague
Jana Temelová, Hedvika Hrychová 203

Learning from „CHINA" or Urban design beyond modern time
Carl Fingerhuth 223

Linking the local and the global:
transnational architects in a globalizing world
Paul Kennedy 231

4. Planning as Politics of Global Urbanism

Large-Scale Urban Waterfront Developments as an Integral Part
of the Metropolitan Transformation Process:
Case Studies from Lyon, Hamburg, and Gdańsk
Alexander Tölle 251

The 'new' Berlin: multiple spatial conceptions of the capital city
in the 'Palast der Republik'/ 'Stadtschloss' debate
Monika de Frantz 261

Towards a sustainable post-suburbia?
The sustainability of new economic centres in European
metropolitan regions
Marco Bontje 279

A society to match the scenery: ordering the spaces of the Veneto
città diffusa
Luiza Bialasiewicz 297

5. Global Urbanism as European Concept?

City of Angels? Lives and Struggles of Migrants in Bangkok
Alexander Horstmann 327

Globalisation and Urbanism: the case of a European peripheral
region, Guadeloupe.
Karine Dupré 341

Contributors

Lionel Arnaud is lecturer in sociology at the Institut Universitaire de Technologie and member of the Centre de Recherches sur l'Action Politique en Europe (CRAPE-CNRS/ Institut d'Etudes Politiques de Rennes / Université Rennes 1). He has published recently: "Sport as a Cultural System. Sport Policies and (New) Ethnicities in Lyon and Birmingham" (IJURR, Vol. 26.3, 2002). He's editor of "Les minorités et l'Union européenne. Politiques, Mobilisations, Identités" (2003). Contact: lionelarno@aol.com

Marco Bontje is postdoctoral fellow at the Department of Geography and Planning of the University of Amsterdam and Marie Curie host fellow at the Institut für Länderkunde in Leipzig. In 2001 he completed his PhD thesis on the results of national urbanisation policy in the Netherlands. His research interests include the urbanisation process, national and regional planning policy and sustainable urban and regional development. Contact: M_Bontje@ifl-leipzig.de

Luiza Bialasiewicz is Lecturer in Geography at the Department of Geography, University of Durham. Her research interests lie with the geographies of European integration and the politics of memory and commemoration in European cities. The chapter in this volume is based on research carried out as part of a project on "Regional Identity and European Citizenship" funded by the Economic and Social Research Council of the U.K. and part of the "One Europe or Several?" research programme. Contact: luiza.bialasiewicz@durham.ac.uk

Karine Dupré is architect and researcher at the Institute of Urban Planning at the Tampere Technological University. She is currently completing her PhD thesis on typo-morphology, modernity and urban development in Guadeloupe, a French Overseas Caribbean Region. Contact: karine.dupre@tut.fi

John Eade is Professor of Sociology and Anthropology and Executive Director of the Centre for Research on Nationalism, Ethnicity and Multiculturalism (CRONEM) at the University of Surrey, UK. His research interests are in identity politics, local/global processes, travel and pilgrimage. His publications include "Placing London: From Imperial Capital to Global City" (2000), "The Politics of Community" (1989), the edited volume "Living the Global City" (1997) and the co-edited "Understanding the City: Contemporary and Future Perspectives" (2002), "Contesting the Sacred: The Anthropology of Pilgrimage and Reframing Pilgrimage: Cultures in Motion" (2004). Contact: J.Eade@surrey.ac.uk

Frank Eckardt is Junior Professor for the Sociology of globalization and is working as an urban sociologist at the European Urban Studies programme of the Bauhaus-Universität Weimar, where he is the local organizer of the "European Cities in Transition Conference" Series. He has finished his PhD at the University of Kassel in political science. Recent publication: "Soziologie der Stadt" (2004). Contact: Frank.Eckardt@archit.uni-weimar.de

Carl Fingerhuth is Professor at the Technical University of Darmstadt, Germany. Architect graduated from the Federal Institute of Technology in Zürich (ETH-Z). He had an office for urban design in Zürich between 1964 and 1978. He worked as an urban designer of the canton in Basel (1979–94). He is since 1995 Consultant for Urban Design. Contact: carl@fingerhuth.com

Monika de Frantz is a Ph.D. candidate in social and political sciences at the European University Institute, Florence. Working at the European Commission and at the United Nations as well as in journalism and urban politics, she has (co-)authored research and publications on European integration, political economy and urban politics. She is about to complete a Ph.D. thesis on cultural aspects of urban governance in Vienna and Berlin. Her research interests encompass the study of spatial concepts in politics and society, urban and regional politics, European integration, multi-level governance, culture and political identities etc. Contact: monika.defrantz@iue.it

Peter Hall is Professor of Planning at the Bartlett School of Architecture, Building, Environmental Design and Planning at the University College, London and director of the Institute of Community Studies. He was previously Professor of Urban and Regional Planning at the University of California, Berkeley, and Professor of Geography at the University of Reading. He is the author of over 30 books in planning and related subjects, including *London 2000, The World Cities, Great Planning Disasters* and *High Tech America*. He has been credited with the invention of the Urban Enterprise Zone concept now widely employed in the USA, the UK and Europe. An advisor to governments and international agencies across the world, Professor Hall is known throughout the world for his contribution both to the theory and practice of city and regional planning. Contact: phall@icstudies.ac.uk

Dieter Hassenpflug is Professor for Sociology and Social History of the City at the Bauhaus-Universität Weimar. He studied ecomomics, sociology and philosophy at the Free University Berlin and Kassel University. He was a lecturer at the Technical University of Berlin, the Berlin College of Economics, Kassel University and at the J. W. Goethe-University, Frankfurt. He was curator of the EXPO 2000 projects in Saxony-Anhalt 1995–2000 and is Director of the Institute for European Urban Studies at the Bauhaus-Universität Weimar and of the EuroConferences Series "The European City in Transition" at Weimar 2001–2003. Contact: hassenpf@archit.uni-weimar.de

Alexander Horstmann is a social anthropologist, specialising on the Societies and Cultures of Southeast Asia. He is currently working on his habilitation thesis on ethnohistory of Southern Thailand/Northern Malaysia at the Institute for Ethnology at the University of Münster. He lectured at Humboldt-University, Berlin and at the University of Bielefeld. He was visiting associate professor at Tokyo University of Foreign Studies. Among his publications are: "Class, Culture and Space. The Construction and Shaping of Communal Space in South Thailand" (2002); and co-editor of "Integration durch Verschiedenheit". His interests cover urban anthropology, borderlands and identity politics. Contact: alexander.horstmann@bitel.net

Hedvika Hrychová is a PhD candidate in urban geography at Charles University in Prague, Department of Social Geography and Regional Development. She is currently working on her thesis focused on inner-city neighbourhoods change; revitalisation, gentrification and globalisation processes in urban structure. Contact: expirata@hotmail.com

Paul Kennedy is a reader in sociology and global studies at Manchester Metropolitan University. He is a founding member and current secretary of the Global Studies Association. Among his recent publications are: 'Global Sociology', co-authored with Robin Cohen;'Globalization and National Identities: Crisis or Opportunity?' co-edited with Catherine Danks; and 'Communities across Borders: New Immigrants and Transnational Cultures', co- edited with Victor Roudometof. Contact: P.Kennedy@mmu.ac.uk

Mark Jayne has taught Cultural Studies and Sociology at the University of Birmingham and Staffordshire University, where he is currently a research fellow in the Cultural Trends Unit. His research interests include consumption, city cultures, urban regeneration, creative industries and cultural policy. Mark is currently co-editing a book (with David Bell) entitled "City of Quarters: Urban Villages in the Contemporary City" (forthcoming). Contact: m.jayne@staffs.ac.uk

Peter Marcuse, a lawyer and urban planner, is Professor of Urban Planning at Columbia University in New York City. He has been involved with urban policy for many years. He was Majority Leader of Waterbury, Connecticut's Board of Alderman (City Council), a member of its City Planning Commission, later President of the Los Angeles Planning Commission, and more recently a member of Community Board 9 in Manhattan and co-chair of its Housing Committee. He was in the private practice of law in Waterbury for over 20 years, then was Professor of Urban Planning, first at the University of California at Los Angeles from 1975 to 1978, since then at Columbia University. He spent two years, 1981 and 1989, in Germany, West and East, and taught in Australia and South Africa. Contact: m35@columbia.edu

M. Margarida Marques is professor at the Department of Sociology and co-director of SociNova/Migration, School for Social and Human Sciences - New University of Lisbon. She is the author or co-author, among others, of: "Politics, welfare and the rise of immigrant participation in a Portuguese suburban context during the 1990s", in A. Rodgers and J. Tillie (org.), *Multicultural policies and modes of citizenship in European cities* (2001); "Ariadne's thread: Cape Verdean women in transnational webs", *Global Networks* (2001). Contact: mm.marques@fcsh.unl.pt

Tuomas Martikainen is a PhD candidate and a teacher at the Department of Comparative Religion at the Abo Akademi University, Finland. He will defend his PhD on immigrant religions in the City of Turku in winter 2003. He has published several articles on immigrant religions in Finland. Contact: tuomas.martikainen@abo.fi.

Olga Mrinska studied Economic Geography and International Economy at the Kyiv National Taras Shevchenko University, Geographic faculty (1998). She is lecturer in the same University since 2002 – courses on management of regional development and regional policy and completed her PhD Thesis 'Experience of Regional Policy in the European Union and Possibilities of its Implementation in Ukraine' at the National Academy of Science of Ukraine. Different publications of regional and spatial development, international and Ukrainian experience of regional policy etc. Since 2002 she is an advisor to the Ministry of Economy and European Integration of Ukraine. Contact: olga@largis.kiev.ua

Gilles Pinson is currently EU Marie Curie Research Fellow of the Centre for Sustainable Urban and Regional Futures of the Salford University, UK. He is also an Associated member of the Centre de Recherches sur l'Action Politique en Europe, Rennes. Among his recent publications: "Political government and governance: strategic planning and the reshaping of political capacity in Turin", IJURR, 26-3, September 2002; "Des villes et des projets. Changement dans l'action publique et institutionalisation de nouveaux territoires politiques", in Fontaine/Hassenteufel (eds) To Change or not to Change? Les changements dans l'action publique à l'épreuve du terrain (2002). Contact: pinsong@aol.com

Leeke Reinders is an anthropologist and works at the OTB Research Institute for Housing, Urban and Mobility Studies, University of Technology in Delft. This paper is based on a four month fieldwork study in Sarcelles. His research topics include the social production and construction of space, and processes of urban renewal and social-spatial segregation in urban neighbourhoods. Currently he is doing research on strategies and practices of image- and identity transformation of restructuring neighbourhoods in the Netherlands. Contact: reinders@otb.tudelft.nl.

Rui Santos is professor at the Department of Sociology and researcher at SociNova/Migration, School for Social and Human Sciences - New University of Lisbon. He is the author or co-author, among others, of: "Politics, welfare and the rise of immigrant participation in a Portuguese suburban context during the 1990s", in A. Rodgers and J. Tillie (org.), *Multicultural policies and modes of citizenship in European cities* (2001); "Ariadne's thread: Cape Verdean women in transnational webs", *Global Networks* (2001).

Jana Temelová is a PhD candidate in urban geography at Charles University in Prague, Department of Social Geography and Regional Development. She is currently working on her thesis focused on real estate development and city promotion, namely on public authorities as developers and investors of "high-profile projects". Contact: dobrickov@hotmail.com

Alexander Tölle is an urban planner and has completed the MSc-course in European Urban Studies at the Bauhaus-University Weimar. He is currently a PhD candidate within the «Europa-Fellows Programme» at the Spatial Economy Department of Collegium Polonicum in Słubice, a joint Polish-German institution of Adam-Mickiewicz-University Poznań and of Europa-University Viadrina Frankfurt/Oder. He is completing his thesis on the conditions for large-scale urban developments in the transformation process of metropolises in France, Germany, and Poland. This year he is co-editing a book on interdisciplinary borderland research from the Polish-German perspective. Contact: atoelle_2000@yahoo.de

Germany, Weimar and the Bauhaus
A Micro-Analysis of Globalization

Dieter Hassenpflug

In the debates on the future of the German society following the elections in September 2002, the word "globalization" was mentioned remarkably often, even more frequently than usually. Evidently "globalization" plays an important role in the strategic orientation of German politics ("our future is global"). On the other hand it serves for a measure to evaluate the present German condition ("Germany is not fit for globalization, yet"). Sometimes it sounds as if "globalization" is the title of a book filled with regulations for up-to-date politics - including the call for shifting down national politics ("the future of Germany is located in Europe"). And some other time it sounds as if "globalization" is the powerful ghost of postmodern times looking like a Sphinx, rapidly changing its expression from the threatening to the promising. So the debates sway between fear and hope, rejection and desire, pessimism and optimism. To put it in one word: In Germany "globalization" has become a synonym for "the big challenge of our times".

Moreover "globalization" has become a kind of source of light illuminating things in a new and different way, a spiritual means of understanding, legitimizing and restructuring things. According to the terminology of contemporary philosophy we call this a "dispositive". The impact of this dispositive can easily be demonstrated in the different way of interpreting the process of the European unification. In the first period following its foundation in the fiftieth the EU (EC) aimed at integrating the western part of Germany into Western Europe. The main instruments to get there were a common market and a strong transatlantic tie (NATO).

In the meantime - already starting before 1989 - the European Union stands for a transnational European response to the challenges of globalization. It is now the existence of the triad North America, Eastern Asia and Europe that seems to give the EU the raison d'être. (c.f.: Ohmae 1995) Gradually the idea of the "United States of Europe" superimposes the former vision of a Europe of the Regions.

By the way: "America". Today it's largely agreed that it's impossible to deal with "globalization" without considering the overwhelming economical, political and cultural influence of the USA. From a European and even more from a German point of view the United States is already a transnational nation, if you like: a globalized nation in itself. While the German cultural identity seems to be more or less exclusive until today, and in the consequence regionally bound, the US cultural identity appears all in all extremely inclusive. As it includes so many different ethnical groups and cultures creating a pluralistic (although highly segregated) societal and cultural universe, the US culture and its corresponding ways of life have this high potential of connectivity that we can experience all over the world. Each culture finds elements of its own in the US-culture using them as a bridge to America. But these bridges are no one way connections. The images and signs of Hollywood, CNN, Disney, Miami, Las Vegas etc. use them for migrating worldwide. So globalization means not only "everything is everywhere" but also "McDonalds, Starbucks, Coca Cola, Microsoft or Halloween, Hula Hoop and Rap is everywhere.

What about Germany? On the one hand it is a highly integrated part of transnational Europe; on the other hand it sometimes appears to me like a fortress, similar to Renaissance ideal city-drawings showing these massive fortifications. If flexibility, flexible regulation, flexible accumulation of capital etc. are describing the post-fordist condition and if post-fordism is an indispensable dimension of "globalization" than Germany is not yet a part of the globalized world. The German social welfare state, although it calls itself a society of dialogue and consensus, appears at present extremely inflexible and unable to communicate and balance particular interests. Predominantly this country seems to be characterized by a very powerful corporatism, only comparable with the role of the various brotherhoods in the former feudal society. In Germany it increasingly happens for example that entrepreneurs, having a well filled order book, refuse to take on additional labour because they fear the consequences of the very strict regulations for protection against dismissal. It's not only the labour unions but also the powerful corporations of medicines, craftsmen, industrials, farmers, health assurances, state officials and many others who block each other and by this contribute to a kind of new German stagnation ("the new German disease" as it is frequently called in certain media). One thing is for sure, certainly: all in all there is still a lack of a culture of individual and civil responsibility and an unbalanced surplus of governmental and bureaucratic patronage in our society.

Amazingly there is a lot of self-confidence concerning the "consensual society" moderated by government. However, most of these practices aim at short-term problem solving with a domestic, i.e. a narrow problem horizon. So it is no surprise that all those who need and want more civil society, i.e. more entrepreneurship, more decentred negotiations and more individual responsibility, but less state or public clientele, i.e. less regulation and less state economy use "globalization" as a kind of weapon. On the other hand: While pointing at the German welfare state fortress critically they hopefully know something about the possibility of co-lateral damaging.

Although Germany is still a strong fordist bastion, the borderless flows of informational, cultural, technological and economical globalization penetrate its heavy armours like X-rays a human body inducing changes in every part and dimension: not only on the institutional level but also in every day life, not only in the physical environment but also in the brains and not only in the economically powerful urban regions in the western and southern parts of Germany but also in the province. So let us zoom down to Weimar located in the state of Thuringia where the biggest city, the capital Erfurt, has less than 200 thousand inhabitants, where less than 2% of the people are migrants (foreigners) and where we have a mortality surplus of 2,5% of the whole population (which indicates strong overaging). This does not sound very global. Anyway - this part of the world is touched by globalization too. Let's start a short micro-analysis of the place where we are right now: the Bauhaus-Universität Weimar.

As known, this institution traces its origins back to the old Bauhaus which was founded in Weimar in 1919. In the 20th this school of arts and architecture has been a contested but nevertheless influential ideological centre of the spatial dimension of fordism. Along with some others (like Le Corbusier) the Bauhaus protagonists gave (first) modernity its spatial image. Ever since fordist space production, being characterized by acceleration, specialisation and economical efficiency, dresses in Bauhaus style. This style, which makes constructions look fast, productive and efficient (even if they are not) refers to a narrative, the myth of the Bauhaus, which prominently migrates totally detached from its local origins in the channels of the global informational flows.

Today the radiation of globalization has also reached the German university. Everybody who knows about the strong influence of the Humboldt ideas connecting "Ausbildung and Bildung" (professional education and intellectual culture) and who additionally knows about the strong traditions of the Prussian institutions can imagine the problems we are facing and the efforts we are undertaking to make this academic body sensitive for the new landscapes, territories and geographies of transnational interactions. To give you an idea about the extension and depth of the changes running, let's have a brief look at the international oriented European Urban Studies programme at the Bauhaus-Universität Weimar which combines four disciplines: urban design, urban sociology, urban management and urban planning.

Right from the beginning the idea of establishing a postgraduate master programme at the faculty of architecture was a reaction on the dramatic changes that take place on the field of post fordist space production. Most of these changes are driven by globalization. During the last 50 years the bachelor and master degree and other Anglo-Saxon certificates and grades have become more or less world wide agreed standards. Four years ago our master programme was one of the first at German universities and it is still the only existing at the faculties of architecture. It's only two years ago when the university started adding bachelor and master studies to the traditional diploma-studies in other faculties. And only three month ago, in October 2002, we started with a European Urban Studies doctoral programme which is sponsored by the DAAD, the world-wide operating German Academic Exchange Service. To emphasize the global impact of this programme they called it PHD which sounds like the Anglo-Saxon doctor-title but the meaning is: Promotionen an Hochschulen in Deutschland (Doctoral Studies at Universities in Germany).

Let's continue our micro-analysis by offering a short interpretation of the term "European Urban Studies". This title expresses our conviction that only profound knowledge about the traditions and features of the European city enables people, students and scholars to participate fruitfully in global debates on and efforts for the future of the cities wherever they are. I am not totally sure if this example fits to what Robertson has called "glocalization". In any case our choice reflects the experience of a general indispensability of difference for any kind of perception and understanding.

Although most of the new bachelor- and master-programmes at German universities are run in English language, we decided to run our programmes in both languages, in English and German. There are several reasons for this. Instead of being neutral instruments of mutual understanding languages are socio-cultural memories and tools of social construction. May be in natural and technical sciences it makes no difference if you communicate in Latin, German or English. However, in cultural sciences and practices language matters. Let me give only one example by picking up the German word "urban" which is quite different from the word "städtisch" - although in everyday language both terms are very often used synonymously. "Urban" refers first of all to the strong and long lasting courteous traditions in Germany and continental Europe in the whole. In a first step you can translate it with 'civil, polite or genteel (urbane) behaviour'.

Simmel, Bahrt and other German sociologists expanded the meaning of "urban" by connecting it with many typical behavioural patterns that are typical for big city dwellers, i.e. for individuals who permanently live under urban conditions characterized by high density, big size and social, cultural and ethnical heterogeneity. Big city dwellers for example seem to be blasé (Simmel decodes this attitude as a psychic reaction, as a kind of protection against the permanent challenge of the crowd), or nervous, they speak faster than people from the country, they seem to be more innovative, open minded, intellectually oriented etc. In the meantime the meanings of "urban" even cover the functional and aesthetical features that are either typical for urban spaces (i.e. the competence of centrality) or, as in normative approaches, responsible for transforming urban space (in the sense of 'städtisch') into urban space (in the sense of 'urban').

Moreover our decision for two languages is an offer for a better cultural integration of students. In the recent years we met many foreign students (e.g. funded by the Socrates-Program of the DAAD) who only visit the still rare English lectures, ending their studies in Germany without being confronted with the academic challenges and chances of German language. Due to the touch of the global flow the portion of foreign students at the university increases from about 2% to now more than 12% in the past three years. (In European Urban Studies the portion reached more than 50% in 2003). Also the number of international congresses and the number of nations and countries participating is increasing rapidly during the last years. For the EuroConference "Urbanism and Globalization" we welcomed participants from 23 nations.

In the meantime we even started to export the design of our European Urban Studies master programme to foreign countries, e.g. the Tonghi-University in Shanghai, China. This project aims at creating a platform for bilateral urban studies. During the UIA World Congress of Architecture in July 2002 in Berlin leading representatives of the Tonghi University signed with us a pre-contract (project agreement) which has become part of a general agreement on the university level signed by the president of the Tonghi-University and the Bauhaus-University in Shanghai in March 2003.

There are more traces of globalization to be find nearby: We are about to install a new internationally oriented professorship titled "Sociology of Globalization" in the context of our Institute of European Urban Studies. Moreover we are examining and changing our curriculum and we adjust the job descriptions of our programmes to globalization: So we do not educate architects or regional planners conventionally. Our programme aims at the new professional identities of urban managers (urban curators or urban imagineers). We detach the job descriptions from the traditional academic disciplines and attach them to real subjects, e.g. to the city. This thematisation of academic studies is a precondition for educating "specialists for interrelations", as Ulrich Beck puts it. As a consequence of all these efforts and changes on the micro level the Bauhaus-Universität Weimar will be pushed gradually into a new international, globalized and very flexible post-fordistic academic landscape.

Let's finally examine some traces of globality in Weimar.

Weimar is one of the most important places of national cultural identity in Germany. One reason for this outstanding prominence is the role some of its inhabitants played at the time of the proto-bourgeois court society in the German enlightenment movement. This movement had, as everybody knows, a global humanistic intellectual horizon. In the periodic system of Robertson it belongs to the "Incipient Phase" of globalization, the period of nation state construction. Some of the most important representatives of this movement lived in Weimar, first of all Herder, but also Wieland, Schiller and Goethe. They all followed enthusiastically the ideas of Emmanuel Kant who is the most important thinker of German origin until today. He was the first German philosopher who really thought globally - although he never left the city of Königsberg during his life time. This biographic note demonstrates, by the way, the ability of true cities (and true cities have always been trading centres) to bring the world, its people, its commodities, its customs and its ideas to the place.

Herder in Weimar was the first who collected songs from all over the world. He called his edition "Voices of the Peoples in Songs" and his philosophical opus magnum was titled "Ideas about the Philosophy of History of Mankind". He already had what we call today a global awareness - although he was living in province most of his lifetime. This biographic note gives us another advice: The civil virtues of people are grounded in their self-consciousness and personality. These virtues are not mere functions of the habitat. There are people who live for long times in places like Berlin, London, New York, Tokio etc. without changing their narrow-mindedness. On the other hand big cities offer social, cultural and spatial opportunities which can help people to open their mind.

There is another side of the Weimar narrative: As everybody knows this city was severely affected by the darkest sides of German history. The keyword is Buchenwald. There are so many reasons for the catastrophe of German nation building, but one of them is of highest interest to urbanism: It's the trend of culture pessimism.

In Germany the process of modernization and the emergence of the big industrial cities in the 19th century were not only reflected as the end of urban history (which was the position of Marx and Max Weber) but also as the end of urban culture which was the position of the culture pessimists. At that time big city criticism arose everywhere in the world where industrialization took place, in France, England, North America etc. But the conclusions drawn from these western countries were pragmatic in general. Take for example the garden city visions starting at the french revolution and not ending in those of Ebenezer Howard. Not so in Germany. Here modernization-criticism and big city-criticism goes deeper and gradually turned into a radical antagonistic position.

Ferdinand Tönnies, one of the outstanding German sociologists of the end of the 19th century, was a representative of this movement. He interprets the emerging big city as an expression of the decline of western civilization. Tönnies: "In the village the oikos (the old agrarian household, oriented to autarky and devoted to the pre-civic idea of "good life") is independent and strong and in the city it survives in the shape of the bourgeois oikos growing into beauty. In the big city the oikos turns into the sterile, narrow, worthless and became a mere shelter detached from any place, a shelter which can be get for money at any time - a shelter being nothing else than a home on the trip, in the world." (Tönnies 1991, 135) He agreed with the categorical system of Marx connecting market economy, society and city on one hand and oikos, community and country life on the other hand. He also accepted his diagnosis about modernity which replaces the urban stage of emancipation by the nation state and - following - the world state. While Marx, however, identified capitalism, bourgeois emancipation and big industrial cities as preconditions for a world wide socialist revolution, Tönnies regarded the same preconditions as the beginning of the catastrophe of modernization. In this respect he's very near to the arguments of his contemporary Oswald Spengler, author of the famous book titled "Der Untergang des Abendlandes" (Decline of the Occident), written during World War II. In 1883 Tönnies stated: "The more the societal condition (pushes back the community condition and) gains influence in a nation or in a group of nations, the more this whole country or this whole world tend to be only one big world wide city." (Tönnies 1991, 211)

The latent enmity against "modernization" (which in this respect is only another word for "globalization") by intellectuals from Heinrich Riehl via Tönnies up to Oswald Spengler has strongly influenced the construction of the ideology of the National Socialist Movement. Here the culture pessimism turned into fanatical, merciless hate against the big city. For these people the terms big city, capitalism, communism and Judaism (Jewry) were nothing but a chain of synonyms.

In Weimar we can study the different aspects of this way of looking at things: First of all it was the favourite city of Hitler. Because of its size (and supported by the loyalty of its dwellers) Weimar was treated by Hitler as a kind of ideal city for his project. He visited it nearly 40 times. He helped his friend Giessler, an architect from Munich, in designing the new Elephant Hotel. It is, in addition, no surprise that Weimar became the first place to realize a so called Gauforum which is a fascist reinvention of the forum romanum. This project expresses the pragmatic change in dealing with the big city during the World War II. The Weimar Gauforum was also designed by Giessler and the only one that was finished in construction.

As a result of both, the history of enlightenment and of fascism, and enriched by many other events like the foundation and the chasing away of the Bauhaus, Weimar became a Symbol for what we can call the German tragedy. Today the myths of Weimar are stronger then ever. They help the city to get hold of a comfortable position in the global landscapes of media or "mediascapes" (Appadurai 1992).

Weimar is a nice looking city, a little "Disneyworld" faking its own images and staging its own narratives. However, everybody who is delighted with the old European charm of its centre should be aware of the fact that the way of looking at its spacial appearance has dramatically changed in the past twenty or thirty years. Its not so long ago when this kind of slow, ornamental, bourgeois, staged and mixed urban textures were experienced in Germany as an aesthetical affront, as the presence of a past that is either poisoned by politics or by an ideologically rejected class. But the post-war period of fordist urban iconoclasm is over. With a little cryptic "help" from a powerful and world wide operating media industry - of Disney, Time-Warner, and many other suppliers of imagineering and citytainment - and completed by a big portion of post fordist reflexivity, we regained our ability to assess the urban and rural spaces not only according to their functional performance but also to their social and cultural meaning, i.e. to their form and aesthetics.

References:

Appadurai, A. (1992) Disjuncture and Difference in the Global Cultural Economy. In:
    Featherstone, M. (eds.) Global Culture – Nationalism, Globalization and
    Modernity. London: Sage.
Albrow, M. (1996) The Global Age – State and Society beyond Modernity.
    Cambridge: Polity Press.
Beck, U. (1997) Was ist Globalisierung? Irrtümer des Globalismus – Antworten auf
    Globalisierung. Frankfurt: Suhrkamp.
Castells, M. (1994) Space of Flows - Raum der Ströme. In: P. Noller; W. Prigge and
    K. Ronneberg (eds) Stadt-Welt. Frankfurt: Campus
Dürrschmidt, J. (2002) Globalisierung. Bielefeld: transcript.
Ohmae K. (1995) The End of the Nation State. London: Harper Collins.
Tönnies, F. (1991) Gemeinschaft und Gesellschaft. Darmstadt: Wiss.
    Buchgesellschaft
Weber, M. (1981) Wirtschaftsgeschichte. Berlin: UTB

Urbanism and Globalization
(Introduction)   *Frank Eckardt*

Urbanism as a way of life has captured the scientific imagination from the beginning of the social sciences. Throughout the course of human history, the construction of urban societies has influenced basic concepts of societal organisation. Although viewed from different perspectives, this incomplete and even accelerated urbanisation form the basis for an analysis of social and political configurations either to regulate and or stimulate the individual life. Observing growth and city-formation might be an impressive phenomenon, but this is far from being a self-explanatory, social fact. Urban life's reflections constitute a broader framework regarding both social life and the political system at large.

"Urbanism as A Way of Life" is the title of a paradigmatic article by a prominent scholar from the Chicago School of urban sociology (Wirth 1938). Louis Wirth, in his contribution to the American Journal of Sociology, concisely defined his perspective on urbanism after three decades of urban research at the Chicago Institute. Most striking was his attempt to crystallize and filter those factors, which evidently constitute the urban context. Wirth identified three prerogative characteristics. Urban life can be found and researched when people gather in large numbers and in considerable density. Urban life, he concluded, is therefore a big city phenomenon. Georg Simmel's psychological approach to define mental life in the big city, as creating a nervous form of self-protecting perceptions, has apparently influenced Wirth's perspective (Simmel 1995). In his article, Wirth reflects not only on the basic ecological approach to urban life but also expresses a scientific perspective, common to public debate on the vitality of city life.

Therefore, it is important for us to move away from theories of symbolic interactionism and their implications for urban sociology. Instead, we have to come to terms with Wirth's approach and the Chicago School The word "urbanism" should be linked to some other form of urban life that transcends the superficial fact that there is human life in cities. We can understand this approach first by looking at human geography of cities and its social implications. One could empathise with the early pioneers and their work and have some mercy with their linking of social sciences to biological comparisons. What is lacking, however, in their analysis of urban life is the basic assumption that society is predominantly grounded. Place matters in the sense, that it is not only the stage for human interaction but also a decisive influence for or that it presupposes urban life. This argument leads us to the question, in which way does place (often seen as the physical site of urban life) and space (mostly viewed as including a societal aspect) are evocating each other. Second, how could we distinguish between place and space analytically?

Recent literature on urbanism, many scholars have expressed their impression that there is a fundamental shift in what once defined relations between the "here" in the objective, environmental, built, and real world and the "abstract", subjective, communicated and mental side of urban life. After more than two decades on world city research, it is common in urban sciences to associate "globalization" with this fundamental yet instinctive tendency. Having once started with the analysis of dependencies and rankings of cities across national borders, the research on how globalization and cities are to be connected in analytical terms has reached a high level of research. Current studies and considerations depict the spectator surrounded with a wide range of sophisticated but controversial approaches and research results. Does this development necessarily mean that we have lost an overview and there has been no progress in our understanding of the apparently interrelated world of the global and the local?

This volume is constructed and written and with the hope and strong belief that confusion is a good starting point for achieving new insights. The editors, therefore, are quite optimistic about the articles presented here. They can contribute to expand our knowledge on the complex relationship between the globalising city and the localizing world. The volume takes the stance that the conceptualization of urban life under global conditions can only be reflected from multiple points of departure. The editors are not advocating a theoretical approach that accepts differences in conceptualizing urban globalities or global urbanism as unsolvable contradictions, fashionable expressions of a wrongly understood postmodernism or the end of the road of rational understandings of the urban chaos. On the contrary, this volume is meant to confront certain aspects of urban discourse to point out and to focus on differences and commonalities. It seeks to exemplify and explore different approaches to "urbanism and globalization" themes. It is obviously impossible to cover all different theoretical perspectives in this debate. Nevertheless, some very basic lines of discourse, their positions and critical contributions are integrated to engage the reader in the differences between various and fragmented lines of argument.

As a useful point of departure, we consider the "world city" hypothesis and later "the global city" debate. These perspectives are seen as leading models in recent, empirical research on hierarchies and city networks. *Peter Hall* draws upon the results of a highly advanced methodology, which provides convincing analysis of these intercommunal flows and dependencies. He points out the particular situation of European cities in the networking world. This perspective could be adopted as a basis for understanding the development of future economic hierarchies and relationships across national borders. *Olga Mrinska* work matches this research agenda. However, she provides an

example that is seldom considered: that of Ukrainian cities for researching urban gateways around the globe. In looking at third tier cities, *Mark Jayne* poses the question what does it mean to look at these hierarchies of cities from below, where cities are not even "latecomers" in the global economy.
Secondly, global city discourse leads to a consideration of "the shadow sides" of these developments. *Peter Marcuse* described consequences for the social fabric of New York, which is often seen as a city most affected by global forces. The question of international migration and the "global diaspora" (Cohen 2001) becomes evident, since these ideas are closely related to his work. In addition to studying urban segregation patterns, the request for a better understanding of transnational communities is an urgent priority. Drawing on the case of Lisbon, *Maragarida Marques* contributes to this debate by considering a European example to analyze migrant's life worlds in a globalized city. *Lionel Arnaud* and *Gilles Pinson* further exemplified this approach with a comparative study. *Leeke Reinders* describes the case of a Parisian banlieue to give another insight into the inside world of globalized cities. And *Tuomas Martikainen* demonstrated which role religious communities are playing in the new developing ethnic mosaik of Turku.
A third perspective focuses more on the actor and on discursive interaction in the "globalizing" city. With *John Eade's* contribution the construction of a global city in the sense of mental processes becomes crucial to the analysis of gloablized urbanism. While Eade has been advocating a shift in sociological terms regarding the framework of a nation-framed society (Eade 1997), the author has demonstrated the history of discourse on London as a Global City and its spatial and societal impact (Eade 2000). In his contribution to this book, he argues in favour for an analysis of the "middle ground" between structural and cultural interpretations of urban globalization.
Jana Temelová and *Hedvika Hrychová* present a case study of Prague. They understand globalization not only as discursive but also as a visible process. Images of Prague depict socio-spatial impacts of globalization and could lead to deeper insights on the role of architecture and other urban forms in globalizing cities. There is a body of literature regarding how both spheres of urban life- the built environment and urban life – space and place in a classical sense – are produced under global conditions. However, Carl *Fingerhuth*'s article makes a unique contribution from the architects' perspective. *Paul Kennedy* has also interviewed architects and questioned them about their engagements in global experiences and perceptions. In this way, we are providing another professional group's version of global urbanism
The fourth approach focuses on political planning and development projects in global cities. This is not far removed from the theme of

architecture in a global city substantial research exists on metropolitan governance and its relationship to globalization processes However, there are only a few examples on what role city planning politics play in this debate. *Alexander Tölle*'s case study of waterfront development projects could be seen as one of the examples, which highlight the influence of new economical tendencies in urban design politics. More focussing on the discourse behind political decision-making, *Monika de Frantz* concentrates more on political-decision making processes. Her example, "Berlin Stadtschloss", demonstrates a particular line of argument, which was used to construct a "new Berlin". This is quite blatant with regards to globalisation with the 1989's reunification of East and West Germany. *Marco van Bontje* provides another example of politics in urban planning. He focuses on the Dutch Randstad. In his contribution, he discusses the concept of sustainability, which has gained so much attention in recent debates. Sustainability is seen, as a response to globalization especially in environmentally concerned movements. This raises the question, which factors are important to consider while looking at the new geography of global urbanism. *Luiza Bialasiewicz*, in her article, seeks to present the societal construction of the globalized urban patterns with regard to the Veneto model as one example.

The fifth debate on urban globalization is critically embedded in external European experiences. The "European City in Transition Series" intends to contribute informed knowledge on recent developments in European cities. Although we use the term, "globalization" to undertake this analysis, it is important to discuss this concept's consistency in a world-wide frame As substantial proof has been acknowledged in the US-American cases, provide concrete proof which tend to lead up to the formulation of formulate major theoretical hypotheses. However, in this volume, these theories, to a certain extent, have been discussed with within the realm of particular European situations. Nevertheless, it can be argued that globalization is not just another postcolonial approach without any significance in the non-OECD world. *Alexander Horstmann's* article provides an insight into how far the concept of global ethnic space, can be used to analyse the world of migrants in Bangkok. His work is deeply inspired by John Eade's reconceptualized concept of globalization. *Karine Dupré's* research presents Guadeloupe as a case of a globalized urbanism in the European peripheral region. Certainly, both contributions are only a starting point to avoid the replacement the American bias in globalization research by Eurocentrism.

This series is by no means the final word on approaches to intensify our research on urbanism and globalization research. However, a few crucial points must be emphasized here. We are we confronted with mayor conceptual challenges, which are intrinsically presented in all the contributions articles and some of them are elaborated expressis verbis. Nonetheless, there are other developing empirical research perspectives that match existing and established traditions of spatial and societal research. In order to develop a deeper understanding to keep up with the momentum of globalization on urban life, both fields of research do complement each other and can serve to re-direct our perspectives simultaneously. In conclusion a few preliminary suggestions are presented here for the reader. It is important to develop an open research strategy that takes different definitions of both "globalization" and "urbanism" into account. We are confronted with a significant – and in sociology traditionally discussed – profound question, namely: What is the relationship between structures (manly cities?) and networks (predominantly globalization?). A metaphor to describe these complex interferences is the hierarchy, which combines positions in a network with the idea of stability. Could this picture be emblematic to characterize the non-economical order between cities beyond the given details of the world city hypotheses and its derivates? Are we developing logic or a mechanism to understand how global networks in general are localized?

The term "globalization" is used in many forms of political discourse. It is often labelled as "neo-liberalism", to legitimize certain political shifts. In this way, scientists have distanced themselves from ideological inclusion in policy-making discourses. What is needed is more in depth study regarding how globalization can be understood in descriptive analysis. This preoccupation to find a definition does not need to be as self-protective and reactive as it might appear. Urban scientists can embrace the opportunity to expand public debate beyond the concepts postulated by Foreign Direct Investment and related types of data. The sociology of global economy, presupposes a new concept of economy, one that has to take into account many "side-effects" such as migration, urban design, cultural and discoursive politics. Our attention might shift from economic globalisation to an economy of globalisation, which focuses on translocal mechanisms.

In that sense, the production of space has been regarded as one of the basis lines of analysis. Which forces constitute global space and which do not? The extent to which space production is linked to a transnational network might be a measurable way to find influential processes that link local society to place. Globalization is seen as a qualitative difference to existing international links and global cooperation in the modern city, is merely based on exchange involving leaving local societies on both sides of the river untouched. In times of global flow, which facilitate exchange – and that would be a definition to prove – that interacts, transforms, and reflects between different nodes of worldwide communication lines in a substantial way.

It is not sufficient to add a cultural dimension to a predominant concept of economical globalization. Instead, we have to understand the underlying concepts of rationalisation and economisation of worldwide cultures. This is not to say that we are allowed to think of a specific form of this „economy of signs and spaces" (Urry and Lash 1999). In recent years, a number of the conceptual tour d'horizone has been undertaken: be it the „glocalization" approach Robertson (Robertson 1994), the postmodern geography discourse by the L.A. School (Soja 1999), John Eade's discourse oriented approach or Arjan Appadurai's analysis of the cultural globalization (Appadurai 2003), ecomune-concept (Hannerz 2002) and considerations of postmodernity (Featherstone 2000), or the concept of a „stretching modernity" by Anthony Giddens, to mention only a few. They all propose a certain way of understanding the global-local relationship with its specific functions

Presently, however, convincing these arguments might be, it is certainly true that we do lack a comparative research framework to verify test, vary and reformulate these primary assumptions regarding the logic of globalizing urbanities. After reviewing the papers presented in this volume, the editor would like to now make some suggstions for furthering the research on „urbanism and globalization": First of all, the research has to transcend disciplinary boundaries and has to be translocal and comparative (Eckardt 2004). This will provide the opportunity to test the globaliation theories in different places as well as to examine the impact of related social facts.

With the choice of this methodological perspective there are other important considerations, which should be taken into consideration. A comparable modus operandi is required that has its basis in related areas of research. It is not clear, whether it would be advantageous or vice versa, if such research seeks to define a conceptual language. More importantly is the focus for translocal globalization research. Possibly the answer to the first question rests within intermediating institutions. For a long tiemnow, the tendency in experience in social science has been to analyse the function, rule production, agenda setting, organisational structure and sysems of power in diffrent types of institutions It might be more productive to consider re-directing this form of research. One could examine local institutions and their – perceived or real – interference with transnational flows of goods, services, organisations, actors, social groups, arguments ideologies, pictures, signs and discourses. In contrast, one could pose the same questions with regard to urban institutions situatedness in the national context. In many cases globalization is very often understood as replacing the significance of transnational networks and structures instead of national ones.

Urbanism is more complex than life in institutions and evolves from a multimultitude of interactions. Thus we cannot solely see the built environment as a certain form of architectural institutionalism or the outcome of city planning and architecture as insitutional settings. We need also to pay particular attention to the world of discourse and the role of the imagination. a research strategy for this field of globalization research seems to require a profound reconsideration of semiotic structures of the „cultures of cities" (Zukin 1995). The city can be integrated as a part of the local-intermedium-global research strategy but only as a part of the strategy outlined above. However, a search for an understanding of globalizing urbanism, leads us to the micro-level of urban sociology with its personal and individual experiences, perceptions, and considerations.

In conclusion, this introduction , expresses a vivid interest in seeing this volume as a progressive starting point for intensified, conceptual empirical, research strategies. The outlines, frameworks, and scientific challenges should become clearer after reading the following pages.

References:
Appadurai, A. (2003) Modernity at large: cultural dimensions of globalization. Minneapolis: Univ. of Minnesota Press.
Cohen, R. (2001) Global diasporas. London: Routledge.
Eckardt, F. (2004) Soziologie der Stadt. Bielefeld: transcript.
Eade, J. (1997) (ed) Living the global city: globalization as a local process. London: Routledge.
-, (2000) Placing London: from Imperial capital to Global city. New York: Berghahn.
Featherstone, M. (2000) Undoing culture: globalization, postmodernism and identity. London: Sage.
Lash, U. and Scott, L. (1999) Economies of signs and space. London: Sage.
Hannerz, U. (2002) Transnational connections : culture, people, places. New York: Routledge.
Robertson, R. (1994) Glocalization: Space, Time, and Social Theory. In: Journal of International Communication. No 1.
Simmel, G. (1995) Die Großstädte und das Geistesleben. In: O. Rammstedt (ed) Georg Simmel Gesamtausgabe. Vol. 7, Frankfurt: Suhrkamp, 116-131.
Soja, E. (1999) Postmodern geographies: the reassertion of space in critical social theory. London: Verso.
Wirth, L. (1938) Urbanism as a Way of Life. In: American Journal for Sociology, No. 44, 1-24.
Zukin, S. (1995) The cultures of the city. Cambridge: Blackwell.

European cities in a global world

Peter Hall

In this article I first want to suggest that there are two alternative ways of looking at cities and city systems, both valid, which need to be combined. Then I look at the performance of the European urban system in the last quarter century. From this, starting from the European Spatial Development Perspective, I want to suggest some lines of policy.

I. Alternative Views of City Systems
There are two alternative ways of looking at cities.

1. The Urban Hierarchy
The first is in terms of a hierarchy of cities – a tradition that goes all the way back to Christaller's classic work of 70 years ago (Christaller 1966 (1933)). But it was developed for a very different age, and it is no longer an adequate description of the European hierarchy: it is dominated by small towns, some of which have ceased to operate as service centres at all, and it totally omits higher-level centres. We therefore need a substitute.

The urban system has been profoundly affected by the changes about which all geographers write: the increasing *globalization* of the world; and the *informationalization* of the economy, the progressive shift of advanced economies from goods production to information handling, whereby the great majority of the workforce no longer deal with material outputs. Manuel Castells has described this as the transition to the informational mode of production: a shift as momentous, in his view, as the shift from an agrarian to an industrial economy in the eighteenth and nineteenth centuries. In typical advanced countries, already by 1991 between three-fifths and three-quarters of all employment was in services, while between one-third and one-half was in information handling; typically these proportions have doubled since the 1920s (Castells 2000, 304-324).

These processes have increased the importance of cities at the very top of the hierarchy, the so-called world cities or global cities. These are not a new phenomenon. Patrick Geddes already recognized World Cities and defined them, as long ago as 1915, in *Cities in Evolution* (Geddes 1915); in 1966 I published a book entitled *The World Cities* (Hall 1966), defining them as cities that performed multiple roles: as centres of political power, both national and international, and of the organizations related to government; centres of national and international trade, acting as entrepôts for their countries and sometimes for neighbouring countries also; hence, centres of banking, insurance and related financial services; centres of advanced professional activity of all kind, in medicine, in law, in the higher learning, and the application of scientific knowledge to technology; centres of information gathering and diffusion, through publishing and the mass media; centres of conspicuous consumption, both of luxury goods for the minority and mass-produced goods for the multitude; centres of arts, culture and entertainment, and of the ancillary activities that catered for them (Hall 1966, 1984).

In the 1980s John Friedmann was the first to deepen this analysis, by suggesting that processes of globalization were resulting in a global hierarchy, in which London, New York and Tokyo were "global financial articulations", while Miami, Los Angeles, Frankfurt, Amsterdam and Singapore were "multinational articulations", and Paris, Zurich, Madrid, Mexico City, São Paulo, Seoul and Sydney were "important national articulations", all forming a "network" (Friedmann 1986; Friedmann and Wolff 1982; q. Smith and Timberlake 1995, 294). And Saskia Sassen has developed the point that the locus of production of advanced business or producer services becomes increasingly disarticulated from that of production:

> The spatial dispersion of production, including its internationalization, has contributed to the growth of centralized service nodes for the management and regulation of the new space economy ... To a considerable extent, the weight of economic activity over the last fifteen years has shifted from production places such as Detroit and Manchester, to centers of finance and highly specialized services (Sassen 1991).

Thus there are contradictory trends: as production disperses worldwide, services increasingly concentrate into a relatively few trading cities, both the well-known "global cities" and a second rung of about twenty cities immediately below these, which we can distinguish as "sub-global". These cities are centres for financial services (banking, insurance) and headquarters of major production companies; most are also seats of the major world-power governments (King 1990, Sassen 1991). A recent study of four world cities (G.B. Government Office for London, 1996) distinguished four key groups of advanced service activity:

(1) *Finance and Business Services:* including banking and insurance, commercial business services such as law, accountancy, advertising and public relations, and design services including architecture, civil engineering, industrial design and fashion;
(2) *"Power and Influence"* (or *"Command and Control"*): national government, supra-national organisations like UNESCO or OECD, and headquarters of major organisations including transnational corporations;

(3) *Creative and Cultural Industries*: including live performing arts (theatre, opera, ballet, concerts), museums and galleries and exhibitions, print and electronic media;
(4) *Tourism*: including both business and leisure tourism, and embracing hotels, restaurants, bars, entertainment, and transportation services.

All these are service industries of the process differs somewhat from sector to sector, but often it involves centrally involving the generation, transmission and consumption of information. The nature a very high degree of immediacy. Whether one considers the investment analyst trading shares, or the lawyer offering advice, or the board of a major corporation in a meeting, or the television producer at work on a show, or the tour guide taking a group sightseeing, specialised information is being processed and transmitted by highly-qualified people in real time. Further, much though not all of this activity involves face-to-face exchange of information, either as a central feature or as an essential ancillary (as when the stock analyst has lunch and picks up important market information). Therefore, an extremely strong force of agglomeration operates throughout these sectors.

It goes almost without saying that these categories tend to be highly synergistic with each other, and that many activities fit effectively into the interstices between them: thus hotels and conference centres and exhibition centres are simultaneously business services and part of tourism; museums and galleries are creative/cultural but also parts of tourism; advertising is both creative and a business service; and so on. For this reason, not only does each of the sectors have strong agglomerative trends set by the need to process and exchange information, but there are also strong agglomerative forces as between the four main sectors.

Work by the GaWC (Global Analysis of World Cities) group at the University of Loughborough (Beaverstock, Taylor and Smith 1999) goes a long way to recognising these trends and developing a new urban hierarchy: it identifies a "global hierarchy" of cities, based essentially on the relationships between different units engaged in delivering advanced services like law and accounatncy. In it, European cities are prominently represented and, of the top six cities, four are in the so-called North West Metropolitan Area of Europe, with London at the top. This is further supported by recent work on the global urban hierarchy based on airport connectivity (Smith and Timberlake 2000).

The christaller central place system (1933)

Type	Market area Radius, Km of town	Population	Population of market area
M (Marktort)	4.0	1,000	3,500
A (Amtsort)	6.9	2,000	11,000
K (Kreisstadt)	12.0	4,000	35,000
B (Bezirkstadt)	20.7	10,000	100,000
G (Gaustadt)	36.0	30,000	350,000
P (Provinzstadt)	62.1	100,000	1,000,000
L (Landstadt)	108.0	500,000	3,500,000

Table 1
Source: Christaller (1966), 67; Dickinson (1967), 51.

The loughborough group "gawc" inventory of world cities
Cities are ordered in terms of world city-ness values ranging from 1- 12.
European cities are highlighted

A. *Alpha world cities*
12: London, Paris, New York, Tokyo
10: Chicago, Frankfurt, Hong Kong, Los Angeles, Milan, Singapore

B. *Beta world cities*
9: San Francisco, Sydney, Toronto, Zürich
8: Brussels, Madrid, Mexico City, São Paulo
7: Moscow, Seoul

C. *Gamma world cities*
6: Amsterdam, Boston, Caracas, Dallas, Düsseldorf, Geneva, Houston, Jakarta, Johannesburg, Melbourne, Osaka, Prague, Santiago, Taipei, Washington
5: Bangkok, Beijing, Rome, Stockholm, Warsaw
4: Atlanta, Barcelona, Berlin, Buenos Aires, Budapest, Copenhagen, Hamburg, Istanbul, Kuala Lumpur, Manila, Miami, Minneapolis, Montreal, München, Shanghai

D. *Evidence of world city formation*
Di *Relatively strong evidence*
3: Auckland, Dublin, Helsinki, Luxembourg, Lyon, Mumbai, New Delhi, Philadelphia, Rio de Janeiro, Tel Aviv, Wien

Dii Some evidence
2: Abu Dhabi, Almaty, <u>Athens</u>, <u>Birmingham</u>, Bogota, <u>Bratislava</u>, Brisbane, <u>Bucharest</u>, Cairo, Cleveland, <u>Köln</u>, Detroit, Dubai, Ho Chi Minh City, <u>Kiev</u>, Lima, <u>Lisbon</u>, <u>Manchester</u>, Montevideo, <u>Oslo</u>, <u>Rotterdam</u>, Riyadh, Seattle, <u>Stuttgart</u>, <u>Den Haag</u>, Vancouver

Diii Minimal evidence
1: Adelaide, <u>Antwerp</u>, <u>Århus</u>, <u>Athens</u>, Baltimore, Bangalore, <u>Bologna</u>, Brasilia, Calgary, Cape Town, Colombo, Columbus, <u>Dresden</u>, <u>Edinburgh</u>, <u>Genoa</u>, <u>Glasgow</u>, <u>Göteborg</u>, Guangzhou, Hanoi, Kansas City, <u>Leeds</u>, <u>Lille</u>, <u>Marseille</u>, Richmond, <u>St Petersburg</u>, Tashkent, Tehran, Tijuana, <u>Torino</u>, <u>Utrecht</u>, Wellington

Table 2
Source: Beaverstock, Taylor and Smith 1999.

World city hierarchy based on air connections, 1997
European cities are <u>highlighted</u>
1 <u>London</u>
2 <u>Frankfurt</u>
3 <u>Paris</u>
4 New York
5 <u>Amsterdam</u>
6 <u>Zürich</u>
7 Miami
8 Los Angeles
9 Hong Kong
10 Singapore
11 Tokyo
12 Seoul
13 Bangkok
14 <u>Madrid</u>
15 <u>Wien</u>
16 San Francisco
17 Chicago
18 Dubai
19 Osaka
20 <u>Brussels</u>

Table 3
Source: Smith and Timberlake 2000.

We can conclude that the Christaller hierarchy now needs to be supplemented by at least two and perhaps three additional levels, producing a hierarchy of perhaps six or seven levels:
(1) *Global cities* (in the Loughborough terminology, "Alpha" Global Cities) typically with 5 million and more people within their administrative boundaries and up to 20 million within their hinterlands, but effectively serving very large global territories: London, Paris, New York, Tokyo;
(2) *Sub-global cities* (in the Loughborough terminology, "Beta" or "Gamma" Global Cities), typically with 1-5 million people and up to perhaps 10 million in their hinterlands, performing global service functions for certain specialised services (banking, fashion, culture, media) and an almost complete range of similar functions for more restricted national or regional territories: all European capitals apart from the global cities, together with "commercial capitals" (Milan, Barcelona) and major provincial cities in large nation states (Glasgow, Manchester, Lyon, Marseille, Hamburg, etc.) (Hall, 1995). This last category may overlap with Christaller's L-centres and may possibly be equivalent to it; but a special category must exist for the national capitals, which do not exist in his scheme.
(3) *Regional* (Christaller's *Landstadt*) (population 250,000-1 million); some of these have characteristics which cause the Loughborough group to describe them as "Showing Evidence of World City Formation".
(4) *Provincial* (Christaller's *Provinzstadt*) (population 100,000-250,000).

Below the provincial level, the five levels which Christaller distinguished have not physically disappeared. But the two lowest levels, his *Marktort* and *Amtsort*, have ceased to perform any significant role as central places; they have lost any service functions they may have had, such as a village store or post office, and have become purely residential villages. The next level up, the *Kreisstadt*, may have very limited village-store type services. The lowest significant level in contemporary Europe is probably his fourth level or *Bezirkstadt*, with a population of 10,000 and a service population of 100,000. It is at about this level, for instance, that one typically finds the establishment of a superstore and of a limited range of national chain stores. All this demonstrates the dramatic increase in mobility and thus in what he termed "the range of a good" in the sixty-six years since he wrote, which has effectively replaced the small village store by the superstore as the basic unit of convenience shopping for the average member of the population.
It is however at the next two levels upwards that some of the most significant changes have occurred, since over wide rural areas, depending on population density, one or other of these usually

represents the largest available central place. They are the typical county market towns of rural Europe, found across much of southern England, southern Germany, and most of France. They have grown because they provide the local services for their populations and sometimes national services (such as universities) also. In the less-developed, depopulating regions of Europe they have acted as magnets, attracting population outflow from the surrounding rural areas; in the more prosperous regions, likewise, they have attracted much of the out-migration of people and the growth of businesses from the major cities at the higher levels of the hierarchy, especially within the transport-rich sectors, as well illustrated by the case of London's western sector. Since 1990 this has been countered by a reurbanisation trend, fuelled in the case of London by migration from abroad and a high rate of natural increase due to a young population. But the net migration trend continues strongly outward.

2. A Geographical-Functional Categorisation: The ESDP

However, the precise form and degree of this development varies significantly from one part of Europe to another. First, it is most marked around the global and sub-global cities, and then predominantly in a few key sectors, representing the most important inter-regional (and sometimes international) transport corridors: around London, for instance, towards the north, west and east.

Secondly, in a few cases this may result in discontinuous corridors or axes of urbanisation, most notably in the so-called "Blue Banana" connecting Birmingham, London, Brussels, Amsterdam, Cologne, Frankfurt, Basel, Zürich and Milan (Brunet 1989).

Third, it is not universal around every major metropolis: Paris, for instance, has disproportionately concentrated its own dispersal into the five giant *cités nouvelles* proposed in the 1965 *Schéma Directeur*, so that – in sharp contrast to London - there has been only minimal dispersal beyond their limits.

Fourth, the precise urban form that results is influenced strongly by the strength of planning powers: there is a sharp contrast between the highly constrained urban growth typical of the United Kingdom and the Netherlands, and the much freer pattern of suburbanisation found in northern Italy. However, in general, because of differential patterns of accessibility set by motorway interchanges and inter-city train stations, market forces by themselves tend to generate a quite discontinuous or punctiform pattern of development around existing central places which remain surrounded by wide green hinterlands. And local resistance, in the form of NIMBY (Not in My Back Yard) movements, tends to limit the growth of many villages and smaller urban places.

Whereas the traditional Christaller central places were linked by radial public transport systems (trains, buses) connecting the towns with lower levels in the system and with villages, the higher levels are directly connected with each other by systems for business travel and information exchange (air corridors, inter-city and high-speed train routes, motorways, telecommunications links for voice and data) and by travel infrastructure in the form of hotels, restaurants and entertainment. This suggests that a new central place system needs to be defined, based on indices of business concentration (international bank transactions, stock exchange transactions, hotels) and flows of people and information. The logic here is that information is exchanged in two ways – by telecommunications and by personal travel – and that the IT revolution almost certainly will *not* mean that the need and desire for face-to-face contact will diminish. On the contrary: the historical record shows very clearly that the growth of telecommunications traffic is paralleled by the growth of personal travel; and this will surely continue to be true in the future. Far from telecommunications reducing the need and desire to travel, it is likely to multiply it: the growth in information exchange will bring with it a necessity for more and more face-to-face. Therefore a key question is where this activity will happen.

All the evidence, even from high priests of cyberspace like Bill Gates or Bill Mitchell of MIT (Gates 1995; Mitchell 1995), suggests that city centres will retain their unique role in providing the most efficient locations for much of this activity, simply because of the accumulated weight of interrelated functions that have historically accrued there, and because radially-oriented transport systems focus on them. Again, the empirical evidence suggests that the hierarchy of cities here in Europe has not changed very much in the last forty years and will not change very much in the future.

The main new influence is likely to be the development of the high-speed train system in Europe, on present plans largely in place shortly before 2010 (Hall 1995a). We know from experience these trains will take about 80-90 per cent of traffic up to about 500 kilometres and about 50 per cent up to about 800 kilometres. This means that by 2010, when the system will connect all the principal cities of Europe from Bari right up to Glasgow and Umeå, virtually all traffic between key city pairs - Naples and Rome and Milan, Milan and Paris, Munich and Cologne, Cologne and Brussels, Brussels and London, Brussels and Paris, Copenhagen and Stockholm - will go by rail. The longer-distance traffic, even within Europe, will largely remain with air. Within the NWMA and specifically what used to be called the Central Capitals Region, business traffic will transfer overwhelmingly from air to rail within the next five years, and a critical planning question will be the linkages at the airports between the two systems. We can already see these at Paris-Charles de Gaulle, and soon at Amsterdam and Frankfurt. The likelihood is that these places will become effectively new urban centres, as Dejan Sudjic suggested a few years ago. They will not only attract a vast amount of business in the form of conference centres, exhibition centres and hotels; they are likely to become shopping centres in their own right, as you can see from the plans for Heathrow Terminal Five. So they will compete with traditional downtown areas as business hubs.

There is thus an emerging contrast between the Central Capitals Region, with its dense cluster of cities closely networked through air, high-speed-train and telecommunications links (London, Paris, Frankfurt, Luxembourg, Brussels, Amsterdam), and the "gateway" or "regional capital" cities in the more peripheral European regions, each dominating a large but less-densely-populated territory (Dublin, Edinburgh, Copenhagen, Stockholm, Helsinki, Berlin, Vienna, Rome, Madrid, Lisbon plus the eastern European capitals of Ljubljana, Budapest, Prague, Warsaw and Tallinn). These cities are connected by air into the central region, even though they may be (and increasingly are) the cores of local high-speed-train systems. Here, we find an interesting degree of competition between a higher-order city that appears to control such a wide sector of the European space, and next-order cities controlling parts of that space (as, for instance, Copenhagen versus Stockholm and Helsinki; Berlin versus Vienna; Madrid versus Lisbon). Additionally, in one or two instances, this critical Euro-regional role is divided between a "political" and a "commercial" capital (Rome and Milan; Madrid and Barcelona).

A system, derived in part from the analysis in ESDP but also from work by the present author (Hall 1993), tries to capture these geographical relationships within the European space as well as to hierarchy; it has provisionally been developed as follows:

- *Central High-Level Service Cities:* major cities (national capitals) and major commercial cities in the so-called "Pentagon": London, Paris, Milan, Munich, Frankfurt, Hamburg, Amsterdam, Brussels, Luxembourg. As the ESDP analysis shows, they have the highest multi-modal accessibility within the European Union. They are connected by dense air corridors now being supplemented by (and even partially replaced by) new high-speed train lines.
- *Gateway Cities (Sub-Continental Capitals):* national capitals and major commercial cities outside the "Pentagon", acting as high-level service centres for major parts of the European space: Madrid-Barcelona, Rome, Athens, Vienna, Berlin, Copenhagen (and the Candidate Capitals: Prague, Warsaw, Budapest). They are normally major air hubs for flag carriers and they are increasingly the cores of regional high-speed train systems which are not however not so fare connected to the "Pentagon" system, and they may be too distant in

some cases for rail to compete effectively. They include some larger commercial cities: Manchester, Lyon, Stuttgart, Leipzig.
- *Smaller Capitals and Provincial Capitals:* these are smaller equivalents of the previous case, commanding less extensive space in terms of population and GDP; in many cases they are at the periphery of the European space: Dublin, Edinburgh, Lisbon, Helsinki, Stockholm (and also smaller, remoter Candidate Capitals: Bratislava, Ljubljana, Sofia). This also includes smaller commercial centres controlling "provincial" territories: Bristol, Bordeaux, Grenoble, Strasbourg, Hannover, Bologna (and, in candidate countries: Poznan, Kraków).
- *"County towns":* this describes the typical rural administrative and service centre for a surrounding area typically 40-60km in radius, of which hundreds exist in the European space. Some, in "accessible rural" areas, are growing very rapidly by dispersal from major cities, thus tending to form highly networked "mega-city regions" as they have come to be known in Eastern Asia (South East England, Delta Metropolis, Lombardy) (Hall 1999). Other, less accessible, examples are experiencing more varied fortunes: some are growing through tourism and migration for retirement, others are stagnant or even (in contracting industrial regions) declining. The last represents a particular problem highly localised in certain parts of Europe, especially the coalfield belt from northern and midland England through Wallonia, Lorraine, the Ruhrgebiet to Upper Silesia (Cheshire and Hay 1989).

II.   Putting the Taxonomies Together: The Recent Record

What happens when we try to put the two different systems of classification together? At the macro-level of analysis, the dominant feature is the contrast between the Central Capital Region, with its dense cluster of high-level cities closely networked through air, high-speed-train and telecommunications links (London, Paris, Frankfurt, Luxembourg, Brussels, Amsterdam), and the "gateway" or "regional capital" cities in the more peripheral European regions, each dominating a large but less-densely-populated territory (Dublin, Edinburgh, Copenhagen, Stockholm, Helsinki, Berlin, Vienna, Rome, Madrid, Lisbon plus the eastern European capitals of Ljubljana, Budapest, Prague, Warsaw and Tallinn). Here, we find an interesting degree of competition between a higher-order city that appears to control such a wide sector of the European space, and next-order cities controlling parts of that space (as, for instance, Copenhagen versus Stockholm and Helsinki; Berlin versus Vienna; Madrid versus Lisbon). Additionally, in one or two instances, this critical Euro-regional role is divided between a "political" and a "commercial" capital (Rome and Milan; Madrid and Barcelona).

These intermediate-size gateway cities have proved relatively dynamic in the 1970s and 1980s. They invariably act as regional airport hubs, with a range of long-distance destinations (Copenhagen, Madrid) and as the hubs of regional high-speed-train systems (Madrid, Rome); they have a wide variety of global service functions, especially where they dominate linguistic regions (as Madrid for Latin America). With expansion of the EU eastwards, the eastern gateway cities (Berlin, Vienna) promise to play new roles in their respective areas, returning to the roles they played before 1914. However, policy does not appear to have played much of a direct role in this development; it is a function of European geography and its relation to the wider global economy.

Smaller cities seem to have experienced some advantages when they are clustered so as to constitute a wider economic area sharing labour markets and specialised services. The outstanding examples are the Greater South East region outside London and the fringes of Randstad Holland. But many other parts of Europe have developed corridors of intense urbanisation along major transport spines, as in the Rhine Valley above Frankfurt, the Rhone Valley below Lyon, or the Emilia-Romagna region of Italy. In a few cases (as in South East England) planning policy has played a conscious role in this; elsewhere, again, it seems to have been a spontaneous evolution. But there is now a general agreement that such a form, which can combine small mixed-use urban developments clustered along strong public transport spines, represents perhaps the most sustainable form of urban development; and some national planning strategies are beginning to adopt it, for instance in the UK.

Many more isolated medium-sized towns, outside these major trans-European corridors but located on national movement corridors connecting larger cities, have shown remarkable dynamism. Examples include Nottingham and Bristol, Hannover and Munich, Grenoble and Toulouse, Naples and Ravenna, Zaragoza and Valencia. The key seems to be first that they are in "Sunbelt" rural regions that are themselves prosperous, either through efficient agricultural production or (more commonly) because these cities themselves have become the main centres for advanced service employment. Public sector spending policies have played a role here, by concentrating such functions as higher education and hospitals in these places. But the sources of growth are more subtle than this, and such places show remarkable variations in fortune, depending on local socio-cultural factors that may go back for centuries - as, for instance, between northern and southern Italy.

How does one try to summarise this mass of partial and sometimes contradictory data? Some kinds of urban area, it seems, are unambiguously growing through in-migration:

First, the hinterlands of the major cities, mainly in Northern and Central Europe, that are benefiting from the exodus from these cities into wider "mega-city regions" - as around London, Copenhagen and Randstad Holland; possibly this trend has weakened since 1980 with the trend to reurbanisation, though rapid growth has continued in the fringe areas.

Second, medium-sized and smaller metropolitan areas in less-urbanised "sunbelt" zones with medium-sized and smaller cities, particularly in the southern UK, southern France, Portugal and central and northern Italy.
Third, a few selected larger urban centres and their immediate hinterlands in the less-developed, less-densely-populated regions of rural out-migration, particularly Scandinavia, Mediterranean Europe, Ireland and some eastern European countries. This tends to reflect the magnetism of such cities at the stage of development these regions have reached, and also government policies in Eastern Europe. It also reflects that there are relatively few such large city regions in these parts of Europe which can act as foci for in-migration.
These trends reflect underlying economic realities. Globalisation and the shift to the informational economy give special value to large cities as centres for efficient face-to-face information exchange. They are the locations of the major hub airports and the high-speed train stations; they also are hubs for commuter traffic. But they also experience some economic disadvantages: high rents, congestion, pollution, the costs of attracting middle- and junior-level staff. So certain activities ("back offices", R and D) tend to migrate outwards: to corridors leading to the airports, to suburban train stations, to country towns in the surrounding ring. Meanwhile, medium-sized cities ("provincial capitals") in "sunbelt" rural regions (Bristol, Hannover, Bordeaux, Oporto, Seville, Bologna) are growing through strong concentrations of public services (higher education, health services), retailing and tourism. Some of these also act as centres of high-technology manufacturing, and/or have attracted longer-distance office decentralisation. Some similar-level cities in older industrial regions (Dortmund, Leeds) have seen a similar growth, though others have been less successful, especially if they are peripheral either nationally or in a European sense. Finally, there are many cases of growth at the next level of the hierarchy: the "county town", or medium-sized administrative-service centre of a rural region, of which hundreds of European examples exist. These centres have grown as local service centres; they often offer a high level of environment (and some, like Freiburg, are outstanding examples); they are attractive both to migration and inward investment.
Thus, the overall picture is not easy to summarise. On the one hand, significant concentrations of activity are occurring in the cores of the very largest cities; they generate wealth and, through multiplier effects, jobs, even though some of the process may be "exported" to commuter towns in the surrounding ring. However, such growth does not generate sufficient

employment to compensate for the loss of traditional manufacturing and goods-handling activities. The result is a paradox: high levels of income generation are accompanied by localised long-term structural unemployment. In terms of employment and population growth, medium-sized and smaller towns are showing more rapid growth than larger ones; and some are benefiting from spillover effects from larger cities into their commuter rings. However, their performance varies significantly from region to region: it is strongest in the zones of deconcentration around the largest metropolitan areas of the Central Capitals region, strong also in "Sunbelt" regions, variable in the peripheral regions of out-migration where the main beneficiaries are at the next level up the hierarchy. In Eastern Europe, cities at this level of the hierarchy tend to be weakly represented.

Another way of looking at the evidence, therefore, is to return to the macro-level of geographical analysis. The Eurocore or Central Capitals region continues to exhibit strong growth, with a reversal of the counter-urbanisation tendencies of the 1970s in at least some of the cities, but with continuing local out-migration which effectively extends the metropolitan area into a huge and complex polycentric structure. The more peripheral political and commercial capitals also exhibit growth, sometimes accompanied by local decentralisation to smaller cities, but sometimes not; here, the pressures for deconcentration, in the form of congestion and other negative externalities, are fewer. The Euro-periphery exhibits general continued out-migration, but accompanied by local migration patterns which benefit a relatively few local service centres.

III. Towards a Spatially Integrated Approach: The ESDP

This is why the European Spatial Development Perspective is highly relevant. It adopts a central principle of polycentricity, allied to decentralised concentration: a principle long ago adopted in Dutch spatial planning, which aims to disperse economic development from congested urban regions, but to reconcentrate it in urban centres in the less developed regions, thus benefiting both kinds of region.

However, it does so at the largest possible geographical scale. The aim is not so much to redistribute some fixed amount of activity in a kind of zero-sum-game; it is to encourage a significantly higher level of growth in less-developed regions and cities, some of which will be older industrial cities in need of restructuring, but a much larger number of which will be cities in the less densely-populated, less-developed fringe regions of western, southern, northern and eastern Europe.

Here, it is necessary to realise that the central word, *polycentric*, needs to be carefully defined: it has a different significance at different spatial scales and in different geographical contexts. At the global level, *polycentric* refers to the development of alternative global centres of power. Presently, there are a very few cities worldwide that are universally regarded as global control-and-command centres, located in the most advanced economies: London appears in all lists, Paris appears on some. Importantly, however, Europe has a number of "sub-global" cities, performing some global functions in specialised fields: Rome (culture), Milan (fashion), Frankfurt and Zürich (banking), Brussels, Luxembourg, Paris, Rome and Geneva (supernational government agencies) (Hall 1993, Hall 1995b, 1995c, Hall 1996).

Within a specifically European context, therefore, one meaning of a *polycentric* policy is to divert some activities away from "global" cities like London (and perhaps Paris) to "sub-global" centres like Brussels, Frankfurt or Milan. But there is also a very important spatial dimension: while some of these cities are found in the Central Capitals region (Brussels, Amsterdam, Frankfurt, Luxembourg), a much larger number are "gateway" national political or commercial capitals outside the Centre Capitals region: they include Helsinki, Stockholm, Copenhagen, Berlin, Vienna, Rome/Milan, Madrid/Barcelona, Lisbon and Dublin. They serve broad but sometimes thinly-populated territories such as the Iberian peninsula, Scandinavia and east central Europe. Because they are national capitals serving distinct linguistic groups, they invariably have a level of service functions larger than would be expected on grounds of size alone; they tend to be national airport and rail hubs, and the main centres for national cultural institutions and national media.

A major issue here is whether it will be either necessary or desirable to concentrate decentralised activity into a limited number of "regional capitals", each commanding a significant sector of the European territory - Copenhagen, Berlin, Rome, Madrid - or whether it would be preferable to diffuse down to the level of the national capital cities, including the smaller national capitals. Essentially, how far should Madrid be regarded as the dominant gateway for south west Europe, or should it share this role with Lisbon, Bilbao, Barcelona and Seville? And likewise with Copenhagen vis-à-vis Stockholm, Oslo and Helsinki. This could be particularly important in eastern Europe, where Berlin and Vienna may develop important roles for their hinterlands reflecting past geographies, but where also there is a real need to reassert the service roles of the different national capitals and selected provincial capitals (Gdánsk, Kraków, Plzeň, Szeged).

At a finer geographical scale, however, polycentricity can refer to the outward diffusion from either of these levels of city to smaller cities within their urban fields or spheres of influence. We have already noticed that such a process has occurred on a wide scale around London, which is now the centre of a system of some 30-40 centres within a 150-km. radius, while (for different historical reasons) Paris and Berlin in contrast have much more weakly-developed urban systems. At the next level, cities like Stockholm, Copenhagen and Milan also show widespread outward diffusion while other cities do not. East European cities, in particular, have had relatively little impact through decentralisation on their surrounding regions, though this may change in the future.

In general, at this scale a policy of "deconcentrated concentration" would suggest adopting the principle fairly widely, but adapting it to the specific development stages and problems of each city and region. Specifically, the general principle should be to guide decentralised growth, wherever possible, on to a few selected development corridors along strong public transport links, including high-speed "regional metros" such as those under construction around Stockholm and Copenhagen, and planned for London, or even along true high-speed lines such as London-Ashford, Amsterdam-Antwerp or Berlin-Magdeburg. These would not of course be corridors of continuous urbanisation, but rather clusters of urban developments, at intervals, around train stations and key motorway interchanges that offer exceptionally good accessibility. Some of these sites could be at considerable distances, up to 150 kilometres, from the central metropolitan city.

In the more remote rural regions, far from the global and sub-global centres, the pursuit of polycentricity must have yet another dimension: to build up the potential of both "regional capitals" in the 200,000-500,000 population range (Bristol, Bordeaux, Hannover, Ravenna, Zaragoza), and smaller "county towns" in the 50,000-200,000 range. The main agents will be enhanced accessibility both by road and (most importantly) high-speed train, coupled with investment in key higher-level service infrastructure (health, education); the systematic enhancement of environmental quality, to make as many as possible of these cities "model sustainable cities"; and finally the competitive marketing of such cities as places for inward investment and relocation. Again, but on a smaller scale, the growth of such centres could be accompanied by a limited degree of deconcentration to even smaller rural towns within easy reach.

We begin to see a potential contradiction in meeting ESDP objectives: dispersal from large cities into "mega-city-regions", which may be occurring around several different kinds of city – Central Cities (London-South East England, Amsterdam-Delta Metropolis), Gateway Cities (Copenhagen-Ørestad, Barcelona-Catalonia) and Provincial Capitals (Stockholm-Mälardalen, Seville-Andalucia) may produce a more polycentric system at the local level but a less polycentric system at a higher, European level. This is why it will be important to measure polycentricity, and its accompanying transport systems, at more than one spatial scale. It is a complex strategy, and its further elaboration will be an important central part of the new programme for the European Spatial Programme Observatories Network which begins work this year.

References:
Beaverstock, J.V., Taylor, P., Smith, R.G. (1999) A Roster of World Cities. Cities, 16, 445-458.
Brunet, R. et al (1989) Les Villes "Européenes": Rapport pour la DATAR. Paris: La Documentation Française.
Castells, M. (2000) The Information Age: Economy, Society, and Culture. Vol. I, The Rise of the Network Society. Oxford: Blackwell.
Cheshire, P.C., Hay, D.G. (1989) Urban Problems in Western Europe: An Economic Analysis. London: Unwin Hyman.
Christaller, W. (1966 (1933)) Central Places in Southern Germany. Translated by C.W. Baskin. Englewood Cliffs: Prentice-Hall.
European Commission (1999) ESDP: European Spatial Development Perspective: Towards Balanced and Sustainable Development of the Territory of the European Union. Brussels: European Commission.
Friedmann, J. (1986) The World City Hypothesis. Development and Change, 4, 12-50.
-, Wolff, G. (1982) World City Formation: An Agenda for Research and Action. International Journal of Urban and Regional Research, 6, 309-344.
G.B. Government Office for London (1996) Four World Cities: A Comparative Study of London, Paris, New York and Tokyo. London: Llewelyn Davies Planning.
Gates, W. (1995) The Road Ahead. London: Viking.
Geddes, P. (1915) Cities in Evolution. London: Williams and Norgate. Reprinted (1998) in: LeGates, R., Stout, F. (ed.) Early Urban Planning 1870-1940, Vol. 4. London: Routledge.
Hall, P. (1966) The World Cities. London: Weidenfeld and Nicolson.
-, (1984) The World Cities. 3rd edition. New York: St. Martin's Press.
-, (1993) Forces Shaping Urban Europe. Urban Studies, 30, 883-898.
-, (1995a) A European Perspective on the Spatial Links between Land Use, Development and Transport. In: Banister, D. (ed.) Transport and Urban Development, 65-88. London: Spon.
-, (1995b) The Future of Cities in Western Europe. European Review, 3, 161-169.
-, (1995c) Towards a General Urban Theory. In: Brotchie, J., Batty, M., Blakely, E., Hall, P., Newton, P. (ed.) Cities in Competition: Productive and Sustainable Cities for the 21st Century, 3-31. Melbourne: Longman Australia.
-, (1996) The Global City. In: International Social Science Journal, 147, 15-23.
-, (1999) Planning for the Mega-City: A New Eastern Asian Urban Form? In: Brotchie, J., Newton, P., Hall, P., Dickey, J. (ed.) East West Perspectives on 21st Century Urban Development: Sustainable Eastern and Western Cities in the New Millennium, 3-36. Aldershot: Ashgate.
King, A.D. (1990) Global Cities: Post-Imperialism and the Internationalization of London. London: Routledge.
Mitchell, W.J. (1995) City of Bits: Space, Place, and the Infobahn. Cambridge, Mass.: MIT Press.
Sassen, S. (1991) The Global City: New York, London, Tokyo. Princeton: Princeton U.P.
Smith, D.A., Timberlake, M. (1995) Conceptualising and Mapping the Structure of the World's City System. Urban Studies, 32, 287-302.

Ukrainian cities as a gateway to the global innovative economy

Olga Mrinska

Ukraine is one of the biggest European countries, which experienced the severest economic crisis and is still recovering from its consequences. The problems of transition period are unequally addressed in different regions of the country and spatial organisation of society has changed drastically during the last dozen years. Big cities are the leaders in progressive innovation-driven model of development and the move towards demand-oriented growth. The analysis of trends in development of 7 major cities of Ukraine is aimed at showing the evidence of prospects for Ukraine as a European state with a rich history and great potential. It is also intended to illustrate the patterns of globalisation of Ukrainian society via metropolitan gateways with simultaneous periferalisation of the rest of the country. This paper is a first attempt to evaluate the readiness of the biggest Ukrainian cities for the sharp competitive environment of modern global economy.

The transition period experienced by former Soviet republics during last 12 years caused fundamental changes in their political and economic systems. The shift from central planning and a command economy to flexible and open market economy and democratic principles brought society in these countries to the new challenges of global innovative economy. Possessing considerable intellectual potential and professional labour skills, the new market economies of eastern Europe have to face the process of continuous catching-up with the progress in the world economy, especially in R and D sector, and consequently to lose some competitive advantages due to limited financial resources and the lack of a proper market institutional framework.

Ukraine is one of the biggest European countries, which experienced the severest economic crisis and is still recovering from its consequences. It lost more than a half of its productive potential and must overcome many difficulties on its way to sustainable economic and social development. The problems of transition period are unequally addressed in different regions of the country and spatial organisation of society has changed drastically during the last dozen years. Big cities are the leaders in progressing innovation-driven model of development and the move towards demand-oriented growth. They are better equipped with the technical and economic infrastructure, education and scientific network, intellectual and financial resources. That is why there are dramatically growing disparities in socio-economic development of the biggest Ukrainian cities – Kyiv, Kharkiv, Donetsk, Lviv, Odessa, Dnipropetrovsk, Zaporizhzhia - and the rest of the country.

The analysis of trends in development of 7 major cities located in different areas/regions of Ukraine is aimed at showing the evidence of prospects for Ukraine as a European state with a rich history and great potential. It is also intended to illustrate the patterns of globalisation of Ukrainian society via metropolitan gateways with simultaneous periferalisation of the rest of the country.

1. The Place of Ukraine in a Global Economy

Ukraine is one of the biggest European states with considerable human, natural and productive potential. Its population is 48,2 million people and its industrial capacity is the most powerful in Eastern Europe. After a sharp decline in major economic indicators over the 90's, Ukraine now is experiencing rapid economic growth which started in 2000. This is particularly evident from the set of indicators (Table 1). However, many analysts relate recent success with the reanimation of old industrial capacities without much new investments, which soon will lead to a slowing down in the pace of growth and further stagnation (Quarterly predictions, 2002). Already in 2002 the growth of national GDP is observed at the level of 4,1%, which is lower than in 2000 and 2001 (6% and 9,1% respectively).

	1997	1998	1999	2000	2001	2002
Economic activity						
GDP, billions UAH	93.4	102.6	130.4	170.1	201.3	213.1*
Real GDP, apc	-3.0	-1.9	-0.2	6.0	9.1	4.1
Real industrial production, apc	-1.8	-1.0	4.3	13.2	14.2	7.0
Real agricultural production, apc	-1.9	-9.8	-5.7	7.6	10.2	3.0*
FDI, millions USD	581	747	489	594	769	600
Labour market						
Population, millions	50.5	50.1	49.7	49.3	49.0	48.1
Real wages, aapc	-0.4	-2.8	-5.7	1.0	20.4	22.0
ILO unemployment rate, %	-	-	11.9	11.5	11.0	10.5
Foreign economic activity						
Exports, apc	0.0	-13.4	-7.9	20.3	8.0	6.0*
Imports, apc	-1.1	-17.0	-19.1	18.9	14.1	4.5*
Current account balance, % GDP	-2.7	-3.0	2.6	4.7	3.7	5.1*
Official exchange rate UAH/USD (average annual)	1.86	2.45	4.13	5.44	5.37	5.33

Tab.1: Macro-Economic Situation of the Ukraine. Source: State Statistics Committee, NBU, Ministry of Finance, Quarterly Predictions(* - forecast, apc – annual percentage change, aapc – average annual percentage change)

In general the situation with national economy of Ukraine is much worse than in neighbouring countries to the East and to the West. It calls for further deep transformation of the economy and social sector, which still possess great deal of Soviet features. Low individual income level and lack of internal investment resources, high corruption index, high risks, including political and financial, make negative influence on the investment image of the country and consequently on its position in world economy.
Being one of the transition economies Ukraine is definitely not the one, which stands at the edge of the process of globalisation. There are not many multinational companies (MNC), it is not that integrated into world economy, especially its financial and banking sector, which unlike industry and services is underdeveloped and can not satisfy the growing demand of local and external investors. Another problem is a lack of appropriate infrastructure, first of all transport and telecommunications. Being one if the strategic "transit" states in Europe, Ukraine still has to develop its transport network intensively in order it to correspond to international standards. Telecommunications are developing quite rapidly over the last 4-5 years and its pace is comparable to those, existing in CEE. Though the scale of this process is still not sufficient for reaching the competitive position of Ukrainian companies on the world markets and for the smooth relations of the country with the rest of the world by electronic means.
In discussing the international competitiveness of the state, one must still remember that Ukraine possesses one of the biggest potential in several crucial modern industries and ranked in world top-ten in such sectors as aircraft industry, space-system engineering, weapon, electronics, highly solid materials, radio-electronics, shipbuilding etc. It has great potential in developing software and modern technologies on the basis of cybernetics, mathematics, physics, though the brain-drain in these spheres is especially high and many of high-class specialists are already working abroad, mainly in highly developed states. It is also necessary to stress, that international companies coming to Ukraine do not import the most advanced technologies and that is why the national R and D sector in its applied sector is getting out-of date without being really "nourished" by investors. Also situation is complicated by the shortage in indigenous investments and lack of venture capital. Fundamental science, which traditionally is financed by the state, is in a very bad condition though still has a respectable position in the world science. For example Philadelphia Institute of Scientific Information regularly calculate the share of each country in the world publication output and for Ukraine this share in 1998 was equal to 0.54% or 26th position. This is better than for New Zealand, Greece, Hungary, Mexico or Turkey. First positions in this rating possess USA, UK, Japan, Germany, France, Canada, Russia and Italy. Though for Ukraine several more years with the financing of fundamental science at

the level of 0,36% of GDP (2002) will lead to its complete collapse. The place of Ukraine in the world global economy and its recent dynamics could be well illustrated by its position in several international rankings.

Source	Nature of Ranking	Date of publication	Position	Position in previous period	Dynamics	Number of countries in ranking
Moody's Investor's Service	Credit Ranking	January 2002	B2	Caa1	+2	-
Standard and Poors Rating Services	Credit Ranking	December 2001	B	CCC	+1	90
Fitch Rating	Credit Ranking	March 2002	B	B-	+1	-
Davos World Forum	GCI – Global Competitiveness Index of state	November 2002	77	69	-8	80 (75)
Foreign Policy Journal	Global	January 2003	42	42	0	62
Heritage Fund	Index of Economic Freedom	November 2002	131	137	+6	155
Transparency International	Corruption Index	August 2002	86	83	-3	102 (91)
CID at Harvard University	NRI – Network Readiness Index	2001-2002	66	-	-	75

Tab. 2: Ukraine in International Rankings. Sources: Institute of Reform; The Global Competitiveness Report; The Global Information Technology Report 2001-2002: Readiness for the Networked World; Transparency International Perception Index 2002; Institute of Reforms; Korrespondent.Net

Ukraine improved its position in different credit ratings over the last 2 years. This is first of all related to the macroeconomic growth, stable situation with national currency, strict budget policy, reduction in debts and increase in national currency reserves. According to JP Morgan in 2001

Ukraine was leading in the list of most investment attractive countries after paying back about 60% of the income from total amount of capital invested in the national economy (Ministry of Economy 2002).

However among the severest "deficiencies" of Ukraine, highlighted by International Organisations and investment agencies, are incomprehensive legislation, lack of intellectual property rights, high corruption (see corruption index), slow process of internal investing due to the existence of wide-scale "grey" economy (about 50%).

The major reason for distortion of the competitiveness of Ukraine under Global Competitiveness Index (GCI) could be an extensive type of national economy. After ten years of constant industrial and general economic decline it strengthens its market positions, but mainly reanimating the old industrial capacities without much investment in new technologies and equipment. The prove of this fact is the structure of national export, which is over weighted by such commodities as ferrous metals (39%), mineral materials (9,6%), agricultural products (6,7%), products of chemistry (10,6%), machinery and equipment (9,3%), non-ferrous metals (5,4%) (State Statistics Committee 2002). Simultaneously the share of innovative products is still not big enough and is expanding slowly.

Despite its high level of human capital, skilled labour force, developed R and D sector, and high potential in producing innovations, Ukraine is a relative laggard in terms of readiness to compete in the global innovative economy. This is primary explained by its underdeveloped infrastructure, inadequate institutional milieu, and lack of efficient links between science and production sector. Being 66th out of 75 countries in the ranking according to Network Readiness Index Ukraine is classified as a state with low teledensity, weakly developed telecommunications infrastructure, lack of sufficient investments in ICT, relatively low population income level (Network Readiness Index Report). For example the index of Internet users per 100 inhabitants is at the factor of 0,39 (7,22 in Poland). The share of Internet users in total population (3,9%) is low comparing to highly developed countries: 65% in Sweden, 60% in Canada, 59% in US, 33% in Japan and 6% in Russia.

However the dynamics of growth in users of Internet in Ukraine is comparable to European tendencies – in December 2000 the registered number was at the level of 500 thousand users and already in October 2001 this number was increased by four times. And this is despite the high costs of Internet for the majority of Ukrainian population (25 US dollars a month). The three major determinants, which influence the growth in the number of Internet users in Ukraine are as follows (Blagodeteleva-Vovk 2002):

- *Education system*, since it provides the basics for forming the information society. The recent tendencies prove that ICT education was at the centre of Government attention and "computerisation" of schools along with the development of ICT training programs is in progress. By ranking in quality of IT education (element of NRI) Ukraine possesses 55 positions – much higher than by integrated index.
- *Income level*, structure of expenditures and unemployment rate, which determine economic conditions for Internet expansion, since any service, including information, has to be paid for. In 2000 (State Statistics Committee) the annual personal income was at the level of 1755 UAH (323 USD) with its maximum in capital Kyiv (1125 USD). Simultaneously the national average annual expenditures and savings amount was equal to 1692 UAH (311 USD) with its maximum in Kyiv (1273 USD). 90% of income is covering basic needs, i.e. excluding Internet. The level of unemployment in 2002 was 11,7 % (ILO methodology), which however does not reflect the specifics of hidden unemployment and grey sector of economy.
- *The level of infrastructure development and hardware*. The number of PC in Ukraine is growing rapidly (more than 50% annually) though it is still lower than in the developed economies (965 thousand on the 1st January of 2001). The number of personal computers per 100 inhabitants is 1,59 (6,89 in Poland). It is worth stressing that 75-80% of all PCs and Internet users are concentrated in 4-5 biggest cities and rural areas have an extremely low degree of coverage by modern technologies. The number of telephone lines per 100 inhabitants is only 22,1 (28,23 in Poland). This particularly explains wide expansion of cellular phones in Ukraine – the number of users in 2001 was increased by 260% and in 2002 – by 65%. In total 3,63 million people use cellular phones (7,5% of population) and it is foreseen that in 2006 this figure will reach 10 million (20% of population). (Korrespondent 2002)

Sub-indices	Rank
Enabling factors sub-indices	**64**
Network Access	68
Network Policy	67
Network Society	66
Network Economy	49
Network Access micro-indices	
Information Infrastructure	68
Hardware, software and support	66
ICT Policy	65
Business and Economic Environment	66
Networked Society micro-indices	
Networked Leaning	67
ICT Opportunities	69
Social Capital	51
NETWORK READINESS INDEX	**66**

Tab. 3: Network Readinnes Index – sub-indices for Ukraine.

It is also interesting to monitor the position of Ukraine according to separate sub-indices of NRI (Tab. 3), which shows the difference in "factor endowment" related to the information economy.

To summarise all above mentioned we can state that:
- Ukraine is one of the most underdeveloped European economies in terms of networking with global economy.
- Ukraine has big potential for ICT development, which is proved by the dynamics of change in major indices, characterising the Information Society.
- Ukraine has considerable social and intellectual potential, which however has no great influence on general productivity due to the weak links between R and D and production sector.
- Ukraine is a rapidly developing economy and potentially big market, which is shown by the pace of development of e-commerce (Networked economy sub-index).
- Providing the steady growth of national economy and personal incomes, which would allow both public and personal investments, the dynamics of development of ICT in Ukraine will be highly positive and according to some estimation will lead to 25% of Ukrainian population to become Internet users by the year 2025.

2. Ukraine's Biggest Cities – Reasons for Being Ambitious

Regional patterns of economic and social development of Ukraine over the last 10 years show a gradual increase in disparities between different regions and territories. It is evident from the fact that the variation between the poorest and richest region according to GVA per capita in 1996 was at a factor of 2.6 while in 2001 this had figure reached the level of 4.4. The geographical distribution of this index in 2000 is presented at Map 1.

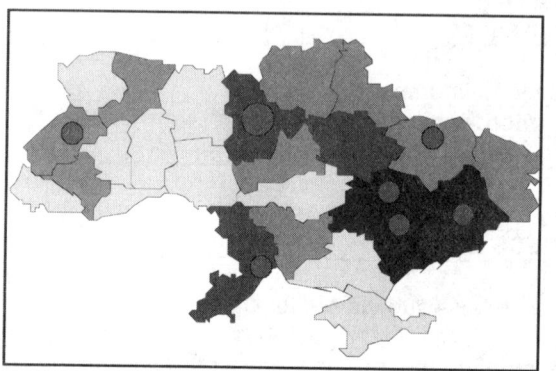
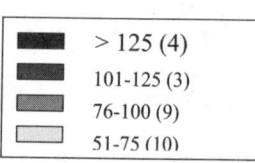

Map. 1. Regional GVA in Ukraine in 2000 (national average =100) and Urkrainian biggest cities. Source: State Statistics Committee, own mapping

The "richest" regions are the most densely populated areas and with the centres, which are the biggest cities of the country. Ukraine have 5 cities-millionaires (Kyiv, Odessa, Donetsk, Kharkiv and Dnipropetrovsk) and also 2 cities could be added as the significant centres of social and economic life – Lviv and Zaporizhzhia. After examination of the spatial distribution of diverse economic and social activities we would highlight all these cities as the major urban centres of Ukraine. Some basic data for them is provided in the Table 4. It is worth mentioning that the present statistical database does not allow full analysis of the trends in development of Ukrainian cities since only Kyiv is identified as a separate unit for statistical purposes and full data is available only for this city. In all other cases official data available at the level of regions (oblasts), this unfortunately does not give a comprehensive picture of the situation. However some data is available via the Association of Ukrainian cities and Web-resources.

Characteristics	Kyiv	Donetsk	Lviv	Odessa	Kharkiv	Dnipropetrovsk	Zaporizhzhia
Population, thous.[1]	2 607	1 042	785	1 002	1 490	1 093	840
GVA per capita[2]	5,96	3,50*	2,16*	2,83*	2,80*	3,56*	3,79*
Personal income[3]	6121	2128*	1256*	1480*	1604*	2455*	1902*
FDI per capita[4]	583	69,1*	-	95,6*	57,2*	87,6*	129,6*
Share in national export[5],%	16,2	18,3*	-	3,7*	2,6*	17,6*	8,2*
Number of universities[6]	66	26*	17*	20*	36*	20*	12*
Students/1000 population	99,6	24*	31*	35,5*	41*	29*	26*
International airport	2	1	1	1	1	1	-
Personal cars per 1000 inh.[7]	147	-	102	-	111	75	161
Telephones /100 households[8]	95	-	66	-	41	-	61
Number of theatres	31	5*	10*	6	10	8*	4*
Number of Internet providers	89	35	12	22	34	17	9

Tab. 4: Ukrainian Cities – Basic Characterstics. Sources: State Statistics Committee, Association of Ukrainian Cities, Institute of Reforms [1] – 01.10.2001; [2]- thousand UAH, 2000; [3] – UAH, 2000; [4] – USD, 01.01.2002; [5] - 2001; [6] - 2000; [7] - 2000; [8] – 2000; * - data for the whole oblast

Kyiv

The capital of Ukraine is one of the oldest cities in Europe, which has a history of more than 15 centuries, "The mother of all Russ cities" as labelled by the historians. With a population of 2,6 million (5,4% of Ukrainian total) the city represents a big potential market with rapidly growing consumer capacity. There is no official methodology for calculating regional GDP and that is why GVA is taken as the major indicator characterising the economic situation. Kyiv has GVA per capita at the level of 214% of national average (the poorest oblast has 51%).

Despite the fact that its share in national GVA and industrial output is equal to 17,4 and 9,3% respectively, it managed to attract almost a half of total amount of Ukrainian FDI, which in January 2003 was equal to 5,2 billion USD.

Kyiv has the biggest international airport of the country (Boryspil), the majority of subsidiaries of foreign companies have headquarters in Kyiv. The city has changed dramatically over the last five years and now can offer quite a high level of quality of life with developed infrastructure, services, modern lodging, entertainment, business sites and other amenities. Kyiv also has very high intellectual and scientific potential, here are located many internationally recognised R and D centres (particularly in the aircraft industry, spatial systems, electric welding, new materials, mathematics, cybernetics, etc.)

Kyiv has the most developed telecommunication network – 4 out of 5 major Cellular Phone operators have their headquarters in Kyiv, here you also can find about 90 Internet providers, multitude of hardware and software agents, integrating companies, Internet-cafes, etc. Kyiv is a culturally rich city with many historical sites, museums, theatres, exhibition and concert halls. For the last several years business climate in the city is characterised as the most attractive in Ukraine and foreigner capital (big companies and private entrepreneurs) feel here quite comfortable.

Donetsk

Donetsk is the industrial capital of Ukraine. This is the centre of traditional industrial region of Ukraine – Donbass, which historically had specialisation in coal-mining, producing ferrous metals, heavy machinery, traditional chemical and construction materials. Nowadays Donetsk is turning into considerable business centre of the country with its own stock market, many banks and financial institutions. It has very intensive links with Russian business and majority of FDI here are Russian.

Since the structure of Ukrainian economy is overloaded by products with low value added and high energy and materials intensity, and since the majority of export commodities are produced in old industrial centres Donetsk now has its "golden age". However, the sustainability of such a profitable situation is fully dependent on city's ability to diversify the structure of output, to strengthen the tertiary sector, sector of SME. The majority of city income is produced by big enterprises in the property of state or big private holdings. The role of local initiative and SME is rather small with an insignificant share of local taxes (up to 5%).

One of the major handicaps for Donetsk to become internationally recognised attractive site for living and doing business is its ecological situation. The degree of pollution here is the highest in the country, which in its turn is reflected in high mortality rate, sickness rate and depopulation.

Lviv
Opposite to Donetsk, Lviv is one of the most ecologically friendly Ukrainian urban zone. "Western capital" of Ukraine, the city which for several centuries belonged to Poland and still has an atmosphere and specifics of traditional Polish city. In Soviet period Lviv was not built-up as an industrial centre and had its specialisation in products of mass demand and services. This is the only Ukrainian city, which in its entirety was declared as world historical heritage under UNESCO auspices. It has magnificent architectural ensembles, which each year attract millions of tourists from all over the Europe and other continents. Polish tourists constitute over the 50% of all foreign tourists coming to Lviv.

The lack of adequate communal and transport infrastructure has to be considered as a serious deficiency and the reform of this sector is a number one in the agenda of municipal authorities. Lviv is a popular place for organising diverse business summits, exhibitions, gatherings, cultural events and festivals. It has a developed network of universities, institutes and training centres with major specialisations in human and social sciences. Local civil society institutions are also amongst the most developed and self-sustainable in Ukraine.

Odessa
This is the "sea gate" to Ukraine – one of the biggest ports of the Black Sea. Odessa possesses one of the strongest potentials in the tertiary sector, having specialisation in transport, logistics and storage services, trade. It has on its territory the Special Economic Zone "Freeport of Odessa" with considerable tax cuts and benefits for international companies. It has a very positive impact on economic growth of the city.

Odessa has unique capabilities in education and science (here is located the only University which provides training for specialists of nuclear power stations, Academy of Low Temperatures and Maritime University). This is one of the most well equipped cities in terms of modern communications and IT. Also Odessa is well known for its cultural life and ethnically diversified environment.

As in many other cities there are serious problems with communal infrastructure and municipal transport system. Though at the same time this is the biggest inter-modal junction of Ukraine having together all means of transport – maritime, automobile, railway, air connection, pipes. The newly constructed branch of oil pipeline Odessa-Brody is one of the biggest strategic investment projects of Ukraine over the last 10 years with the aim of integrating Ukraine firmly into the European oil transit system. Also newly constructed fast railway line for the containers and lorries to Lithuania benefited to establishing smooth and less bureaucratic connection for those transporting the goods from Black to Baltic sea (time span dropped down in 3 times).

Kharkiv

It used to be the capital of the Ukrainian Soviet Republic in the 1920's and its inhabitants still have the aspirations of "a capital city". This is also called "a city of students" – it has the greatest number of universities and institutes and the biggest number of students per 1000 inhabitants after Kyiv.

Kharkiv is a centre of Ukrainian machinery complex and used to be one of the biggest centres of the Military Industrial Complex in USSR. So now it possesses great intellectual and scientific potential in such domains as aircraft industry, weapon, transport and energetic machinery, producing software and hardware, innovative technologies in medicine and microbiology. Kharkiv is one of the biggest transport junctions having intensive links with neighbouring Russia. In its new strategy the city proclaimed its goal to become the business site for Ukrainian and international companies looking to Eastern markets as their future.

Dnipropetrovsk

This is one of the biggest industrial cities of Ukraine. Dnipropetrovsk region by many indices (GVA, industrial output, export, and investments) possesses 2-3 position among Ukrainian regions. The city has a developed financial sector with 11 commercial banks and 2nd position in amount of provided loans. There are 20 commodity stocks. Dnipropetrovsk is a capital of ferrous metallurgy, machinery, especially precise, spatial-system and transport machinery. Here are located the most important factories, which produce spatial technologies and appliances, which have strong competitive positions in world markets and participate in many international projects (e.g. Sea Launch).

Zaporizhzhia

Out of 7 cities included in this analysis this one is the least "big". However it has several features, which in the present model of development of Ukraine makes Zaporizhzhia one of the growth points of the national economy. One striking fact – even after several years of economic growth Ukraine has now reached only 63% of its 1989 GDP level. Zaporizhzhia as a region achieved greater success – it reached 100% of 1989 figure already in 2000. This is one of the biggest centres of ferrous and non-ferrous metallurgy, transport machinery. Here is concentrated the industrial capacity of one of the biggest foreign investors - "AutoZAZ-Daewoo" (motor-cars construction) as well as the "Motor Sich" factory producing aircraft and missile engines.

3. Any Chance to Become European Centres?

The phenomena of big cities is well-explored in the scientific literature of the last century though still the precise definition of a world, global, international, European city or mega-city is in the process of formulation. There are different approaches to the functional identification of the role of the largest cities in the global scale based upon either external or internal characteristics, or both.

Fundamental research in the middle of 20th century (Hall, 1966, Hymer, 1972) proposed that the global city gained its role due to the functional inner pre-conditions in such spheres as politics, trade, communications, finance, education, culture and technology. And this is all the result of process of urbanisation. Others (Cohen, 1981, Friedmann, 1986) put emphasis on the corporate power and location criteria associated with the activities of Multinational corporations.

At the same time there is an opposite approach of Sassen (1991, 1994), which puts aside detailed analysis of the inner organisation of the city and explains the phenomenon of world cities as a symbiosis of two processes: globalisation and organisational structure of the producer service and finances. The less broad approach and more finance-concentrated is the one proposed by Reed (1981). He constructed a five-tier hierarchy of world cities according to the existence of international finance centres.

The recent findings of "Globalisation and World Cities Research Group and Network" (London) propose a classification of world cities in terms of their role as global service centres. On the basis of deep analysis of empirical data in 4 major sectors – accountancy, banking, advertising and legal services - were identified 55 world cities in three levels (Alfa, Beta and Gamma) and also 68 cities (split into 3 sub-groups) with the indicators of formation of world cities' features (Beaverstock, Smith and Taylor 1999)

For Ukraine there is bad news – none of its cities is in the list of world cities. There is also good news – Kyiv is in the list of "candidates" (2nd sub-group) showing some evidences of becoming the World City someday. The question is how Kyiv should perform in order to catch-up with such cities as Prague, Warsaw, Istanbul (Gamma metropolises) and what progress Odessa or Donetsk should make to qualify as the potential world cities as much as St Petersburg, Dresden or Tashkent (3rd sub-group of candidates).

Unfortunately this brief analysis does not give us an opportunity to present a comprehensive account based on the presence of MNC in each particular city and hence the degree of integration of Ukrainian biggest cities into the world business environment. We are basing our conclusions on the analysis of primary factors and some secondary indices, which in fact could prove the presence of strong demand from the business community, both national and international. However deeper research based on empirical data showing the presence of major service companies in Ukrainian urban centres and their linkages with world centres is needed in the future.

We also do not come up with the definition of possibilities for Ukrainian cities to become world cities. We are more concentrated on their potential to become considerable urban centres in European scale. That is why further reflections concern the chances of 7 cities to become "European cities" in terms of not only functional characteristics in some strategic service sectors but also based on their cultural, intellectual and social potential.

Though basing our conclusions on those few facts, presented in this paper, it is possible to say that Kyiv has strong chance to become the World City in a relatively short time horizon if the present pace of development is sustained. This is possible not only because of the development of major service sectors, but also because of the role of Kyiv as a cultural, social educational and scientific centre of Eastern Europe. This is the place where you can get the utmost concentration of Ukraine in all its aspects – geographical, economical, social, national, and ethnic. And that's the place the one should come if wants to find out something about East Europe and Slavonic world. There are real opportunities to communicate with the people in the same language, with the same level of education and very similar mentality, with people, who have own deep-rooted traditions, and who know and respect European and world traditions. So along with being well equipped technically, socially and economically for integration into the global economy Kyiv proposes a concentrate of 48-million European nation with millenniums history.

Speaking about the European chances of other biggest Ukrainian cities it is worth to highlight the following. Out of 6 cities Odessa, Donetsk and Lviv are the most promising to become the centres of European significance, especially on the map of a newly shaped continent without the dividing lines of Cold War period. They represent regional capitals of three Ukrainian parts – South, East and West – which are very different not only from a cultural, historical or social point of view but differ from each other by the mode of making business, degree of personal initiative and entrepreneurial potential.

Odessa may become a capital of the hi-tech sector of Ukraine and having the beneficiary regime of a Free Port it could attract foreign companies specialising in this sector. Local universities and research centres would supply the high-skilled employees with the condition of maintaining tight links between R and D and enterprises. Another great potential of Odessa is a Black Sea transport multimodal node, standing on the cross-road of the strategic routes from the North to the South and from the East to the West of Europe.

Lviv is going to be a significant service centre in the event that all necessary arrangements for the improvement of infrastructure according to international standards will be made in the coming years. Enlargement of EU in 2004 will lead to the situation when Lviv will be located only some kilometres from EU border. In case there would be a chance to omit the appearance of new Iron Curtain between new members and "the rest of Europe", Lviv has a chance similar to the chance of Western Polish cities, which gained a lot from the neighbouring Eastern Germany after borders were opened up.

Donetsk is the most controversial case of all mentioned. It definitely has all signs of becoming city of European scale – due to the rapid development of finance sector, services, building modern amenities and infrastructure. At the same time it is a capital of traditional industrial region, which in several-years term in case major reforms will not be implemented, will sink into the "deep water" of crisis and social exclusion. Present technologies and producing capacities are depreciated for 70-80%, new technologies are being introduced at a very low pace. The main component – training and re-training – does not correspond to the needs of modern economy and companies working in the city. So by symbols Donetsk is a strong centre with potential to become big Eastern European business site. But by nature this city could turn into "the ghost" after national economic structure will be changed considerably and emphasis in production and export will be shifted from raw materials and low value-added products to the competitive innovative commodities and services.

Among the other three cities only Kharkiv has a chance to become European City. These assumptions are primary based on its high intellectual, technical and scientific potential. However radical changes in the sphere of R and D and education are needed in the next few years in order to match the demand of enterprises with the supply capabilities of universities and institutions. Special emphasis should be put on formation of integrated structures such as technology parks and incubators where science and practice could co-exist in harmony enriching each other in the process of reproduction. A well-developed transport infrastructure, financial and other services, good ecological conditions and developed modern amenities would be stimulating to the formation of a significant business centre in the east of Ukraine.

Dnipropetrovsk and Zaporizhzhia unfortunately have very narrow specialisation in the production sphere, which has its impact on establishing of educational and other social institutions. These cities would remain important national-scale or even CIS-scale centres

(Commonwealth of Independent States), though their potential is not enough for creating the sound fundamentals of European cities.

Conclusions

This paper is a first attempt to evaluate the readiness of the biggest Ukrainian cities for the sharp competitive environment of modern global economy. There is no deep analysis of particular evidences of metropolitan cities in Ukrainian reality. But still proposed picture outlines major specifics of Ukraine as a player in the global innovative economy. The present chances for Ukraine to win are not that high but rapid economic growth and fundamental changes in political and social spheres give all reasons to envisage an optimistic scenario of future development. And this optimism is based primary on the dynamics of development of the biggest cities. This is the place where major changes are occurring and where the one can find the signs of building a modern Ukrainian economy.

Each of these 7 cities has unique features and gravitation power for certain economic and social activities. But they are first of all a gateway for the rest of the country to the external world and simultaneously a gateway for the world which wants to know more about Ukraine and wants to make business here.

References:
Beaverstock J., Smith R., Taylor P. (1999) A Roaster of World Cities. In: Cities, 16 (6).
Blagodeteleva-Vovk S. (2002). Evaluation of Internet Potential Users in Ukraine by the Year 2005. Marketing in Ukraine.
Cohen R. (1981) The new international division of labour, multinational corporations and urban hierarchy. In: M. Dear and A. Scott (Eds.), Urbanisation and Urban Planning in Capitalist Society. London: Methuen.
Doroshenko O. (2002) Perspectives and Threats of Globalisation Facing Ukraine in the 21st Century. Research Paper.
EBRD Transition Report 2001 Update.
Friedmann J. (1986) The world city hypothesis. In: Development and Change, 17.
Hall P. (1966) The World Cities. London: Heinemann.
Hymer S. (1972)The multinational corporation and the law of uneven development. In: J. Bhagwati (Ed.), Economics and World Order from the 1970s to the 1990s. Collier: MacMillan.
Investment Rating of Ukrainian Regions (2002). Institute of Reforms (Kyiv).
Korrespondent (2002). 'Mobile Communications in Ukraine – Future Development', October 16 – www.korrespondent.net
Major Social and Economic Indices of Ukrainian Cities – Members of the Association of Ukrainian Cities (2001). Association of Ukrainian Cities (Kyiv).
Monitoring of Social and Economic Development of Ukrainian Regions in 2001 (2002) Ministry of Economy and European Integration, UNDP (Kyiv).
OECD Economic Outlook Vol. 69 July 2001.
Quarterly Prediction (2002) Ukrainian economic survey. October (Kyiv).
Reed H. (1981) The Pre-eminence of International Financial Centres (New York,

Praeger).
Report on Implementation of Economic Policy in 2001 by the Government of Ukraine (2002) Ministry of Economy and European Integration of Ukraine (Kyiv).
Sassen S. (1991) The Global City. Princeton: Princeton University Press.
-,   Cities in a World Economy. London: Pine Forge Press.
Statistical Yearbook of Ukraine 2000 (2001). State Statistics Committee (Kyiv).
The Global Competitiveness Report 2001, The Global Information Technology. Report 2001-2002: Readiness for the Networked World. Executive summaries, available at World Economic Forum's site www.weforum.org.

Globalization and third-tier cities: the European experience

Mark Jayne

Literature surrounding urbanism and globalization has overwhelmingly focused on global and national cities. The aim of this paper is to take a step, or two, down the urban hierarchy and investigate flows of capital, culture and people associated with third-tier (or lesser) cities. I argue that Europe is characterised by a relatively high number of small- and medium-sized cities, and the ways in which they have faired in an increasingly globalized urban hierarchy (characterised by intense inter-urban competition) deserves increased theoretical attention and empirical research. However, as Thrift (2000) shows, cities are not homogenised entities - not all cities are the same; one story of urbanity cannot tell all - at any level of the urban hierarchy. This paper therefore presents fragments of political, economic, social, cultural and spatial practices and processes relating to third-tier European cities. In doing so, I interrogate the utility of conceptualisations of the globalized post-industrial/post-Fordist/(post)modern city, and also unpack the idea of the 'European city' as an archetypal example of urbanity.

Urbanism and Globalization:
The Post-Industrial/Post-Fordist/Post-Modern City

The past two decades have witnessed the global reconstruction of economic, political and social, cultural and spatial practices and processes, which have had a profound effect upon the nature of everyday life. This has been theorised in terms of a movement to late or advanced capitalism, underpinned by a shift from Fordism to flexible accumulation. Related to this profound change has been the decline of manufacturing industries and an increase in the importance of service industries. This has been coupled with social and demographic forces that saw the simultaneous increase in mass unemployment, and the rise of a 'new petite bourgeoisie' (Giddens 1973). These processes have been mapped onto the landscape, and reproduced in space by conditioning and reflecting the social production of the built environment (Knox 1987). In time with these changes, North American and European cities were hit with recession that led to a dramatically declining manufacturing base, unemployment and physical decline. This 'urban crisis' was met with 'a new urban politics', which saw city authorities (previously focused on local provision of welfare and services), being forced to adopt a more outwardly orientated stance designed to foster local growth and economic development (Harvey 1989). Risk taking, inventiveness, and the driving necessities of promotion and profit,

engendered an entrepreneurial outlook by local government agencies in an attempt to respond to economic, social and cultural change.
Theorists such as Zukin (1982), Knox (1987), Soja (1989), Harvey (1989) and Davis (1990) have presented these new socio-spatial urban configurations - variously described as post-industrial, post-Fordist, or post-modern – as being very different from their predecessors. This 'new' city is not only characterised by new public-private partnerships or programmes of place promotion, but is visibly more spectacular. Revitalised city centres and agglomerated business and financial districts feature gleaming high-rise office blocks, waterfront developments, heritage centres and 'urban villages' - such as London's Canary Wharf, Barcelona's Olympic Marina, Paris' La Defense, Vancouver's Pacific Plaza, New York's Battery Park, and Sydney's harbour. This economic and symbolic (city) centre, is surrounded by high-technology business clusters, out of town mega-malls, and a veritable archipelago of elite enclaves, fragmented neighbourhoods and 'edge cities' (Zukin 1982; Knox 1987; Soja 1989).
It is in this context that increased competition has arisen around the efforts of cities to create new images in order to attract speculators, businesses, and consumers. Place promotion and marketing strategies have been augmented by speculative developments and partnerships with private capital. If cities were/are to be successfully rejuvenated, local authorities became aware that they would be forced to initiate redevelopments that were often speculative in nature, high profile, and had symbolic significance in attempting to represent progressive socio-cultural and economic trends. These physical and symbolic attempts to improve the urban environment are what Landry and Bianchini (1995) consider as initiatives, to promote a 'creative city'. These encompass aesthetic improvements of 'soft infrastructure', ranging from the building of squares and fountains to the greening of streets, the provision of benches and improved public spaces and establishment of late night shopping and 'happy hours', cultural events and festivals such as music, literary or street theatre - all designed to make the city more 'liveable'. Augmenting this has been the promotion of creative and cultural industries such as advertising, architecture, the art and antique market, crafts, design, designer fashion, film, interactive leisure software, music, performing art, publishing, software, television and radio. With buildings and facilities such as theatres, art galleries, convention and exhibition centres, as well a supporting cast of café bars, restaurants, fashion boutiques, delicatessens and other cultural facilities - the buzz of 'creativity, innovation and entreprenurialism' - which is thought to be associated with these activities, is seen as crucial to contributing to the competitiveness of cities (Florida 2002).

It is clear, then, that in this vision of the restructuring of cities - particularly those that have most successfully moved from a focus on manufacturing production to a service and consumption based economy - that particular social and spatial forms of urban life have been produced. For example, while some urban spaces are developed around the consumption practices of the 'new petite bourgeoisie', it is suggested that in other parts of the city (such as inner city or suburban residential areas) there is an ever-widening gulf between the 'haves 'and 'have-nots'. For example, the declining industrial city with unemployment, fiscal problems from the erosion of the tax base, and poor households in poor areas, is characterised as being plagued with housing abandonment, arson, vandalism and sometimes riots. Moreover, new kinds of flexible deregulation of the labour market ensure that it is only low paid, insecure and low status jobs that are generated by the demands of gentrifiers, conference delegates and other affluent consumers. It is this regime of flexible accumulation that creates these new spatial and social relations. However, such uneven development is not only manifest within but also between cities (Harvey 1989; Savage and Warde 1993): landscapes of consumption and devastation exist in intimate relationship to one another (Zukin 1982; Harvey 1985; Davis 1990). The combination of economic, political and cultural morphology has been reflected in new spatial and social formations, and academic attention has been concerned to map their impact upon the changing city.

The Urban Hierarchy and Uneven Development
The extent and degree of this urban morphology is thus seen to be uneven. The restructuring of urban employment and the physical infrastructure is a global process that has generated new international developments and connectedness between capital, labour and resources as well as social identities, lifestyles and forms of sociability. Castells (1989, 1997) identifies how the relationship between places and spaces of flows of capital and culture is being recast, noting how cities' relationship to global flows and their ability to generate these new urban spaces is crucial to the ability of cities to compete in a post-industrial economy.
As such, Castells (1989, 1997) suggests cities must be viewed as a nexus point of these different, complex flows and relations – a place where they become 'visible'. Thus, a city is both a spatial manifestation (physical and social) and a place in space – it exists in a space of flows with relationships to other places. Harvey (1989, 14) argues that it is the very nature of this economy which ensures 'the ideology of locality, place and community has become central to the political rhetoric of urban governance' - as cities attempt to make themselves more attractive to those flows of capital and culture.

Addressing this contradiction between 'fixity' and 'motion' in conceptualising the territorial organisation and historical geography of the spatial scales of cities is a pertinent concern (Brenner 1989). Thus, Massey's (1993) conceptualisation of power geometry and space is an important theoretical and empirical tool. Massey shows how individuals, groups, cities, and regions are placed in very distinct ways in relation to the flows and interconnections of political, economic, social and cultural process of globalisation. Some initiate flows while others are on the receiving end of them. So those who are 'doing' the making and the communication are in a position of centrality. Thus, in terms of seeking to understand the transformations (or not) of cities, consciousness of links with the wider world (which integrates in a positive way local, regional, and national and supranational political, economic and cultural influence) is necessary. In presenting a more progressive 'sense of place', Massey highlights how theorising the transformations of cities is about successfully conceptualising a global construction of place. What is important here then, is that while cites are presented as a nexus point for flows of capital and culture, Massey depicts cities as dynamic, social constructions; the result of historical processes where different political, economic and cultural practices have sculpted the character of the city.

Such an understanding suggests that the ability of cities to compete at particular nodes in the post-industrial urban hierarchy is in part delineated by complex interaction of political, economic, social, cultural and spatial practices and processes that operate at particular spatial scales. For example, global/supranational/national/regional cities are such because of the physical and symbolic infrastructure, political, economic, social and cultural facilities and structures that they developed and sustain. In essence, global cities have the highest concentration of financial and business institutions; political and economic centrality; and the right mix of lifestyles and social relations - which importantly *represent* those cities as socially and culturally successful, innovative and attractive. The social and spatial reorganisation of capital, which has resulted in new functions for financial markets, has created this re-ordering of the significance and influence of cities across the world. However, this has also ensured that while some cites can successfully compete in this post-industrial economy, others are disadvantaged. In essence, intra-city spaces/places, and regions monopolise control functions, while others are subordinate (Massey 1993).

Thus, where city spaces are envisaged or refashioned by city imagineers, altering the prevailing social construction of space, the changes (physical or cultural), can only be fully understood in terms such as the sedimentation of local social relations, and geographical dimensions of regional, national and global spaces. There is a need to ground understandings of such urban morphology in theoretical and empirical study in order to highlight how deeply embedded cultural systems affect places (Savage and Warde 1993).

It is the contention here that, in seeking to explain epochal urban change and presenting the political, economic, and social changes associated with particular periods of (post)modernity, theorists have overwhelmingly concentrated on those cities which seemed to establish and best highlight their arguments concerning urban paradigm shifts. While this is perhaps understandable, as academics seek to promote breakthroughs in critical discourse, it has been cities near the top of the urban hierarchy - global cities such as Los Angeles, London, Singapore and Sydney, or cities in the western industrialised world with national or regional significance, such as Barcelona, Indianapolis, Manchester and Birmingham – which have mainly been the focus of theorists. However, as Thrift (2000) states, cities are not homogenised entities - not all cities are the same; not all cities (or spaces/places with cities) compete at the same social or spatial level; one story of urbanity cannot tell all. It is suggested here that if debates about the nature of the post-industrial/post-Fordist/post-modern city are to be more fully developed, then cities throughout the urban hierarchy must be considered. Savage and Warde (1993) note that such a process in turn interrogates the very notion of such archetypal city formations.

In a similar vein, research has also tended to be overly deterministic in its theorisation of factors such as the social construction of the social relations, identities, lifestyles and forms of sociability that contribute to the nature of everyday life in our cities. In sum, the ways in which space and place make a difference to their discursive construction has been under-theorised (Savage and Warde 1993; O'Connor and Wynne 1996). When studies consider archetypal identities which have been associated with urban change (whether they be new petite bourgeoisie, industrial working class, bohemian artists, immigrants, lesbian and gay, youth and ethnic social groups - or any other consumption identity couplet which could be mentioned), it must be understood that although there are groups of consumers who share similar lifestyles across national boundaries and continents, there the also important differences between them (Glennie and Thrift 1992).

As such the consequences of globalisation have been undertheorised and current literature impoverished in several ways; firstly, insufficient attention has been paid to the way in which regional, national and global processes influence the 'local' cultural politics of place. Secondly, little regard has been paid to the way in which urban trajectories are embedded in particular constellations of 'stubborn' local social and spatial relations that are consumed, negotiated and contested in light of multiple institutional and public discourses. This 'reflexivity' in local contexts has been presented by Giddens (1991) as a reaction to people being socialised in the light of global knowledge. This is elaborated by Spybey (1996, 67) who suggests 'towards the end of the twentieth century the individual, as never before, is subject to a continuous array of global influences. But the important factor is the way in which people reproduce social institutions in the light of these pervasive global models. This alone reveals the true meaning of globalization, which is essentially a reflexive process involving both global cultural inputs and the local act of reproduction. Globalization can only exist when, on a global scale, people take up and reproduce institutions in their local milieu'. Spybey describes this in terms of the shift from Fordism to post-Fordism, and globalisation of culture as key elements in multiplying the complexity and density of global-local interdependence.

However, it is important to understand that while diverse city cultures incorporate communities into an uneven and unequal world, the dynamics of globalization creates pressure for local variety, which potentially in turn, can be institutionalised on a global scale. As Spybey (1996, 1), suggests a 'mass participation society' mediates how the dynamics of globalization effects the local level and shapes a societies labour markets, its patterns of inequality, its health, political stability and the life chances of its people. Interpenetration is a concept which depicts the two way relationship between the global and the local and is 'central to our comprehension of globalizing process as major structuration of the world as a whole ... tied together as part of global nexus' (Spybey 1996, 102).

In sum, interpenetration describes both concrete global-local interdependence and consciousness of the global whole. However, the key to this pervasive quality of the globalizing process is as Robertson suggests, 'reflexivity ... vis-a-vis structure and/or individuals' (1992, 33). This highlights how globalization is a contested process that carries reflexive connotations and objectives increasingly interconnecting the local and the global in mutual reference and influence. Robertson depicts a process of 'Globalization [which] influences the reproduction of social institutions by continuously presenting us with a globally derived and cumulative cultural background to inform the reflexive monitoring process in social behaviour', (1992, 12). As such, there is great relevance in discussing the ways in which regional, national and global factors impact upon the local economic, political and cultural trajectories of cities throughout the urban hierarchy.

Multi-Scalar Urbanity
While it is clear that cities compete in terms of the prevailing modes of a 'globally integrated' economy, this creates multi-sector uneven development which can only be fully theorised by extending theories of 'glocalisation' (Robertson 1992) to a more progressive multi-scalar

perspective. The ability of localities to undertake meaningful action in the face of globalisation has been a dominant theme in much social science literature over past two decades. Literature has reflected on the globalisation of cities and culture, the new international division of labour, the globalisation of finance and investment, the emergence of transnational frameworks, the hollowing out of the nation-state, and the political response of entrepreneurialism (Boyle and Hughes 1991; Cox 1993, 1997; Cochrane et al 1996; Hall and Huddard 1996). However, the central motif of this literature has been the impact of globalisation on cities, communities and localities through a dichotomous interpretation of the global-local dialectic. This ignores that it is processes of interpenetration that discursively constitute global-local structures. Moreover, this also makes invisible the understanding that such interpenetration is constituted by flows which reverberate (or not) with multifarious regional, national, and supranational influence to effect the nature of specific cities and visa versa (see Robertson 1992). Such an interpretation has potential to provide a fuller picture of the nature of the post-industrial/post-Fordist/post-modern urban hierarchy.

Such a project begins to appear in Brenner's (1998) consideration of the contradiction of notions of fixity and motion in the circulation of capital. This asserts capital's necessary dependence on territoriality or place and its space annihilation tendencies (in generating so-called generic placeless places). Lefebvre (1974) adopts a Foucauldian stance to argue that the scalar structures of both cities and territorial states have been moulded even more directly by the contradictions between fixity and motion in the circulation of capital since the nineteenth century, when a 'second nature' of socially-produced socio-spatial configurations were consolidated on a world scale. As such, the current round of multi-dimensional re-scaling in political, economic, social and cultural terms represent cities and states being reterritorialised in the conflictual search for 'glocal' scalar fixes. As Brenner suggests, '[t]he production of spatial scales, and the notion of 'scalar fix' to theorise the multiscalar configurations of territorial organisation, allow understanding of hierarchical patterns of interdependence and the constitution of a seemingly relevant, fixed and immutable geographical infrastructure for each round of capital circulation' (1998, 462).

As such, any progressive theorisation of the politics of scale must be attuned to both aspects of geographical scale: its (potential) mutability as well as its (provisional) fixity. For example, Wood (1998) suggests that the literature on urbanisation and globalization is on theoretically and empirically impoverished ground in their consideration of entrepreneurial governance and the way in which scale and concepts of the local and the global have been mobilised. Thus, while the notion of a socio-spatial dialectic is evident in global-local restructuring and competition between places, there is a need to distinguish the social, physical and cultural character of *place* as being discursively constructed with local, regional, national, supranational and global influences. Wood argues there is a need to move away from a view that concerns itself with consigning social processes to particular global and local spatial scales. In order to fully understand the processes shaping both specific urban arenas and the constitutive role of the local in shaping the broader changes associated with globalisation, it is necessary to adopt a theoretical perspective which not only focuses on the relationship between spaces and networks and flows but also the political, economic, social, cultural and spatial constituents which mediate them. The second half of this paper elaborates this argument with reference to third-tier European cities

Globalisation and third-tier European cities
I suggest that given the structure of the urban hierarchy in Europe any conceptualisation of an archetypal European city must be that of a third-tier city and not a city which is a global or supra-nationally significant city. Furthermore, while that it is conceptually useful to generalise about third-tier cities as part of a globalized urban system - and there have been interesting case-studies presented from third-tier cities in Brazil, Japan, South Korea and the USA (see for example, Markusen et al 1999) - it is important that the discursive construction of that third-tier urbanity is more fully explored. The focus here, then, is to outline some broad urban discourses, in conjunction with examples of fragments of political, economic, social, cultural and spatial practices and processes associated with specific European third-tier cities.

Political Economy
In a globalized urban hierarchy not all cities have the capacity or ability to be successful in attracting global capital, developing financial and service economies, or providing the spaces/places to appeal to new residents, visitors and tourists. Not all cities have the institutional expertise to successfully instigate public-private partnerships with the potential to facilitate 'spectacular' developments or infrastructure improvements which produce the spaces/places and ambience associated with post-industrial/post-modern identities and lifestyles. Similarly, not all cities are sufficiently economically, spatially and/or socially diverse to innovate and significantly alter the physical and symbolic resonances of their past heritage; to render industrial and working-class employment and lifestyles marginal; or to socialise a significant proportion of the population to desire jobs, lifestyles and spaces/places associated with the post-industrial/post-Fordist/post-modern economy.

For example, cites such as London, Paris and Berlin are able to exploit their position as central nodes in a global economy and attract large amounts of capital, inward investment, all the skilled workers they need and financial, managerial and white-collar industries. National cities such as Leeds, Milan, Dublin and Hamburg, while not as successful as the previous group, prosper as rich, well-endowed cities seemingly able to attract workers and businesses. Elsewhere, other cities such as Bristol, Seville, Cambridge, Bonn, Lisbon, and Plymouth can claim to be significant at national levels because they are able to fully exploit their location as regional hubs, successfully sustain less dense post-industrial centers, or attract flows of money and people relating to educational expertise or the presence of military bases. On the other hand, third-tier cities such as Rennes and Perugia have struggled to maintain their roles as administrative and tertiary centers, whereas Bergamo has sold itself as Italy's city of production hosting agricultural and industrial fairs. Other third-tier cities such as St Etienne and Stoke-on-Trent have been less successful in finding an economic specificity beyond traditional industrial lexicons.

Self-imaging and place promotion have been identified as central to the political rhetoric of urban governance and are moreover constitutive of a 'glocalised' ideology of 'locality, place and community' (Harvey 1989, p. 14). Entrepreneurial urban practices therefore attempt to produce attractive and distinctive locations in the face of intense inter-urban competition. However, what has not been fully developed is an understanding of the extent to which the characteristics of particular cities (or places/spaces within cities) dictate their degree of (potential) success in the post-industrial economy. Many cities (and areas within cities) are less concerned with economic growth than economic stability, or with halting a spiral of decline by producing more 'liveable' conditions. This often involves not 'spectacular developments' but rather cosmetic renovation of declining city centres; attempting to produce a competitive advantage in localised economic, cultural or spatial terms; or simply by 'greening' initiatives, community projects or retraining in order to improve the job prospects of the (post)industrial workforce. Such diversity in the entrepreneurial orientations of urban governance highlights how issues of scale, scope and efficacy must be central to any conceptualisation and evaluation of 'glocalised' urban renewal projects (Hall and Hubbard 1998). This is not only an important goal in itself, but also helps us to examine how local cultures mediate, contest and negotiate their trajectories and how different groups, with differing mindsets and agendas, view cities.

It is perhaps understandable that research has presented cities (and places/spaces within cities) at the top of the urban hierarchy as facilitators and beneficiaries of global economic restructuring, and those lower down as recipients and victims of new regimes of capital accumulation. Likewise, it is often evident through the visible extremes of wealth and poverty that certain places and people within the city are celebrated and are economically and culturally central while others are marginalised. However, the imposition of such stereotypical growth-coalition models of entrepreneurial success and failure can obscure more than it reveals (Hall and Hubbard 1996). Such generalisation ignores the most important feature of globalised urbanity: that political and economic priorities, orientations, objectives and actions, are mediated through a complex matrix of specific localised social, cultural and spatial factors.

Bagnasco and Le Galès (2000) identify a range of practices and processes which can be associated with the political economy of European cites. For example, while economic globalisation has led to fiscal crisis, unemployment and the undermining of strong European welfare states, state intervention and relatively stable job market in some sectors (for instance, the relatively high proportion of workers in the public-sector) has ensured that there has been little altering in the ranking of cities or indeed a pressing need to significantly restructure and agglomerate financial and economic command functions. Third-tier European cities are strongly embedded in historic and relatively stable regional and local networks and are not necessarily overly-dependent on high levels of global flows of capital, culture and people.

The literature on new urban politics and entrepreneurial governance provides valuable insights into changes in cities, but exhibits a crude conception of the relations between the local and the global. This has led to over generalisations about the mobility of economic and symbolic capital at different scales. Instead of the local being considered as mutable and the global as abstract, linking them through the intermediate scales allows a fuller understanding of how fluidity and flow discursively construct the character of place/space. As such, 'globalisation is not a matter of the construction of a global economic space or arena, but of the expansion of networks and flows (of money goods and people) and of their articulation with areal or regional spaces at different scales' (Low 1997, 244).

These kinds of themes have begun to be more fully theorised and explained by writers arguing that it is an increasingly common strategy for cities and regions to approach multi-sector uneven development (and the constraining and enabling factors of opportunity, location and action) by pursuing 'structured complimentarity' (Jessop 1998), 'comparable regionalism' (Cisneros 1995), or 'internal regionalisation' (Hall 1997). This means that regeneration projects are tailored to the particular spatial scale in which the city (or place/space within the city) is competing. For example, 'flagship' projects often surround the creation of new types of urban places/spaces for living, working and playing, and attract producer services and people consuming a 'mix and match lifestyle' (Mort 1998). Market hubs or gateways, off-centre retailing, new cityscapes with multi-cultural 'urban villages' (such as gay and ethnic quarters), meanwhile, attempt to refigure or redefine the urban hierarchy to produce a new physical, social (and even cybernetic) infrastructure. Such methods of space and place production create location-specific advantage for the production of goods and services and other urban activities relating to new markets and class fractions, modifying the spatial division of consumption through local, regional, national and global levels of competition.

A political-economy analysis suggests that invariably it is cities with distinct indigenous economic potential that have been more proactive in shaping local, regional, national, supranational and global economic competitiveness. Bigger cities have a higher functional centrality and degree of urban spatial influence. Smaller, more locally-based markets with a less pronounced economic identity have less utilisable economic specificity and have difficulty identifying and promoting specificity beyond the boundaries of the city. For example, Herrschel (1998) describes the ability of particular cities in Eastern Europe to compete following the transformation from post-Socialist modes of accumulation and regulation. Inevitably, bigger cities were quick to utilise existing specificity, individuality and inter-local distinctiveness, and adapted quicker to shape a diverse indigenous economic base.

Those competing at higher levels of the urban hierarchy are (and must continue to be) more dynamic, pro-active and constantly innovating in a pro-growth procurement model of competition. This involves remaining attractive to global capital, fostering dynamic public/private partnerships, securing state and supra-national (for example, European Union) funds, having more aggressive place- marketing, and constructing the multi-cultural places and spaces necessary to compete in the urban 'international beauty contest'. Such strong competition is facilitated by political, economic and social conditions oriented to capturing and influencing economic and cultural flows. The political, economic and social conditions of those cities pursuing only 'soft competition' ensure that cities lower down the urban hierarchy are more concerned with the 'search to capture mobile factors of production and therefore prone to zero sum competition of mobile investment and re-configuration without expansion' (Jessop 1998, 98). Such uneven development not only highlights competitive inter/intra regionalism (as people and places/spaces between/within cities compete for resources), but also the efficacy and sustainability of entrepreneurial practices and policies as spatially and socially specific.

Hence, it is important to understand that the willingness and ability to pursue sustainable entrepreneurial activity is socially embedded in the complex world of political, economic, social and physical opportunity tailored by dominant local values and their negotiation and contestation (Loftman and Nevin 1998). The way in which political and public discourses collide and conflict leads to negotiation over issues of economic competitiveness and the social and cultural orientations of collective consumption. However, where awareness of structured complementarity and intra/inter city level opportunities for competitive advantage are ignored, many examples of over-adventurous and unsustainable entrepreneurial policies have led to tax payers picking up the cost of speculation and uncertainty (Harvey 1989; Beck 1992). 'Best-practice' blueprints are regularly replicated in 'me-tooist' strategies, where any advantage is ephemeral. While there is a ubiquitous 'narrative of enterprise', necessarily designed to promote policies of local growth and attracting inward investment and jobs, Jessop (1997) identifies different *levels* of entrepreneurial activity. These surround the spatial and social orientation of particular urban economies, and their ability to attract economic and symbolic capital and to provide local/regional/national/global cityscapes which (re)define the urban hierarchy at specific levels.

Thus, often glaring disparity of investment in many cities has led to community, employment and small-business oriented projects, and less spectacular entrepreneurial activity designed to alleviate deprivation and poverty and to enhance the liveability of cities. These economic and business-orientated initiatives include agglomeration economics, technopoles, undercutting, re-skilling the workforce, enhancing local and regional gateways, and developing new sources of supply to enhance a city's economic base (Painter 1997). Public-private partnerships have also been activated to pursue economic development and community oriented projects (Jacobs 1992). The funding of ethno-religious initiatives, crime management projects, health and poverty programmes, community centres, the physical enhancing of problem estates, greening and infrastructural improvement to housing, street furniture and CCTV, the targeting of employment black spots and problem estates, and projects to improve participation in local politics have all been initiated in this context (see Jewson and McGregor 1997).

It is clear, then, that there is no 'quick recipe' for successful entrepreneurial policies and practices. Similarly, the potential for successful mobility, with those dominant cities aggressively exploiting past success, is limited. Even middle-ranking cities (such as Dublin and Barcelona) have few opportunities for economic expansion in the face of stubborn centre-periphery relationships (Jessop 1998). Thus cities develop strategic approaches that take into account strengths and weaknesses. Cities such as Cheltenham, Swindon and Bristol in the UK are not growth, management oriented, concentrating on attracting the market segments of high-tech industries and providing the residential environment to satisfy professional and managerial workers (Hall and Hubbard 1996). Similarly, the variety of innovative techniques for generating liveable and creative projects is site- and opportunity-specific (Landry and Bianchini 1995). In Italy the rich array of medium sized cities and dispersed financial institutions and strong hold of political subcultures as ensured the upholding of local identities and businesses above others (Oberti 2000). Scandinavia and its famed welfare orientated cities have been able to maintain provisions to relatively high standards because of the power base of actors such as trade unions, the green party, feminist and pensioner groups – despite increasing unemployment in the light of global restructuring (Lehto 2000).

In sum, the political-economy analysis asserts that entrepreneurial policies can be episodic and politically, economically or spatially oriented to particular market segments or class fractions. As such, the scale, scope and efficacy of urban renewal is very much location- and condition-specific. However, it has been argued that in order to fully conceive this diversity it is important to move beyond describing global-local processes as dichotomous poles, and to consider instead how cities and different parts of cities are discursively constructed in relation to flows of capital and culture at other spatial scales. In order to understand the multi-scalar dimensions of the construction of cities it is important to more fully theorise the interface of particular political and public discourses and social structures which mediate the nature of urban renewal and dictate concerns for spatial orientations, economic growth, collective consumption and welfare issues.

Cultural Economy
Richard Peet, who has persistently been a staunch 'economistic' theorist of urban change, has recently called for a new type of critical enquiry, called 'cultural economy'. Such an approach seeks to marry the political-economy approach, – which has predominately theorised urban change in terms of a rational choice-model of economic and political decision-making – to the ways in which culture, aesthetics and symbolic process interpenetrate the political economy of different cities. His argument promotes the need for an understanding of beliefs and logics in local and regional contexts, so that cultural influences on the ways in which political and economic systems are discursively constructed can be revealed. Theorists have found it difficult to show how cultural characteristics translate into economic and political productivity. As Peet (2000, 1217) shows, 'culture and agency disappear swiftly behind falling curtains of economics'. Peet thus employs the work of theorists such as

E.P Thompson, Raymond Williams, Antonio Gramsci, and Max Weber to discuss the embeddedness of social networks. This highlights the role of cultural materialism and the social imaginary (imagination as a social, material and experiential process) in affecting the ways people and institutions engage subjectively (rather than objectively) in 'rational' decision-making. Notions of the embeddedness of economic action must therefore engage with a vision of economic actors immersed in networks of social and cultural relations.

However, conceptualising the relations between political, economic, social and cultural praxis of life, which meld into one another, is not an easy task. One way to attempt this is to '[s]ketch out an economic geography of cultural production in modern capitalism and to show the images that better, more forcefully define how our cultural environments emerge out of concrete production systems and their geographical milieu' (Scott 2000, 204). Such an approach is invaluable to understanding of the trajectories of third-tier European cities

For example, Crewe and Lowe argue that;

> [i]ncreasingly what distinguishes one place from another is the strength of their 'consumptional identities' ... the complexes of services available. As places compete for limited investment funds their vitality and viability increase ... depending on sustaining and nurturing an image and central to such place-selling strategies is a 'conscious and deliberate manipulation of culture in an effort to enhance the appeal and interest of places'... Places are thus being promoted and sold not simply as centers of economic growth but as culturally rich places in which to live and work ... and the quality and quantity of consumption opportunities are crucial elements in generating such place myth. What is crucial here, then, is how contemporary consumption is intrinsically linked to quality of life, the key being the symbolic content of such services...(1995, 1880-1881)

However, there has been a tendency to over-generalise about these urban conditions, with little attempt to contextualise the cultural politics of place and the socio-economic experience of class, gender, ethnicity and sexuality in constituting the construction of social life.

Thus, it is possible to argue that a majority of third-tier European cities have struggled to innovate and significantly alter the physical and symbolic resonance's of their past heritage; to render industrial and working-class employment and lifestyles marginal; or to socialise a significant proportion of the population to desire jobs, lifestyles and spaces/places associated with the post-industrial/post-Fordist/post-modern economies. Bagnasco and Le Galès (2000) suggest that this is due to small and medium sized European cities being populated by a relatively large proportion of working-class people. Such cities cannot therefore generate a critical mass of post-industrial business, managerial and professional employers and employees; nor do cultural producers and consumers who will create a cosmopolitan ambience which in turn attracts, capital and tourists and other creative people (see Florida 2002).

This helps us to understand why global cities are more successful in attracting to the local milieu 'thick' economic and symbolic capital, and in developing diverse spaces/places of consumption. Economic competitiveness is pursued by promoting the presence and visibility, of institutions, infrastructure, buildings, and spaces/places where different market segments of producers and consumers work, live, shop and relax. On the other hand, such insights help to explain why not all cities or parts of those cities compete at the same spatial scale or social level. For example, weaker local states are forced to focus on local issues, often pursuing unclear development potential or internal re-organisation. While this may have some success in making particular areas of the city socially, culturally or economically distinct, such practices have little generic impact upon the flows of capital or culture outside the city, region or country.

For instance, Stoke-on-Trent a city of around 250,000 in the English Midlands has a global reputation for its production of ceramics. However, due to the nature of the ceramics production process - capital was tied up in the production process and there was little need for significant administrative, financial, banking institutions or retail infrastructure, because goods were exported around the world but people did not come to the city to purchase ceramics products - the city has never had a large representation of middle-class residents. As such there is a resistance at political and vernacular level to any post-industrial strategy or development, which are seen as yuppish or pretentious (O'Connor and Wynne 1996). The city thus remains dominated by working-class industrial production and consumption cultures that are not easily capitalisable on in an urban hierarchy dominated by middle-class values (Jayne 2000, 2003).

In a similar vein, Jon Binnie (2000) argues that the globalization of an urban sexual economy has ensured that spaces and places in large cities have become sites where lesbian and gay lifestyles, identities and consumption have become visible and identifiable as part of a global network. However, cities in for example, middle -England, middle-America, and middle-Europe are not necessarily tolerant of indigenous communities or welcoming of cosmopolitan 'otherness' - in terms of ethnicity, gender, sexuality, and also fashion sub-cultures. Binnie describes these as spaces of unsophistication – a useful concept to describe the often 'provincial outlook' of third-tier cities. Binnie argues that we need to do more than to articulate a metropolitan gaze onto the nom-metropolitan, but rather investigate the mutual interdependence of categories and identities such as provincial and metropolitan. Such an approach is central to understanding the relationship between cities throughout the urban hierarchy.

One of the ways for third-tier cities to attempt to raise their profiles in a global marketplace is to show the world that they *do* possess a creative, innovative and entrepreneurial post-industrial political-economy and cosmopolitan (non-provincial) social and cultural ambience and infrastructure. Of course, one tried and tested way to undertake a 'quick-hit' place promotion campaign is through sporting, arts and cultural festivals or expos. For instance, Roth and Frank (2000), argue that culture, (and I suggest cultural economy), is often seen as crucial to the regeneration of third-tier cities – festivals can be used to express urban distinctiveness and competitiveness.

For example, Weimar confronted with the closure of big factories, which was not off-set by emerging commercial enterprises and malls attempted to proliferate images of internationalisation and cosmopolitan during its time as Cultural Capital of Europe in 1999 (Roth and Frank 2000). The well known problem with festival is of course, whether the host cities remain attractive to visitors and capital once the festival has left town. Similarly, whether the branding of third-tier European is actually underpinned by a cultural economy of creativity and innovation, or whether third-tier European cites such as Weimar actually have a critical mass of creative industries to support significant production and consumption milieux at national or global, and not just at local and regional levels is debatable. Mollencopft suggests that; "the successful urban region is one that evolves the right mix of lifestyles and cultural, social and political forms to fit with the dynamics of capital accumulation" (1983, p. 61). While third-tier cities can sell themselves as possessing cultural-economies which generate such critical-mass it is often the case that such cities are likely only to be politically, economically, socially and culturally legible at regional rather than national or global levels.

Space and Place
It has been argued that in order to establish archetypes of the post-industrial/post-Fordist/(post)Modern city theorists have overwhelmingly concentrated on global and national cities and spaces and places within them. In Europe, only Paris and London have justifiable claims to global city status. National cities such as Barcelona, Berlin, Frankfurt, and Rotterdam have been well represented in urban literature. However, given that the European urban landscape is characterized by the relatively high number of small- and medium-sized towns of between

100,000 and 1-2 million the literature on third-tier cities is relatively under-developed. The 'European City' as a model of urbanity *has* been utilized in order to contrast to American cities that are predominantly organized around geometric grid-pan. This is presented in opposition to the European city characterised by a built-up area as a focal point, with administrative and public buildings, churches, open spaces, and central agglomerated areas for commerce and trade. It is often suggested that there is a relative lack of social segregation in city-centre due to the fact that the bourgeoisie had not wholly fled to suburban areas. It is suggested that because most European cities have seen their infrastructure grow over the centuries that the provision of public-services are the heart of municipal planning. Finally it is argued that where city-regions have suffered de-industrialization, cities can remain relatively prosperous (although this can be fragile) because they are more firmly embedded in regional and national political and economic practices and processes than they are reliant on globalized flows of capital and culture (Bagnasco and Le Galès 2000).

Cattan et al. (1994, 23) suggest that 'for an urban population that is 30% higher than that of the US, the European urbanized community alone counts 3 times as many urban areas over 10,000 inhabitants (3,500 as against 1,000)', which are located fairly close to one another. Cattan et al (1994) show that the top thirty American cities are markedly larger that the top thirty European cities and while small and medium sized 'middle America' urban areas have received some academic attention this is not usually in the context of discussing globalized urbanity through spaces and places associated with the McDonaldization and Disnyification of small-town 'main street' American life (Ritzer 1998).

In the UK, a perceived European model or urbanity has been used at national policy level to seek to instigate movements of people and capital back into city centers and halt movements to the suburbs and regional dispersal of economic activity - to create an *'Urban Renaissance'* (Rogers 2000). By promoting cities as sites of consumption of European style street and cafe culture, and lifestyles such discourses have provided a useful rhetorical tool to imagine urban spaces and places – and, of course, have provided useful for government and local authorities to tap into European funding streams. In these terms the concept of the (third-tier) European city does represent a useful resource in political and economic restructuring of space and place.

However, unpacking the diverse and differentially constructed political, economic, social and cultural practices, processes and processes associated with cities responses (or not) to global urban restructuring of third-tier cities it is clear that not one story can tell all. While there are useful generalization to be made about entrepreneurial governance, place promotion, and attempts to attract post-industrial employment in third-tier cities, there are of course wide variances in the scale, scope and successes of such cities in the light of increased globalized urban hierarchy. Thus while it is useful to draw similarities between cities in Europe with those in Brazil, USA or Japan to highlight the situation facing cities beyond the metropolis there are marked differences that must be investigated. However, given that third-tier urbanity is a predominant model in Europe then this continent is a good place to start to generalize about such cities as a globalized model, as well as investigating the differential construction of the political, economic, social, cultural and spatial practices and processes which constitute the differences which characterize each city.

Conclusions

This paper seeks to contribute to debates on uneven economic development and the nature of political, economic, social, cultural and spatial constructs of the post-industrial/post-Fordist/post-modern urban hierarchy. While at times the analysis of the economic, political and social phenomenon noted in third-tier European cities may read as an 'negative ideal type' (of the post-industrial/post-Fordist/post-modern metropolis), the concern of this paper is to be 'at the middle level between pure theory and outright empiricism ... fundamentally, the theoretical curiosity informing the ... research is that in global times it is sill sensible to... look at local cultural differences between cities and to treat them as having a social significance and continuing cultural prominence and impact' (Taylor *et al* 1996, xi-xii).

It has been made clear that localities do not operate as discrete localised economies, rather that economic fortunes are increasingly tied to global economic trends. As such, globalisation is a major factor in urban trajectories, and the new urban politics can be considered predominantly as the by-product of local reaction to broader forces of national and international social and economic transition (Knox 1987; Robertson 1992; Short *et al* 1998). However, as the concept of interpenetration suggests, cities are not helpless pawns; local political, economic, physical, social and cultural factors influence and direct approaches to multi-sector uneven development and particular multi-scalar orientations. This in turn grounds the idea that political, economic and social transformation is mediated through institutional structures which in themselves can take various forms and operate in a multiplicity of ways (Weber 1968; Giddens 1984). In these terms, reactions to global changes exemplifies a specificity of action which potentially provides a benchmark to pursue an understanding of how cities, political structures and people have responded to wider structural changes.

I have argued that while the depiction of archetypal spaces/places of production/consumption, and their associated identities, lifestyles and forms of sociability is undoubtedly useful in delineating arguments about epochal periods of (post)modernity - research has only begun to consider how the discursive construction of the political, economic and socio-spatial and cultural constituents of space and place effects uneven development. It is understandable that in order to formulate the above broad theories of localised political responses to global processes, researchers have concentrated on providing generalisable accounts that have predominantly been grounded in case studies of cities, spaces/places or projects within cities near the top of the urban hierarchy. Such a research agenda is only now beginning to broaden and produce multi-disciplinary conceptualisations of globalised urbanity that seek to include a wider spectrum of cities at all levels of the urban hierarchy. This will potentially provide a more satisfactory understanding of how a complex matrix of political, economic, social, cultural, environmental and spatial factors not only dictates the nature and competitiveness of cities, but is also constitutive of global processes. Importantly, then, the ability to achieve or sustain the sectoral shifts associated with the post-industrial/post-Fordist/post-modern economy, to attract global financial institutions, producer and communication services, and to innovate with cultural and consumption-led regeneration, is now being more critically considered in terms of reflexive reactions to the constraining or enabling factors of location and opportunity. Thus, while debates around post-modernity have produced important depictions of epochal urban change, archetypal spaces/places of production/consumption, social identities, lifestyles and forms of sociability - and related these to particular periods of post-modernity - research has tended to be over- general, deterministic and romantic. Individuals/social groups/neighbourhoods/cities/regions are not helpless pawns reacting to global influences, but that 'people take up and reproduce institutions in their local milieu' (Spybey 1996, p. 36), and that they do so in very different ways that reflect specific constellations of political, economic, socio-spatial and cultural practices and processes.

To conceptualise an archetypal European city, via practices and processes which have been associated with urbanism and globalisation, masks the different ways in which European cities are integrated into global flows of capital, culture and people. However, due to the structure of the European urban hierarchy to talk about an archetypal European city, is to talk about a third-tier city. We can thus learn a lot about globalization by looking at urban practices and processes at a level of the urban hierarchy which has remained relatively under-theorised. Thus, the utility of concepts such as an archetypal European city or indeed the post-industrial/post-Fordist/(post)modern global city is that they provide a schema to elaborate specificity in the face of global urban change. However, to apply Jon Binnie (2000) concerns to European third-tier cities, we need do more than to articulate a metropolitan gaze onto the non-metropolitan (to discuss smaller cities through the lens of the metropolis), but rather investigate the mutual interdependence of categories and identities such as provincial and metropolitan. Such an approach is central to understanding practices and processes of urbanism and globalization and also to elucidate the relationship between cities (and spaces and places within cities) at different levels of the urban hierarchy.

References:
Bagnasco, A.; Le Galès, P. (2000) Cities in Contemporary Europe. Cambridge:xxx
Beck, U. (1992) Risk Society: Towards a New Modernity. London:xxx.
Binnie, J. (2000) Cosmopolitanism and the Sexed City. In: Bell, D./Haddour, A. (eds) City Visions. Essex:166-178.
Boyle, M./Hughes, G. (1991) The Politics of Representation of the 'Real. Discourses from the Left in Glasgow's Role of European City of Culture. In: Area. (23). pp3-28.
Brenner, N. (1998) Between 'Fixity' and 'Motion', Accumulation, Territorial Organisation and the Historical Geography of Spatial Scales. In: Environment and Planning D: Society and Space. (16). 459-481.
Castells, M. (1997) The Rise of the Network Society: The Information Age, Economic Social and Cultural, Volume 1. Oxford.
Cattan, N. ; Pumain, D. ; Rozenblat, C. ; Saint-Julien, T. (1994) Le Systeme de Villes Europeennes. Paris.
Cisnernos, H. (1995) Urban Entreprenurialism and National Economic Growth. Washington, D.C.
Cochrane, M.; Peck, J.; Tickell, P. (1996) 'Manchester plays Games – Exploring the Local Politics of Globalisation'. In: Urban Studies. (33). 1319-1316.
Cox, K. (1995) Globalisation, Competition and the Politics of Local Economic Development. In: Urban Studies. (32). 213-225.
-, (1993) The Local and the Global in the New Urban Politics: A Critical View. In: Environment and Planning D: Society and Space. (11). 433-448.
Crewe, L.; Lowe, M. (1995) Gap on the map? Towards a geography of consumption and identity. In: Environment and Planning A. (27) 1877-1898.
Davis, M. (1990) City of Quartz: Excavating the Future in Los Angeles. New York.
Florida, R. (2002) The Rise of the Creative Class. New York.
Giddens, A. (1991) The Consequences of Modernity. Cambridge.
-, (1973) Review of Class Struggle of Advanced Societies. In: British Journal of Sociology. (29) 10-15.
Glennie, P.D.; Thrift, N. J. (1992) Modernity, Urbanism and Modern Consumption. In: Environment and Planning A. (10) 432-443.
Hall, T. (1997) (Re)Placing the City: Cultural Relocation and the City Centre. In: Westwood, S./Williams, J. (eds), Imagined Cities: Scripts, Signs, and Meaning. London:
-, /Hubbard, P. (eds) (1998) The Entrepreneurial City: Geographies of Politics, Regimes and Representation. London.
-, (1996) The Entrepreneurial City: New Urban Politics, New Urban Geographies?. In: Progress in Human Geography. (20) 2, 153-174.
Harvey, D. (1989) The Urban Experience. Baltimore: John Hopkins University.
-, (1985) The Urbanisation of Capital. Oxford.

Heikkinen, T. (2000) From The Margins: The City of Culture 2000 and the Image Transformation of Helsinki. In: International Journal of Cultural Policy. Vol 6. No 2, 201-218.

Herrschel, T. (1998) From socialism to post-Fordism: the local state and economic politics in East Germany. In: T. Hall/ P. Hubbard (eds).

Jacobs, B. (1992) Fractured Cities; Capitalism, Community and Empowerment in Britain and America. London:

Jayne, M. (2003) Too Many Voices, "Too problematic to be plausible": representing multiple responses to local economic development strategies. In: Environment and Planning A. (in press).

-, (2000) Imag(in)ing a post-industrial potteries. In Bell, D./Haddour, A. (eds) City Visions. Harlow:

Jessop, B. (1998) The Narrative of Enterprise and the Enterprise of Narrative: Place Marketing and the Entrepreneurial City. In: T. Hall/P. Hubbard (eds).

-, (1997) The Entreprenurial City: Re-Imagining Localities, Re-Designing Economic Government, or Re-structuring Capital?. In: Jewson, N./McGregor, D. (eds).

Jewson, N.; McGregor, S. (eds) (1997) Transforming Cities: Contested Governance and New Spatial Divisions. London:

Knox, P. L. (1987) The Social Production of the Built Environment: Architects, Architecture and the Postmodern City. In: Progress in Human Geography. 21 (3), 154-377.

Landry, C.; Binachini, F. (1995) The Creative City. London.

Lefebvre, H. (1974) The Production of Space. trans. Donald Nicholson-Smith. Oxford.

-, (1971) Everyday Life in the Modern World.

Lehto, J. (2000) Different cities in different welfare states. In: Bagnasco, A./Le Galès, P. (eds).

Loftman, P.; Nevin, B. (1998) Pro-Growth Local Economic Strategies: Civic Promotion and Local Needs in Britain's Second City. In: Hall, T./Hubbard, P. (eds).

Low, M. (1997) 'Representing Urbanisation: Globalisation and Democracy'. In: Cox, K. (ed), Politics of Globalisation: reasserting the Power of the Local. New York. 240-280.

Markussen, A. R.; Lee, Y-S.; DiGiovanna, S. (eds) (1999) Second Tier Cities Beyond the Metropolis. Minnesota.

Massey, D. (1993) 'Power-Geometry and a Progressive Sense of Place'. In: Bird, J./ Curtis, B./Putnam, T./Robertson, G./Tickner, L. (eds), Mapping the Futures: Local Cultures, Global Change. London. 54-69

Mollencopft J, (1983) The Contested City. Princeton.

Mort, F. (1998) 'Consumption, Masculinities and the Mapping of London Since 1950'. In: Urban Studies. 35 (5-6). 889-907.

Oberti, M. (2000) Social structures in medium-sized cities compared. In: Bagnasco, A./Le Gales, P. (eds).

O'Connor, J./Wynne, D. (1998) 'Consumption and the Postmodern City'. In: Urban Studies. (35) 5-6. 841-864.

-, (eds) (1996) From the Margins to the Centre: Cultural Production and Consumption in the Post-industrial City. Aldershot.

Painter, J. (1997) 'Entrepreneurs are Made Not Born: Learning and Urban Regimes in the production of Entrepreneurial Cities'. In: Hall, T./Hubbard, P. (eds).

Peet, R. (2000) 'Culture, Imaginary, and Rationality in Regional Economic Development'. In: Environment and Planning A. (32). 1215-1234.

Ritzer, G. (1998) The McDonaldisation Thesis. London.
Robertson, R. (1992) Social Theory and Global Culture. London.
Rogers, R. (2000) Towards an Urban Renaissance: The Report of the Urban Task Force. London.
Roth, S.; Frank, S. (2000) Festivalization and the Media: Weimar, Cultural Capital of Europe 1999. In: International Journal of Cultural Policy. Vol 6. No 2. 219-241.
Savage, M.; Warde, A. (1993) Sociology, Capitalism and Modernity. New York.
Scott, A.J. (2000) The Cultural Economy of Cities: Essays on the Geographies of Image Producing Industries. London.
Short, J. R.; Kim, Y-H. (1998) Urban Crisis/Urban Regeneration: Selling the City in Difficult Times. In: Hall, T. and Hubbard, P. (eds).
Soja, E. (1989) Postmodern Geographies: the Reassertion of Space in Critical Social Theory. London.
Spybey, T. (1996) Globalisation and World Society. Cambridge.
Taylor, I.; Evans, I.; Fraser, P (1996) A Tale of Two Cities: Global Change, Local Feeling and Everyday Life in the North of England. A Study of Sheffield and Manchester. London.
Thrift, N. (2000) Not a Straight Line but a Curve, or, Cities are Not Mirrors of Modernity. In: Bell, D./Haddour, A. (eds), City Visions. Essex. 233-264.
Weber, M. (1946) Class, State, Party. In: Bendix, R./Lipset, S.M. (eds), Class, State and Power. Gelcoe, IL. 63-75.
Wood, A. (1998) Questions of Scale in the Entrepreneurial City. In: Hall, T./ Hubbard, P. (eds).
Zukin, S. (1982) Loft Living: Culture and Capitalism in Urban Change. Baltimore.

The Dark Side of Really Existing Globalization

Peter Marcuse

Globalization has had multiple implications for human settlements, some favorable, some unfavorable[1], some indeterminate as yet. But globalization is a term used in many different senses; as used here, it is intended to mean that combination of 1) technological advance, particularly in communications and computerization, and 2) concentration of wealth and economic power, particularly through sophisticated financial instrumentalities, both extending across national borders, that we have witnessed increasingly since about 1970. The two are of course related to each other, but not necessarily in the forms we see them today. What we see today might be called really existing globalization, because other forms of globalization might easily be envisaged; we return to a brief comment on such alternative globalization possibilities at the end of this discussion. It should be clear that globalization as used here is not a brand new phenomenon, but rather a magnified continuation of existing trends. It should also be clear that some of the trends to be discussed below only in part have to do with the international, cross-border aspects of globalization; most in fact represent processes developing - and developing in quite differentiated form in different countries and cities - within countries, accelerated and modified by international connections.

We first discuss the general trends that result from real existing globalization. But it should be clear that these are trends only: that they vary widely from city to city, nation to nation, continent to continent. But there are substantial variations, important more than descriptively. They show the impact that specific policy decisions taken at the local and at the state level can have on existing trends. Globalization is not some immutable historical force that operates everywhere free of the influence of individual agents, actors, cities, states; it consequences can be affected, even its nature can perhaps be changed, by the deliberate acts of men and women. We take up some of the variations thus produced in the course of our description of the underlying trends, and at the end summarize some of the key countervailing actions/trends that are to be seen around the world today.

---

[1] Favorable is here used in terms of the generally accepted goals of Habitat: quality of life, health, environmental quality, equity, democratic participation.

The Direct Physical Reflections of Globalization

The changing relationship between manufacturing and service sector activities is sometimes taken as a key hallmark of the age of globalization. Its impact on settlement patterns is obvious, and profound: cities that had been the hub of bustling manufacturing enterprises in the period of rapid urbanization are losing that industry, and instead becoming the seats of concentrated clusters of commercial and financial and management activities: FIRE, finance, insurance, and real estate prominently among them. Manufacturing plants, instead, have been moved to the suburbs, sometimes to rural regions, and to a significant extent from older industrially more developed countries to less developed ones. Where the move has been to less developed countries, the direction of development is ultimately often similar to that in older countries: Sao Paulo, for instance, fifty years ago the relocation target of major automobile plants, is now seeing them leave for regions in the interior of Brazil, and instead is watching its cluster of high-rise internationally-oriented commercial office buildings proliferate. The Asian tigers are similarly seeing competition in industrial labor for other less developed Asian countries, and are maintaining their position by shifting towards higher tech production as a matter of deliberate policy.

These developments are not the simple consequences of technological advances. They are in large part determined by changes in the organization and concentration of wealth and the policies of government, which in turn determine how (and where) new technology will be used. The shift from manufacturing to services, for instance, only in part represents technological progress. For the total amount of manufacturing activity in the world, whether measured in value or in employment, is increasing, not decreasing. That it is moving from its older locations, often the locus of past worker organizing efforts, strong trade unions, and high wages, to other areas where greater profits can be made with a cheaper work force, is not a function of technology, but of the quest for higher profits. Advances in communications technology facilitate, but do not mandate, centralization of command functions; the particular constellation of power dictates the use of these technologies, nothing inherent in the technologies themselves. The greater facility at creating forms of entertainment and distributing them widely could as well be used to support a proliferation of diverse cultural experiments as a homogenization of culture; that United States movies dominate international television is not a function of the medium, but of the messengers. The complex intertwining of technology and power directly produce the consequences unfavorable to traditional conceptions of good urban life described above.

Cross-border activities have even more direct impacts. Certain unfavorable trends that represent causes of alarm are even more directly and obviously related to that component of really existing globalization that is represented by the impact of increased air traffic, for instance, is one of the most visible consequences of globalization. It has resulted in serious noise and air quality pollution in those cities having airports near in, such as Washington, D.C. or Los Angeles. Where airports are further from the city, as in New York City or London, problems of traffic congestion are heightened. As important are the implications of the growth of air commerce on regional forms of habitation: the clusters of "airport cities" that have sprung up around major hubs, such as Frankfurt or Dallas/Fort Worth, have siphoned off business activity, and with it commercial life, from many downtowns, and severed connections of these activities from the life of the cities which explain their existence. The ability to develop mega-projects, including but not limited to the skyscrapers that are becoming an essential component of the image of any city that wishes to call itself global, would not be possible in most cases without cross-border financing. In further pursuit of that image, a uniformity of architecture claiming international stature but often more characterized by its plushness and pretentiousness than by its aesthetic quality; is found.

We focus, in this discussion, however, on the most deep-seated of the potentially unfavorable effects of globalization on cities: the increase in inequality, and its concomitants.

The Major Issue: Inequality and the Quartering of the Space of Cities

Increasing inequality is more and more recognized as an accompaniment of existing globalization. The process leading from globalization to inequality is clear; it results from the use of advancing communications and transportation technology to enable the concentration of wealth in the hands of a few, to the comparative, and often absolute, detriment of the majority. The increasing mobility of capital, and the increasing span of control newly possible, have resulted in an increasing concentration of wealth at the top, and an increasing gap between the holders of that wealth and the poor of the world. The poorest 20% of world's population has seen its share of global income decline from 2.3% to 1.4% in the past 30 years, the share of the richest 20% went from 70% to 85%. [2] Social welfare policies significantly affect the level of inequality; thus the states traditionally associated with such policies, from Sweden and the Netherlands to Singapore, show lower levels, but even in these countries the gap between rich and poor is increasing.

---

[2] From United Nations Development Program, 1996, Human Development Report, 1996. New York: Oxford University Press

These two major aspects of globalization: the restructuring of manufacturing and services, and the widening inequality or polarization, have their reflections in shape of cities and the activities they harbor. The most fundamental of these in the quartering of urban space.

The Quartering of Urban Space

The link between inequality and urban space is not so much the division of society into two simple parts, not the dual city, the city of the rich and the poor, of Disraeli, but the quartered or divided or partitioned city of today. It is the indirect, but essential, product of really existing globalization. Inequality, in this broader sense, has been extensively documented in the literature as a world-wide phenomenon. It has two distinct aspects. One is inequality, which for purposes of the issues discussed in this paper, has four aspects: an increase in the relative numbers of those who are rich and those who are poor; an increase in the distance between them, the rich being richer and the poor poorer (the phenomenon of exclusion); a greater differentiation among the groups between rich and poor, so that one may speak of a four or five part division of classes rather than a simple division into two; and sharper differentiation among the groups from each other. Polarization, as used in this report, refers to the increase in inequality, to the processes by which inequality comes about under conditions of globalization.

This process of polarization is reflected in the residential spaces of cities, in a pattern we may call quartering, a partitioning of residential space, and its four aspects are each reflected in the physical space of cities. The *enclave* is its most typical spatial form for all but the poorest. Harking back to the origin of the term in the enclaves of the imperial powers in the colonies, the enclaves accompanying globalization similarly represent the effort to wall some in and keep others out.

The resulting residential pattern in cities consists of five separate formations, at the top "non-spatial" in the sense that it floats freely[3] in multiple locations in and outside of the city, the other four forming and based on traditional neighborhood quarters. Each with its source in a parallel economic differentiation induced by globalization, each with its own form of separation from the others, each with its own dynamics of development.

One may thus speak of five increasingly separate *residential cities*, one free-floating, four in quarters, each with its parallel (although not always congruent) *cities of business and work*. For business, the spatial patterns

---

[3] Manuel Castells has coined the phrase "space of flows" as non-place based locations, but, as Saskia Sassen has pointed out, those spaces need to be based in specific places (she argues global cities, but all cities are to some extent globalizing), and what we here call the luxury city and its business correlate, the city of control, are those places.

include areas in which people of many occupations, classes, status, living in many different residential areas, and work in close proximity. Yet, if we define economic divisions by the primary activity taking place within them, one may again get a four or five-part division:

The Free-floating Citadels of Wealth and Business

The *luxury areas of the city*, the residences of the wealthy, while located in clearly defined residential areas, are at the same time non-spatially-bound. The very rich, in terms of residential location, are not tied to any quarter of the city, just as the men that whipped the horses that pulled apart the quartered prisoner are not linked to any one of the resulting quarters. For the wealthy, the city is less important as a residential location than as a location of power and profit. The restructuring of cities has led to an increased profitability of real estate, from which the already wealthy disproportionately benefit.. Joel Blau cites figures that indicate from 1973 to 1987 additional revenue from property constituted 45% of the income growth among the top 1% of the population. It is for them first and foremost a profit-making machine. They profit from the activities conducted in the city, or (increasingly) from the real estate values created by those activities; they may enjoy living in the city also, but have many other options. If they reside in the city, it is in a world insulated from contact with non-members of the class, with leisure time and satisfactions carefully placed and protected. If the city no longer offers profit or pleasure, they can abandon it; 75% of the chief executives of corporations having their headquarters in New York City lived outside the city in 1975.[4] The pattern is repeated throughout the world. The wealthy want and need cities, and cities of a particular kind, but which city is almost an arbitrary choice. Any given city is disposable for them.

The *controlling city*, the city of big decisions, includes a network of high-rise offices, brownstones or older mansions in prestigious locations, perhaps the old colonial mansions of the imperial powers in the Third World. It is less and less locationally circumscribed. It includes yachts for some, the back seats of stretch limousines for others, airplanes and scattered residences for most. But it is not spatially rootless. The controlling city limited as to location, although the places where its activities at various times take place are of course located somewhere, and more secured by walls, barriers, conditions to entry, than any other part of the city. But its choice of locations is large.

Yet the controlling city tends to be located in (at the top of, physically and symbolically) the high-rise centers of advanced services, because those at the top of the chain of command wish to have at least those below

---

[4] Steven Brint, in Mollenkopf and Castells, p. 155

them close at hand and responsive, and so it goes down the line. Our interviews with those responsible for planning the then new high-rise office tower for the Bank für Gemeinwirtschaft in Frankfurt revealed professionals who had concluded that a separation of functions, with top executives downtown but all others in back office locations, was the most efficient pattern for the bank, but were over-ruled by their superiors, with only the advantage cited above as their reasoning. By the same token, Citibank in New York City wants its next level of professionals directly accessible to its top decision-makers where they are; credit card data entry operations may move to South Dakota but not banking activities that require the exercise of discretion. Those locations, wherever they may be, are crucially tied together by communication and transportation channels which permit an existence insulated from all other parts of the city, if dependent on them.

The controlling city parallels in its occupancy and character, but is not congruent in time or space, with the luxury areas of the residential city. When they are together, we have the fullest form of an age-old phenomenon, but now in its market incarnation: the citadel. The recognition of the centrality of the control function in this upper segment of the city is by now wide-spread, and the citadel is its extreme form. In the citadel, the type form of the free-floating luxury residential city and the controlling city of business come together in space. Here also the phenomenon of walling (in and out) is at its extremes. The citadel, a word first used in this context by John Friedmann 30 years ago, is where those at the top of the economic hierarchy live, work, and recreate in protected spaces of their own; in Friedmann's striking phrase, citadels are where the international elite set down when they are not in the air traveling from one citadel to another. Many years ago their residents were concerned to protect their separate space in the city by public instrumentalities such as zoning.[5] Today, each private high-rise condominium has its own security, and elsewhere literally walls protect the enclaves of the rich from intrusion. Such citadels are to be found from New York City to Tokyo, Vancouver to Shanghai, Johannesburg to London, Paris to Moscow.

The Quarter of Gentrification

The *gentrified city*[6] serves the professionals, managers, technicians, yuppies in their 20's and college professors in their 60's: those who may

---

[5] 1969 Zoned American, Grossman, New York

[6] I use the term here, not in its narrower sense, as a portion of the city in which higher class groups have displaced lower class (see definitions in Marcuse, P., 1985. " Gentrification, Abandonment, and Displacement: Connections, Causes, and Policy Responses in New York City," Journal of Urban and Contemporary Law, Volume 28,

be doing well themselves, yet work for and are ultimately at the mercy of others. The frustrated pseudo-creativity[7] of their actions leads to a quest for other satisfactions, found in consumption, in specific forms of culture, in "urbanity" devoid of their original historical content and more related to consumption than to intellectual productivity or political freedom.[8] The residential areas they occupy are chosen for environmental or social amenities, for their quiet or bustle, their history or fashion; gentrified working class neighborhoods, older middle class areas, new developments with modern and well furnished apartments, all serve their needs. Locations close to work are important, because of long and unpredictable work schedules, the density of contacts, and the availability of services and contacts they permit.

The *city of advanced services*, of professional offices tightly clustered in downtowns, with many ancillary services internalized in high-rise office towers, heavily enmeshed in a wide and technologically advanced communicative network. The skyscraper center is the stereotypical pattern, but not the only possibility. Locations at the edge of the center of the city, as in Frankfurt/Main, outside it, as in Paris at La Defense or outside Rome or what investors hope will be the Docklands at London, or scattered around both inside and outside a city with good transportation and communications, as in Amsterdam. Social, "image," factors will also play a role; the "address" as well as the location is important for business. Whether in only one location or in several in a given city, however, there will be strong clustering, and the city of advanced services will be recognizable at a glance.

The city of advanced services parallels in the economic city the characteristics of the gentrified residential city. They compose the most rapidly growing quarter of cities, on an international level. Where they are located outside the center of the city, they fall into the pattern of enclaves typical of groups both above them and below them in the hierarchy of the globalized economy.

St. Louis, Washington University, 195-240), but in the broader sense of areas occupied by, or intended for, the professionals, managers, technicians, described earlier in this paper, which may include newly constructed housing as well as housing "gentrified" in the narrower sense of the word.

[7] The reference here is not to creative artists, to what in earlier days would have been called Bohemians, who cannot generally afford the prices of the gentrified city, and are more likely to live somewhere between the abandoned and the tenement city. To the extent that they tend to congregate in specific neighborhoods, they may serve as precursors of gentrification (Damaris, R. 1984., 47-74), who differentiates sharply among different categories of gentrifiers.

[8] Häusermann, H.; Siebel, W., 1987. Marcuse, P. in John Allen and Chris Hamnett, 1991, 118-135.

Suburbanization Inside and Outside the City

The *suburban city* of the traditional family, suburban in tone if not in structures or location, is sought out by better paid workers, blue and white collar employees, the "lower middle class," the petit bourgeoisie. It provides stability, security, the comfortable world of consumption. Owner-occupancy of a single family house is preferred (depending on age, gender, household composition), but cooperative or condominium or rental apartments can be adequate, particularly if subsidized and/or well located to transportation. The home as symbol of self, exclusion of those of lower status, physical security against intrusion, political conservatism, comfort and escape from the work-a-day world (thus often substantial spatial separation from work) are characteristic. The protection of residential property values (the home functioning as financial security and inheritance as well as residence) are important. Archie Bunker is the pejorative stereotype; the proud and independent worker/citizen is the other side of the coin.[9]

The *city of direct production*, including not only manufacturing but also the production aspect of advanced services, in Saskia Sassen's phrase, government offices, the back offices of major firms, whether adjacent to their front offices or not, located in clusters and with significant agglomerations but in varied locations within a metropolitan area. Varied, indeed, but not arbitrary or chaotic: where customers/clients (itself an interesting dichotomy!) wish to be in quick and easy contact, inner city locations are preferred (as in the industrial valley between Midtown Manhattan and the Financial District for the printing industry, or Chinatown and the garment district for textile production, in New York City).

For mass production, locations will be different. Here the pattern has changed dramatically since the beginning of the industrial revolution. At first factories were near the center of the city; indeed, to a large extent they led to the growth of the city around them, as in the manufacturing cities of New England or the mid-west or the industrial cities of England. But more modern manufacturing methods require more single-story space, vastly more, with parking for automotive access rather than paths for workers coming on foot, and many more operations are internalized; so land costs become more important than local agglomeration economies, and suburban or rural locations are preferred.

The city of direct production parallels but is not congruent with, in either space or time, the residential suburban city.

---

[9] I still find Damaris R., 1980; 71-76, one of the best pieces dealing with the very ambiguous relationships of homeownership to political position.

The Old Working Class Quarter and the Immigrant Enclave

The *tenement city* must do for lower paid workers, workers earning the minimum wage or little more, often with irregular employment, few benefits, little job security, no chance of advancement. Their city is much less protective or insular. In earlier days their neighborhoods were called slums; when their residents were perceived as unruly and undisciplined, they were the victims of slum clearance and "up-grading" efforts; today they are shown their place by abandonment and/or by displacement, by service cuts, deterioration of public facilities, political neglect. Because they are needed for the functioning of the city as a whole, however, they have some the ability to exert political pressure, to get public protections: rent regulation, public housing, were passed largely because of their activities, although often siphoned up to higher groups after the pressure went off. When their quarters were wanted for "higher uses," they were moved out, by urban renewal or by gentrification. The fight against displacement, under the banner of protecting their neighborhoods, has given rise to some of the most militant social movements of our time, particularly when coupled with the defense of the homes of their better off neighbors.

The *city of unskilled work* and the informal economy, small-scale manufacturing, warehousing, sweatshops, technically unskilled consumer services, immigrant industries, closely intertwined with the cities of production and advanced services and thus located near them, but separately and in scattered clusters,[10] locations often determined in part by economic relations, in part by the patterns of the residential city. Because the nature of the labor supply determines the profitability of these activities, the residential location of workers willing to do low-paid and/or unskilled work has a major influence. Thus in New York City sweatshops locate in Chinatown or the Dominican areas of Washington Heights, in Miami in the Cuban enclave, or in the slums of cities throughout the world.

The economic city of unskilled work parallels the tenement city. In the more industrialized countries, residence will be separate from work. For older "smokestack" industries, that will be true in developing countries also; major automobile plants in Brazil or China draw on pools of workers from various residential areas, often from large informal settlements, squatter colonies, not very propitiously located in their vicinity. For other types of work, in particular but not only textiles and forms of light manufacturing, homework is again coming into vogue as a cheap and flexible form of production, combining place of residence with place of

---

[10] See, for instance Sassen, S. (1989) with brief but provocative comments on the intra-city spatial aspects of the trends she describes.

work and avoiding the necessity of investing in a separate work-place entirely. The separation of such workers from the core of the city is further enhanced.

Exclusion, Abandonment, and the New Ghetto of Exclusion

The *abandoned city*, economic in the United States, racial, and in other parts of the world ethnic or tribal, is the place for the very poor, the excluded, the never employed and permanently unemployed, the homeless and the shelter residents. In older industrialized countries it will have a crumbling infrastructure, deteriorating housing, the domination of outside impersonal forces, direct street-level exploitation, racial and ethnic discrimination and segregation, the stereotyping of women, are everyday reality. The spatial concentration of the poor in such areas is reinforced by public policy; public (social, council) housing becomes more and more ghettoized housing of last resort (its better units being privatized as far as possible), drugs and crime are concentrated here, education and public services neglected. In less industrialized countries the excluded will live on the fringe of the city, often in informal accommodations, often lacking proper sewage, water supply, or other basic infrastructure, and often without protected legal tenure. Whether in developed or less developed countries, the residential areas of the excluded are abandoned by the formal structures of government and denied the public services considered normal in other parts of the city.

Here will also be, in economic terms, the *residual city*, the city of the less legal portions of the informal economy. In the third world it will overlap with the abandoned city: marginal and illegal work will take place where its participants live. In industrialized countries, it will be the city of storage where otherwise undesired (NIMBY) facilities are located, the location of abandoned manufacturing buildings, generally also congruent with the abandoned residential city. But for political protest many of the most polluting and environmentally detrimental components of the urban infrastructure, necessary for its economic survival but not directly tied to any one economic activity, are located here: sewage disposal plants, incinerators, bus garages, AIDS residences, housing for the homeless, juvenile detention centers, jails. New York City's recently adopted Fair Share regulations are a reflection both of the extent of the problem and its political volatility.

Social exclusion is a characteristic of the abandoned and residual city, and the excluded ghetto is its newer and extreme form in the First world; the ostracized settlement, the apartheid township, are its often older parallels in the Third. The recognition of the excluded ghetto is by now widespread in the United States, where its presence is most widespread.[11] Two separate streams of analysis have contributed to the discussion, differing in their starting points and emphases, but not necessarily inconsistent with each other. One places the central emphasis on race, the other on economic change and class. The former has been developed, logically enough, in the United States; the latter, while also receiving major attention here, has greater linkages to European experience. The key text dealing with the racial ghetto is Massey and Denton's *American Apartheid*,[12] although a significant further literature developing some of the issues has also appeared.[13] William Julius Wilson has been the most productive of the commentators stressing the role of economic change and its relationship to class; his use of the term "the underclass" has probably been the most provocative contribution to the sociological literature in the last twenty years.[14] Wilson's substitution of the term "ghetto poor" for "underclass"[15] suggests the linkage between race and class and its spatial component.

The presence or absence of the excluded ghetto, of the apartheid township, depends very much on the social and economic policies of government. Thus workers from the former Dutch colonies in Indonesia cluster together in Amsterdam, immigrant quarters exist in Stockholm, Turkish is the dominant language in sections of Frankfurt, but the welfare policies of these states are strong enough to preclude the type of ghettoization found in the United States, to which its much longer-resident African-American population is subject. The dangers of the global pattern are visible around the globe, but they are recognized and countered with much greater will and effort in some countries than in others.

Putting the lines of residential and business division together, then, a general pattern emerges, in which the lines of separation are more or less congruent, and the social, economic, political, and cultural divisions largely (but not completely) overlap. One may thus speak of five distinct cities co-existing within the single "city" of municipal boundaries and popular reference. The lines of separation in this five-part division are complex; they overlap with differences in family composition, disparate

---

[11] For a recent discussion, Marcuse (1996)

[12] Massey and Denton (1993)

[13] Among the best recent studies are: Goldsmith and Blakeley (1992); Bullard, Grigsby and Lee (1994)

[14] Appropriately enough, the other contender for that honor is probably John Friedmann's "world cities" or Saskia Sassen's "global cities."

[15] Wilson (1991) p. 6

situations of women, ethnic minorities, immigrants, children, the elderly, alternate life styles and sexual preferences. As one progresses down the scale both in the quarters of the residential city and of the economic city, in the United States the proportion of black and Hispanic and immigrant household increases and the proportion of women heading households increases. Race, class, ethnicity and gender create over-lapping patterns of differentiation--invidious differentiation, for there is no doubt that the differences are not simply of "life-styles" or "special needs," but reflect positions in a hierarchy of power and wealth in which some decide and others are decided for. And the lines of division, and the reflection of polarization, are sharpest and most visible at the two extremes of the scale: the citadel and the ghetto. How sharp and how visible will depend both on the intensity of the impact of existing globalization and on the extent to which the various actors, in government and without, move to counter their negative features.

Walls between the Quarters
The poor are walled in by clear social convention, the definition and stigmatization of neighborhoods, often social housing which has become more and more housing of last resort for the very poor. The rich wall themselves in, forming the gated communities, the walled enclaves, the security zones in the central cities, the hi-tech protected high-rises, of large cities around the world. For the poor, the demarcation of boundaries may be along the lines of streets or slopes of hills or freeways or open (usually deserted or under-maintained) spaces; they may be artificial or natural barriers (highways or railroad tracks, hills or rivers), architectural barriers and indicators (the forms of housing, the placement of public facilities). For the rich, the walls are more likely formally constructed (community walls, barbed wire fences, doormen and security systems).[16] In both cases, the meaning of the walls is recognized by all sides.

In between, the residents of the enclaves of the gentry, the middle class, and the working class of the formal labor market also seek to separate themselves out for "the others," each as to those below them, and all as to the very poor and excluded. Thus the new architecture of shopping malls, skywalks, and policed pedestrian malls is a striking physical mirror of the social separation. Downtown skywalks, for instance, can both symbolically and physically permit the men and women of business and shoppers with money to spend to walk over the heads of the poor and

---

[16] See incredible walls at Chacara Flora in São Paulo, and walls at Courtyard Village, Rua Conde D'Eu, of Coelho da Fonseca, of which I have photos. Even the name gives it away.

the menial.17 The market serves as the desired stratifying force; walls, intended physically to keep out the very poor, function socially and economically and symbolically to keep out any lower group. The selection of public facilities and private shared facilities within each division reinforces boundaries (occasionally it may reinforce aspirations towards upward movement); thus retailing is geared to the market level of each division and located near the centers in each, public services such as school districts are geared to the level of demand and reinforce the differential attractiveness of each. However created and walled, the movement towards the hardening of boundaries between the quarters of the city is everywhere visible and can be, and often is, mapped, whether in newspaper accounts showing the curfew lines after the civil unrest in Los Angeles or in ads showing the security zone around the office clusters in the center of Johannesburg.

The awareness of the process has led some governments to attempt counter-measures, often with significant success. Thus in the Netherlands the up-grading of areas with high concentrations of poverty has been a deliberate policy, as it has in other welfare states in western Europe. The danger, of course, is the upgrading may lead to gentrification and its concomitant displacement, the concern that now pervades Harlem in New York, where the goal – neither ghetto nor gentrified enclave – remains elusive. The Debasing of the Urban Cultural Environment.

The particular historic character of a city often is submerged in the direct and overt quest of international image and international business. From Shanghai to Johannesburg, from Buenos Aires to Melbourne, from Hanoi to St. Petersburg, an international business class fashions downtown offices and stores and hotels and resorts and condominiums in its own image. Local identity becomes an ornament, a public relations artifact designed to aid marketing. Authenticity is paid for, encapsulated, mummified, located and displayed to attract tourists rather than to shelter continuities of tradition or the lives of its historic creators. Cultural critics speak of the international disneyfication of entertainment and recreation, but the process affects the built form of cities as well. Disneylands, because of their scale, remain outside dense urban settlements, but Disney stores, ubiquitous fast food franchises with their trade mark architecture, malls of greater and greater scale, chain stores and international franchises, dot the urban landscape, suburbs as well as downtowns. In fact, there is convergence in the cultural suburbanization of the central areas of cities, proceeding in parallel with the urbanization of the periphery, to change regional form from concentric to multi-centric

---

[17] Marcuse (1988) 15-122 ; Barnett (1989)131-5.

to shapeless (although remaining dependent on a single center for key financial, governmental, and control functions).

Such developments have both favorable and unfavorable sides. The favorable are perhaps more obvious, McDonalds brings fast food and pleasure to may people, and that the Disney stores are successful indicates a real market for what they sell. The unfavorable aspects lies in what is lost by this addition to the range of choice: a submergence of identity, a loss of cultural traditions, a feeling of powerlessness, that has contributed to the growth of what is neo called "identity politics" around the world. The line between reclaiming identity and separatism akin to tribalism is a thin one. Many governments recognize this, and the quest for a meaningful multi-culturalism that is between submergence of identity in assimilation to the majority, on the other hand, and primacy to separate identity in enclavization on the other, is still being sought. In HCM, "to officials, blighted tracts within the inner city were unwelcome sights because they not only deter investments but also undermine the image of an economically strong and healthy modern city that they wish to project.[18]

The Declining Public Orientation of the State and the Distortions of Land Use by the Market

While the economic aspects of globalization explains a great deal of this, it could not develop as it has without the support of changing state policies, the reflection of the changing political balance of power that is likewise the result of globalization. The emphasis on the "competitiveness of cities" (as if a "city" were competitive, rather than just particular businesses and groups within it, with widely different impacts on different groups within it, as the opposition to Olympic bids within cities as diverse as Atlanta, Capetown, Sydney, and Berlin shows) that is taken as essential for a city's political leadership in a global age, has the effect of apotheosizing the private market. The private market will naturally segregate; it takes public action to overcome that result, to produce a measure of equality in the use of the space of the city. But public policy working in that direction is less and less evident.

The extent of government's role in shaping cities is an ideologically controversial topic. The facts are hardly in issue: without a very active governmental role, cities could not exist: traffic could not move, the danger of fires would be uncontrolled, health hazards would multiply, cities would be unlivable. What is controversial is rather the direction of governmental activity: whether it should be directed solely at efficiency,

---

[18] International Development Research Centre, Canada, and Hanoi Architectural Universit, Vietnam. 1997. Shelter and Environmental Improvement for the Urban Poor: Summary Report. October, 82.

reinforcing the current distributions of wealth and power, or whether it should play a redistributive role, creating a social minimum standard for quality of life of all of its residents. The attack on public planning, epitomized by the policies of a Thatcher or a Reagan administration, question the redistributive aspects of such planning, rather than the planning itself. For it must be recognized, regardless of ideology, that the market abandons brownfields, wastes land in speculation, pollutes, sprawls, has four gas stations at an intersection, dead malls all over, dead centers in the middle. Only with effective government action can such types of wasteful results be avoided.

The tendency thus is to call for the separation of planning from (potentially redistributive) politics; to technocratize it, make it the province of a specialized bureaucracy, and remove it from public scrutiny. Protests in the name both of equality and of democracy counter this trend, with varying effect in different countries. The move to greater local initiative and greater local participation that Habitat itself has strongly encouraged in general supports the redistributive direction of governmental action, although there is perhaps some ambivalence in the degree to which the role of government is explicitly emphasized in some of the practices and models that Habitat has encouraged.

The Residualization of Social Housing
The place of social housing in cities may be taken as a litmus test for the extent of inequality in its residential structure. In no country in the world does the market provide adequate housing for those unable to make payments for it at the prevailing rates of return, nor would the market be expected to. That is true regardless of globalization; globalization has added to the perennial problem an increase in levels of inequality and a process of exclusion that has made the plight of those at the bottom of the economic ladder even more desperate. Governmental action is thus indicated to protect those the market does not serve. In the immediate post-war years, most governments took energetic action, the extent varying with resource availability, to secure adequate housing for their populations: whether returning war veterans or devastated communities, the need was dire, and acknowledged. In many countries, the dominant force in housing construction was public, and broad sections of their populations were eligible for government supported housing. Today, that situation is true only in a handful of countries; the pattern is rather that of privatization of social housing, reduction of government's role in housing provision, a pattern most strikingly evident in the formerly state socialist countries of eastern Europe, where the income gap is likewise growing rapidly, but also in most countries in both the first and the third world. . The result has been a residualization of social housing in the developed countries, and a stratification of its occupants in less developed

countries. The unwillingness to subsidize "unproductive" investment in housing is a consequence, at least in part, of the competitive pressures felt by governmental leaders from perceived global competition; it has led to a heightened segregation and inequality in housing provision around the world.

In summary, then: major unfavorable trends have resulted from the increasing globalization of economic activities and their political consequences. Most fundamental of those trends in the increase in inequality, and its reflection - and reinforcement - by the quartering of the spatial structure of cities, with the attendant insulation of the citadels and enclaves of the rich and the walling in and segregation of the ghettos of the poor. Along side this increase in spatial separation are other unfavorable consequences of globalization: the restructuring of central business districts as manufacturing relocates and services grow; the debasing of older cultures, with homogenization of new culture; and the residualization of social housing, a part of the general movement away from the use of government in a socially redistributive capacity towards a more technocratic and efficiency-oriented mode.

But there are countervailing trends also.

The Countervailing Favorable Trends: The Democratization of Decision-making

The greatest single positive feature of the development of cities in the last thirty years has been in the increasing role of their residents in participating in the decisions as to their future. Citizen participation in planning and local government has been on the increase almost everywhere in the world, and has been a major thrust of Habitat efforts also over the years. Participation, of course, is not the same thing as influence, and certainly not the same thing as decision-making; yet it is an essential element in each. How far it will develop to change decision-making depends on the existing relationships of power, which in so many ways globalization has rather served to reinforce. But the movement is there. Decentralization of governmental powers to cities, a characteristic policy of many countries, is ambiguous in this regard: since the resource base of economies are not effectively taped at the local level, if responsibility is devolved from national to central with a parallel devolution of resource, devolution may more increase inequality than reduce it.

The impact of globalization on resident participation is still unclear. Two opposite tendencies can be discerned. On the one hand, the domination of a mass media, increasingly multi-national in its ownership and homogeneous in its content and centralized in its control, permits a manipulation of popular opinion which the established holders of power are well able to exploit. On the other hand, the speed and ubiquity of communications technology can help social movements organize, citizens groups to hammer out agenda, protests to be coordinated, and, above all, the information necessary for effective action to be distributed. By the same token, while the mobility of capital far exceeds that of labor, the internet has provided a channel of communication world-wide that has permitted local groups, organized around particular local problems, to share information with other groups having encountered similar problems. At the extremes, it permits citizens protest to be organized on a global basis, and a global public opinion to be formed, that may exert a countervailing influence to globally-organized established power.

Three social movements go well beyond the local and individual cities, but have strong local implications. The women's movement and those organized around freedom of sexual preference, the militancy of ethnic groups organized around issues of civil rights, and the environmental movements, all have supra-urban bases but important impact on the future of cities. The women's movement has put in the forefront the question of the impact of urban developments of globalization generally on human welfare, as well as on the disproportionately negative impact on women. Not only are women's pay scales still substantially below those of men for equal work, not only is much of women's work entirely unpaid and unrecognized, but also in the distribution of public facilities and services in most cities women's needs a subordinated to those of the business community and the men who dominate in it. Issues of child care, of security in the streets, of accessibility - of rights to the city - have been effectively raised by women and organizations of and for women.

Identity politics, alluded to above, has direct urban impacts, heightened in a period of globalization. Because inequality in income, education, and political power is so often directly related to ethnicity and color, campaigns against discrimination on the basis of race, creed, and color are in general also campaigns for greater equality. Affirmative action, long a progressive slogan in the United States, may be on the defense there, but it is increasingly recognized as a necessary accompaniment to the effort to reduce inequality, whether in South Africa, Singapore, or Sweden. The forms it should take are matters of discussion in most of these places, but that it involves explicit recognition of ethnic and color bases of inequality is increasingly recognized.

The environmental movement is probably that movement that has most explicitly dealt with the unfavorable consequences of globalization, both in natural areas and in cities. Environmental quality and equality are closely connected: pollution, lack of clean water, inadequate sewage disposal, polluting industries, lack of green space, are all characteristics of poor communities; the escape of the rich to environmentally more friendly suburbs on protected enclaves only reinforces the inequality in the distribution and location of environmental detriments and benefits.

This relationship between environmental concerns and inequality has come out very clearly, on a global basis, in the international conferences devoted to each subject separately, and certainly both in the first and the second Habitat conference.

The Advance of Knowledge: Best Practices and Best Policies

At the beginning of the third millennium it is safe to say that the technical knowledge exists to deal with the unfavorable manifestations of globalization in urban areas that have been described above. The spread of the social knowledge likewise necessary, but not sufficient, to put that technical knowledge into practice also exists. We have the scientific knowledge to avoid and to control environmental degradation; we have the planning competence to improve housing, to plan cities well, to equalize educational opportunity, to open the doors to a better quality of life for all of the residents of cities throughout the world. Globalization has significantly increased both out technical and our social know-how. But inequalities of power, accentuated substantially by existing globalization, stand in the way of the uses of that knowledge to socially favorable purposes. Whether existing forms of globalization may be channeled into alternative and more positive forms remains to be seen. The result will be decisive for the future of cities around the world. The tremendous variety that already is to be found among cities shows that the possibility is there. It shows that what people actively do in their environment, although not always in circumstances of their own choosing, can make all the difference in the world.

References:
Barnett, J. (1989) Redesigning the Metropolis: The Case for a New Approach. Journal of the American Planning Association, Spring, vol. 55, No. 2, 131-5.
Brint, S. (1969) Zoned American. In Mollenkopf and Castells, Grossman. New York. p. 155
Bullard, R., Grigsby E, and Lee, C. (1994) (eds). Residential Apartheid: The American Legacy. Los Angeles: Center for Afro-American Studies, University of California at Los Angeles.
Damaris, R. (1984) Rethinking gentrification, Environment and Planning D: Society and Space, vol. 2, 47-74
-, (1980) Toward a Re-evaluation of the Political Significance of Home-Ownership in Britain. In Political Economy of Housing Workshop, Conference of Socialist Economists, March 1980. Housing Construction and the State, London, 71-76
Goldsmith, W. and Blakeley E. (1992) Separate Societies: Poverty and Inequality in U.S. Cities. Philadelphia: Temple University Press
Häusermann, H. and Siebel, W. (1987). Neue Urbanität. Frankfurt am Main, Suhrkamp.
International Development Research Centre, Canada, and Hanoi Architectural University, Vietnam. (1997). Shelter and Environmental Improvement for the Urban Poor: Summary Report. October, p. 82.

Marcuse, P. (1985) Gentrification, Abandonment, and Displacement:
  Connections, Causes, and Policy Responses in New York City. In: Journal of
  Urban and Contemporary Law, Volume 28, St. Louis, Washington University,
  195-240.
-, (1991) Housing Markets and Labour Markets in the Quartered City, in John
  Allen and Chris Hamnett (eds) Housing and Labour Markets: Building the
  Connections, London: Unwin Hyman, 118-135.
-, (1996) Space and Race in the Post-Fordist City: The Outcast Ghetto and
  Advanced Homelessness in the United States Today. In E. Mingione, (ed)
  Urban Poverty and the Underclass. Oxford: Blackwell.
-, (1988) Stadt - Ort der Entwicklung. In Demokratische Gemeinde, November,
  . 115-122.
Massey, D. S. and Denton, N. (1993) American Apartheid: Segregation
  and the Making of the Underclass. Cambridge: Harvard University Press
Sassen, S. (1989) New Trends in the Sociospatial Organization of the New York
  City Economy. In: Beauregard, R. A. (ed) Economic Restructuring and
  Political Response, Newbury Park, Calif.
Wilson, W. J. (1991) Studying inner-city Social Dislocations: The Challenge
  of Public Agenda Research. American Sociological Review, Vol 56, February.
United Nations Development Program, 1996, Human Development Report, 1996.
  New York: Oxford University Press

Welfare and Immigrants' Inclusion in a Context of Weak Civil Society: Associations and local politics in Oeiras (Lisbon)[*]

M. Margarida Marques and Rui Santos

Migrants may melt in the host society, settle and form communities (Castles 2001), become transmigrants (Portes et al. 1999), or adopt other mobility patterns. Either way they are part and parcel of the thread interweaving the various processes engaged in globalization. As 'quasi-citizens', they enact the human rights' global umbrella (Soysal 1994); as 'citizens to be' of new forms of global governance still to be devised, they are a challenge to the cooperative structures squeezed inside the nation-state (Bauböck 1998; Castles 2001).

Civic and particularly 'political incorporation' of immigrants has therefore become one of the important topics in the political agenda of both earlier and later immigration receiving societies. A recent project adopted by UNESCO[1] focused precisely on how and how far immigrants and their descendants were being brought into the political arena, as active actors (MPMC [1997]; Penninx 1998), in social and political contexts where, until very recently, immigration had been treated as a transitional phenomenon (Bauböck 1994, Soysal 1994). The analytical framework adopted by the MPMC project and elsewhere, whenever clear guidelines and criteria are needed for comparative purposes, reveals some bias in the way questions are asked that makes it difficult for empirically based research in a context of late immigration such as Portugal to conform to such guidelines (Marques and Santos forthcoming).

This seems to be the case when discussion about immigrants' political inclusion refers to a 'liberal state' context, as if this could only mean a strong, democratic, fully developed welfare state. This is an important issue entailing two derived and closely related questions. The first concerns the diversity of 'incorporation regimes' and the way they are shaped by the institutional matrix of the host societies (Soysal 1994)

---

[*] Research funded by Praxis CSH/840/95 and SOC/12104/98 projects and ESF. A first draft of this paper was presented at the IVth International Metropolis Conference, Washington DC, 8-11th December 1999; we are indebted to the Luso-American Foundation for Development, as sponsor of the Metropolis Portugal group, for making it possible for us to attend the conference. We owe a special note of appreciation to Tiago Ralha for his collaboration in the first draft and to Pedro Tavares de Almeida, to whom we are deeply indebted for his precious suggestions in several informal conversations.

[1] *Multicultural Policies and Modes of Citizenship in European Cities* (http//www.unesco.org/most/p97.htm), involving 6 cities from late receiving countries (Athens, Barcelona, Milan, Oeiras, Rome, and Turin) among the total of 17.

which cannot be analysed separately from the historical processes of civil society building (Hall 1995, Mouzelis 1995) and their connections with state building (Bendix, Bendix and Furniss 1987; Scockpol 1999). The second is about the ways formal and informal dynamics articulate when the state is unable to entirely fulfil modern welfare functions (Bermeo 1999; Oxhorn 1995).

R. D. Putnam's analysis on Italian regional politics (1993) made a strong case for the importance of civil society in the performance of democratic states. This point was also made concerning immigration issues: the stronger the civic communities built by dense associative interaction, the more immigrant populations tend to participate politically in the institutional settings of the host society, and therefore to exert some control over state intervention in ways that are congenial with their interests (Fennema and Tillie 1999, *inter alia*). But what if we are dealing with a weak liberal state, where, as in Portugal, some particularistic and local identifications and commitments that still prevail paradoxically render state intervention 'necessary for almost everything'? (Lucena 1982: 909)

Building on the idea that the welfare state is the 'arena in which the divergent interests of the state and civil society are joined' (Bendix, Bendix and Furniss 1987: 19; see also Esping-Andersen 1994), we intend to address the possible effects, in a context of weak civil society and state, of welfare inputs in drawing articulation devices between these two instances which are (1) effective in bringing together immigrants' associations as interlocutors of public authorities; and (2) able to legitimate representatives at both levels (state institutions and the constituencies the associations are supposed to represent).[2]

General features of Portuguese society include deep mistrust toward state institutions' performance and opportunity structures in general (Villaverde Cabral 1997), and low and fragmented associative participation (Ambrósio *et al.* 1983; França et al. 1993; Bacalhau 1994; Villaverde Cabral 1997, 2000) - which is the hallmark of a still important 'familist' tradition.[3] The often diagnosed weakness of the welfare state is

---

[2] We thank D. Papademetriou for calling our attention to this aspect and especially providing us factual information about the specific problems which arose in the USA with Latin American associations.

[3] This concept, coined by British and American anthropologists for describing the particular social structures they found in the Mediterranean basin and recently used by Karin Wall (1998) in a study of Portuguese rural society, was part of a theoretical framework which has been harshly critized (Pina-Cabral 1991, *inter alia*). B. S. Santos sees in these traditional orientations of Portuguese society one of the underpinnings of a 'welfare society' (1994: 64). We still prefer the term familism. On the one hand, 'welfare society' in this context seems to be a contradiction in terms, in the sense that formal welfare institutions evolved to take the place of missing society

the other side of this coin (Esping-Andersen 1993; Wall 1995). In this context, the present analysis of the particular situation of immigrants' participation in a Portuguese municipality aims to assess the effects of the ability of public catering for collective needs in 'bringing in' this particular segment so far excluded from civic participation.

Perceptions of equity are undoubtedly a condition of democratic civil society building (Bermeo 2001). Subjective well-being, optimism about life chances and effective security and welfare rights may be strong determinants of generalized trust and civic participation (Offe 1999, Inglehart 1999, Uslaner 1999, Warren 1999). This seems to make sense in a context of full-fledged welfare states, where redistributive devices and norms have been routinized. Is this to be equally expected where welfare resources are comparatively meagre, and redistribution mechanisms are not stabilized, often being perceived as biased or unfair? (Mingione 1996) On the other hand, social perceptions of needs and satisfactions are not stable. They evolve in a dynamic way, as once basic needs are satisfied, new needs tend to arise concerning higher order issues and generating new perceptions of absolute or relative deprivation, according to Maslow's (1963) hierarchical model.

In Oeiras, the effects of providing socio-economic resources by local government coincided with important policy developments at the central level, concerning immigrants' legalization, vote, and representation through consultative bodies. This raises the issue of the legitimacy of representatives. We argue that two different legitimating processes occur. One is the granting of legitimacy by public institutions to national level immigrants' associations as representatives in governmental consultative bodies. This legitimacy is based on past performance as advocates, and the social capital they can draw next to national political elites (Portes 1998), without significant participation by immigrant population. In keeping with the very fragmented character of Portuguese civil society and its low levels of participation, these national associations are not federations of local associations, and incipient attempts to bring about federative institutions have been so far unsuccessful.

The second legitimating process lies on the trust placed by immigrant population in local associations. These originally developed at neighbourhood level, based on interpersonal relationships and generated

---

links and to develop a whole range of new functions. On the other hand, 'welfare society' has been used in the context of *full fledged* welfare states referring to the reversal of the trend from state concentration of welfare functions, towards the development of *new* welfare policies depending on civic organizations (Offe 1999). This is clearly not the Portuguese situation, where the driving trend of welfare state building is far from complete, and family based support is a traditional asset rather than a postmodern development in civil society's functions.

trust based on familiarity, or ethnic and local identities, and on their ability to provide some services to local populations. As it assumes the form of 'particularized trust', it is encapsulated in its local contexts, and is by itself insufficient to build trust and legitimacy for larger scale representation (Offe 1999). In fact, evidence points to this kind of trust as being adverse to civic participation (Uslaner 1999) unless it is tied to translocal networks (Scockpol 1999). The problem thus translates into whether and how local particularized trust based on familiarity and informal relations can be geared into more generalized trust necessary to formal instances of representation at the national political level; and what are the effects of inclusion in public welfare redistribution on this process. In this case study, we intend to show that, besides the formal institutional context (Penninx 1998), the effective ability of providing public resources is also a prime determinant of the opportunity structures moulding immigrants' civic inclusion. It is not enough to create formal structures of participation, unless public authorities can achieve some sort of effective redistribution of public goods, and the extension of welfare rights that build the state's 'performance legitimacy' to previously excluded segments of civil society (Bendix, Bendix and Furniss 1987; Marshall 1992). Furthermore, the assumption of some welfare functions by local actors, in a context of a weak central state, brings about forms of political and civic mobilization which rely on the combination of formal and informal processes (cf. Oxhorn 1995 for Latin America). This development may lead to the creation of fuzzy channels of articulation. Through them political agents involved in central political arenas can eventually feed the legitimacy they get at the central level into their ability to be accepted at the local level. Conversely, local agents' access to central agents may strengthen their ability of acting as local interests' representatives. We suggest therefore that an effective model of political representation and mediation should link both sources of legitimacy, the local and the central and acknowledge both formal and informal incorporation processes.

We shall undertake the case study exploration (1) starting with the presentation of changes occurred in the associative landscape following both the large scale re-housing process at the municipal level and the reshaping of the political opportunity structure occurred at the central level; (2) we shall then describe and characterize the linkages between local actors and between them and central level institutions, trying to evidence the distinct dynamics they involve; (3) a discussion will ensue on the central problem of how local and central levels, and formal and informal mechanisms are interrelated.

Data were collected through interviews with relevant actors in 1998 and 1999. Interviews were conducted with:

1) Leaders of 4 local and 2 national associations who either formally aim to represent Cape Verdean interests, or whose constituencies and leadership are mainly made up of Cape Verdeans (the larger immigrant group present in Oeiras). These interviews focused on associations' histories, aims, activities, resources and recruitment; on their involvement with local and national processes; and on their relations with akin associations, other civil society organizations, local government and national state agencies, and with institutions abroad (such as sending country governments and EU institutions).

2) Three leaders of local associations without Cape Verdean constituencies or leadership, with whom associations in 1) have established some kind of relation.

3) Oeiras local government: 7 elected officials (the Lord Mayor; 2 aldermen for housing and culture; 1 municipal parliament and 3 parish[4] board members coopted from local immigrants' associations); 4 appointed officials and 4 technical staff dealing with relevant issues. Interviews focused on local government policies concerning immigrants and ethnic minorities, on processes involving these local populations (such as re-housing, immigrants legalization and local elections), and on local government's relationships with local immigrants associations and other intervening actors.

4) Two national government officials in state departments dealing with immigration and citizenship issues, and 1 MP related to immigration issues. Interviews focused on public policies towards immigrants and ethnic minorities and policy induced processes, and on relationships by these state agencies with immigrants associations and other types of actors listed.

5) Three representatives of local and national civil society organizations, not mainly composed of, nor led by immigrants themselves but addressing immigrants' and ethnic minorities' rights. Interviews focused on their aims and intervention guidelines, and relationships with immigrants' associations, national and international organizations and, where relevant, with Oeiras local government.

6) One member of the Cape Verdean Parliament elected by the emigrants' constituency in Europe.

Transcripts were analyzed according to the themes defined by the research problems above. Relational data (among themselves and between them and other organizations they mentioned) were codified as to their nature and stored in a sociometric matrix, from which was drawn the network graph we will present below.

---

[4] The parish ('*freguesia*') is the smallest administrative district in Portugal.

Besides this core of interview data, we also relied on information collected in field research ongoing for several years, including interviews and survey data on inhabitants of municipal neighbourhoods and of remaining shanty towns (Marques, Santos, Santos and Nóbrega 1999; Marques, Santos, Araújo and Nóbrega 2001). These data provided information on population attitudes towards civic and political participation, trust in institutions and opportunity structures, and the re-housing process.

1. Changing dynamics of representation induced by new patterns of settlement

Immigration is a recent phenomenon in Portugal. Official records on foreigners with a legal residence permit show that they were less than 5% of the total population in 2002. If one includes return migration, figures on migrants add up to more than 10%, according to Ferrão's (1996) computations. Should one concentrate on migrants from Portuguese speaking countries, and particularly from former African colonies, available data reveal high concentration in metropolitan areas (Pires et al. 1987). A tentative census made by a Catholic organization in 1995 estimated the population of African origin (including only black and mixed individuals) settled in Oeiras' poor neighbourhoods at around 6% (Cachada et al. 1995b).

Oeiras municipality harbours less than 200 thousand inhabitants, lies in the outskirts of Lisbon along a large waterfront on the Tagus estuary. Its urbanization process reveals three coexisting layers: the inheritance of a past summer resort, which lasted until the 60s; the suburban vicinity where Lisbon could centrifuge its lower middle classes and suburban nuisances, mainly during the 70s and the early 80s; later developments conferred to Oeiras the status of a natural spreading of the capital city, concentrating some of its most affluent segments and prestigious hi-tech corporations (Fernandes 1997 for further details).

It was during the second period that vast slum areas, which began to be built by internal migrants and were later inflated by large international migrant populations and their offspring, have risen along the border with Lisbon municipality. Most of that population, a large part of which is of Cape Verdean origin, lived highly concentrated in five slums laid in a specific area to the East of the municipal territory.[5] In recent years a huge municipal re-housing process was undertaken, the former slums are now dismantled and their inhabitants scattered throughout the municipal territory, living in municipal estates.

The map in Fig. 1 compares the former slum concentration to the present dispersed settlement pattern of municipal neighbourhoods.

---

[5] Further details in Marques, Santos, Ralha and Cordeiro, 1998.

Fig.1

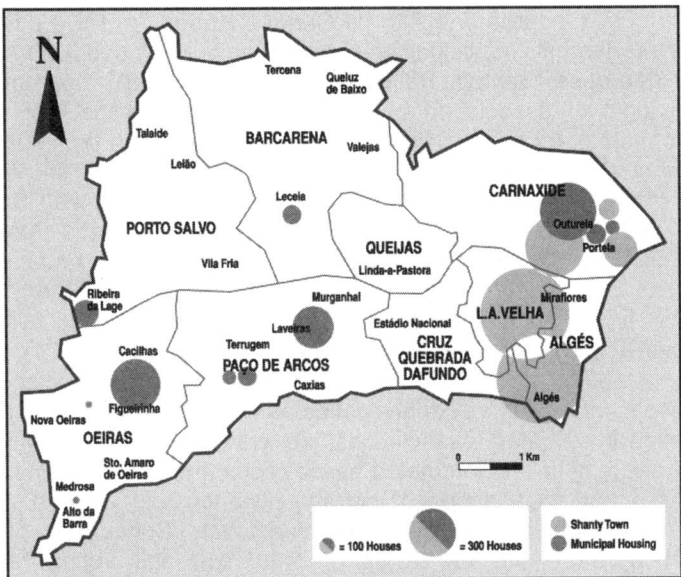

Source: Adapted from A Fernandes, *A geografia de Oeiras. Atlas Municipal*, CMO, 1997.

Local grassroots associations, suddenly unable to maintain the same type of face-to-face interaction in which they thrived within a now scattered community, experienced important challenges due to the conjunction of this spatial de-confinement with a new political conjuncture in which immigrants achieved some political weight. This was notably the case of being allowed to enrol as voters in local elections (since 1996), and to operate as interlocutors in mediating structures, with a right to say on migration policies, at local and central levels of governance.

It is not easy, however, to assess the exact extent of change occurred during the process. To begin with, there is only one locally based association formally claiming the status of an immigrant association (ECC-CO), which aims to act at a national level. Furthermore, among the associations having significant participation of immigrants and ethnic minorities, as listed in official sources in the mid-nineties, some have indeed disappeared following these new settlement arrangements, while others never really existed, and yet others rely on very informal arrangements.

Most of the 15 associations whose existence we were able to directly confirm were concentrated in three areas: seven in two shanty towns (Pedreira dos Húngaros and Alto de Santa Catarina) and five others in one of the largest municipal re-housing neighbourhoods (Outurela-Portela) (Marques, Santos, Ralha and Cordeiro 1998). This confirms that the logic of association building followed the spatial settlement pattern of immigrant and ethnic minority populations, and thus suggests a dominant type of activities concentrated on a particularistic scope, indeed confirmed by survey and interview data (Marques, Santos, Santos and Nóbrega 1999; Marques, Santos, Araújo and Nóbrega 2001). This is not significantly different from the mainstream situation.

Portuguese civil society is weak in organizational terms; although some corporatist type institutions are being framed since the early 80s (see references above). As Y. Soysal (1994) and P. Ireland (1994) put it, immigrants tend to espouse the dominant matrix of the host society. This is the case insofar as the evidence collected until now shows: concerning participation in voluntary associations, we found low rates of adhesion, extreme diversity of uncoordinated associations, many of them having a very limited and local scope of activity, distance and even suspicion toward more formalized levels of representation. Concerning political participation, there are low rates of enrolment and voting turnout, mistrust toward middle and higher levels of representation, and scarce articulation between local and national levels of ethnic representation. Most of the local grassroots associations were committed to very specific aims: promoting the preservation of the original cultural heritage, sports activities, coaching the youngsters in school works, etc...[6] Others included concerns about local living conditions improvement and thereby worked as pressure groups next to municipal authorities. Relations with each other and with outside actors were irregular, and no stabilized form of articulation existed. It comes as no surprise then that the political representation of immigrants or citizenship issues ranks low (if present) in local associations' agenda.

More recent observations show that the associations who 'survived' continue to evidence these main features. Yet, when the massive re-housing started scattering people throughout different neighbourhoods, which occurred simultaneously with the acquisition of electoral rights by Cape Verdeans and some other migrants, people and institutions started to become more integrated in supra-local levels of activity and connections.

---

[6] Details of existing associations in the Lisbon area in Cachada et al. (1995a) and Albuquerque, Ferreira and Viegas (2000).

Along with the considerable decrease in the number of associations with large immigrants and ethnic minorities' participation[7], observation reveals that surviving asociations grew more internally differentiated and aim at a wider scope of action. Their participation in transnational activities (cultural, sportive and political) is worth mentioning, as is their ability to get funds for projects against social exclusion.

Another aspect worth mentioning is the increased formalization of relations between public authorities and these local organizations. In the re-housing neighbourhoods, associations use municipal facilities and, in order to be granted any sort of support by local authorities (financial, logistics ...), the associations must present a plan of activities fulfilling a series of requirements. Their dependence on the compliance with formal normative criteria to get municipal support also operated as a selection mechanism[8] leading to the disappearance of a kaleidoscope of small associations and to strengthen the systematic work of a few others. Furthermore, becoming a tenant creates the need for more formal claims making towards the City Hall, and consequently more formalized interest representation. Oeiras Town Hall, however, does not have a formal mediating structure aiming at addressing migration policies.

2. Taking off into politics: underlying processes

The spatial reorganisation induced by the re-housing process coincided with wider policy developments. This course of events had major consequences in the structure and dynamics of the associative field in Oeiras. On the one hand, a few remaining associations rose to higher levels of participation. On the other, new subjects and opportunities for their action emerged. We shall now depict the emerging structure through a conceptual framework describing the organizations' participation space.

---

[7] In 1998 we found only eight of the fifteen original associations still active (Marques, Santos, Ralha and Cordeiro 1998: 49).

[8] See also Albuquerque, Ferreira and Viegas (2000).

Table 1

		ARENAS			
		Immigrant Groups	Immigrant Associations	Civil Society Organisations	Political Institutions
LEVELS	*Supra-national*	Diasporas; transnational networks	International Federations	Political parties in sending countries; International religious organisations; International NGOs	UN; EU; Cunsultative bodies (EU Forum); Political institutions in sending countries; CPSP*
	National	Immigrant communities and networks	Immigrant associations and federations; Immigrant press; Immigrant entrepreneurial associations; Immigrant-specific religious organisations	Political parties; Human rights, anti-racist, etc. associations; Catholic Church; Entrepreneurial associations; Trade unions; Press	Political institutions; HCIEM** Consultative Council
	Municipal	Immigrant communities	Immigrant associations	Voluntary associations; Entrepreneurial associations; School associations (pupils, parents)	Municipal and parish political institutions; Municipal consultative councils
LEVELS	**Neighbourhood**	Immigrant communities	Immigrant associations	Residents' associations; Voluntary associations; School associations (students', parents')	

From Marques and Santos (forthcoming). Actors specified in the cells are meant to be examples, not exhaustive listings.
* Community of the Portuguese Speaking Countries; ** High Commissioner for Immigrants and Ethnic Minorities.

We conceive the participation space as defined by two ordered axes dealing respectively with participation *arenas*, ranging from the communities to the decision-making institutions, and participation *levels*, ranging from local neighbourhoods to supra-national spheres of action. In both dimensions, participation processes can be defined as *top-down (activation)*, *bottom-up (mobilization)* or combinations of the two.[9] The intersection of these two axes defines a map such as shown in the table

---

[9] The terms were coined in the MPMC project conceptual framework (MPMC [1997]) and further discussed in Marques and Santos forthcoming).

below, on which we can plot the relative positions of the various actors and their relationships.

Figure 2 portrays graphically the network that emerged out of the aforementioned developments, as far as we were able to elicit it from interviews and information gathered in fieldwork.[10] Owing to the composition of the immigrant population in Oeiras, we concentrated on Cape Verdean-led associations. Several kinds of connections are considered, namely collaboration, support (e.g. financial or logistic), and interlocks through common personnel and close personal ties (for instance, in spite of their links to rival political parties, the presidents of Assomada [ASSOM] and Pedreira dos Húngaros Sports Association [PHSA] are brothers). A specific kind of relation was drawn for the placement of associations' members into other political institutions. We also considered overt competition or conflict. In this respect the refusal of the Oeiras Town Hall [CMO] to accept external organizations as interest group mediators is very salient in their position against [SOS R], an active left wing anti-racist organization, and also against national and local level catholic groups [CCH] [CRA] who tried to establish themselves as intermediaries speaking for slum minorities. It should be noted that these relations may be ambivalent, as competition and collaboration or interlocks may coexist between two given actors (as is the case with the residents' associations of two adjoining neighbourhoods, white working-class 18th May [18M] and mainly Cape Verdean Outurela-Portela [RESID], and with [ASSOM] and ECC-CO).

---

[10] We don't intend the graph to be exhaustive, especially as some informal connections may have eluded the interviews. On the other hand, some simplifying steps were taken to make its reading easier, namely the suppression of some actors with scarce links that didn't add to the interpretation, and the conflation of a few others into one single position (for instance, several Catholic organisations into Catholic Church [CCH]). The HCIEM, though an important actor by itself, was subsumed under the Government tag (GOV). The HCIEM Consultative Council, however, was retained as a specific organisation. Furthermore, as we only considered institutional actors, an area of 'invisible networking' is left open between the organizations and the local communities themselves.

Fig. 2

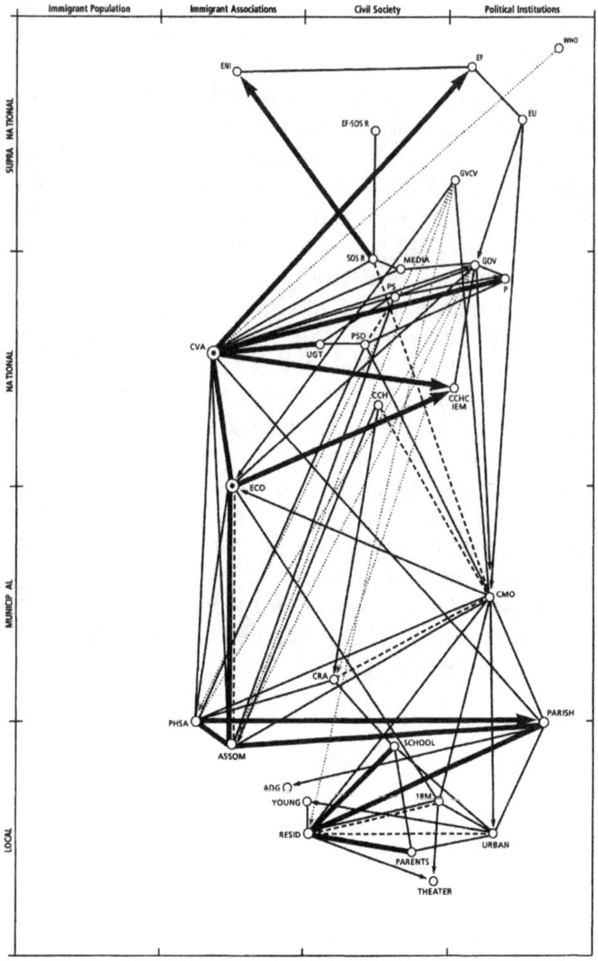

EU - European Union
EF - European Forum
EF - SOS R - European Federation of SOS Racism
ENI - European Network of Immigrant Associations
GVCV - Capeverdian Government/ National Assembly/ Political Parties
GOV - Portuguese Government
P - Portuguese Parliament
MEDIA - Media
SOS R - SOS Racism
PS - Socialist Party
PSD - Centre right Social Democratic Party
CCHCIEM - Consultative Council of the High Commissioner for Immigrants and Ethnic Minorities
UGT - Trade Union
CVA - Capeverdian National Association
CCH - Catholic Church
ECO - Oeiras Municipality Capeverdian Community Space
CMO - Oeiras Town Hall
PHSA - Pedreira dos Húngaros Sport and Cultural Association
ASSOM - Assomada Association
SCHOOL - School
PARISH - Parish Board
ADG - African Dances Group
YOUNG - Youngsters Club
RESID - Outurela/Portela Residents' Association
18M - 18th May Residents' Association
PARENTS - Outurela/Portela Parents Comission
URBAN - Oeiras Municipality European Urban Project
THEATRE - Outurela/Portela Theatre Group

Personal link: placement (organisation at rear end placed at least one member into organisation at arrow end)
Personal link: interlock (at least one common member in both organisations)
Current support (organisation at rear end currently gives financial or logistic support to organisation at arrow end)
Current co-operation between the two organisations
Competition
Past support for specific activities

We see that both at the neighbourhood and municipal levels, on the one hand, and at national level, on the other, there are very connected clusters of organizations bridging across the several arenas, namely between immigrant associations or civil society organisations addressing a largely immigrant public, and political institutions. These connections can, and have proved to be, effectively used for lobbying, voicing discontent and influencing political agenda setting.

Between local (i.e. neighbourhood and municipal) and national levels, however, bridges are thinner and more concentrated on a small number of mediators, along two main kinds of channels. There is one mediation path through the political institutions and political parties, where the main mediating position is held by the Town Hall. The other we might call the ethnic organizations channel, where the mediating position is divided between ECC-CO, who enjoyed a comparatively privileged relation with the Town Hall [CMO] and with the by then Cape Verdean government [GVCV], and the Capeverdean Association [CVA], who can mobilize much more diversified social capital at national and international levels, although its links to municipal political institutions in Oeiras, consisting of people elected in the opposition party lists, were thinner. Mainly through the same mediators, there are also links between the two channels.

Channels thus seem to be available for the local associations to mobilize into political representation of interests, and for national level associations to activate the local ones and draw legitimacy from their local social capital. That possibility, however, is very contingent on the dynamics through which these channels emerged, and on the ability of local agents to keep the local 'particularized trust' that they enjoy from eroding as they evolve into more formalized and openly political forms of action. We should therefore take a closer narrative look at those case features.

Following the re-housing process the surviving associations, whose former neighbourhood constituencies became scattered throughout the municipality, were drawn upward from confined neighbourhood activities to the municipal level. In the process, they also came to redefine their place in the participation arenas, moving from local sports and culture associations to more explicit claims of immigrant representation into the municipal political institutions (e.g. [PHSA] football team participation in national and international African tournaments, and their regular articulation with national level [ECC-CO] association with siege in Oeiras). Within the proposed framework these shifts have a double sense in apparently opposite directions, both of which, however, reinforce rather than contradict each other. As they move upward into the municipal level and more formally inward the political arena, these associations also seem to move back from an ethnically non-particularist civil society position into an ethnically defined one. This double movement reflects changes in the political opportunity structure following policy programs and political framework changes targeted toward the inclusion of immigrants and ethnic minorities, and forms the basis for privileged ties into the political mainstream.

In fact, this was a combined effect of several factors. Re-housing not only redefined the associations' ecological setting but also put the populations into closer contact with the Town Hall and led to the articulation of new demands. These in turn led to the rise of new and strong associations at neighbourhood level, namely residents' associations, tending the interests of the new municipal re-housing neighbourhoods much more effectively than the former shanty town associations could in this new context. A major instance of this fact and of its implications on associative structure was the organized outbreak of protest against rent increases in 1995, after the Town Hall updated old leases and imposed tighter control over eligibility for subsidies. Immigrant led neighbourhood associations then emerged as actors, gaining unprecedented mobilization, collaborating with older white working class residents' associations and getting heard by the Town Hall.

On the other hand, along with re-housing, the Town Hall, albeit its claim to disregard any form of collective representation, also contributed to the selection process and to the rising of former neighbourhood associations to the status of political partner. The recent grant of voting rights to immigrants in local elections, first held in these terms in 1997, also played a major role, forcing the main political competitors to address a new potential constituency and to recruit eligible candidates of immigrant origin from local associations into their lists. Former neighbourhood associations, along with the new residents' associations, thus came to take hold of a new set of opportunities for participation in the municipal political struggle. The taking of this role, however, is hindered by the political position held by the Town Hall of not recognising any forms of collective interest representation in dealing with citizens' demands, a stance that only recently began to be opened to discussion.

At the national level, the comparatively dormant immigration issue came to light in the early 90s and reached large public opinion segments with the first immigrants' regularization process in 1992/3 and the ensuing political debates on the way it was conducted (Machado 1993; Guibentif 1996). National level immigrants' associations, allied to sectors of the Catholic Church and civil rights organizations, then earned enhanced visibility in the political arena and came to some political agreements with the Socialist Party then rallying collective interests opposed to the decade-long centre right party in office.

After the Socialist Party came into office in 1995, the shift in government policy towards immigrants and ethnic minorities led to a higher political framing of immigration issues. Honouring pre-electoral commitments, a second regularization process was undertook which, contrary to the first, largely relied on participation by both national and local immigrants' associations. Its promotion next to the immigrant populations and its implementation led to added opportunities for local associations to link with national ones and to widen their scope of action, both in terms of arenas and of levels of participation. Also a new institutional actor was created within the government, the High Commissioner for Immigration and Ethnic Minorities (HCIEM), who eventually appointed a Consultative Council with representatives of the larger national groups, deemed to give advice on policy and to carry over the needs and claims of immigrants. Previously established or newly engaged links between the uprising municipal associations and the national level ones thus became indirect paths into mainstream political institutions at the national level, just as electoral recruitment established a direct one at the local (municipal) level.

One important dimension of these shifts is the refashioning of the associations' social capital (in Fennema and Tillie's [1999] terms). Local associations got directly linked to (or more strongly so than before), and interlocked with, municipal political institutions and to national immigrants' associations. Through both these channels, they were connected to others at national and international level, across the whole range of institutional arenas. Conversely, as the political dimension of immigration issues was amplified by the changes in the electoral system and by the creation of national and local[11] immigrants' representative bodies (among other factors), the problems of recruitment and representativeness took a larger share of the national associations' concerns, who had to further activate their links or establish new ones to local level actors. Indeed, the Cape Verdean Association's position as a representative in the Consultative Council of the HCIEM was legitimized by an unprecedented suffrage by local associations (in which, however, not all of the most important associations in Oeiras took part). Also at the international level, Cape Verde government was monitoring their nationals' communities in Portugal. Steps were taken to activate federation among associations (a process that aborted, though the idea remains), and even the building up of a new association, politically closer to the party in office in Cape Verde by that time, was encouraged.

As a result of these combined developments, structural conditions seem to have evolved towards an enhanced participation of immigrants' representatives in local political institutions, and to a possible role in some future developments of national level representation. But the

---

[11] In some of the neighbouring municipalities of the Lisbon Metropolitan Area with large immigrants and ethnic minorities populations; not in Oeiras, though.

possible growth of that participation raises the problems of trust and legitimacy, in a context where mistrust towards organized forms of collective action and extremely low associative affiliation rates predominate - among immigrants no less than among the autochthonous population (see references above). The much particularized nature of the local legitimacy of these associations is a major problem in this respect.

In fact, this movement toward an apparent formalization of political representation procedures is underpinned by very informal dynamics. It relies heavily on the local associations' leaders. The typical association leader was also its founder, besides being its main activist and the core of its staff. As formal participation by the population, through formal enrolling, fee paying or meeting attendance is in fact very low, associations depend on the very personal commitment of these few people. They are immigrants, having Portuguese or dual citizenship, who are strongly embedded in the local communities. The associations were very much born as personal projects, through large use of their private resources such as time, money and social ties – and still depend very much on these resources to keep working. Through their activities, they have developed personal relationships of service rendering inside their community, and became known and systematically called upon as possible mediators for individual interests next to local institutions, whereby they came to gain charismatic prestige and central roles in the communities' networks through these brokerage activities (Boissevain 1974). It is mainly on this personal charismatic basis, rather than a formal political role of representatives of mobilized associations, that they got recognized by local political leaders and were invited to take part in local election lists, and eventually elected into office. Their community reputation, which they hold as particular individuals, is the main vote-inducing asset that political parties count upon for electoral dispute.

Thus, both the local associative phenomenon, as expressed in the number of active associations, and its incipient move into politics in fact rest on low formal associative participation and on informal interpersonal dynamics with charismatic and to some extent clientelar contents. So the question arises as to how effective and lasting this move into formal political representation will prove to be in the future. And that in turn will largely depend on whether it will stimulate formal participation by their constituencies, through formal voluntary associations and voting, in order to achieve lasting legitimacy for political representation. Following Mouzelis (1995), should this process follow the 'clientelism' form of incorporation; it might reinforce the intermediary role of the associations and thus contribute to strengthen civil society, through a specific articulation mechanism between formal and informal dimensions. Should the 'populist' incorporation prevail, and the association leaders' cooptation obey a veiled purpose of control by political parties, then the chance of creating that articulation, so important in contexts of late civil society building (Oxhorn 1995), could be jeopardized. Anyway, one should keep in mind that the *particularized trust* placed by local population on their association leaders, as incumbents of local offices, might erode, as a consequence of general mistrust against formal politics. A mistrust that is mirrored by the very same people who were newly drawn into party politics, who are prone to declare themselves and their associations as non-political.

3. Discussion

As mentioned above, in this particular Town Hall, political orientations have been clearly against the idea of creating an immigrants' and minorities' consultative body. Instead, the 'open administration philosophy' favours the unmediated individual citizens' search of solutions to arising problems. Yet, in practical terms, Oeiras associations of immigrants have been frequently treated as intermediary bodies – not only for national policies implementation (legalization, electoral registration ...), but for decisions at the local level as well (how to deal with school drop-outs, to encourage youngsters' professional training...).
The explicit guidelines at the central level are much more balanced, between the multicultural and the republican stances. Yet, here again direct access to public authorities by associations' leaders and the public in general is possible, sometimes even encouraged. Local and central level authorities, formally of the 'liberal neutrality' and 'liberal multiculturalism' types (Penninx 2000:11-12), respectively, seem to share a dominant pragmatic stance.
Yet, contrasting with the results obtained among Portuguese population as a whole, trust in public authorities and opportunity structures, and reliance in mediating structures is, among immigrants and their children living in Oeiras, comparatively high (Marques, Santos, Araújo and Nóbrega 2001), relying on the 'loyalty' type attitude (Hirschman 1970). After re-housing, however, the 'voice' stance (namely concerning housing issues) seems to be gaining ground, with local associations as part of the chorus. Thus, the stress on the 'populist incorporation' form (Mouzelis 1995:234-237) in Oeiras, congenial with atomized forms of participation, does not seem to have brought about the melting of the intermediary bodies – on the contrary.
Local associations originally emerged as responses to immediate survival needs, mainly concerning the utter situation of exclusion faced by migrants and their offspring in the slums. As depicted by Oxhorn (1995) for Latin America, by Danese (2001) for Italy and Spain, and by Ireland (1994) and Soysal (1994) for Switzerland, supra-local civil society institutions (Christian churches and NGOs, among others) stepped in, in that context, providing important assistance in civil society building and

welfare. Catering for all sorts of support, from commodities to information and other services aimed at these populations' self-organization.[12] As Ireland (1994) pointed out, exclusion from the welfare state leaves room for other agents to strive (including sending countries authorities) and favours identification with homeland – against local disaffiliation as a foreigner.

In this context, the municipal re-housing process appears as a watershed. Local public authorities took in charge the welfare function of providing basic resources, thus mitigating some of the needs the associations were supposed to meet – together with municipal housing, there was also the creation of public facilities or public funded services (e.g. occupational training for the youngsters, daily care for children and the elderly ...). It also helped to dislodge other supra-local civil society organizations from their role of civil society coaching (namely, the Catholic Church). This relieved local associations from some of the supra-local level actors' competition for resources – as Danese (2001) also noted elsewhere –, getting their hands free to extend their autonomous influence.

Some local associations thus seem to have gained a lot with the re-housing process, namely more freedom to act as autonomous bodies, to make plans for the future (not being so intensely dependent on responding to urgent, pressing, everyday needs), to organize to meet interests above the local level immediate needs, and to engage in activities (old and new) which further the civic inclusion by framing it in regular, formalized settings. A *caveat* is in order, though, since the dependence on municipal resources somehow mitigates the autonomy thus achieved.

In sum, we contend that the assumption of wider redistribution functions by local authorities created favourable conditions for the local associations to 'play the game' and further their claims as stakeholders. This, in turn, naturally had far-reaching consequences on the attitudes toward the opportunity structures.

The re-housing process has in fact generated welfare through the satisfaction of basic needs, as shown by survey indexes of residential satisfaction. This would be expected to lead to enhanced trust in the opportunity structure and in the institutions that shape it, and that trust would in turn lead to more formal participation. However, the relationships are not quite so linear.

---

[12] The *Nô Djunta Môn* [Holding Hands] project for health and education, funded by the UN and co-ordinated during the 80s by the Cape Verdean Association, is a good example of this. Another is the claims made to the City by a Dutch missionary who lived in a slum, since demolished, and by local Catholic groups.

In keeping with Maslow's (1963) hierarchical model, the satisfaction of old needs is turning into a range of new ones, and the Maslow paradox is in play: the satisfaction of a given level of needs is a determinant for frustration at a higher level. As basic needs of housing conditions and residential security were partially met by the re-housing process, new ones arose that translate into concerns about fairness, equity, and self-esteem aspects of welfare. And again according to Maslow, the satisfied needs (along with the means used for that purpose) become undervalued as against those basic needs not yet fulfilled and new emergent ones, on which new deprivation perceptions are construed.

On the other hand, the re-housing process accrued to the Town Hall position of a purveyor of public goods that of a landlord who imposes rents, with whom housing conditions and repairs have to be discussed, and to whom new sets of responsibilities are committed. This change in the role of the public institution brought about a whole new set of grievances.

So, dissatisfaction with some aspects of the re-housing conditions and neighbourhood equipment is very manifest in interviews. House rent levels and associated expenses are currently seen as an important downside to the re-housing benefits, both in interview and survey data. New houses for which rent is paid also seem to raise expectations about living conditions and about the landlord's responsibilities in keeping them. New rationally designed neighbourhoods invite criticism about urban forms and functions which were unthinkable in the slums, and worry for the perceived residential stigma associated to them. And in this case the landlord and the city planner are one with the welfare provider, all these roles being performed by the Town Hall.

The effect of welfare redistribution on expressions of trust in the institutions is therefore ambiguous. Trust earned by past performance in fulfilling welfare functions is tainted by distrust about equity in the procedures, and about commitment to provide for new expectations. And the fact that loyalty-type trust was very vocally turned into voice-type distrust (Hirschman 1970) during the protest against rent increases leads us to the second point. Once a threshold of trust about institutional performance was attained, it was distrust about equity and fairness that triggered the most important mobilization process to date. At least episodically, trust in political institutions was transferred to voluntary representatives, namely residents' associations. And this eventually was one of the recruitment channels of migrant leaders for electoral lists. So, distrust and protest against political institutions turned into trust in representatives and a move into formal political participation.

In this case, it seems that the effect of welfare provision, enhancing both trust in the redistribution functions of the political system and the level of demands on political institutions, along with the changes in associative structure and roles it brought about, may prove to be instrumental in fostering the ground conditions from which more sustained participation can take advantage of the newly created opportunities in the political system.

In this new setting, the relative disjunction between immigrant associations' actions and legitimacy grounds at local (municipal and neighbourhood) levels, on the one hand, and at national or international levels, on the other, constitutes a problem. If the latter fail to gain recognition by the former there will be negative consequences for the building and functioning of democratic mechanisms for representation.

Given the current growth of the political relevance of immigration, the trend for increasing participation by immigrant associations in the political competition, and the very rules of the democratic game, the legitimacy issue is paramount in order to establish acknowledged representation of interests and institutional mediating roles. This is indeed a very explicit concern in many of our interviews. As things stand, the way the two forms of legitimacy outlined above (closeness to national and international political institutions and closeness to local populations' problems) may coalesce and thus reinforce each other will condition the outcome of how the associations will be able to keep playing the political game. The sometimes very informal and personal networking between associations at different levels, even when conflicts arise and political allies seem contradictory, is probably at present the possible, albeit fragile, backcloth for the building up of trust among immigrant organisations and for progress toward more stabilised forms of mediation (Fennema and Tillie 1999).[13]

This may be of importance even if the institutional mediating channel is to be privileged, for it depends on the inclusion by mainstream institutions and political parties of immigrant personnel in their ranks, which in turn depends on how much importance these actors will place on immigrant vote in local polls, and on naturalized immigrant vote in national ones. Should immigrant population voting turnouts prove to be ineffective, because of lack of trust in their representatives or in the political system as such, the structure of political opportunities which has started to open up for their participation might regress.

Two main hypotheses stem from this case study.

First that welfare redistribution should not be taken for granted when

---

[13] While dealing with immigrants' participation in local political institutions, one shouldn't however lose sight of the relatively autonomous influence of supra-local actors on policy making (e.g. through lobbying procedures), which may in turn feed back, *via* acknowledged results, into the reliance that the populations come to place on them.

dealing with the role of the state in shaping the inclusion of immigrants: in comparative perspective, welfare is a variable, not a constant. Furthermore state redistribution performance may be a necessary precondition for creating trust in formal articulation and forms of representation, but it may as well be a sufficient condition to rise the level of claims making to political institutions. These two effects combined may in turn dislodge political attitudes from the 'loyalty' ('we are being taken care of') to the 'voice' (we have to state our demands and act to get response') stance. Enhanced political participation in representation bodies may follow – provided these are able to foster trust and generate representation mechanisms. This is neither automatic nor irreversible.

Second, as suggested also by Oxhorn (1995), informal networking and formal participation can have a reciprocal shaping up effect in enacting forms of democratic participation: as long as the first one can achieve some autonomy from particularistic dynamics, and the latter can add some grassroots legitimacy into its representation claims.

References:
Albuquerque, R., L. E. Ferreira and T. Viegas (2000) O Fenómeno Associativo em Contexto Migratório: Duas Décadas de Associativismo de Imigrantes em Portugal, Oeiras: Celta.
Ambrósio, T. et al. (1983) Situação, Problemas e Perspectivas da Juventude em Portugal, Vol. VIII, Conferência - Comunicações e conclusões, Lisbon: IED, Cadernos Juventude.
Bacalhau, M. (1994) Atitudes, Opiniões e Comportamentos Políticos dos Portugueses: 1973-1993, Lisbon: Ed. M. Bacalhau and T. Bruneau.
Bauböck, R. (1994) Transnational Citizenship: Membership and Rights in International Migration, Avebury: Aldershot.
-, (1998) The crossing and blurring of boundaries in international migration. Challenges for social and political theory. In: R. Bauböck and J. Rundell (eds) Blurred boundaries: Migration, ethnicity, citizenship, Aldershot: Ashgate.
Bendix, R. J. Bendix and N. Furniss (1987) Reflexions on Modern Welfare States and Civil Societies. In: R. G. Braungart and M. M. Braungart (ed.) Research in Political Sociology, Vol. 3, 1-38.
Bermeo, N. (1999) 'What's Working in Southern Europe?', South European Society and Politics, N. Bermeo (ed.) Special issue on Unemployment in Southern Europe: coping with the consequences, 4/3, Winter, 263-287.
-, (2001) A Teoria da Democracia e as Realidades da Europa do Sul, Lisbon: Difel.
Boissevain, J. (1974) Friends of Friends. Oxford: Basil Blackwell.
Cachada, F., et al. (1995a) Imigração e Associação: Associações Africanas, Outras Associações e Instituições Ligadas à Imigração na Área Metropolitana de Lisboa. Lisbon: Cadernos CEPAC 1.
-, (1995b) Os números da imigração africana. Os imigrantes africanos nos bairros degradados e núcleos de habitação social dos distritos de Lisboa e Setúbal. Lisbon: Cadernos CEPAC 2.

Castles, S. (2001) Migration and Community Formation under Conditions of Globalisation. Lisbon: SociNova WP, FCSH-UNL.
Danese, G. (2001), 'Participation Beyond Citizenship: Migrants' Associations in Italy and Spain', Patterns of Prejudice, 35 (1), 69-89.
Esping-Andersen, G. (1993) Orçamentos e Democracia: o Estado-providência em Espanha e Portugal, 1960-1986. In: Análise Social, 28/122, 589-606.
-, (1994) Welfare States and the Economy. In: N. Smelser and R. Swedberg (ed.) The Handbook of Economic Sociology. Princeton: Princeton University Press and New York: Russel Sage Foundation, 712-732.
Fennema, M. and J. Tillie (1999) Political Participation And Political Trust In A Multicultural Democracy. Civic Communities And Ethnic Networks In Amsterdam. Paper presented at the Multicultural Policies and Modes of Citizenship workshop, Liège, November.
Fernandes, A. (1997) A Geografia de Oeiras. Atlas Municipal. Oeiras: Câmara Municipal de Oeiras.
Ferrão, J. (1996) Três décadas de consolidação do Portugal demográfico moderno. In : A. Barreto and C. V. Preto (eds.) A situação social em Portugal 1960-1995. Lisboa: ICS, 165-190
França, L. (ed.) (1993) Portugal. Valores Europeus e Identidade Cultural. Lisbon: IED.
Guibentif, P. (1996) Le Portugal Face à l'Immigration. In: Revue Européenne des Migrations Internationales, 12/1, 121-140.
Hall, J. (1995) In Search Of Civil Society. In: J. Hall (ed.) Civil Society: Theory, History, Comparison. Cambridge: Polity Press, 1-31.
Hirschman, A. (1970) Exit, Voice and Loyalty. Cambridge: Harvard University Press.
Inglehart, R. (1999) Trust, Well-being and Democracy. In: M. E. Warren (ed.) Democracy and Trust. Cambridge University Press, 88-120.
Ireland, P. (1994) The Policy Challenge of Ethnic Diversity. Immigrant Politics in France and Switzerland. Harvard University Press.
Lucena, M. and C. Gaspar (1991) Metamorfoses Corporativas? Associações de Interesses Económicos e Institucionalização da Democracia em Portugal II, In: Análise Social, 27/115, 135-187.
Lucena, M. (1982) Transformação do Estado Português nas suas Relações com a Sociedade Civil. In: Análise Social 18/72-73-74, 897-926.
Machado, F. L. (1993) Etnicidade em Portugal: O Grau Zero da Politização. In: M. B. N. Silva et al. (eds.) Emigração/Imigração em Portugal. Lisbon: Fragmentos, 407-414.
Marques, M. M. and R. Santos (forthcoming) Immigrants' Participation in Civil Society in a Suburban Context: Between "Top-Down Activation" and "Bottom-Up Mobilization. In: M. Martiniello, R. Penninx and S. Vertovec (eds.), Immigrant participation in Local Politics and Political Systems. A Comparative European Perspective [provisory title].
Marques, M. M., R. Santos, F. Araújo and S. Nóbrega (2001) Renovação Urbana em Oeiras: um estudo sociológico. Oeiras: Ed. C.M.O.
Marques, M. M., R. Santos, T. Ralha and A. R. Cordeiro (1998) City Template: Oeiras. Multicultural Policies and Modes of Citizenship in European Cities (MPMC) (http://www.unesco.org/most/p97oeira.doc).
Marques, M. M., R. Santos, T. Santos and S. Nóbrega (1999) Realojamento e Integração Social (vol. II-III). Lisbon: Colibri.
Marshall, T.H. (1992) [1950] Citizenship and Social Class. In: T.H. Marshall and T. Bottomore, Citizenship and Social Class, part I. London: Pluto Press, 3-51.

Maslow, A. (1963) Motivación y Personalidad. Barcelona: Sagitario.
Mingione, E. (1996) Urban Poverty In The Advanced Industrial World: Concepts, Analyses And Debates. In: E. Mingione (ed.), Urban Poverty and the underclass. A reader, Cambridge: Blackwell, 3-40.
Mouzelis, N. (1995) Modernity, Late Development And Civil Society. In: J. Hall (ed.) Civil society: Theory, history, comparison. Cambridge: Polity Press, 224-249.
MPMC [1997] Conceptual Framework (http://www.unesco.org/most/p97.htm).
Offe, C. (1999) How Can We Trust Our Fellow Citizens? In: M. E. Warren (ed.) Democracy and Trust. Cambridge University Press, 42-87.
Oxhorn, P. (1995) From Controlled Exclusion to Coerced Marginalization: The Struggle for Civil Society in Latin America. In: J. Hall (ed.) Civil Society: Theory, History, Comparison, Cambridge: Polity Press, 250-277.
Penninx, R. (1998) European Cities and Their Citizens: Problem, Challenge, Opportunity? Introductury lecture to the conference Ethnic Minorities and Local Government, Amsterdam, January (http://www.unesco.org/most/p97lect.htm).
-, (2000) Participation Of Immigrants Through Their Organizations: Political Visions On Multiculturalisms And Their Implications. Lisbon: SociNova Working Papers, FCSH-UNL.
Pina-Cabral, J. (1991) As categorias de comparação regional: uma crítica à noção de Mediterrâneo' in Os contextos da antropologia. Lisbon: Difel, 69-89.
Pires, R. P. et al. (1987) Os Retornados, Um Estudo Sociográfico. Lisboa: IED.
Portes, A. (1998) Social Capital: Its Origins And Applications In Modern Sociology. In: Annual Review of Sociology, 24, 1-24.
Portes, A., L. Guarnizo and P. Landolt (1999) The Study of Transnationalism: Pitfalls and Promise of an Emergent Research Field. In: Ethnic and Racial Studies, 22 (2), 217-237.
Putnam, R. D. (1993) Making Democracy Work: Civic Traditions in Modern Italy. Princeton University Press.
Santos, B. S. (1994) Pela Mão de Alice. O Social e o Político na Pós-Modernidade. Porto: Afrontamento.
Scokpol, T. (1999) How Americans Became Civic. In: T. Skocpol and M. P. Fiorina (eds.) Civic Engagement in American Democracy, Washington, D.C.: Brookings Institution Press and New York: Russell Sage Foundation, 27-80.
Soysal, Y. (1994) Limits Of Citizenship. Migrants and Postnational Membership in Europe University of Chicago Press.
Uslaner, E. M. (1999) Democracy and Social Capital. In: M. E. Warren (ed.) Democracy and Trust. Cambridge University Press, 121-150.
Villaverde Cabral, M. (1997) Cidadania Política e Equidade Social. Oeiras: Celta.
-, (2000) O exercício da cidadania política em Portugal. In: M. Villaverde Cabral, J. Vala and J. Freire (eds.) Atitudes Sociais dos Portugueses. Trabalho e Cidadania. Lisbon: ICS/ISSP, 123-162.
Wall, K. (1995) Apontamentos Sobre a Família na Política Social Portuguesa. In: Análise Social 30/131-132, 431-458
-, (1998) Famílias no Campo: Passado e Presente em Duas Freguesias do Baixo Minho. Lisbon: D. Quixote.
Warren, M. E. (1999) Democratic Theory and Trust. In: M. E. Warren (ed.) Democracy and Trust. Cambridge University Press, 310-345.

Shaping the identity and mobilising the "ethnic capital" in three European cities

Lionel Arnaud and Gilles Pinson

Studies on the devices of urban governance (Stone 1989; Le Galès 1995) have revealed a new research perspective centred on the development of a capacity of collective action in cities. Cities are indeed places where the main political and social problems occur. It is also the place where resources are concentrated, and where various groups and social interests meet and clash with each other. The aim of urban governments is therefore to build a political ability to organize coalitions of actors and groups, to connect interests, and to organize them according to objectives that have been collectively defined. Urban governance is more and more about collective action: its aim is to create and/or reactivate urban identities and to integrate the many existing groups and interests into these identities. This will enable the city to play a collective role, to act in a cohesive manner and to develop a strategic vision (Bagnasco and Le Galès 1997).

By making the creation of partnerships between various local groups a condition to the payment of various grants, the European construction has greatly contributed to the building up of these urban coalitions. The specificity of European grants is that they tend to "bypass" the national level by encouraging the creation and the development of "territories" as privileged interlocutors. Faced with these changes at a local level, we wish to study their impact on the status and position of ethnic minorities. They may actually be directly affected by this reconfiguration, which might alter their social status in cities, but they are still dependant on the "philosophies of integration" (Favell 1998) in force in each national state. Our hypothesis is that these types of mobilization, which increasingly take the shape of collective action, form a new kind of citizenship defined as the involvement of individuals and groups in processes of public and collective action. This new definition of citizenship may allow ethnic minorities to integrate in other ways: the question of legal status becomes less important than the promotion of identity through action and the involvement in local action groups (Melucci 1988; Castells 1999). One could call this a "differentiated citizenship" to describe the overcoming of a perspective where legal citizenship sanctions the existence of a "natural" community of interests on a given territory (Rhodes 1997). Differentiated citizenship refers to a context where a variety of communities coexist with their own identities and interests, and where the government's action consists in implementing processes of action that will enable these different communities to converge and to cooperate (Gelli and Pinson 2001). Citizenship is thus seen less as a status than a process of cooperation during which common interests will be discovered. In a context of ever increasing territorial competition, the reshaping of urban identities can thus lead on to processes of collective action that may in turn provide new ways of integration.

In order to verify this hypothesis, we have compared the policies aimed at ethnic minorities[1] in three big European cities: Birmingham in the United Kingdom, Lyons in France and Turin in Italy) These cities (are facing similar problems resulting in particular from deindustrialisation and globalisation; they also have various links (twinning, Eurocities network), which gives them the opportunity to swap experiences regarding urban policies[2]. We have focused on specific initiatives that value existing identities in order to further the involvement of various groups and actors, and that promote interactions between these groups in order to gather their interests and identities. Examples of this type of initiatives are the *Convention Quarter* in Birmingham, the organisation of the *Défilé de la Biennale de la Danse* in Lyons and the urban regeneration of the area of *Porta Palazzo* in Turin. These initiatives are peculiar in that they simultaneously enable cities to shape their identity, and also potentially provide new ways of integration for ethnic minorities.

After showing that globalisation, the reshaping of national States, European integration and competition between territories lead to a general reconfiguration of urban policy making and of the integration of ethnic minorities, we will then see that integration is more and more the expected result of the involvement of individuals and minority groups in collective action in cities. In the third part, we will describe the way in which cities try to involve social networks and ethnic identities in order to build a new image.

1. European policies and territorial reorganisation

Historically, the national State was built on a relatively passive and homogeneous idea of citizenship, usually based on the submission to a same corpus of rights and of duties (Badie 1995; Burns 2000; Leca 1991, Tilly 1992). If each Nation-State managed very differently the place and the political status of ethnic minorities on their territories at the

---

[1] Apart from designating a variety of statuses and populations from post-colonial immigration in the three countries studied, the notion of "ethnic minorities" is built on a "conceptual category", according to Glaser and Strauss (1967): it is a pertinent theoretical abstraction regarding the integration policies implemented in European cities, but it is also the expression of a change in the place and status of these populations at a local level.

[2] This research is based on around twenty interviews and on an analysis of official publications and documents, complemented by a direct observation of the implementation of the projects studied. Please refer to Arnaud, 2002b, as well as Gilles Pinson's PhD thesis, 2002b.

national level, one notices strong similarities in the way policies aimed at ethnic minorities are defined and implemented by French, British and Italian urban governments when shifting the focus to a local level. This convergence is the result of two types of phenomena which appeared in the 1980s and 1990s. First, the urban governments, notably in France and in Britain, have experienced the limitations of the undifferentiated and passive integration policies implemented in the 1960s and 1970s as a result of the extension of the welfare State. The policies regarding housing and health and the development of social and educational facilities show their inability to cater for the specific needs of the inhabitants in general and those of ethnic minorities in particular. The shortcomings of these urban policies gave rise to the development of social movements, and even urban riots (notably in Birmingham and Lyons), which have attracted the attention of experts and scholars since the late 1960s (Castells 1977; Anwar 1986; Ball and Solomos 1990; Lapeyronnie 1993). Urban policies must henceforth handle these identities carefully and possibly use them as a resource.

Following this trend, the European Union policies developed in the 1980s and 1990s promoted a more active definition of political citizenship. By encouraging partnerships, the mobilisation of citizens and the development of socio-cultural resources, the European Fund for Regional Development (EFRD) and the European Social Fund (ESF) contributed to a shift in social and regional policies from an "allocation centred approach" in which central governments had the upper hand, to a "mobilisation centred approach" that puts local actors in a more prominent position. The "bottom-up" method of implementation, the support of trans-national and trans-regional cooperation, and the emphasis on community objectives and priorities (particularly obvious in Community Initiative Programmes like *Urban* or *Equal*) contribute to bypassing the national level. In this part, we will try to define the effects the European integration has had on the modes of participation of ethnic minorities in two different contexts. On one hand, in countries that, like France and the United Kingdom, have a long tradition of integration policies, we will show that the influence of European integration policies is *indirect*. On the other hand, in countries such as Italy, which are only just starting to address these issues, we will see that the influence is *direct*. The main consequence of these policies has been in all cases to turn the identity of ethnic minorities into a local resource.

1.1. Indirect effects: partnership and entrepreneurship
In France and Great Britain, the mobilisation of ethnic minorities since the late 1970s has played an important role in questioning a concept of

citizenship that was insensitive to local and identity specificities. In France, following urban riots in summer 1981 in the suburbs of Lyons, it was decided to set up various local services offering leisure or cultural activities to youngsters from deprived areas. The peculiarity of what has been then called *"La politique de la ville"* was that it did not address directly the problems of ethnic minorities or racial discriminations but tried to cop with the problems of suburban local communities in areas that had been selected according to urban and socio-economic criteria among which the concentration of people of foreign origins (Chevalier 1996). Throughout the 1980s and the 1990's, *"La politique de la ville"* tried to involve youngsters and local associations in projects initiated but did not succeed in resolving the huge social problems of the large social estates in the suburbs of French cities neither in coping with racial discrimination. This was notably highlighted by the riots of Vaulx-en-Velin in the outskirts of Lyons in 1990, which raised again the issue of the integration of young French nationals of foreign origin.

In contrast to this, the question of equal opportunities was the proclaimed priority of the Labour team that won over Birmingham city council in 1981. Encouraged by the central government to deal with race equality, the local government launched various initiatives addressing the problem of discrimination. For example, a quota system (*Ethnic Monitoring*) was implemented within the local council to ensure a better representation of ethnic minorities. However, the willingness to promote the participation of ethnic minorities through the creation of local committees was hindered by a better organisation of the "white" population that tended to have a stronger influence on the running of these new structures (BCC 2001a). Violent riots in the area of Handsworth in 1988 were the reason for the local council to initiate a regular consultation with community leaders via the *Standing Consultative Forum* (SCF), at the risk of reinforcing an already problematic "ethnicisation" of local politics. Local press thus accused the *Race Relations Unit* of wasting public money (Solomos and Back 1995). In parallel to this, a seemingly widespread feeling of aggression by minority activists in Birmingham led to social tensions that then invaded the political arena. The *Race Relations Unit* was finally replaced in 1997 by the *Equalities Unit*, which was supposed to deal with inequalities in general. But the problem of representing the interests of ethnic minorities remained unsolved. One of the great objectives of the local council in 1996 was "the involvement of the population in decisions that are relevant to them" (BCC 1996). Progressively, the integration policies in Birmingham have shifted from a focus on racial discrimination in the workplace and in public services to an emphasis on the political participation of ethic minorities.

Faced with similar problems, the local governments of Birmingham and *"Grand Lyon"* (i.e. a political and administrative authority enlarged to the outlying city councils) shared their experiences within the frame of their twinning and of the *Eurocities* network. Then, in 1999, they put a joint application in for the European programme *Equal*. Aimed at helping disadvantaged citizens take over a business or set up their own, this initiative is directly in line with the objectives of the ESF. This collaboration has several consequences on the integration policies in both cities. Lyons is following the example set by Birmingham in its methods of entrepreneurship and of development of human capital: the purpose of these methods is to base the integration of ethnic minorities on their ability to get organized, to be creative and finally to get involved. Reciprocally, the partnership approach adopted in Lyons over the past twenty years in urban policies is progressively being adopted in Birmingham to replace a policy of "racial relationship" based on a kind of "community corporatism". Following the European campaign *"All different, all equal"* and various reports (in particular those that followed the racist murder of young Stephen Lawrence in 1993, cf. BCC 2001a) that underlined on the necessity of a coherent political action between the institutions, the *Equalities Unit* and the SCF were replaced by the *Birmingham Race Action Partnership* (BRAP). Its aim was to encourage all members of the community to work together on issues such as housing, criminal justice, urban regeneration, etc. From this point of view, the role of the BRAP is to switch from an action centred on community leaders (as in the SCF) to an "empowering" of ethnic communities. In order to do so, the BRAP is trying to *"show the potential added value that communities can bring the city and stop them being perceived as a problem. The stress is put on the need for the institutions to innovate and to find out more efficient ways of working with various communities"* (BRAP 2001a). In both cities the combined action of Community Initiative Programmes (CIP) like *Equal*, of a "sharing of experiences" and of legal demands regarding the fight against discrimination, has induced many changes. These changes have in turn contributed to a new definition of the role and place of ethnic minorities within the local community.

1.2. Direct effect: networks and social regeneration
In Turin, a sudden phenomenon of non-EU immigration at the end of the 1980s led to social and political tensions. The fact that the new immigrants have settled down in central locations or in inner-city areas like *San Salvario* and *Porta Palazzo*, and not in the suburbs, increased their visibility and therefore violent reactions against them (Allasino *et al.* 2000). The precarious situation of these new immigrants forced them quickly into marginality (prostitution, delinquency, drug addiction). The question of immigration systematically associated with insecurity, thus became a major issue on the local political agenda: indeed it was the main focus during the local elections in 1997 and citizens' committees

were being created to put pressure on local government to solve the problems associated with immigration. In response to this, the centre-left local government launched a few initiatives like the *Consulta degli Stranieri* (consultation committee of immigrants). But it was mainly the very dense network of catholic and secular non-profit organisations that addressed the problems of the immigrants and that provided them with services.

In Turin, like in most Italian cities, the European programmes have directly contributed to shape a previously non-existent integration policy. This influence is evident in *The Gate*, an integrated project of urban, social and economic regeneration of the area of *Porta Palazzo*. This area in the city centre is known for having the largest market in town and for facing problems of precariousness and marginality, mostly amongst its immigrant population. This project has been financed since 1996 by the European Union under the scheme of the *Pilot Urban Projects* (ESFR)[3]. Here again, the stress is put on the development of links and social networks. Discrimination is seen as the result of "*a lack of links between the existing services*" and between these services and the population. Thus, the part of the project dealing with security ("*Networks of security*") involves immigrant communities in the struggle against crime and marginality. A specific action has been to create a cultural mediation team for drug-addicts of foreign origin. Another action was the creation of an information centre aimed at foreign residents, *Extra-Informa*. This centre provides information to immigrants and keeps a record of situations of exploitation in the workplace or in housing. Some cultural and sport activities, like for example the financing of the Italian-Arabic cultural centre *Dar al Hikma* (various courses, discussion groups, exhibitions), have also been offered to develop links between different communities. Another part of the project called "*Alla ricerca dei legami perduti*" ("searching for some lost ties") aims at using the economic and commercial activities of the area to create some links of knowledge-sharing and mutual recognition between the various communities living in that area. A further initiative targets the creation of a "multi-ethnic gastronomic district" with two main aspects: to provide support and training services for starting up and running a business and to set up a cooperative structure to manage the common spaces of the market. The general aim is to help the immigrants communities build an internal structure to integrate individuals and to cooperate with other components of the local community. The involvement of individuals and groups is

---

[3] The launching of the project in 1996 was accompanied by the creation of a project committee, a private law entity directly responsible to the European Commission and made of local council representatives, social workers, consultants and representatives of tertiary sector associations and of the population.

regarded as "a means to revitalize the territory and to establish all possible links".

1.3. European competition and rebirth of urban identities

As envisaged within the frame of European programmes, the increasing involvement of ethnic minorities in urban policies has other aims than to make local life more "democratic". One can even point out that its main aim is to gather their abilities to make local economy more dynamic in a context of economic difficulties and of increasing competition between cities. If urban competition is a powerful incentive for local mobilization and networking, if it can lead urban elites to reactivate some kind of urban identities, one should not forget that the local authorities concentrate their efforts on "reviving" city centres by attracting businesses and valued social groups (Soldatos 1991). This concomitant rebirth of a "town culture" under the conjoined action of some changes in the productive system and some new urban policies has taken the shape of great initiatives in town-planning and city centres regeneration policies. In those policies, the emphasis is put on economic solutions to urban and social problems. In this sense, the contribution of the EFRD plays an active role in regenerating the identity of cities and their inhabitants through economic development projects. The attempt to encourage integration through economic activity, to link social approaches and economic approaches show that the identities of ethnic minorities, and more generally the culture of cities, are nowadays seen as a capital, as an economic resource (Zukin 1991).

From this point of view, it may be useful to remember that the industrial tradition has left Birmingham, Lyons and Turin with little presence in the booming services industry, which could have helped compensate job losses in industry and the bad image of "industrial cities". These problems have been exacerbated by the nature and the rhythm of the redevelopment of Birmingham from the 1950s until the 1970s: it is responsible for considerable demolitions in the historic centre following the bombings of the Second World War. This centre was rebuilt with cheap and unattractive functional buildings surrounded by a vast motorway infrastructure. Birmingham then became *"motor city"*, not anymore because of its tradition of car industry, but because of its *Inner Ring Road* and its *Spaghetti Junction*, which are the symbols of a town *"through which one drives (usually at high speed), rather than visits, works, lives in or invests"* (BCC 2000). Situated in the heart of the *Convention Quarter*, *Brindleyplace* is the likely symbol of the "urban renaissance" of Birmingham, with its café terraces along the canals. Young executives from the surrounding businesses and offices like to meet there whenever the sun is out, while those attending the *International Convention Centre* (ICC) – which opened in April 1991 with the help of a £50 million funding from Europe – have a chat next to the classical music lovers of the *Symphony Hall* and the tourists who have come here to visit the Aquarium... But this idyllic vision of the new centre-to-be of Birmingham is in stark contrast with the state of decay of the immediately surrounding areas. On a symbolic level at least, the new "post-modern" buildings of the *Convention Quarter* are not only very different from those in low cost areas: they also display an academic culture that does not have much in common with the preoccupations of the inhabitants in neighbouring areas. The stake of the regeneration of Birmingham city centre is therefore not only urban: it is also cultural, as the question of spatial and "racial" segregation remains a central issue in Birmingham. Yet (official) statistics announce clear previsions: in twenty years ethnic minorities will be a majority in the city (BCC 2001a).

The context of European Unification, of globalization, of the multiplicity of identities and of technological renewal also opens new perspectives of economic, social and cultural development for Lyons and its surroundings. Like in Birmingham, the risk of segregation of a certain number of popular areas or some peripheral suburbs of the city of Lyons represents a major challenge, both on an urban and on a cultural level. In this specific local context however, it would be more appropriate to speak of "relegation" because the problematic of the integration of "ethnic minorities" is seen here in terms of spatial and socio-economic exclusion, and much less in cultural terms (Delarue 1991). In Lyons, the creation in 1998 of a prospective and strategic Mission called *Millénaire 3* aimed at implementing an initiative involving various components of the community from Lyons and its suburbs. Some discussion forums have regularly taken place about various issues like education, citizenship, health, security, culture, memory, environment or new technologies. More than 20 reports have been published since February 1998. From its European and International perspective, this structure has helped impose the idea that the development of Lyons should be based on its opening-up, as is explained in the urban project of the "*Grand Lyon*":

> Nowadays, this opening-up is a major element of social cohesion. Several hundreds of thousands inhabitants of diverse ethnic, cultural, religious and national origins have been present for years or decades in the city and its suburbs and are settling down here. It is only by adopting an attitude of open-mindedness, of dialogue and of recognition of cultures and differences that these rapid and often brutal changes will enrich and benefit the "Grand Lyon", and not create tensions, or even ruptures within the community of Lyons. It is also an essential condition to the economic development of the region. In all its

history, Lyons has never shone as much as since it opened up to the world. (Grand Lyon Prospective 2000a.)

Unlike Birmingham however, Lyons' urban heritage has remained nearly unchanged for a century and has been looked after and shown off to advantage (notably through a policy of lighting of the monuments). Thus, in 1998, the city has received the prestigious award of world heritage of Humanity by the UNESCO, thanks to a strong mobilisation of its economic and cultural actors. From this point of view, Lyons' concern is less to reconstruct its built environment, as is the case in Birmingham, but rather, like Turin, to develop an urban identity that is a necessary condition to its economic competitiveness.

In the case of Turin, the link between developing community resources and the identity of ethnic minorities through urban policies, on one hand, and reshaping the identity of the whole town appears clearly in another initiative launched by the mayor Valentino Castellani. The strategic plan *Torino Internazionale* intends to grant Turin an international status, notably by showing that the town has successfully entered the so-called multi-cultural society. The strategic plan *Torino Internzionale* is based on the idea that the overwhelming presence of the largest Italian industrial group, FIAT, Turin has always ignored anything that was not directly involved in the industrial process: its patrimony and cultural treasures (the baroque architecture, the gastronomy, its status as the birthplace of cinema), its social richness (dense associative network, competent catholic and secular support groups) and its cultural diversity. The aim of this strategic plan was to bring these hidden resources to light in order to turn Turin into an international, diverse, plurifunctional and open city. Highlighting the ethnic and cultural diversity was part of this willingness to open up and to strive for socio-cultural internationalisation.

2. The local ways of implication

Overall in Turin, Lyons and Birmingham, the democratic and "basist" ambitions of urban policies implemented to promote the integration of ethnic minorities have been largely amended with the development of the economic crisis, of economic liberalisation and its effects on urban territories. Even if certain councils have been able to put into practice some of their projects in the matter of local democracy and of citizen's participation in town-planning projects, they were quickly forced to relegate these matters to a position of secondary importance on their agenda. The worsening of social problems (unemployment, insecurity, racism) is often an obstacle to the "communicational ethics" that these "new policies" advocate (Healey 1996). The social management of deprived communities is then transferred from the public to the private sector. On the pretext of "democratisation" and "autonomisation", the call for projects, market, businesses or associations enables to avoid a global definition of the problem of discrimination to the profit of a more pragmatic approach, by substituting auto-responsibility to state and administrative regulations (Castel 1995; Boltanski and Chiapello 1999). In this perspective, it seems that resorting to European funds and to a definition of integration linked to economic involvement has enabled cities to bypass national traditions that were still trying to make ethnic minorities adopt the principles and values of the country they settled in. It has also enabled them to rethink political integration in terms of project, individual and collective mobilisation, economic integration, entrepreneurship, cultural integration and valorisation of terms of identity resources. In the final part, we study in detail the new forms of mobilisation "from the top" that the European construction still encourages at a political level (substitution of an active citizenship to a passive citizenship), at an economic level (entrepreneurship is preferred to the old protection system), and at a cultural level (the diversity of identities, seen from an esthetical point of view, becomes a resource that *serves* social regeneration).

2.1. The project as a new form of political mobilisation
With regard to public policies, the notion of project has originated in town planning. It refers to the various planning techniques that intend to break with the functionalist and rationalist precepts inherited from the modern Movement in architecture that limit the relations between individuals and social groups and the city to a strictly instrumental relationship between the place and its users. The functionalist urban production modes have reduced the city to a pure undifferentiated structure, a place to organise production forces, a spatial continuum without an identity (Tomas 1995; Toussaint and Zimmermann 1998). The project takes the opposite view of this model. It consists in developing collective goals in open planning processes that intend to discover and valorise the proper assets of a specific space or a specific community. Whereas, in traditional rational planning, the emphasis is put on centralisation of decision making and allocation of resources, in project approaches, it is rather put on self empowerment and proper resources mobilisation. With regard to this, we must stress that one of the privileged uses of the project was build following a reflexion on the pedagogical problems encountered in the insertion training of disadvantaged people, who were excluded from the production process (youngsters with little qualifications, long-term unemployed people, people with disabilities, etc.). Inherited from the North American pragmatic approach, the pedagogy of project aims at a progressive pedagogy, also called open pedagogy, in which the

individual becomes responsible for his training through concrete apprenticeships or practices that are relevant to him/her (Boutinet 1993). Such an approach has spread widely in France within the scope of popular education and socio-cultural animation policies of the "post-1968" period (Augustin and Gillet 2000). It is at the heart of the initiatives developed to organise the *Défilé de la Biennale de la Danse*, one of the most spectacular projects of "Grand Lyon" that relies on the cultural awakening of popular suburban areas around Lyons. Following the model of Brazilian samba groups, the socio-cultural structures of "Grand Lyon" have been invited to come together with professionals (choreographers, costume designers, set designers, musicians...) to prepare during one year a one-day parade in the city centre of Lyons. After four parades, the *Défilé* has now become a regional, national, indeed even an international event that made the headline of *The Herald Tribune* (among others). Beyond the visual symbol, the *Défilé* is presented as a medium of integration, which has been the main concern of its organisers from the start. It is financed largely through the *Contrat de Ville* (the contractual scheme that associates the central and local governments in the financing of measures targeted at deprived suburban areas). The local central government representative for urban policies (*Sous-préfêt à la ville*) chairs a piloting committee that is in charge of ensuring that the socio-cultural and local development objectives are met. These objectives are clearly set by the *Fonds d'Action Sociale* (FAS – quango in charge of integration), the *Direction Régionale des Affaires Culturelles* (DRAC – the central government office in charge of cultural matters in the région) and the association *Inter Service Migrants* (ISM – an association dealing with the immigrant population), all of which are actively involved in the project. An "insertion" section has besides been added in 1998. It aims in particular at supporting projects that chose to mobilise participants who *"are facing social, economic and/or psychological difficulties, around the artistic support provided by the* Défilé" (*Biennale de la Danse de Lyon*, 2001).

This project soon met the ambitions of the prospective and strategic mission *Millénaire 3*. In 1997 a socio-cultural analysis about the inhabitants of "Grand Lyon"[4] showed an "acceleration of changes, henceforth led by a large elite of "ordinary" people: employees, working women, secondary school leavers, inhabitants of the suburbs". According to this analysis, the most pioneering and innovative forces are to be found in particular in towns from 20 000 to 100 000 inhabitants (Bron, Caluire, Vénissieux, Meyzieu, Rillieux, etc.) where the majority of the "ethnic minorities" live. From then on, it becomes necessary to

---

[4] A study conducted within the scope of the elaboration of a Master Plan in the development and urbanism of "*Grand Lyon*" (Schéma directeur "Lyon 2010").

reintegrate these active forces into the social fabric and to make up spatial segregation with some "*popular events and projects that stem from metropolitan social life; in a word to grow richer in mutual differences*" (Grand Lyon Prospective 2000a, 8). Under these circumstances it is not surprising that "*the exceptional place of the Défilé de la Biennale de la Danse (...)*" is celebrated "*in the heart and the mind of* "Grand Lyon's" *actors (...) In the* Défilé, *it is the suburbs that are welcomed at the heart of the city centre!*" (Grand Lyon Prospective 2000b). In giving access to a common public space to the diverse social and ethnic groups that inhabit the city and its surroundings, the parade symbolically incorporates images of the city (the centre and its suburbs) and different cultural practices (street culture and academic culture) into a common public culture. From this point of view, ethnic minorities and artists themselves become a cultural means of producing city space while confirming the cultural hegemony of the city centre, where it takes place.

On the other side of the English Channel, the massive investments that were made over the past ten years in the creative industries[5] have been the most talked about initiatives in the matter of urban regeneration. This sector is particularly attractive from a strategic point of view because it contributes to the local growth and also because it channels the strengths and the abilities of the young population, particularly those of ethnic minorities. Spatially, a lot of these sectors have shown an ability to expand and concentrate in the city centre by contributing to the development of places of consumption and of cultural production. Supplemented by affordable and innovative accommodation targeted mainly at young residents, these zones have become dynamic areas of economic growth and also an important and distinct part of the city's image and identity (Banks et al. 2000). The report 2001 on Birmingham's strategic repositioning in order to be among the 10 cities most favoured by new industries in 2010 thus identifies "*the new media and other creative and entertainment leisure industries*" as one of the six developing key sectors (BCC 2001b). From this point of view, Birmingham's application to be the European Capital of Culture in 2008 has initiated a vast assessment and consultation of the city's cultural strengths. The meetings *Highbury 3* in February 2001 were held to gather these "strengths" and define the city's needs and potentials: the stake was in particular to transform the image of a grey and industrial city tainted by the racial tensions of the 1980s and 1990s, into a harmonious, modern and pleasant city (BCC 2001c). From then on, the team in

---

[5] The British government's definition of this vast sector includes : advertisement, architecture, arts and antiques markets, craftwork, design, fashion, cinema, interactive entertainment software, music, living arts, publishing, software, television and radio (DCMS, 1999).

charge of the application focused on the assessment and the organisation of "black" cultural initiatives into a network. Coupled with the council's initiative to organise a national "*Black History Month*" each October, the purpose of which is to celebrate the strengths of local ethnic minorities and their cultural action, and with the Regional Arts Board for the West Midlands's initiative for "black art" and that of "ethnic minorities" (WMA 2001), a certain dynamic seems to be in place to support the cultural development of ethnic minorities[6]. From this point of view, culture and aesthetics must help activate "*the potential of Birmingham's rich cultural mix*" (BCC 2001c, 46).

In Turin, the local administration and the Committee in charge of the project *The Gate* have focused on the deletion of the social links and the relations of knowledge-sharing and mutual recognition between the various local components. This deterioration of the social fabric was responsible for turning the formerly very lively borough of *Porta Palazzo* into a mere transit area. Hence the slogan of this operation: "*Living, not leaving*". The area being the largest open-air market in Turin, one of the aspects of the project is to use commercial links and networks to help improve the living conditions of the immigrants who are in a precarious economic and legal situation, and to improve their relationship with the Italian population. The question of immigration and of marginality is addressed mainly from the perspective of a lack of social ties, loose social networks and a lack of recognition of local resources. This reflects the predominance of the themes of local development, of "*community building*" and of social capital in some Italian public policies. These themes are also found in the European doctrine of integrated approach, partnership and governance. The project *The Gate* has chosen the *Action Planning* approach, which consists in gathering together members of the local council, social workers, town-planning specialists, experts and local inhabitants regularly from the construction of the problem to the elaboration of concrete lines of action. The *Action Planning* is defined by *The Gate*'s committee as "*an interactive design practice*" designed to involve the people who will benefit from the action in its construction and, furthermore, to build the local community's ability to organise itself. The presumption behind the *Action Planning* is that the local community does not lack resources or abilities, but it does lack an organisational structure that would enable some cooperation links to be developed.

---

[6] Thus, in October 2001, during a cultural forum organised by the *Birmingham Race Action Partnership* (BRAP) and significantly called "*Black City, White Mask*", links have started to be established between various actors of the "*Black Cultures*" in the presence of numerous participants belonging to the "black cultural world", and some local and regional representatives (*BCC Leisure and Culture* and *West Midland Arts*), in order notably to fight against "institutional racism" in public administrations.

This has led to the willingness to enable ethnic minorities to make use of their own resources – such as identity, culture or organisational skills. This orientation appears also clearly in the plan *Torino Internazionale*. The plan conveys the idea that a city can only reach a good position in European urban competition if it is able to build a strong identity and the presence of structures ethnic communities could help to develop this cosmopolitan identity. One of the strategic orientations of the plan emphasizes the necessity for Turin to open up to the multicultural society and to base its status of metropolis on the recognition of its ethnic and cultural diversity. However, the theme of multiculturalism is only one of the dimensions of the strategic plan. One could even wonder whether this aspect has not been neglected in the mobilisation that followed the plan *Torino Internazionale*. Many interlocutors pointed out to us that two very distinct types of networks had developed during the elaboration of the plan. One of them gathered together the representatives of social associations and of the third sector, whereas the other was formed of economic and political elites. As we will see in the following section, the imperatives of economic development seem to dominate in the different projects and to retain a very cosmetic vision of ethnic and cultural diversity.

2.2. "Creative" entrepreneurship and development of human capital
The development of creative industries in the *Eastside Quarter* of Birmingham is a major element in the new plan to use European structural funds over the period of 2000-2006. The area has been chosen as one of the main priorities of the cities within the scope of the EFRD, in aiming at developing creative media, new technologies, tourism and the leisure industry (Barber 2001). The *Birmingham and Solihull Entrepreneurship Consortium* (BASEC), co financing organism set up to support the European program Equal, bases its local development project on *"the creation of new businesses through the active involvement of disadvantaged groups"*, notably in *"sowing the seeds of entrepreneurship culture – promoting the image of entrepreneurship, particularly among the youth"* and in *"introducing new markets"* in a zone inhabited by 22% of *"Non-Whites"* (BASEC, 2001). In this sense, Equal aims at stimulating the artistic and entrepreneurship creativity of ethnic minorities who are "trading" their cultural assets within the scope of the reconstruction of the city's image. The development of *"creative industries"* has been especially encouraged within the rehabilitation of Birmingham's city centre: they form an important urban project where artistic and craft potentialities, as well as abilities in the matter of new technologies and new media must enable unqualified youngsters to integrate and value the know-how of the various cultures.

This ambition is also at the heart of the initiatives implemented within the scope of the *Plan local d'insertion par l'économique* (PLIE – a plan focused on integration through economic ways) in Lyons: this plan tries to combine artistic work and economic insertion by relying for example on the dynamics created by the *Défilé de la Biennale de la Danse*. This approach is not new to a growing number of actors on the socio-cultural scene. They have long recognised the socio-economic impact of the artistic initiatives involving disadvantaged people in and around Lyons. The European Union is directly involved, not only by helping Lyons and Birmingham share their experience, but more directly by financing the PLIE and by making it part of the Objective 3 of the ESF. In this perspective, one of the main recommendations that followed the assessment of the 1998 *Défilé* was to stress the necessity of a closer monitoring of the PLIE regarding the construction and the choice of staging points in the people's route, and finally to reconsider the EU's recommendations regarding the *"path of insertion"* (ASDIC, 1999, p.31). At this level, the involvement in a European project tends to legitimate a renewal of the actions concerning training and employment, which move progressively from a notion of "repair" to one of "accompaniment", within the scope of joint economic growth. Some costume designers who took part in the parade in 1998 and 2000 have thus continued their insertion by working on the rehabilitation of the *Passage Thiaffait*, a deprived area in the City Center. This initiative takes place in the former "silk" quarter of the *Croix Rousse*, in the 1st *arrondissement* (ward), which has been redeveloped around the fashion and textile industries, and is directly in line with the three axes of intervention mentioned by the ESF in the form 2.1. of the Objective 3[7] : it sees the professional involvement of ethnic minorities as one of the key elements of economic competitiveness.

Through activities offering various ways of insertion, either in the citizen community or in the legal labour market, the city of Turin with its "*The Gate*" project produces positive integration policies that make up for the lacks of national legislation, which only deals with the conditions of entry on the territory and the rejection of the flow of illegal immigrants. Here again, the local strategy is valorising the integration effects of economic activities. Within the scope of the action line "*If economy is social*", an action consisted in opening a council desk help for immigrants working illegally and willing to enter the legal labour market. Another, which was not aimed specifically at foreign communities, was to further the creation of cooperatives liking market traders of foreign origin working at the daily local market. Structuring immigrants economic activities is seen as a

---

[7] Help to set up businesses and activities through specific support given to the initiators of a project, mobilisation of economic actors within the scope of territorial dynamics, professionalizing of the actors involved in town policies.

promising way to structure and integrate foreign communities to the local society. . Within this scope, the association *Apolié* was created to offer ways of insertion to illegal workers and to help immigrants set up their own business. The project *The Gate* clearly focuses on central themes like social capital, the development of an ability among foreign communities to organise themselves and to cooperate. The idea of "*imprenditorialità*", of *entrepreneurship*, is part of this general willingness to structure foreign communities in order to integrate them in a local community that is able to create its own forms of cooperation and organisation. In this respect, and as claimed on *The Gate*'s website: "*La razza (sic) reinforza economia*", race (sic) reinforces economy.

Conclusion

The cooperation between cities and the European Union around integrated projects of urban regeneration reinforces a vision of territories where their competitivity builds itself through the activation of synergies between the various actors and through the involvement of human and social capital (Rouault 2001). Local identities and social networks are henceforth resources that are essential to the construction and implementation of local policies. These policies mobilise the ethnic minorities and help them to develop their resources through a process of action, in terms of identity, *entrepreneurship* and social networks of cooperation. A new way of integration can thus potentially develop through the implication of ethnic minorities in project devices.

Through incentive initiatives, it seems that the EU has supported the changes in theory and in practice that have transformed the role and the place of difference in the society. Without really questioning the fundamental principles of the "integration regimes" of national States, it now views the "ethnic" identity as a resource. There was a move from a social way of dealing with ethnic minorities, seen at its best as being "assisted", and at its worst as being "submissive", to more responsive and territorialised policies, which require these minorities to become actively involved in the transformation of their living conditions and of the modalities of integration in the urban society.

But while territorial competition[8] gives an impression of urgency and forces the local representatives to select the "places" in their city with the most exploitable "genious", the project is most of all a means to point out the most "fashionable" places or social groups within the scope of a communication plan. The efforts to improve the living environment have been made mostly in places that have been chosen to convey an urban

---

[8] This feeling of competition is widespread amongst elected representatives, civil servants and the inhabitants of cities, whatever their size (cf. J. Bouinot and B. Bermills, 1995).

identity seen as the exportable image of the city. The "city project" is designed to give the city as a whole a specific identity and various strategic vocations that are defined mainly in economic terms. It "formulates a general ambition, shared by all the urban actors, in the form of a wanted future in the long term" (Bouinot and Bermills 1995, 85). Urban euro competition occurs between collective actors, which are the result of the building of coalitions between political, economic and social interests. The more they share a common and strong identity, the stronger and durable these coalitions are (Pinson 2002b). In order to ensure this sharing of an urban identity, local elites may consider that gathering "ethnic" identities into the urban identity is essential to give the image of an urban community assembled around a joint project.In this way, by objectivising in what resembles an "ethnic capital" all the cultural resources linked to groups that have common properties but also that are linked by frequent, sometimes even permanent, useful contacts[9], cities try to reduce the multiple dimensions and conflicts that shape a culture and identity into a coherent image. This concept of culture as a "way of life" is indeed incorporated in "cultural products" – in other words ecological, historical, festive or architectural materials, which are developed, implemented and even "sold" by cities in the European competition. Because culture has become a system of production of symbols, any attempt to encourage people to "buy" these products is made within the scope of a cultural industry in which cities are nowadays implicated. And in a world where styles developed in the streets are then recycled by the mass media, especially magazines and fashion and music programmes, or even television series, "*the cacophony of demands for justice is translated into a coherent demand for jeans*" (Zukin 1995, 9). The merging of commercial culture and "ethnic" identity becomes henceforth an essential element of competition between European cities.

---

[9] In this sense, the "ethnic capital" can be defined as the combination of a social and a cultural capital. More precisely, the incorporated and objectivated cultural capital of "ethnic minorities" forms a specific kind of social capital. Once institutionalised, this capital is able to provide privileges and profits, like economic capital in other social fields, by regarding collective resources of populations with an ethnic background as a *heritage* (see Pierre Bourdieu's analysis, 1979, 1980). In fact, this notion stresses the ambiguity of policies which, by trying to mobilise and develop the identity of immigrant populations, are tempted to reify the link between culture and society and in the end to institutionalise a notion of ethnicity that yet entails a strong subjective and relational dimension (Amselle and M'Bokolo 1985; Barth, 1969).

References:
Allasino, E./Bobbio, L./Neri, S. (2000) Crisi urbane: che cosa succede dopo ? Le politiche per la gestione della conflittualità legata all'immigrazione. In : Polis. VIX. 3. déc. 431-49.
Amselle, J.-L./M' Bokolo. E. (1985) Au cœur de l'ethnie. Ethnie. tribalisme et Etat en Afrique. Paris. La Découverte.
Anwar, M. (1986) Race and Politics. Ethnic Minorities and the British Political System. Londres. Tavistock.
Arnaud, L. (2002a) Sport as a Cultural System. Sport Policies and (New) Ethnicities in Lyon and Birmingham. In: International Journal of Urban and Regional Research. 26.3. sept. 571-87
-, (dir.) (2002b) Les minorités ethniques dans l'Union européenne. Politiques et identités. Rapport final. Programme CNRS « L'identité européenne en questions ».
ASDIC (1999) La mobilisation autour de la compagnie Zanka dans le Défilé de la Biennale de la Danse. Rapport établi pour le PLIE de Lyon. Association ALLIES.
Augustin, J-P./Gillet, J-C. (2000) L'animation professionnelle. Paris. L'Harmattan.
Badie, B. (1995) La fin des territoires. Essai sur le désordre international et sur l'utilité sociale du respect. Paris. Fayard.
Bagnasco, A. (ed) (1990) La città dopo Ford. Il caso di Torino. Torino. Bollati Boringhieri.
-, (1988) Torino : la fabbrica e la città. In : Spazio e società. 42. juil-sept.
-, (1986) Torino : un profilo sociòlogico. Torino. G. Einaudi.
Bagnasco, A./Le Galès, P. (eds.) (1997) Villes en Europe. Paris. La Découverte.
Ball, W./Solomos, J. (1990) Race and Local Politics. London: MacMillan.
Barber, A. (2001) The ICC. Birmingham : A Catalyst for Urban Renaissance. The University of Birmingham.
Barth, F. (1969) Ethnic groups and boundaries. The social organization of cultural differences. Bergen/Oslo. Universitetsforlaget.
BASEC (2001) Birmingham and Solihull Entrepreneurship Consortium. Leaflet.
Biennale de la Danse (2001) Le Défilé 2002. Leaflet.
Birmingham City Council (2001a) Challenges for the Future. Race Equality in Birmingham. Report of the Birmingham Stephen Lawrence Inquiry Commission.
-, (2001b) Repositionning Birmingham to be one of Europe's Top 10 Preferred Locations for New Industry and Commerce by 2010. Report of the Director of Economic Development to Cabinet.
-, (2001c) Highbury 3. Dynamic. diverse. different. Report of proceedings.
-, (1996) Policy Framework 1996/1997.
Boltanski, L./ Chiapello, E. (1999) Le nouvel esprit du capitalisme. Paris. Gallimard.
Bouinot, J./ Bermills, B. (1995) La gestion stratégiques des villes. Entre compétition et coopération. Paris. Armand Colin.
Bourdieu, P. (1979) Les trois états du capital culturel. In : Actes de la Recherches en Sciences Sociales. 30. 3-6.
-, (1980) Le capital social. In : Actes de la Recherches en Sciences Sociales. 31. 2-3.
Boutinet, J.-P. (1993) Anthropologie du projet. Paris. PUF.
BRAP (2001a) Birmingham Race Action Partnership. Leaflet.

-, (2001b) Black City. White Mask. Race. Racism and the Cultural Services : Issues for Birmingham. Leaflet.
Burns, D. (2000) Can Local Democracy Survive Governance?. In: Urban Studies. Vol.37. 5-6. 963-973.
Castells, M. (1999) Le pouvoir de l'identité. Paris. Fayard.
-, (1977) La question urbaine. Paris. François Maspero.
Castel, R. (1995) Les métamorphoses de la question sociale. Une chronique du salariat. Paris. Fayard.
Chevalier, G. (1996) Volontarisme et rationnalité d'Etat. L'exemple de la politique de la ville. In : Revue française de sociologie. 27. avril-juin. 209-35.
Delarue, J.-M. (1991) Banlieues en difficulté. La Relégation. Paris. Syros.
Favell, A. (1998) Philosophies of integration : immigration and the idea of citizenship in France and Great-Britain. London. MacMillan.
Gelli, F. / Pinson, G. (2001) Federalization Process, Participation and Democracy in Italy. The examples of the Veneto Region Constitutional Chart and of the City of Turin New Urban Policies. Paper for the Joint Sessions of Workshops of the European Consortium for Political Research, Grenoble, April 6th 2001.
Glaser, B./Strauss, A. (1967) The Discovery of Grounded Theory. Chicago. Adline.
Grand Lyon Prospective (2000a) Une agglomération compétitive et rassemblée. 21 priorités pour le 21ème siècle. In : Les Cahiers Millénaire 3. 21.
-, (2000b) Le défilé de la biennale de la danse vu par Millénaire 3. Leaflet.
-, (1998) Analyse socio-culturelle des habitants de l'agglomération lyonnaise. Spécificités et évolution. Rapport réalisé par la Cofremca. In : Les Cahiers Millénaire 3. 2.
Healey, P. (1996) Planning through debate: the communicative turn in planning theory. In: Campbell, S., Fainstein, S. (eds) Readings in Planning Theory. Oxford, Blackwell.
Lapeyronnie, D. (1993) L'individu et les minorités. La France et la Grande-Bretagne face à leurs immigrés. Paris. PUF.
Leca, J. (1991) Nationalité et citoyenneté dans l'Europe des immigrations. In : Costa-Lascoux. J./Weil P. (dirs). Logiques d'Etat et immigrations. Paris. Kimé. 13-57.
Le Galès, P. (1995) Du gouvernement des villes à la gouvernance urbaine. In : Revue française de science politique. vol. 45. 1. février. 57-95.
Melucci, A. (1988) Getting Involved: Identity and Mobilization in Social Movements. In : Klandermans. B.. Kriesi. H.. Tarrow S. (eds) From Structure to Action. Greenwich. CT. JAI Press. 329-348.
Pinson, G. (2002a) Political Government and Governance: Strategic Plan and the Reconstruction of a Political Capacity in Turin. In : International Journal of Urban and Regional Research, 26.3, September, 477-93
-, (2002b) Projets et pouvoirs dans les villes européennes. Une comparaison de Marseille. Venise. Nantes et Turin. Thèse de doctorat de Science Politique. IEP. Université Rennes 1
Rhodes, RAW (1997) Modern Governance. London. Macmillan.
Rouault, S. (2000) De l'insertion professionnelle à la valorisation du capital humain : un changement de paradigme accompagné par l'Union Européenne ?. Politique européenne. 2. septembre. 49-66.
Soldatos, P. (1991) Les nouvelles villes internationales. Profil et situation stratégique. Aix-en-Provence. SERDECO.
Solomos, J., Back, L. (1995) Race. Politics and Social Change. London: Routledge.
Stone, C. (1989) Regime Politics. Governing Atlanta 1946-1988. University Press of Kansas.

Tilly, C. (1992) Contrainte et capital dans la formation de l'Europe. 990-1990. Paris. Aubier (orig. ed. : Coercion. Capital and European States. Cambridge MA. Blackwell. 1990).
Tomas, F. (1995) Projets urbains et projets de ville. In : Les Annales de la recherche urbaine. 68-69.
Torino Internazionale (1998) I dati fondamentali. Informazioni sintetiche per la costruzione del piano. Torino.
-, (2000) Il piano strategico della città. Torino.
Toussaint, J.-Y./Zimmermann, M (dirs.) (1998) Projet urbain. Ménager les gens. aménager la ville. Sprimont. Mardaga.
West Midlands Arts (2001) Shifting Perspectives. West Midlands Arts Black and Minority Ethnic Arts Action Plan.
Zukin, S. (1995) The Cultures of Cities. Malden. Blackwell.
-, (1991) Landscapes of Power. From Detroit to Disney World. Berkeley. University of California Press.

Baby Bronks: Place and Identity in a Parisian Banlieue

Leeke Reinders

The dichotomy of location
In ten years, between 1955 and 1965, a new city rose up some fifteen kilometres to the northeast of Paris. Sarcelles was built for the new postwar age and was intended to make a radical break with history. The buildings that rose up were made of modern materials such as steel and concrete, standardized production methods ensured rapid and cheap construction, and the rational design of the neighbourhoods were designed to mould the residents into a community. The city provided accommodation on one-and-a-half square kilometres for about forty thousand people. Several years after the completion of the first dwellings, with the infrastructure still not in place and many services and facilities still lacking, the concept began to erode. Fantastic stories spread through the city like wildfire. Journalists and raconteurs wrote about a monotonous landscape, populated by lost, lonely, and isolated residents. In Sarcelles symptoms of a rare virus were said to have appeared. The disease appeared first of all in the form of a depression, or psychosomatic symptoms. Later this 'sarcellitus' developed into anxiety and hypersensitivity, which led to suicidal tendencies and other nervous diseases. People also showed a tendency to alcoholism, tobacco dependence, and excessive use of pharmaceutical substances. People suffered from functioning difficulties and behaved in a strikingly obsessive manner. Women acquired a phobic urge to clean and polish their houses and turned their young out of their parental homes. These youths settled outdoors into lawlessness, committing violent and sexual offences. It became apparent towards the end of the 1960s that living between long terraces and high-rise flats was far from satisfactory (*cf.* Domenach 1995: 40-41; Jannoud and Pinel 1974:7-47; Mezrahi 1986: 154-189 and Plas 1997: 20-22).
The legend of Sarcelles is an absurd story, but it puts the finger squarely on an influential notion about the new towns, such as those that were set down after the war at the edge of European and North-American agglomerations. In the middle of the 1960s there was a turn around in the thinking about modern architecture, a 'second grade criticism', as Choay writes, in which the new towns, which were themselves based on a critical view of society, were in their turn put through the mangle (1965:53). The media reported about desolate and monotonous neighbourhoods, and scientists demonstrated that a hygienic city does not necessarily produce residents in good mental health. From the viewpoint of environmental psychology, for example, a field in which efforts are made to clarify the interaction between the individual and the

environment, studies appeared on the effects of overpopulation and the causal connection between criminality and specific forms of urban architecture. Such social-psychological research was supposed to demonstrate that 'vertical living', living in high-rise flats, forms a source of dissociation and disintegration. Architects were accused of an academic and authoritarian attitude and from then on their dwellings were called 'straitjackets', 'reproducible cells' or, as Castells writes, "inhumane urbane forms" (1983:73). People, it was said, prospered better in cluttered and 'organically' grown neighbourhoods than in rationally designed and theoretically thought through situations. The key item in this criticism is a statement dating from 1961, in which Jane Jacobs expounded the view that neighbourhoods should not be planned from top down, but should grow as a natural organism. Modern town planners have failed to understand the city, according to the sociologist. They elevate it to a work of art and ignore the true nature of city life. "Impersonal streets," she warns, "make faceless masses" (1994:69).

In the debate about the new towns two opposite views are set against each other. On the one hand we see the hallmark of architects, planners and other policy makers involved in the construction of the city, to direct the behaviour of people and communities with their creations. On the other hand there are critics who reject the project. They have found the city unsuitable for human living. In spite of the conflicting conclusions they draw, a common perspective lies hidden in the position of both parties. Underlying both the utopian longing for a new city and the mocking creation of the sarcellitus virus is the idea that architecture determines the social behaviour and the mental condition of people. Both those in support and those against the city believe ultimately that space is a determinant of human behaviour. In this paper, in a certain sense I turn this train of thought around. Residents, I suppose, do not allow themselves to be squashed into the latticework and patterns of the town planner. People make up their own city.

The question how space influences human behaviour and how behaviour influences space has led to many headaches. Within geography, planning, sociology and other disciplines directly involved in thinking about and structuring urban space, there is a continuing search for ways to comprehend this dilemma. Numerous concepts are thought up, usually in terms of dichotomies, such as between mass and space, absolute and relative space, physical and social space, abstract and differential space, place and space, and potential and effective environments (*cf.* Madanipour 1996). These concepts share a common theme. Here I refer to what Sonnenfeld calls the *dichotomy of location*, an awareness of the coexistence of the 'objective dimensions' of a physical environment and the 'subjective dimensions' of a social environment (1972:244). Space is in some sense like a blank page. The way people perceive and use buildings, streets, parks, or squares is not decided in advance. As English and Mayfield see it, space is empty. It needs binding and identification by a group or an individual for an interaction between humankind and the environment to be recognized (1972:214). Once a building, street, city, or other physical space is realized, it is up to its users to capture and recreate it, to make it their own. As the anthropologist Lévi-Strauss once put it, the city is first and foremost a social work of art (1962:112).

The relationship between man and environment is central to this paper. The fundamental point raised is that, stated directly, people make their own city. Henceforth, I refer to this domain as the 'soft city', a term derived from a treatise by Jonathan Raban on the 'plastic' nature of urban existence. For next to the 'hard city' of architects and town-planners there is another city which people live by and live through. The notion of a soft city serves as a guiding idea in the active role people play in inhabiting a city an idea. It concerns the way people perceive and use, appropriate, and transform their environment. There is however something deceptive about these conceptions of physical and social spaces. On the one hand, a material environment is by no means physical, but is rather a social and historical object, shaped by human thoughts and activities. Residents on the other hand, while arranging their environment, are not free to act as they please, but are bound in many ways by spatial restrictions. Thus it seems fruitful to see how both concepts interact rather than treat the physical and the social as isolated poles.

In this paper I explore the intermingling of hard and soft city on the basis of a fieldwork study on the social spatial behaviour of young people in the Parisian banlieue of Sarcelles. This paper focuses mainly on the use of public space by young men, and leaves women and other groups out. These youths form an unruly group of residents to whose account the decline of the city is largely laid. It is the second generation of youths we are concerned with here, who in contrast with their parents were born in the city and/or grew up there. Youths form a dominant grouping in the city. Not only does the category up to twenty years form the biggest age group (Mabrut 1995, Vieillard-Baron 1994), they also make their presence in the city felt in an emphatic manner. *Les beurs*, as these migrant kids are also known, use obscene words and gestures, go around dressed in trainers and tracksuits, cluster together at suspicious places, write on walls, and make offensive rap noises. In contrast with what is often assumed without further ado, these forms of expression are no empty poses or sloganeering. The verbal and non-verbal texts and pictures are parts of a sign language, which youths men use to give their environment meaning.

In this paper we see how the schism between such deviant groups and the dominant *mainstream* society works out in the public space of Sarcelles. I have therefore divided this paper into two parts. The first part consists of two sections in which I describe the hard city of Sarcelles. Here we see how ideas, which underlie the design, the construction and the management of the city, fall back on post-war developments in urban architecture and on dominant ideologies about city and society. We consider here in particular the presence of the state in public space and the manner in which architecture and urban space reflect the existing balance of power. In the second part, the accent is on the form and substance youths give to the soft city. Here we see how, with the help of 'minor means of communication' such as graffiti, rap and other verbal and non-verbal language signs they use the city as the context in which to give sense and meaning to their existence. Here youths are as it were the 'second architects', turning their living environment into a cultural domain. The paper ends with a conclusion, in which I interweave the conceptions of hard and soft city.

Concept and plan of modernistic architecture
Architects meet a practical need for dwellings, workshops and other places, but they tend to operate on the premises of an artist. In the hands of architects and town-planners, cities become works of art and people become superfluous. There is something irrevocable behind architecture, however. Architects put an ineradicable stamp on the environment. In contrast with a painting or a play, one cannot alter an architectonic work of art other than by blowing it up or pulling it down. Streets, squares, buildings and parks form the physical structure within which social life takes place. This hard city of architects, town-planners and local authorities, the city as it is designed, built and managed, is considered in the next two sections. Here the analysis of the different elements of the "symbolic realm of urban imagery" in their historical context is featured (Nas 1993:2). Underlying the hard city of Sarcelles are specific aesthetic and ideological themes related to abstract ideas about the city and society. Our exploration of the hard city starts at the beginning of the twentieth century, when suddenly, *un, deux, trois, soleil*, a Swiss-French architect saw the light.

Le Corbusier was a man of his time. The American novelist Tom Wolfe described him as "the perfect wire figure of the Machine Age" (1989:118). He wore close-fitting, tailored clothes. Underneath his black suit, white shirt and black tie, there was a pale thin body. His spectacles had thick round frames, and on his balding head he wore a black bowler. He liked to portray himself as an enlightened person. Photographs show him staring absent-mindedly into the future with one of his recent plans in the background and a ruler or some other instrument in his hand. His

favoured form of transport was a white bicycle. Now and again he would cycle anonymously through Paris on his nice, clean bicycle. But what he saw there did not please him in the slightest.
After the Industrial Revolution, Paris developed into an urban region. Private property and private investments had obtained a juridical base and town planning had for the most part become dependent on fluctuating price developments. Economic prosperity led to excessive building activities, which came to a standstill during periods of economic decline. Because speculators in the city centre forced up real estate prices, many citizens took stock and left. People who could not afford city centre housing prices moved out of town and businesses and corporations became established on cheaper land on the city's edge. In this way the city grew and control from above was lost. The government implemented a policy of *laissez faire* and allowed housing development to proliferate. Like other European cities, Paris turned into what Benevolo refers to as a 'liberal city' (*cf.* Benevolo 1993). In the mid-nineteenth century the French government had intervened. Napoleon III ordered his prefect Baron Haussmann to subject the historical centre of Paris to a renewal programme. Napoleon let Haussmann build an open city with wide boulevards, great parks, stations, bridges, sewer systems, and prestigious public works. But next to these stately results of urban renewal there were whole districts totally lacking in colour or style. An uncomfortable situation was allowed to develop, particularly in slums like the *bidonvilles*, with people living tightly packed together in small buildings and without proper sanitation. Epidemics broke out, which cost many lives. At this point, the local government authority set up institutes and marked an 'unhealthy rows of houses' on the city map. During the interwar period, many social projects were launched and sixteen garden cities were built.
To Le Corbusier, the nineteenth-century city was an eyesore. It was crowded, unhygienic, chaotic, and inhabited by people with parochial habits and conventions. "Paris is cancerous," he wrote (1963:7). In these words resounded the nineteenth-century ideas of such political thinkers as Matthew Arnold and Charles Fourier, who saw the city as a breeding ground of disorder and social anarchy, and of Karl Marx and Friedrich Engels who criticized the unplanned growth of industrial towns. As they saw it, the Industrial Revolution and capitalist economy had a fatal impact on life in the city and on the mental and moral state of its citizens. At the time some ideas were put forward, which showed how things could be better done. There was Robert Owen's 'Village of Harmony and Society' and Charles Fourier's collective living space called the *phalanstere*. In these ways they drew attention to the future of the individual, who had apparently become estranged from the big city. The city of the future had to be a 'free space', logically constructed, clean, simple and without any unnecessary fussiness. Next to this 'progressive model' stood the ideas of

John Ruskin, William Morris, and Augustus Pugin, who became worried about the threatening gap between the old city center and its outer fringes. In their 'cultural' city models, they reverted to the past ideal stage of the organic community, in which the social group and not the individual was central (*cf.* Choay 1965). Le Corbusier took up this view of the future. One could hear his voice in the narrow and dim alleys of the Quartier Latin, the chaotic *logements* of the *bidonvilles* and the *bric-à-brac* of Montmartre and Montparnasse. "Attention," he wrote later, "Attention! Some day it will be fulfilled. A new civilization, a whole new world!" (1958:32). He had created a vision in his head that would transcend far across his time.

Le Corbusier was quite sure that people had to live in order and harmony, far from the hustle and bustle of the city center. Society needed a plan and it was up to the architect to create one. With that thought, Le Corbusier ascribed revolutionary powers to himself and town-planners in general. According to him, the harmony of society was a matter of building. Le Corbusier incorporated his plans in a city of the future. This city had to be a miniature society without any class structure. Large numbers of people - he once designed a city for three million inhabitants - would live under the roof of a city. Guided by the principle of 'freedom through order,' he created a place guided by laws and rules. Le Corbusier thought of the sun breaking through in the city. It would be green and full of air and space. For example, large high city towers stood there, 'vertical cities' as he called them. Many people could be housed in a small area, every room would have enough sunlight, and all the residents would have an unfettered outlook over their surroundings. The buildings looked like cubistic blocks. Le Corbusier built them in modern materials such as steel and concrete, and banished all unnecessary details. These 'machines for living' could be obtained by order and completed in very little time with the help of modern production techniques. Surrounding the buildings lay great parks, Le Corbusier wanted to bring the *conditions de nature* back to the city. So on his drawings the apartment blocks always stood against the setting of a natural landscape; in the foreground there would be a bush or tree. Around the apartment blocks the streets formed a system of straight lines and right angles, and every spot had its own specific function. And right across the city ran a diagonal road, providing the pathway for car traffic. Le Corbusier eliminated the street, which for him was a source of anarchy and barbarism. The new city represented speed; there was no room for alleys or pavements. Simple, straight, high, and grandiose, that was how he wanted it.

Le Corbusier travelled throughout Europe with his plans and joined up with a group of architects, which included such people as Mies van de Rohe, J.P. Oud, Gerrit Rietveld, and Walter Gropius, who founded the Bauhaus Art Centre on the ruins left after the First World War. Urged by the effects of the industrial revolution and the idea of an upcoming new society, these new builders wanted to get rid of everything that recalled past times and traditions. In the pamphlet entitled *Charte d'Athenes,* they wrote down the architectural principles which future cities had to incorporate. This signalled the start for a future of rational cities built according to modern standards. This school fitted the purist Le Corbusier as if it had been made for him. He had created a *salon d'automne* that was detached from time and place. It was a reproducible thing that could be built from scratch on any piece of land imaginable. How completely a new city would change social life! In the closed society of art, Le Corbusier was treated as a star. From that time on, his colleagues addressed him endearingly as 'Corbu'. His drawings, maps, dioramas and plaster castings were never accepted beyond that circle, however. In France, Le Corbusier did not manage to recruit a single moneylender. For sure, he had created a utopia, but The Radiant City was never built.

Paris after World War Two was confronted with a housing shortage. People came to the city from all directions. Repatriates returned home from former colonies, people left the countryside, and many immigrants came looking for work. The city was soon confronted with an acute shortage of living space. Many houses were dilapidated or had been destroyed during the war, the housing market was in an economic crisis, and the existing legislation held up the execution of plans. The government implemented a defensive policy to stabilize the population level in the Parisian agglomeration. In the beginning of the 1950s, however, the authorities developed laws to stimulate the construction industry to build on a larger scale, and established teams of engineers who had sophisticated building techniques at their disposal, and encouraged the building of many new towns as cheaply possible on special zones outside the city centre. A post-war explosion of building projects followed, which radically changed the map of Paris. Between 1954 and 1982 the number of residents in the periphery, the *petite* and *grande couronne,* doubled (*cf.* Scargill 1983). After the development of an industrial agglomeration and the extension of the city boundaries the new towns marked a third phase in the development of the conurbation of Paris (*cf.* Lecoin 1988).

Sarcelles is an enlightening example of the wave of construction in the 1950s and 1960s. The city is referred to as a *grand ensemble,* a term used for a large-scale project consisting of eight to ten thousand housing units, including a combination of apartment blocks in five or six storey buildings, providing accommodation for thirty to fifty thousand people. Many of these complexes were set up with the help of standardized building methods and constructed on the spot like a model building set. To relieve the pressure on the centre of Paris, as many people had to be accommodated as cheaply and as quickly as possible. Notwithstanding the limited time available, the building activities were not set out at random. The heavy hand of the architect can be seen in the design and layout of the city when viewed in the context of post-war developments in town planning. Sarcelles is a "big composition" writes Chaslin; as an example of modernistic architecture, various futuristic ideas were effective (1987:75). In Lochères, as the new town of Sarcelles was called, an extreme division of functions was carried through separating places for living, working, and recreation. The city was divided into four, with each quarter provided with a community centre, a school, and a shopping centre. In the middle of the project an indoor shopping mall was built where, as Le Corbusier advocates, municipal services and office space are located. Sports facilities are laid out between the old village core of Sarcelles and the city centre and some businesses and corporations are located on recently created *zones franches*.

In the division between living and working spaces, we see a city as it was first intended to be. Sarcelles is set up as a peaceful and quiet living area, counterbalancing the crowded inner city. We see evidence of this motivation of creating the outside city as an orderly place in the street pattern. In contrast with the small, concentric streets of the old village core of Sarcelles, the new town has an orthogonal system of straight roads. These wide, gritted streets played a part in well-functioning car traffic, but also stood for clarity and order, and so formed a counterpart to the narrow alleys of the pre-war slums. "For good circulation, a straight line is required", wrote Le Corbusier. "Straight things are healthy, the crooked line is dangerous, and it ruins and paralyses" (1925:10). Adopting this policy, the city of Sarcelles has many apartment blocks which, especially in the latest building constructions, stand out as landmarks between lower buildings. With this *urbanism of towers*, as it was developed in Lochères, scarce land was used efficiently. The apartment blocks also gave an impression of open space and sunlight breaking through. They could not be too high, according to Le Corbusier. From the fourteenth floor upwards one was living, as he saw it, in pure air. In addition to the high buildings and straight streets, the 'free' or 'green spaces' are also fundamental to the town-planning concept of Sarcelles. The city is like a living body, with lungs provided by a huge park. Between the buildings lie large and open places, alongside the streets stand trees and plants, and family gardens are laid out to meet the desire of city people for quiet places outside the city; these are used especially during the weekends. In a municipal brochure, the mayor Lamontagne describes Sarcelles as a *ville fleuri*. It has a total of two hundred hectares of lawns, grass plots and meadows, seven hundred trees, five thousand square metres of flowers, and one hundred thousand plants (1995:11). This theme of urban nature recurs repeatedly in the promotional material. Sarcelles has an own *service cadre de vie*, which, operating under the slogan 'for a clean, beautiful and green city' keeps up and maintains the stock of trees and plants. Each

year the fresh start of a new season is introduced by the planting of some new trees. In 1997 the municipality presented a new logo, with three birds spreading their wings and flying towards the sun against a clear blue background.
The new towns surrounding Paris and other French cities have been built from a strong belief in progress. In France came a new era, which demanded new ways of living. The 1950s and 1960s, writes George Ross, were thought of as a turning point in the country's history. These decades would mark a transitional period, a "take-off to a modern era." As their political leaders expressed it, France stood at the eve of a new industrial order, a modern society modelled on the American example. But the moment that France stepped into the new era, Le Corbusier had pitched his tent somewhere else. He was designing cities in Algiers and Chandigarh and was working out his ideas in separate buildings. But the new towns surrounding Paris drew eagerly on his storehouse of models. In the naming of the new towns, the underlying concept and their outward appearance, his voice resounded again. All the ingredients of modern society - economic and technical advancement, an expanding urban population, higher living standards, an increase in the use of cars, and a strong belief in high-rise buildings and large-scale urban planning - were present in Le Corbusier's model-city. He, it is now reported, hit on the core questions of the modern city. Although these days the architect is seen as the personification of the evils of post-war developments in town planning, one great quality was assigned to him. The man, Evenson writes, knew how to put bad ideas in an attractive package (1987:247).

City and state
Function separation, straight streets, free spaces and high buildings; we have seen above the ingredients of an urban development plan laid out. However, the hard city incorporates not only design and construction, but also management and maintenance. In this section we consider the hard city as integrated in this top-down approach. The design, the construction and the conservation of the city incorporate a concealed, influential idea about the layout of the city and society. Modernism was in this respect no fantasy of a solitary architect, or an ideologically underpinned movement (*cf.* Gold 1998), but a radical physical manifestation of what is referred to as the 'culture offensive'. The philosopher Richard Sennett writes in this connection about the *tyranny of intimacy*, the manner in which, in western cities in the course of the twentieth century, ideas derived from the private domain permeate to an increasing extent through to the public domain (*cf.* Sennett 1990). Sennett sees in the increasing personalism, the process of individualization and the rise of the private or *etui* person as a 'new puritan ethic'. The basis of this 'culture offensive' lies in a deep distaste and antipathy for urbanism, such as we noted in

the ideas of Le Corbusier. In the formation of modern urban communities we see then also a community hidden behind a protective screen and driven by anxiety for the unknown and potentially threatening, the avoidance of violence, and the repression of deviant elements.

The most striking aspect of this culture offensive is the ideology of multiculturalism as we encounter it in Sarcelles. The *grand ensemble* is an urban concept that, as the term suggests, emphasizes the collective. *Ensemble* means literally the 'whole', or the 'combination', 'the musical chord'. The architect Emile Aillaud, who designed Chanteloup les Vignes in the 1970s, a neighbourhood to the south of Paris, considered this as an "imperative" of his time, in which the individual was imbedded in a collective. Aillaud had, following Le Corbusier's principle of 'liberty through order', an urban collective in mind, in which people would find their liberty within a strict order. "The city as one house" is how he describes his project (1978:9). The collective housing form of the grand ensemble embodies an ideology, which lies at the basis of the French united state. Since the process of economic and cultural unification following the Revolution of the 18th century, France has been governed by a strongly centralized state apparatus. It functions as a *communion nationale*, an administrative and legal unity that proclaims the national identity above ethnic, religious, and linguistic identities. According to the anthropologist Emmanuel Todd, with this Jacobean-Republican ideal the French State takes up a special position within the European community. From the end of the nineteenth century and in particular during the interwar period, in comparison with other countries, the state was able to incorporate the arrival of immigrants without any great problems, and although in France economic lines of separation have also appeared and the immigration issue has led to heated public debates, in principle forms of inequality within society are rejected. "French culture is complex and heterogeneous", writes Todd, "but at its heart there is the idea of the rightness, the necessity, of equality. It is the fundamental doctrine of the Republic" (1997:26).

We see the fundamental principle of the Republic, a combination of an administrative unity with an ethnic diversity (*cf.* Todd and Le Bras 1981), worked out in various ways in the physical environment of Sarcelles. The public domain of Sarcelles is furnished with various national symbols. The French tricolour hangs in prominent places, and the city is also provided with a national symbolism in the naming of the streets. Besides the central *Place de France* and *Avenue du 8 mai 1945,* the avenues and streets bear the names of twenty-three painters, twenty-seven novelists, eight philosophers, six sculptors, nineteen composers, and an actor. Only significant figures in French (art) history who lived and worked in the eighteenth and nineteenth centuries are included. A local government brochure praises Nicolas Poussin for his "idealistic view of nature",

Antoine Watteau for his "humane vision", Charles Peguy for his "socialist and humanist line of reasoning", and Jean-Jacques Rousseau for his insights into the liberty and equality of citizens. Also exemplifying the presence of the state in the public space of Sarcelles are the folders and magazines published under the auspices of the city government, which keep the residents informed of the comings and goings of their local government authority. In these newspapers, which function as a disguised forum for local politicians and building contractors, we see the preservation of the conception of the *grande ensemble* referred to above. *Sarcelles le Magazine* for example begins every edition with a short, rhetorical article, written by the mayor, elaborating on a sense of community and solidarity. Several standard rubrics follow these introductory words, reviewing the history of the city and introducing forthcoming plans about town planning renewal, safety and employment. The paper also features notable people and groups, who talk or write about their memories of the city in their youth, which they for that matter left behind them a long time ago. Under the headline 'a mosaic of societies,' *A Sarcelles*, a monthly magazine about the clubs and social events, calls repeatedly for a sense of community, solidarity and brotherhood. It is time for a "big meeting", writes the local council through the mouth of an antiracism committee. "We struggle to defend the values to which we all adhere: justice, tolerance, brotherhood, citizenship" (1997:1). Local government authority officials often point out the three-day market as an example of intercultural meetings and ethnic integration. *L'écritoire*, a freely distributed paper, recommends the market as an oasis in a violent environment, a "lively spot" where "traders from all parts of the country offer their exotic wares," from mint leaves to perfumed rice.

Hidden transcripts: power relations in public space

In the previous two sections I described the hard city of Sarcelles. We saw the physical environment as a social and historical object, shaped by the ideas of planners and architects, and maintained by local authorities. The following sections analyse the various ways youths struggle to escape the watchful eye of the authorities and infiltrate the public domain with their messages. Forms of expression, in which youths provoke the public and upset the established order, are involved here. We can consider the public behaviour of youths in this sense as a cultural practice, an everyday strategy by which they react to and shape their direct social and spatial environment (*cf.* Welz 1991). Before I discuss various elements of such verbal and nonverbal forms of expression, let me notice some things on the nature of public space.

In Sarcelles the way things actually run differs markedly from what planners and architects first had in mind. Sarcelles has the reputation of being a violent place. In Sarcelles, which is only surpassed in the regional crime statistics by Argenteuil and Cergy, 4693 criminal offences were reported during 1996 (*La Gazette du Val d'Oise*, 12-2-1997). As a consequence, a climate of anxiety and danger has been created that has its repercussions on public space. In Sarcelles many eyes are keeping watch. Security personnel walk round supermarkets, the police patrol the streets, and on certain public places videos cameras keep constant watch. On the main roads around the city, houses are laid out like forts. There are no front gardens, most of the shutters are closed night and day, and watchdogs stand alert behind the walls and fences. The local newspapers moreover encourage such spatial processes. They bring the abuses taking place in the region to the attention of their readers. Every week the *Gazette du Val d'Oise* and *Le Parisien Seine-Saint-Denis* report under such headlines as 'deeds and misdeeds' and 'sundry facts' a host of criminal activities in the region. These newspaper reports cover a variety of events - break-ins, pursuits, destruction, attacks, verbal aggression - but are put together according to a specific stereotype. Depending on the seriousness of the crime, under a pithy leading article and an introduction there may follow a detailed reconstruction of an event. Date, day, time, place, perpetrator and victim are reported, leading into an exciting story. There are usually two main figures. One is a youth, marked out as a 'young offender' whose behaviour is described with customary surprise by a usually faceless reporter; the other is the police officer who eventually restores public order. The report ends with the arrest or escape of the offender or suspect.

Such scribblings are read in a society. The style of journalism is part of what Champagne refers to as the "medialising of social problems" (1991:67). Journalists operate in this context as a summary executioner. Although they are usually based on an eyewitness account and written in the objective style of a police report, these newspaper articles all share a suggestive undertone. Facts are served up, but the background is omitted. Such representations and reconstructions of criminal facts play a large part in the discourse of anxiety, such as is seen in the *banlieue*. Ideas of violence and danger provide in a certain sense the handles that people are looking for to help them restore order. Body-Gendrot uses for this the term 'social deregulation'. Complex communities in which important and rapid mutations take place, she writes, weaken the mutual value structure. Particularly in places like Sarcelles that accommodate a kaleidoscope of nationalities, the public space comes under pressure. "The city is a space in flux," writes Body-Gendrot, "where individuals traverse neighbourhoods, but where agreement on a common space and on rules of coexistence fade away" (1995:531). In such fragmented communities anxiety eventually forms the link between segments, which otherwise seldom come in contact with each other. Gerald Suttles, an urban ethnologist who has carried out research in a multi-ethnic urban district in Chicago, writes in this connection of 'social distances'. "Complex urban societies," he writes, "seem to produce such great social distances that those at the extremes can do little more than build myths about one another" (1976:5). Body-Gendrot perceives in such constellations a political trend to ascribe the problems of the community in a specific neighbourhood to a particular category of people. This trend is different from the case of the ghetto-ization of North American inner cities, since it is age, not ethnicity, which is usually considered to be the most important factor in the decline of the city. Not only do youths form a numerical majority, but also a highly visible group, which in various ways makes its presence felt in the public domain and distances itself from the rest of society. The asocial behaviour patterns which they resort to and which I discuss below constitute, in the view of those in authority, a threat to public order. "Youths," writes Wacquant, "are widely singled out by older residents as the chief source of vandalism, delinquency, and insecurity, and they are publicly held up as responsible for the worsening condition and reputation of the degraded *banlieue*" (1993:376).

Sarcelles does not seem to be very well suited to young people. Many youths feel that the city is a boring place. They have the feeling of being shut in and isolated, far removed from the speed and action of an urban existence. Youths often complained for example about the lack of entertainment facilities in the city, such as discos and cinemas. "Amusement is impossible to find here", said one boy about the lack of entertainment in the city; "here there aren't any weekends". The local politicians, well aware of the boredom that is rife among large groups of youths, have tried to fill the gap through courses, programmes, and projects. A host of projects are being run on art, sport, and education, and the police try to recruit youths. Occasionally, a graffiti-wall is made available for some unruly youths, or a rap course may be given for beginners. The local politicians try, as protectors of the public order, to preserve the hard city as a respectable place. Nevertheless, large groups of youths form a dissonant note in the whole. The domestication of rap and graffiti, pillars of the hip-hop culture, and the grouping together of undesirable elements and behaviour labelled as 'deviant' and 'delinquent' can therefore be seen as a form of exercising power. They have, as Scott writes, the aim "to stigmatize activities or persons that seem to call into question official reality" (1991:55). Stigmas ought eventually to distract attention from the real claim that youths are making.

The public space of Sarcelles, as we can deduce from reports in the media and from the environment as laid out by the state, is a power-loaded domain. In Sarcelles, social reality is held together in a painstakingly laid out and maintained public space. It is an imaginary community based on an *act of will* rather than on an *act of experience* (*cf.* Sennett 1970). We can consider the city in this respect as a political setting or 'urban arena', consisting of social places that are used in different ways by different parties. A "war of places" takes place, as Arantes describes, in which various groups fight for their right to exist (*cf.* Arantes 1996). Levitas writes in this connection of the city as a 'multi-clientele organization', in which groups adapt to their environment with the help of various strategies (*cf.* Levitas 1978).

Inscribing identity

In Sarcelles a social-spatial process takes place, in which parts of the city are claimed and marked out. Parts of public space are transformed into a cultural domain, locations within which people create and propagate their identities. Sarcelles bears traces of the process of appropriation and turning round described above. Here and there in Sarcelles texts and pictures are scribbled, scratched and sprayed with paint. These graffiti, expressly manifest in Sarcelles, are a superficial but meaningful medium that can provide us with some insight in the balance of power within the urban arena. Graffiti are cultural leftovers, temporarily or permanently observable remnants of human behaviour. They function as an adaptive form of communication, in which physical objects in the environment are used as messengers. A tree, a boulder or, in our case, the exterior of a city, are provided as it were with a second, meaningful layer. With graffiti, people transform a physical object into a cultural artefact, thereby marking and anchoring their identity in the immediate environment. This cultural act sits in the definition of the word. *Graffiti*, in the singular *graffito*, is derived from the Italian g*raffiare*, meaning scratching of scraping, and the Greek word for write, *grapho*. The graffito is carved, and its maker literally puts a stamp on the environment, witnessed in public by others in his or her presence. By writing in a public place he or she, however marginally and insignificantly, proclaims a demand for a place in the urban system. To be sure, graffiti have been grafted as transnational signs on the iconography of a worldwide body language, but they are not to be seen apart from a local context, set in the specific messages for city and residents. Not everyone is altogether enthusiastic about that.

Graffiti in French suburbs are a controversial topic. Cleaning teams free the neighbourhoods, some of which are under strict supervision, from 'paint vandalism', and graffiti writing and drawing are taken up in the byelaws as illegal practices. The government authorities in Sarcelles turn a blind eye to graffiti in certain designated places to control the urge to paint graffiti. Shop fronts and roll-down shutters are painted on request, and in certain places the local government authority has dedicated some walls. In the context of the counteraction of undesirable graffiti, projects are set up to encourage youths to develop their wall drawings into frescos. This domestication of graffiti, to enrich the colouring of the townscape, nevertheless has no legitimacy. Graffiti touch on persistent conceptions about the public domain. The hard city of the designers and administrators is, as we saw before, a clean and respectable place. Graffiti do not fit in with that picture; they make the city 'ugly' and 'chaotic'. Graffiti are *crimes of style*, writes Ferrell. "They [the power holders] constitute a sense of beauty grounded not only in control of property and space, but in the carefully coordinated control of image and design, in the smoothed-out textures of clean environments. They embody a demand that material culture reflect planned and routinized human activity" (1993:180). Young people recapture by means of graffiti parts of the planned city, they "carve a bit of cultural space from the enforced monotony of the environment" (1993:176). In this respect graffiti form, as Kohl writes, an antithesis to the formalized, academic and legitimate world of adults and institutions (1972:109). Around graffiti a division arises. Against the care for the face of the city of the authorities stands the urge of revelation of youth. Illustrative of this is a graffito painted in the Jewish quarter of the masturbating cartoon dog Goofy, with a chastity sticker stuck on it that would be difficult to remove. Once set in an eye-catching place, the social mechanism of censorship comes into force.

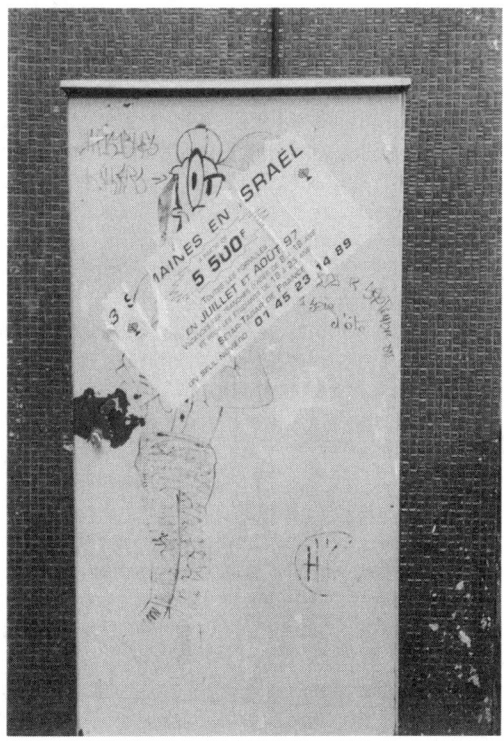

There is a close connection between graffiti and spatial behaviour (cf. Ley and Cybriwsky 1974). The wall texts in Sarcelles are not all of the same size, but follow a specific path. In addition to physical restrictions - underground passages are sometimes too dark or the walls are too high to reach, a reason why all texts only reach to arms length - graffiti are spread unevenly over the city. In particular, places where surveillance is strict, such as the Jewish synagogue, the Catholic Church, the University of Technology, the central shopping centre and relatively prosperous residential districts consisting of stacks of owner-occupied dwellings and private parking garages, are largely devoid of graffiti. Graffiti are concentrated in specific parts of the city, where the intensity of smells and the amount of rubbish is also relatively high. In particular, the sorts of space in which graffiti are found are significant. The nature and content of graffiti texts are related to the sort of space in which they are set.

In this respect we can distinguish two sorts of space in the public domain of Sarcelles. On the one hand the city consists of *espaces collectives*, the central meeting places of the city, such as squares, parks and shopping centres. These spaces form what Strauss refers to as the *locales* of a city, places intended as meeting places for various social groups (cf. Strauss 1970). In such spaces, where social control is relatively great, youths usually take up a position on the sidelines. In these eye-catching locations, such as the façades of buildings, texts are particularly explicit, giving voice to the antagonism and dissatisfaction with the wider society. These graffiti are usually set out in short sentences and obscenities deriding various institutions such as the police, the law, and politics and, with reference to neighbourhoods in New York and Los Angeles, denouncing racism and discrimination. Graffiti are moreover often oriented to concrete, physical manifestations of the power apparatus. During my research period there was uproar about the school system. Reports trickled through regularly about break-ins, fights, truancy and conflicts between teachers and students. Graffiti lay these controversies bare. School complexes that may not be well guarded after closing time function as regular meeting points and are favourite objects for graffiti artists.

Moving from the central spots to the marginal locations of Sarcelles, the form and content of graffiti change. Sarcelles harbours many 'urban voids', undefined locations, such as the spaces between buildings and roads. They are marginal locations, the frayed edges of the public domain, which for the most part escape the monitoring eye of the authorities and are therefore considered exceptionally suitable places in which to hangout. Strauss refers to such places as *locations*, places where the segregation between the segments of a society is maximal. The opposition is set out here in a subtle and implicit manner. Graffiti are concentrated on passageways such as alleyways and galleries, around such places as basketball courts, school buildings and parks, or in objects which have fallen into disuse such as artworks and empty buildings, and on the concrete fencing of transit routes and metro lines. Graffiti function here as markers of the *action space* of the young, transforming a physical environment into a social space. Texts such as 'this street is mine' and 'the world is ours' claim parts of the public domain and lay down firmly the limits of their territory. Wuertz refers to graffiti as a form of 'monopolization' of the public space, in which people privatize parts of the public space for themselves (1991:66). Exemplifying such a claim is the emblem of 'Golden Man' drawn on the door of an electricity cupboard and a synonym for an active group of graffiti artists in the city. A figure is depicted on the emblem, with arms raised and legs curled round like the claws of a scorpion, and accompanied by a warning: "Whoever moves one step forward here is finished." The claws make a pinching movement, and a cloud of dust is all that remains of the victim. In the group's emblem, in which various ornaments are worked, more names are written, crossed out, and added. Such graffiti, in which territories are demarcated and claimed, are numerous. Youths set or scratch by visual means a cultural layer on the outer side of the city. Round the corner and out of sight youths make their presence felt, dropping their anchor in the space in which they live.

The appropiating of space is also done with the help of body language. Here is to be found minor nonverbal language signs by which in various ways youths take bodily possession of the public domain. Public objects and spaces are taken into possession in an ostentatious manner by hanging around on the streets, spitting on the ground, and using street furniture in alternative ways. There is a whole range of sitting positions for the benches placed round the edge of public squares, varying from sitting on the arm to standing and placing their feet on the seat. Youths also use various facial expressions to challenge the passer-by, such as a stare, or a mocking grimace. These appear to imply openness, but have the intention of shocking others and wrong-footing them. This ambiguity is also buried in *bougér*, a distinctive, quasi-nonchalant way of walking, in which the head and shoulders move loosely backwards and forwards.

A striking process is revealed in the social spatial behaviour of youths. They appropriate to themselves parts of the urban environment, so that the central and the collectively laid-out spaces, felt by many to be insecure, ambivalent and marginal places, acquire a marginal meaning and fulfil a central role. These *other places* become a breeding ground for groups, which - whether they seek it or not - have their being outside the maelstrom of society. Hetherington describes these places as 'heterotopias', "sites of social centrality for the *reproduction* of marginal or outsider identities" (1991:34). "Margins become centres, centres become margins, and the meaning of centres and margins becomes blurred. Those who see themselves as marginal see such places as socially central to their alternative values and beliefs" (1996:39).

Anonymity and pseudonyms
Graffiti express in a certain sense a longing for visibility. They are written in the public domain and with the intention of being seen and noticed. According to Kokoreff, graffiti form a commentary on the faceless city life. The graffiti are in their appearance products of a media-driven society, in which visibility operates as an "ontological principle". Youths distance themselves from the mass, withdrawing from their anonymity. A twofold process is involved. What strikes outsiders as incomprehensible, ugly or anarchic, forms for insiders a revealing source of information. Although by means of graffiti youths express in a direct manner their opposition to the urban system, they turn away from it in an implicit manner. In their provocation and reversal of the established order they put up a front between themselves and the outside world. Many wall texts, set on inaccessible locations and read by few people, are not addressed to outsiders. Graffiti are usually set in codes, masking and mystifying, and as a result only have a select audience in mind.

A rudimentary form of the mechanism described above is the use of *tags*. A tag is a stylized signature, in which letters are worked into a logo or anagram. In Sarcelles this mostly involves separate scribbles in which a name or a nickname is spelt out in full, or with just the initials. Some tags cover several city neighbourhoods; others mark out small-scale places, such as a neighbourhood, street, or alleyway. The tag functions as a pseudonym. With them, the writers make their presence in public evident, but in a veiled manner. They make themselves knowable but unrecognizable to outsiders. Graffiti function in this sense as a means of communication in which youths attach themselves to a group, movement, neighbourhood, city or region. One may be confined to a group name, another makes from the names of others a list of fingered names, possibly supplemented with specific qualities set in code, such as the size of the genitalia, or the rank within a group. Such lists are often finished off with a covering term. This can be a group name, the name of a city or neighbourhood, an ethnic association, a postcode, a house number, or an expression of strength. A form of interaction takes place on the walls, with names and texts crossed out, overwritten, improved, or added. Graffiti make up part of the social network, with the wall functioning as a medium to enter into a dialog with each other. The use of graffiti as a means of communication illustrates moreover the formation of a second, alternative identity. Where youths in the wider society lack status and respect, they turn that around to their own benefit. With a lack of legal options, youths choose and invent a medium along an informal path. With a frequently bizarre nickname, in combination with drawings of male genitalia or such objects as jewellery, cars, dress, and weapons, they acquire a status position. A self-chosen name is a medium of identification and differentiation.

These distorions and mystifications are also found in language. Graffiti contain many twists and distortions (verlan), invented terms and expressions (argot), word games and metaphors. Next to his or her identity, the graffitist hereby can disguise his message. These language distortions concern mostly cultural sensitive information. A whole vocabulary exists, consisting of synonyms for police, seksual organs, men and women, money, clothing, drugs and alcohol. These are significant themes or central elements in the daily life of young boys. With this flexible use of language graffitis and rappers bridge a gap between worlds. Their langage is transparant for insiders, their own group, but also functions as a unpenetrable front to outsiders.

Fantasy and the romanticisation of ghetto culture
In addition to a journey in search of and in confirmation of their own identity, the wall texts also form a reflection on their own world. The walls of Sarcelles are then not only a medium for the transmission of anonymous messages, but also a reflection of the world in which they live. The distinction drawn between 'public' and 'private signs', often found in the literature on graffiti, does not apply to Sarcelles. In the public domain of the city we also find for example the 'latrinalia', a term which refers to signs set in semi-public spaces by which people may allow themselves to be driven by unconscious impulses and conflicts and free from social restrictions, they relieve themselves of social restrictions. In the graffiti of Sarcelles ideas about violence, money, and in particular sexuality play an important part. The virility-centred perspective that dominates the wall texts is striking. Graffiti often include aggressive and 'dirty' signs and texts, such as sexist terms and portrayals of raised middle fingers and disproportionate genitalia, in which youths expose their vision of man-woman relationships. Women are usually caricatured, with long curly hair, pouting lips, exceptionally long legs spread out, fat buttocks, whether or not penetrated by distorted, usually unidentifiable penises without an attached body, with testicles staring out like two frog's eyes.

The scene in the photo above exemplifies the game with fiction and reality that is carried on in graffiti, in which everyday objects—a pit-bull terrier, a car with an open roof, shades, baseball cap—are transformed into elements of an idealized world. Here we see how fantasy functions as a social weapon. In contrast with their inferior position in real life, graffiti are a means to revenge. Many expressions are in use, like 'arriving on the front', 'launching' and 'strike a pose', in which they aim at the system in all its appearances. A retaliatory action is aimed for. Many lyrics describe the inventivity and originality with which the established order is turned upside down. 'Faire le truc' as the expression goes; misleading and making fun of police officials, depicting themselves as victors in the midst of a conflicting environment.

Graffiti represent a stylised world, within which youths associate themselves with the poor image of their city, in which stigmas and stereotypes are turned into status objects and prominent places in the city are claimed as objects of opposition. In this romanticizing of and identification with their own marginality and the peripheral location of their city, youths draw fully on the style resources of American hip-hop. In addition to the graphic design and the use of English language catchwords and phrases, various American icons such as clothes labels, sports stars, pop stars, films and TV series are worked into graffiti, which are also integrated into their own existence. With such icons youths follow the example of their American predecessors. In depictions of their living environment also many references are included to the apartheid regime in South Africa, de slave trade, the nuclear threat, the bomb on Hiroshima, the conquested areas in Gaza, and the North American inner city ghetto. These are identifications with other marginal groups, creating a discours of dissidence, in which the black ghetto, functions in their imagination as an almost mythical place. Youths draw and write with their sign language to turn their own city into a mythological domain, styling themselves and their world as a model city in which they have the upper hand.

Conclusion

This paper began with a modern city legend. The story about the sarcellitus virus is based on an influential idea about the relationship between space and behaviour. Modern architecture ought, according to a view still expressed, have a modifying influence on the psychological and social being of a society. Above, with the help of Raban's concept about the plasticity of the urban existence, I have parried this dominant idea and shown how people make their own city. I concentrated on the cultural practices young men use to make the city the context in which to give sense and meaning to their existence. In this soft city they transform the existing space into a habitat, give colour to an inhuman, dismal, empty and grey living space. I first formulated an idea about the hard city, designed by architects and planners and maintained by local authorities. Underlying the urban development plan of Sarcelles, as we saw, are ideologies which link back to the *trentes glorieuses*, the post-war years in France steered by a strong belief in progress. The time was ripe for the conceptual world of the utopians of the nineteenth century and beginning of the twentieth century. With function separation, high-rise building, straight streets and green spaces Sarcelles was built along the same lines as the Radiant City, a maquette of the modern city designed by Le Corbusier. Underlying the modernism such as that which was constructed in Sarcelles, there was also a conception about the French Republic. It involved the manner in which the local politicians tried to arrange the collective form of living of the *grande ensemble*.

Other voices penetrated through the cultural surface of the hard city. The public domain functions as a political setting, in which youths express their dissatisfaction with existing institutions in a struggle with local authorities. Youths make use of a sign language in which they infiltrate the public domain with their messages in a concealed manner. Here the hard city, round the corner and out of sight, undergoes a transformation in which ill-defined, marginal spaces are transformed into social-central places in daily life. We directed our attention to the verbal language signs of graffiti. Graffiti is linked to the hip-hop movement, in which youths anchor their identity in the immediate living space. They are behaviour traces, in which youths appear in an anonymous manner in public. The wall texts form a sort of *folk utopia's*, with stylized pictures and stories about their own reality. Where the immediate environment leaves little to the imagination, youths take refuge in fantasized worlds. With their identification with the ghetto and with other marginal groupings, the symbolic revenge on authorities and the implementation of an internal and mutual competition, young people bring their own discourse into life. In this distortion of reality a remarkable reversal process takes place, in which a marginal position is elevated to a status object and marginal spaces of the public domain to central places. Youths use their masculinity, money, status, sexuality, and illegality as a protest to claim their dominance. They bring to life a substitute world, within which they describe themselves as victors.

There is some evidence here of an ambiguous discourse. The impenetrable smile, the coded French rap language, the recognizable and yet unrecognizable wall texts, the private spaces in a public domain; with one leg inside and the other outside society, the youths appear in public to demand the respect and build up the self-confidence that ordinary society denies them. Youths demand their place in the urban system, but at the same time they position themselves *out of place*. The soft city goes beyond the locality, but is anchored in their own, weekendless city.

References :
Aillaud, E. (1978) Chanteloup Les Vignes, quartier La Noé. Propos sur l'art urbain. Paris: Fayard.
Arantes, A.A. (1996) The war of places: symbolic boundaries and liminalities in urban space. In: Theory, culture and society, 4:81-92.
Benevolo, L. (1993) De Europese stad. Amsterdam: Agon.
Bernard, M. (1964) Sarcellopolis. Paris: Flammarion.
Body-Gendrot, S. (1995) Urban violence: a quest for meaning. In: New community, 4:525-536.
Castells, M. (1983) The city and the grassroots. A cross-cultural theory of urban social movements. London: Edward Arnold.
Champagne, P. (1991) La construction médiatique des 'malaises sociaux'.In : Actes de la recherche en sciences sociales, 90:64-75.
Charles, G. (1994) Jours agités à Sarcelles. In: L'express, June 9, 70-73.
Chaslin, F. (1987) Les années de béton. In: L'histoire, 102:74-78.
Choay, F. (1965) L'Urbanisme, utopies et réalités. Une anthologie. Paris: Seuil.
Chobeaux, F. (1994) L'identité collective de jeunes en difficulté d'insertion sociale. In: Hommes et Migrations, 1180:23-29.
Domenach, N. (1995) Fallait-il construire Sarcelles? Entretien avec François Chaslin. In: L'histoire, 192:40-41.
Eade, J. (ed.) (1997) Living the global city. Globalization as a local process. London: Routledge.
English, P.W. and R.C. Mayfield (eds.). (1972) Man, space and environment. Concepts in contemporary human geography. New York: Oxford University Press.
Evenson, N. (1979) Paris. A century of change, 1878-1978. Yale University Press.
Evenson, N. (1987) Yesterday's city of tomorrow today. In: H.A. Brooks (ed.) Le Corbusier, 241-255. New Jersey: Princeton University Press.
Ferrell, J. (1993) Crimes of style. Urban graffiti and the politics of criminality. Boston: Northeastern University Press.
Fyfe, N.R. (ed) (1998) Images of the street. Planning, identity and control in public space. London: Routledge.
Gold, J.R. (1998) The death of the boulevard. In: N.R. Fyfe (ed.), Images of the street. Planning, identity and control in public space. London: Routledge.
Gumperz, J. (1973) The speech community. In: P.P. Giglioli (ed.) Language and social context. Harmondsworth: Penguin.
Hannerz, U. (1969) Soulside. Inquiries into ghetto culture and community. New York: Columbia University Press.
Hannerz, U. (1980) Exploring the city. Inquiries toward an urban anthropology. New York: Columbia University Press.
Hebdige, D. (1988) Hiding in the light. On images and things. London: Comedia.
Hetherington, K. (1996)Identity formation, space and social centrality. In: Theory, culture and society, 4:34-52.
Jacobs, J. (1994) The death and life of great American cities. London: Penguin.
Jannoud, C. and Pinel, M. (1974) La premiere ville nouvelle. Paris: Mercure de France.
Kokoreff, M. (1991) Tags et zoulous: une nouvelle violence urbaine. In: Esprit, 169:23-36.
Lamontagne, R. (1995) Toujours pour Sarcelles. Montmorency: RDVA.

Lecoin, J.P. (1988) Paris and the Ille de France. In : H. van der Kammen (ed.), Four metropolises in Western Europe. Development and urban planning of London, Paris, Randstad Holland and the Ruhr region. Assen: Van Gorcum.
Le Corbusier. (1925) Urbanisme. Paris: Crès.
-, (1958) Het elektronische gedicht. Puteaux: Editions de Minuit.
-, (1963). Manière de penser l'urbanisme. Paris: Gonthier.
Lévi-Strauss, C. (1962) Het trieste der tropen. Reisverslag van een antropoloog. Antwerpen: Aula.
Levitas, G. (1978) Anthropology and sociology of streets. In: S. Anderson (ed.), On streets. Cambridge: The MIT Press.
Ley, D. and R. Cybriwsky. (1974) Urban graffiti as territorial markers. In: Annals of the Association of American Geographers, 4:491-505.
Mabrut, B. (1995) Locheres, logements, population. Sarcelles.
Madanipour, A. (1996) Design of urban space. An inquiry into a socio-spatial process. Chichester: John Wiley and Sons.
Mezrahi, C. (1986) Regards et temoignages sur Sarcelles. Sarcelles: Idéographic Editions.
Nas, P.J.M. (1993) Introduction. In: P.J.M. Nas (ed.), Urban symbolism, 1-12. Leiden, New York and Keulen: E.J. Brill.
Piatier, J. (1964) Sarcellopolis ou le meilleur des mondes.In: Le Monde, July 4.
Plas, E. (1997) La seul vaccin contre la sarcellite.In: L'unité, 247:20-22.
Raban, J. (1974) Soft city. Glasgow: Fontana/Collins.
Ross, G. (1991) Introduction: Janus and Marianne. In: J.F. Hollifield and G. Ross (eds.), Searching for the new France. New York: Routledge.
Scargill, I. (1983) Urban France. New York: Croom Helm.
Scott, J.C. (1990) Domination and the arts of resistance. Hidden transcripts. New Haven: Yale University Press.
Sennett, R. (1970) The uses of disorder. Personal identity and city life. London: Allen Lane.
-, (1990) The conscience of the eye. The design and social life of cities. New York: Alfred A. Knopf.
Sonnenfeld, J. (1972) Geography, perception and the behavioral environment. In P.W. English and R.C. Mayfield (eds.).
Strauss, A. (1970) Life styles and urban space. In: H.M. Proshansky, W.H. Ittelson and C.G. Rivlin (eds.), Environmental psychology. Man and his fysical setting. New York: Holt, Rinehart and Winston.
Suttles, G.D. (1979) Urban ethnography: situational and normative accounts. In: Annual review of sociology, 2:1-18.
Todd, E. (1997) The French exception. In: Newsweek, June, p.26.
Todd, E. and H. Le Bras. (1981) L'intervention de la France. Atlas anthropologique et politique. Paris: Pluriel.
Vieillard-Baron, H. (1994) Qui habite Sarcelles? In: Hommes et Migrations, 1181:11-18.
Wacquant, L.J.D. (1993) Urban outcasts. In: International journal of urban and regional research, 3:366-383.
Welz, G. (1991) Streetlife. Alltag in einem New Yorker Slum. Frankfurt: Notizen.
Wolfe, T. (1989) Het geschilderde woord / Van Bauhaus tot ons huis. Amsterdam: Uitgeverij Bert Bakker.
Wuertz, K. (1991) Van geranium tot graffiti. Een visuele antropologie van het wonen. In: P.J.M. Nas and W.J.M. Prins (eds.), Huis, cultuur en ontwikkeling, 61-75. Leiden: DSWO Press.

The houses of foreign gods

Tuomas Martikainen

Many European countries have received a significant influx of immigrants from various non-western societies since the 1950s (Forsander 2002: 16-17). Among other issues, questions relating to culture and religion have become a major thread in the general debate on immigrants (Rex 1994; Ylänkö 2002). Around the continent, immigrants have formed thousands of religious associations, built large numbers of shrines as well as contested social practises in their new host societies at large (Davie 2000: 13-14, 124-126). Europe that seemed to be on the verge of forgetting religion altogether faces suddenly a situation where religion is again a major force in contemporary society. One of the most intense issues with regard to immigrants' religious activity has been the building of mosques and other temples. Local residents have opposed fiercely some building projects and sometimes succeeded in transforming the plans (e.g., Karlsson 2000; Karlsson and Svanberg 1995: 10-12; Martikainen 2000a). At the same time, other religious communities have built their own churches in peace. How is it possible that in the supposedly free religious climate of a 'secularised' Europe, religion can still heat up feelings to the verge of violence?

Buildings and the built environment embody significant symbolic power (Park 1994: 197-199; Raivo 1996: 15-16). Immigration to Europe has mainly been targeted to urban settlements, especially to large cities and metropolitan regions. Thus, changes in the built environment have mostly taken place in urban areas. Many European cities have significant, and also visible, ethnic minorities that have transformed the landscape in the areas where they live and beyond. The contemporary European city is in many ways 'a global village', where many cultures are settled in one place. Even the material dimension bears witness to that in the form of multilingual signs, 'ethnic' dress codes and, sometimes, architecture (e.g., Eade 1997). This fact has not gone unnoticed by the majority population.

In this paper will be presented three cases of building 'houses of foreign Gods' in Finland. The building projects are a Sunni Muslim Islamic Centre, a Vietnamese Buddhist Cultural Centre and a Russian Orthodox chapel, all in the City of Turku in South-western Finland. By comparing these three cases we can see what types of arguments are used in the debate, and what are the practical hindrances in the building process. The paper analyses the cases by setting them into a perspective of global migration and media. It is suggested that these cases can be best understood as examples of the conjunctures of the *global mediascapes* and *ethnoscapes* (Appadurai 1996). Local argumentation draws its material from globally mediated images of religious practises from far away, and implements it to the locality without asking the immigrants in question, whether their activity bears any resemblance to that of the media-based representations. However, there are significant differences in the ways in which different religious traditions are handled. In a particular local community, these processes can be understood in the framework of *glocality*, where the local is seen as the nuclei for the process of globalisation (Robertson 1995).

Globalisation, ethnoscapes and mediascapes

Globalisation has been a major research interest since the late 1980s. The process of globalisation has been defined and understood in a myriad of different ways (Held et al. 1999: 2-10). I shall follow the line of reasoning as suggested by the sociologist Roland Robertson (1992,8):

> Globalization as a concept refers both to the compression of the world and the intensification of consciousness of the world as a whole.

Robertson's refers with 'globalisation' both to the compression of the world - taking place in cultural, economic, political and social processes - and to the creation of a 'global ethos'. The latter point stresses that everyone has become a part of a global humanity and that the Globe has become a meaningful category to understand human relations. The definition also implies that in order to study almost any social relations a global perspective can or will be useful.

A further development of the notion of 'globalisation' has been to view it as 'glocalisation', which means that a significant aspect of the global cultural, economic, political and social processes is to be found in their local manifestations, which ultimately define the particular form of globalisation in question. Glocalisation refers to a particularistic understanding of the process of globalisation. There are no necessary outcomes of the process, but rather a multiplicity of options that happen in the framework of *glocality*. Glocality is the condition of the global-local relations in a local context, where locality itself can be understood in many cases as a result of extra-local and extra-societal processes and action, and, ultimately, that it is a part of and scene for globalisation. The view not only ties developments in local communities to a larger perspective, but it also stresses that localities exist only in relation to the world outside (Robertson 1995).

Global migration and media have been elevated by some researchers to the main carriers of cultural change in the global condition (e.g., Appadurai, 1996; Hannerz, 1996). Arjun Appadurai's (1996: 3, 27-47) model of the global cultural economy takes media and migration as the most central carriers of cultural change that he conceptualises as 'scapes' (originally from land*scape*).[1] The *ethnoscape* refers to the "landscape of persons who constitute the shifting world in which we live: tourists, immigrants, refugees, exiles, guest workers... (Ibid. 33)". The *mediascape* refers to the "distribution of the electronic capabilities to produce and disseminate information ... and to the images of the world created by these media (ibid. 35)". The 'scapes' function largely by their own logic and independent of each other. However, in some cases they meet and produce a joint effect; these conjunctures are profoundly unpredictable. A telling example of the unpredictability of these conjunctures is the responses in the European Union member states to the September 11th 2001 terrorist attacks in New York. While the general response in all cases was immediate and large-scale, it led to highly differentiated reactions in different member states (Allen and Nielsen 2002).

To sum up, in the framework of globalisation contemporary local communities can be defined as glocal spaces. In these glocalities the global ethnoscapes and mediascapes make their encounters or conjunctures in unexpected ways. The specific encounters of global mediascapes and ethnoscapes may produce consequences that are not understandable solely from the context of a particular local community. Furthermore, the particular conjunctures can have further consequences in different localities that are not directly connected to the original one.

Immigration and religion in Finland

Finnish post-war migration patterns in a European perspective
European post-war immigration patterns can be divided into two phases. The first phase lasted from the 1950s to the early 1970s, when Germany, France, Sweden, the United Kingdom and other growing European economies recruited significant numbers of guest labour from abroad. The migrants were mainly from less developing European countries, but also from non-European societies. The latter ones were often from the old colonies of the states in questions. It was at first thought that the migrants would later return to their countries of origin, but this assumption was - in retrospect - wishful thinking. Actually, the migrants not only stayed in their new home countries, but later also brought their wives and children with them (Forsander 2002: 15-19).

The second phase of the post-war migration to Europe started in the 1980s, and was less based on labour migration and more on global

---

[1] The original model includes five different 'scapes' (ethnoscape, technoscape, finanscape, ideoscape and mediascape), but as only the ethnoscape and mediascape are essential for the current study the others are left out.

refugee flows. This has not only changed the type of migrants coming to the continent, but also changed the rhetoric with regard to immigration issues in general. While the debate during the first wave of migration was centred on *economic issues*, the discussion during the second phase is characterised by notions related to *culture and ethnicity*. This reflects the fact that European economies were not as lively as earlier, and also that many of the second phase migrants were from non-western societies. The second phase has also affected many societies that were not immigrant receiving societies in the first phase, including Finland (Forsander 2002: 15-19).

Finland was a country of net emigration during the post-war decades, when almost half-a-million Finns emigrated to Sweden for work. However, Finland became a country of net immigration during the early 1980s and increasingly so in the 1990s. This was due to Finland's changed international position and the collapse of the Soviet Union. During the 1990s Finland's foreign population grew from 21,000 (1990) to 88,000 (2000). Now the immigrant population constitutes circa two percent of total population, and it is estimated to further double in the coming decade or so, depending on economical development. Even though the number of people of immigrant-origin is still relatively small in a European perspective, the change has been very significant in the national context and has created intense interest in questions on immigration, multiculturalism and ethnicity. Issues related to cultural diversity and immigrant populations were before practically unknown in the country (Forsander 2002: 17-18, 25, 63-69).

Migrants to Finland come from several parts of the world, but mostly from regions near by. Even though there are about 160 different nationalities present, some geographical areas and nationalities dominate the general picture (Statistics Finland 2001a). The migrants can be divided into four large groups that also reflect their area of origin:

1) Finnish returnees, who come mainly from Sweden and the former Soviet Union,
2) foreign spouses of mostly European origin,
3) labour immigrants and students mainly from Europe, and
4) refugees, asylum seekers and family reunions from the recent crises regions of the world (the former Yugoslavia, the Middle East, Somalia, Vietnam).

Most of the people of immigrant-origin in Finland are first generation migrants, even though the size and importance of the second generation is growing all the time. Significant differences exist also in how the various groups have adapted to Finnish society (Forsander 2002: 105-126).

The post-war immigration history of Finland is thus twofold. From the 1950s to the 1970s Finns emigrated in large numbers to work abroad, mainly to Sweden. After that Finnish emigration has been much smaller, but Finland has become a target for international migration, especially from the 1990s onwards. This has lead to a level of ethnic diversity previously unknown in the country. Issues related to immigrants have become a central topic in many discussions about life in the country and about the future of the nation. Discussions have also had strong tendency to take culture and ethnicity as central features of the new immigrants, especially the non-Europeans. That is also the general frame in which religious matters have been discussed.

Immigrant religions and media attention
Finland has been fairly homogenous in its religious composition both historically and even in contemporary times. The national Lutheran Church has dominated the religious milieu of the country, even though there has been a small - mainly Protestant Christian - religious plurality since the late nineteenth century, which was supplemented by the so-called New Religious Movements and New Age spirituality from the 1970s onwards. In 2000, 85,1% of the population were members of the Lutherans Church, and only 2,2% belonged to other registered religious organisations. In reality the latter figure is too small, but still no more than about 5% of the population are members of other religious communities. Today, there are over 100 religions active in the country, even though the majority of them are quite small (Heino, 1997).

The establishment of immigrants' religious communities in Finland has happen in two distinct periods. The first period coincided with the time when Finland was a part the Russian Empire (1809-1917). Before that most non-Lutheran forms of religion were illegal in the country. Due to Russian immigration to Finland were established parishes of the Russian Orthodox Church[2] as well as a handful of Jewish and Tatar Muslim congregations. Also some Catholic activity started. All of these were religious communities strictly for the immigrants. Native Finns were not allowed to take part in their activities, not to mention conversion. The Orthodox Church enjoyed a special status, but the Jews and Muslims were merely tolerated. They received official status first after the independence of Finland in 1917. Religious freedom was established in

---

[2] There have been Orthodox Christian Finns ever since the faith was introduced in the region at the turn of the first millennium. However, most of them have lived in eastern parts of the country, and the Orthodox faith was introduced as a distinctly immigrants' faith community in the main part of the country. The situation after the Second World War is more complex, but not of major significance for the current argument. For further information, see Heino 1997: 64-69.

the country in the early 1920s, when also the small Catholic community could officially organise its activities (Heino, 1997: 64, 70-71, 212-215). The second period of the formation of immigrants' religious communities started in the 1980s due to increased immigration. The recent nature of immigration also implies that most of the new immigrants in Finland are first generation migrants, and that second generation issues have only risen to the forefront lately. While we are still lacking basic demographic and organisational knowledge of the migrants' religious communities, it can be stated that the new immigration has resulted in the birth of tens of new religious communities as well as it has affected a large number of previously existing communities. Most of the new immigrant congregations are in cities, as elsewhere in Europe. The largest national immigrant centre is the Helsinki region, where almost half of the migrants live. The rest of them are in other large urban centres, for instance in the Cities of Oulu, Tampere and Turku. Today, immigrants' religious communities belong to the most lively and rapidly growing religious sector in the country (Martikainen, 2000b; Sakaranaho and Pesonen, 1999).

With regard to religious diversity, the increased immigration has brought new elements to the national religious scene. The main development has been the rapid increase of the national Muslim population, which is now the largest new immigrant religion in the country. Today there is circa 20,000 Muslims in Finland and about two dozen apartment mosques. Other groups that have grown due to migration are Lutherans (West Europeans and Ingrians from the former Soviet Union), Orthodox (Russians and Eastern Europeans), Catholics (South Europeans, Iraqis and Vietnamese) and Buddhists (Vietnamese and South East Asians). Also some other minor groups have arrived, including Protestant Christians, Mandaeans, Zoroastrians and Ahl-i Haqq-all from the Middle East (Martikainen, 2000b; Sakaranaho and Pesonen, 1999).

During the 1990s, certain topics having to do with immigrants' religious practises have received significant attention in national media. These include male and female circumcision, ritual slaughtering and the building of religious meeting places. Often Islam has been positioned at the centre of the debate (Martikainen, 2000a: 338-341; Männistö, 1999: 112; Sakaranaho and Pesonen, 1999: 13-15; Sarlin, 1999). Media attention towards immigrants' religious practices is to a large part about what can and what cannot be accepted in Finnish society. This is obvious in the cases of ritual slaughtering and male or female circumcision as these practises conflict with national traditions and to some extent legislation, but it is less obvious with regard to the building of immigrants' prayer halls. There is religious freedom in the country and as long as the communities in question follow national legislation the building of temples, mosques and churches is perfectly legal in Finland.

Controversies that are related to migrants' sanctuary building projects are not unique to Finland. They take place in many other countries as well (Eck, 2001; Karlsson and Svanberg, 1995: 10-12). What makes them especially interesting, is that in all of the places where the controversies take place, already exist a large number of mosques and other temples that have been able to function without greater public controversies. The main difference with the existing and planned shrines is that the previous ones are usually *non-visible* to the outsiders as they are in apartments, abandoned factories and the like. The planned projects, however, tend to be *to-be-visible-landmarks* that would alter the local landscape to some degree. Therefore, the building projects should be viewed as a kind of public architecture that embodies significant symbolic value.

The building of immigrants' shrines in Turku

The City of Turku is the largest urban centre in South-western Finland and the fifth largest city in the country with 175,000 inhabitants in 2002. The local religious field is in many ways close to the national average. The Lutheran Church is dominant, but there is also a rich grass-root level, religious pluralism. Turku is also the second largest national immigrant centre after the capital region and about five percent of the local population have immigrant background. Recently established local immigrant religions include several Christian (Catholic, Orthodox, Protestant), Muslim (Sunni, Shiite) and Buddhist communities, as well as some other minor groups. Remainders of the nineteenth century immigration include Catholic, Orthodox, Jewish and Tatar Muslim congregations (Martikainen, 1996).

The local cityscape includes many religious elements, but as a whole it cannot by any means called distinctly religious. The only significant religious monuments in the cityscape are a couple of large Lutheran churches that dominate a part of the locality's skyline. Immigrants' religious presence is mostly visible in the dress code of certain new immigrants and in the Orthodox and Catholic churches as well as in the Jewish synagogue in the city centre from the first period of immigration to Finland. The careful observer would, of course, find many other religious elements in the city, but by and large they are invisible to the by-passers, and the more so, because they do not stand out because of their architecture or appearance (Martikainen, 2002). Let us move to take closer look at two building projects that challenge the non-visibility of the new immigrants' religious communities. The projects in question are a Sunni Muslim Islamic Centre and a Vietnamese Buddhist Cultural Centre. After that will be shortly presented a less visible, but nevertheless illustrative chapel project of the new Russian Orthodox migrants.

The Sunni Muslim Islamic Centre Project
The local immigrant Muslim population started to grow slowly during the 1980s, and more rapidly since the early 1990s. In autumn 1991, the new migrants took the initiative to organise a place of prayer for themselves. The first meeting places were rooms in the International Meeting Point governed by the Cultural Centre of the City of Turku. As the group continued to grow new possibilities for meeting places were sought and two apartment mosques were founded. The initial division was based on the differences between the Sunna and the Shia. Later both of these communities have been further divided into two, and thus there are now four recent Muslim, apartment mosque communities for the local population of some 3,000 Muslims. Furthermore, there has been living a small group of Tatar Muslims in the city already since the late twentieth century, but they have stayed outside of the recent developments and not had significant contacts with the new Muslims (Martikainen. 2000a).

The Islamic Society of Turku (in Finnish, Turun islamilainen yhdistys ry) was founded in 1993. The society is the largest Sunni Muslim group in the locality and has several hundreds of people attached to it. The group has had its own meeting place since its foundation, but the facilities were not large enough. For example, women did not have the opportunity to take part in the Friday prayer, because of the lack of space. Beside ritual activities the society provides teaching in culture, language and religion. Additional space was also needed for the education of children. The society started a plan to build an Islamic Centre in 1996. The place would include space for a mosque, kindergarten, school, shops, restaurant, festival hall, apartments, library and an exhibition hall. A reservation for land close to central Turku was announced in July 1997. The cultural centre would have become a significant landmark. After the announcement of the land reservation started a heated debate in local media; television and radio programs as well as newspaper reports were done about the matter. The case also made its way to national media. The local debate lasted for a couple of months. A local politician also started a petition against the mosque plan (Martikainen, 2000a).

The debate about the mosque plan can be summarised as follows. After the initial announcement of the plan several letters to the editor were published in the leading local newspaper *Turun Sanomat*. Most of the published letters were critical towards the planned mosque. Various arguments about Islam as a religion were at the core of the debate. Islam was seen as alien in Finnish society and its expansive ideology was considered a threat to the Finnish way of life. Other issues that were mentioned included women's rights, terrorism and the loss of property value in the designated building area. Several writers also stated that the designated place was not suitable, and criticised the planned minaret that would not fit into the Finnish landscape. In other instances also

practical matters about parking problems and increased traffic were mentioned. The Islamic Society of Turku did not participate in the debate, as they considered that it would only make things worse (Martikainen, 2000a).
The society had applied finances from Saudi Arabia, but did not receive them. Thus, the building plan has so far not been finalised, as the organisers have not been able to secure the finances of the project. More recently, the society changed its plans and has expanded its current facilities so that the question of space is not acute anymore. The mosque still functions as an invisible apartment meeting place close to the centre of the city. However, we may expect that some time in the future the issue comes to the fore again and when this happens, we can expect a new debate on the matter. In the local media the issue is taken up every now and then when other similar projects are planned.

The Vietnamese Buddhist Cultural Centre Project
The local Vietnamese community started to take shape in the late 1980s. With regard to religious affiliation, the Vietnamese refugees are mainly Catholics and Buddhists. The Catholics were integrated to the local Catholic parish, but the Buddhists have not had a meeting place of their own. Nor could they receive help of other Buddhist societies as those were very small and did not have any permanent localities for their own use. So far the Vietnamese Buddhists have arranged various events in hired localities (Martikainen, 1996: 118). There are circa 3,000 Vietnamese Buddhists living in Finland, of whom about 10% are settled in the Turku region (Statistics Finland, 2001b: 68). Among the Vietnamese Buddhists rose the idea that they would build a cultural and religious centre that would serve the national Vietnamese Buddhist community. Different places were sought and finally a place close to Turku was found in 2001 where the land was reserved for building a community centre. One reason for the choice of locality was also that leader of the national society lives in Turku (Turun Sanomat, 11.1.2001; Vinh Tuyen, 16.1.2003).
The Vietnamese Buddhist Cultural Centre would be built in three phases: first a cultural centre with a meeting hall, then a *pagoda* - a Buddhist type of religious building - and lastly a tower and gate. The community has even considered applying for the right to build a burial ground next to the complex. The designated place for the centre is an area where there are only few neighbours close by, situated on the outskirts of Turku. That was how the planners wanted it, because they did not want to create any controversies with neighbours. However, people living in the neighbourhood were still worried about the plan and complained about it to the city. The neighbours' motivations to oppose the plan were worries about increased traffic and other practical matters. In late spring 2003

the complaints were dismissed by the city authorities and the plan could then proceed. The community leader hopes that the building process would start in the coming two years. In order to finance the project the local Buddhists have collected money and applied for transnational financing from the Buddhist community in France (Turun Sanomat, 21.12.2000, 11.1.2001, 7.6.2003; Turkulainen, 10.1.2001; Vinh, 16.1.2003).

In comparison to the Sunni Muslim Islamic Centre the Buddhist plan has not created any significant public controversies, but interestingly enough there have been hindrances in the project because of the planned Islamic Centre. A local politician asked for a thorough analysis of the process, because of the mosque controversies (Turun Sanomat, 21.12.2000). The spokesman of the Vietnamese Buddhists stated in a newspaper article that "[m]any Finns ask whether we have noisy services. Only few know that we are very quiet, because our religion is meditative (Turkulainen, 10.1.2001)". Thus the images of the Islamic Centre have affected the way in which the Buddhists are met in the planning process.

The Russian Orthodox Uspenije Chapel
The Orthodox Church of Finland is historically an offshoot of the Russian Orthodox Church, and in many ways it still has close links to its origins. The local parish was founded in the early part of the nineteenth century for Russian officials and migrants the living in the city. After the independence of Finland in 1917 the parish remained a small, mainly Russian and partially Swedish-speaking community, but after the resettlement of Karelians in the post Second World War period the community soon became mostly Finnish speaking. After the independence the church became separate from its mother church (Martikainen, 1996: 65-66; Repo, 1999). The local Finnish Orthodox parish functions in a large area in south-western Finland, of whom almost 60% of its members live in or near the City of Turku. The church's membership was fairly stagnated until the 1990s, but it has risen c. 25 % during the last 10-15 years. The growth in membership has been largely due to immigration from Eastern Europe. The current membership is c. 2,500 and the current members represent several language-groups. Languages used on a regular basis are Finnish, Swedish, Church Slavonic and sometimes Romanian. Sunday service attracts on weekly basis 60-70 people (c. 3%) of the parish members. The parish has two full-time priests of whom the other travels around the parish (Ratilainen 21.11.2002).

In October 2002 Turku received its second Orthodox congregation that functions under the jurisdiction of the Russian Orthodox Church, but also has good relations with the local Finnish Orthodox congregation. At the time a new chapel - called *Uspenije* - was opened that has activities directed towards the new local Russian migrants. The local Russian consulate played a key role in the establishment of the shrine. The chapel is situated next to the consulate and there are services arranged now on a regular basis. The Russian monk in charge of the chapel estimated that the congregation has circa 100 members. In the small chapel are gathered usually 20-30 people. Many local Russians welcomed the chapel as there are certain differences between the Finnish and Russian churches, for example with regard to calendar (Nikita, 31.1.2003).

Local newspapers made small articles about the chapel, but no further debate took place. A feature that is missing from this case is that of finding a suitable building site. The City of Turku had agreed to give the old, small warehouse next to Russian consulate for the congregation's use, but no public debate about the matter took place nor was neighbours consulted. The chapel is not visible from the street nor does it carry any large signs indicated its usage (Nikita, 31.1.2003; Turkulainen, 25.1.2003).

Glocal controversies
The debates on the planned Sunni Muslim Islamic Centre and the Vietnamese Buddhist Cultural Centre in Turku are examples of local events with controversies that cannot be understood from a purely local perspective. Instead a wider view is needed. They are also examples of how contemporary immigrants' religious communities try to make use of transnational connections in order to further their local aims. Both projects have tried to use transnational financial connections - the Muslims from Saudi Arabia and the Vietnamese from France - but neither of the groups has been successful so far. A likely reason for that is that the national migrant populations are still too small when seen from the outside. However, let us now turn back and analyse the two building projects from a glocal viewpoint. In the following analysis the Orthodox chapel, also an immigrant church will provide a different viewpoint to the logic of glocalisation.

The presence of refugees and immigrants in contemporary Finland is based on Finland's changed international position and was made possible by international agreements; both developments related to the globalisation of politics. As contemporary refugee policies can resettle large groups around the world, so Finland has also received people from countries, with which it has traditionally not had much contact, including Muslims from the Middle East and Buddhist from Vietnam. Consequently the new religious minorities have established themselves in the country and started to plan how they could best practise their religion and culture in the social environment. The plans to build mosques and temples are a part of that. Also the growing presence Russians in Finland is related to globalisation, more specifically to the collapse of the Soviet Union and to the rearrangement of political boundaries. The local and national consequences of these developments can be understood as results of the intensification of transnational movement of people or global ethnoscapes that are a part of globalisation.

The discussion about the building plans follows a different logic. The debate on the Sunni Muslim plan was based on popular, stereotyped images of Islam. It had very little to do with the local or national situation of Muslims in Finland, but rather concentrated on images from the global media: terrorism, women's rights and expansionist Islam as seen on television, and mediated by large transnational companies. Furthermore, discussion about the position of Christian minorities in certain Muslim societies was seen as a justification for opposing Islam in Finland. The goals of the local Muslims were understood as an extension of the globally mediated images. Thus the people opposing the project reasoned that if we do not yet have terrorism in the country, the planned mosque would certainly bring it in. Later, the example of the mosque controversy scared some people whether it would create a similar debate, and thus the Buddhist community's project has been made more difficult because of that.

The conjuncture of the global ethnoscapes and mediascapes took first place in the public debate with regard to the planned Islamic Centre. The images presented of Islam were not based on the experience of Muslims living in Finland, but rather on images from the Middle East, the former Yugoslavia and Saudi Arabia. Local actors drew material from far, far away to motivate their actions. The core of the debate was nevertheless local; what can be accepted in Finland and, specifically, in Turku. The idea of a minaret rising in the local skyline was too alien for many participants and was considered a threat towards their way of life. Landscape's symbolic meaning as an embodiment of the Finnish way of life was an undercurrent in the debate.

The Orthodox chapel provides a significant modification to the argument above. Even though the Russian Orthodox are basically facing similar challenges in their religious organisation and practice in Finland than the rest of migrants, their building project did not gain any noteworthy public attention what so ever. The likeliest explanation for this was that Orthodoxy was an already well-known and generally respected religion in the county, which did not provide any threat to local people. In this context it should also be noted that was not always the case, but rather that Orthodox Christianity lived in a rather hostile environment until the 1970s, especially because of its relations to Russia. That the *Uspenije* chapel did not involve public planning was obviously one factor as well, but at this stage I would still argue that it was because of the positive public image of the *Finnish* Orthodox Church that the *Russian* Orthodox community did not face any negative publicity.

The Muslim and the Buddhist building plans are examples of local projects functioning in a glocal structure that neither the locals nor the migrants can control and which may have effects on them. On the one hand, images from the global media are an important factor how local migrants are met and what they are seen to represent. On the other hand, migrants themselves can feel helpless in trying to persuade local inhabitant to see them in a different perspective. Thus, local social reality in connected in many ways to developments taking place elsewhere, which cannot be either controlled or influenced. In this sense local reality is glocal, even though purely local developments also have a role to play. However, as argued with regard to the Russian Orthodox *Uspenije* chapel, we are still faced with a selective local process of which matters become topical. This implies that even though the local community is inherently connected to a wider whole that can be called glocal, the local reasoning and attitudes are, nevertheless, highly significant.

Discussion

In this article was discussed to which extent local realities are embedded in a larger global social reality. The relationship between the local and the global was defined as glocal, to show their deep structural interconnectedness. The empirical cases presented were three building projects of immigrants' religious shrines in the City of Turku in Southwestern Finland: a Sunni Muslim Islamic Centre, a Vietnamese Buddhist Cultural Centre and a Russian Orthodox chapel. In addition to that was given a general picture of the history and contemporary situation of immigrant religions in Finland. The study came to the conclusion that even though the global cultural flows affect local life to a large degree, the local component is still there, even though in sometimes unexpected ways. Globalisation is, thus, a complex process that does not create even conditions in different localities, but rather sets a general structure in which we will find various outcomes.

Global migration flows provide challenges and will continue to do so for urban development in contemporary Europe. Features that were present in most debates concerning 'the houses of foreign Gods' in Turku can be divided into practical and symbolic matters. The practical matters included parking problems, increased traffic and the like, which can be avoided by good planning. The symbolic matters are more difficult though. As some people seem reluctant to see foreign religious symbols to be elevated above their heads, controversies are bound to rise, at least as long as global media feeds stereotyped images of non-Christian traditions and, especially, Islam. An easy solution would be to raise the new shrines to peripheral places, where they are out of sight, but that does not solve the main problem. In my understanding the wish to raise the new monuments from the migrants' point of view has to do with the symbolic acceptance of their presence in society. The question is thus who owns right for the symbolic landscape. How can urban planners take into account the creation 'ethnic landscapes' in the increasingly diversifying Europeans cities? How to integrate architectural monuments to local cityscapes that have their origins in different cultural traditions than the European? Can urban planning help to overcome discriminatory discourses, so easily combined with the planning and the raising of religious shrines originally foreign to the European eye? There just are no simple answers to these questions, but one thing is for sure: they are to be glocally solved.

References:
Allen, C. and Nielsen, J.S.(2002) Islamophobia in the EU after 11 September 2001. Vienna: European Monitoring Centre on Racism and Xenophobia.
Appadurai, A. (1996) Modernity at Large: Cultural Dimensions of Globalization. Minneapolis: University of Minnesota Press.
Davie, G. (2000) Religion in Modern Europe: A Memory Mutates. Oxford: Oxford University Press.
Eade, J. (ed.) (1997) Living the Global City: Globalization as a Local Process. London: Routledge.
Eck, D. (2001) A New Religious America: How A "Christian Country" Has Become the World's Most Religiously Diverse Nation. New York: HarperSanFrancisco.
Forsander, A. (2002) Luottamuksen ehdot: Maahanmuuttajat 1990-luvun suomalaisilla työmarkkinoilla. Helsinki: Väestöliitto.
Hannerz, U. (1996) Transnational Connections. London: Routledge.
Heino, H. (1997) Mihin Suomi tänään uskoo. Helsinki: Wsoy.
Held, D.; McGrew, A.; Goldblatt, D.; Perraton, J. (1999) Global Transformations: Politics, Economy and Culture. Cambridge: Polity.
Karlsson, P. (2000) 'Making Room for Islam – Mosques in Sweden', Nils G. Holm (ed.) Islam and Christianity in School Religious Education,183-202. Åbo: Åbo Akademi.
Karlsson, P.; Svanberg, I. (1995) Moskéer i Sverige: En religionshistorisk studie i intolerans och administrativ vanmakt', Tro and Tanke 1995:7.
Martikainen, T. (1996) Moniarvoinen Turku: Käsikirja uskonnollisista, maailmankatsomuksellisista ja etnisistä yhteisöistä. Religionsvetenskapliga skrifter 32. Åbo: Åbo Akademi.
-, (2000a) 'Muslim Groups in Turku', Journal of Muslim Minority Affairs 20(2) 329-345.
-, (2000b) 'Muslims in Finland: Facts and reflections', Nils G. Holm (ed.) Islam and Christianity in School Religious Education: Issues, approaches, and contexts, 203-247. Religionsvetenskapliga skrifter 52. Åbo: Åbo Akademi.
-, (2002) 'Uskonto kaupunkimaisemassa: esimerkkinä Turku', Lena Marander-Eklund et al. (eds.) Kulturell miljö, natursyn och symboliskt landskap — några aspekter på kulturmiljöstudier, 65-85. Religionsvetenskapliga skrifter 55. Åbo: Åbo Akademi.
Männistö, A. (1999) 'Suomen muslimit lehtikuvissa', Tuula Sakaranaho and Heikki Pesonen (eds.) Muslimit Suomessa, 112-127. Helsinki: Yliopistopaino.

Nikita (31.1.2003) The leader of the Uspenije chapel in Turku. Interview.
Park, C. (1994) Sacred Worlds: An Introduction to Geography and Religion. London: Routledge.
Raivo, P. (1996) Maiseman kulttuurinen transformaatio: Ortodoksinen kirkko suomalaisessa kulttuurimaisemassa. Nordia Geographical Publications Vol 25:1. Oulu: University of Oulu, Department of Geography.
Ratilainen, P. (21.11.2002) The leader of the Finnish Orthodox Parish of Turku. Interview.
Repo, M. (1999) 'Ortodoksinen Suomi', Markku Löytönen and Laura Kolbe (eds.) Suomi: Maa, kansa, kulttuurit. Helsinki: SKS, 290-302.
Rex, J. (1994) 'The Political Sociology of Multiculturalism and the Place of Muslims in West European Societies', Social Compass 41(1) 79-92.
Robertson, R. (1992) Globalization: Social Theory and Global Culture. Sage: London.
-, (1995) 'Glocalisation: Time-Space and Homogeneity-Heterogeneity', Mike Featherstone, Scott Lash and Roland Robertson (eds.) Global Modernities, 25-44. London: Sage.
Sakaranaho, T.; Pesonen, H. (1999) 'Johdanto. Muslimit monikulttuurisessa Suomessa', Tuula Sakaranaho and Heikki Pesonen (eds.) Muslimit Suomessa, 8-22. Helsinki: Yliopistopaino.
Sarlin, T. (1999) 'Muslimit päivälehtien sivuilla', Tuula Sakaranaho and Heikki Pesonen (eds.) Muslimit Suomessa, 128-143. Helsinki: Yliopistopaino.
Statistics Finland (2001a) 'Foreigners and International Migration 2000', Population 2001:8.
Statistics Finland (2001b) 'Population Structure 2000', Population 2001:6.
Turkulainen (10.1.2001) 'Moisioon hankkeissa buddhalaistemppeli'.
Turkulainen (25.1.2003) 'Nikita ja Nikolaus'.
Turun Sanomat (21.12.2000) 'Turkuun aiotaan rakentaa buddhalainen temppeli'.
-, (11.1.2001) 'Buddhalaiselle temppelille varattu tontti Paimalasta'.
-, (7.6.2003) 'Valitukset buddhalaisten rukoushuoneesta hyllytettiin'.
Vinh, T. (16.1.2003) The leader of the Vietnamese Buddhist Society of Finland. Interview.
Ylänkö, M. (2002) 'The two faces of globalization: migration and globalization of cultures', Annika Forsander (ed.) Immigration and Economy in the Globalization Process: The Case of Finland, 10-47. Vantaa: Sitra.

Living the globalising city: globalisation in the context of European urban development.

John Eade

1. Globalisation, Europe and European Cities

Globalisation became a 'buzz word' during the 1990s, both in academic discourse and in the wider world of political and media institutions. The process seemed to refer to something new - the accelerating speed in which people, capital, goods, information and images flowed around the globe and the limited ability of nation-states to control the rapid growth of global flows. Indeed, many governments decided that they had no alternative in an increasingly globalised world but to reform their national practices in order to attract global capital. Socially and culturally the effect of these economic and political forces was to disembed localities (see Giddens 1990), and stretch them out across the globe through the dynamic interplay between global and local which Robertson describes as the process of 'glocalisation'.

Globalisation is not simply an economic process in other words, despite the widespread tendency to equate globalisation with neo-liberal policies pursued by nation-states, global elites and powerful transnational corporations. Furthermore, globalisation is not the same as modernisation or Americanisation. Cross-border flows indicate a more complex process than that indicated by Western-centred models of modernisation and Americanisation. American economic hegemony has been challenged by the emergence of regional transnational formations, such as the European Union, NAFTA and the Pacific Rim. However, the conflict in Iraq during March and April 2003 revealed the limited power of these regional transnational formations. American global military hegemony contrasted sharply with the deep divisions between members of the European Union and the extremely limited ability of even America's closest military ally – the UK – to influence American policy. Although economic globalisation is not the same as Americanisation, the American state's use of its wealth to maintain a vast military-industrial complex enabled it to pursue political and economic interests in defiance of its global competitors. Clearly global flows are shaped by an uneven geometry of power where the USA retains a hegemonic position despite economic competition from the European region.

The growth of the European Union has encouraged debate about what might be distinctive to Europe as a region and European cities in particular. Yet attempts to ground 'Europe' on some essential cultural or political foundations such as Christianity or modernity are belied by historical and contemporary dissension. As Malmborg and Stråth (2002) point out, 'Europe is a contested concept that must appear in the plural' (2002:1). Multiple interpretations have been created:

> Because there has never been such a thing as 'Europe', in an essentialist sense, but only as imaginations. Europe has existed as an invention of states, before the French Revolution of groups of states, and after the Revolution and the Napoleonic Wars by nation states. (2002:3)

Likewise, care must be taken not to produce an essentialist interpretation of European cities. Sophie Body-Gendrot (2000, 2002), for example, is right to point to important, historically rooted differences between American and European cities in such areas as urban civility and citizenship (see also le Galès 2002). However, she runs the risk of setting up a stereotypical and essentialised concept of the European city. Clearly, there are different types of European city – not one essential form of such a city – and these differences are shaped not only by varying local/national histories but also by varying engagements with the American mode of free market capitalism (see Sykes, Palier and Prior 2001). While Body-Gendrot may be correct to talk about *European* cities in contrast to those in the USA (2000: 258), within Europe the differences *between different types* of globalising cities are just as – if not more – important as nation-states engage in diverse ways with global processes.

2. Global Cities, Ordinary Cities and Transnational Urbanism

Debates concerning globalisation and European cities overlap with the discussion about the advantages of describing a select few, e.g. Frankfurt, London and Paris, as 'global cities'. The discussion has been deeply influenced by Sassen through her publications (*The Global City* 1991, *Globalisation and Its Discontents* 1998 and her collaboration with the Globalisation and World Cities Network research team at Loughborough University (UK). Two themes in her work have attracted both support and criticism – firstly, her emphasis on a hierarchy of cities with three at the top (New York, London and Tokyo) and secondly, the growth of a new spatial order shaped by the socio-economic polarisation between global business and financial elites, on the one hand, and the poor who service these elites, on the other. The 'global city' label suggests that a certain place has reached the specific state of being global but, as Marcuse and van Kampen (2000) point out, this suggestion directs us away from examining globalisation as a process where no particular city becomes simply or totally global and the varying impact of global flows on all cities around the world, not just those in such dominant regions as Western Europe, N. America and the Pacific Rim. Globalising cities, therefore, are not the sites for a new spatial order but places where earlier trends, bound up with the history of global capitalism, are reinforced in diverse ways.

These criticisms are echoed in a recent article by Robinson, who points to the Western-centric focus of urban studies, generally, and the global/world cities debate, in particular. She builds on post-colonial critiques and urban anthropology to argue for a variety of perspectives. For example, '[t]he criteria for global significance might well look very different were the map-makers to relocate themselves and review significant transnational networks in a place like Jakarta, or Kuala Lumpur, where ties to Islamic forms of global economic and political activity might result in a very different list of powerful cities' (2002: 539). She points to the lessons we can learn from earlier urban research undertaken by social anthropologists, such as Clyde Mitchell who worked in Central Africa during the immediate post-1945 period. (Vertovec has drawn on Mitchell's model of networks in recent work undertaken by his Transnational Communities Research project at Oxford). As Smith points out in his book, *Transnational Urbanism* (2001), we need to focus on 'mediated differences in the patterns of intersecting global, national and local flows and practices in particular cities' – a task which is far 'more important than cataloguing the economic similarities of hierarchically organized financial, economic, or ideological command and control centers viewed as constructions of a single "agent" – multinational capital (2001: 70). The interplay of transnationalism from above and below produces a complex world of dual identities, multiple homes and a middle ground created by transnational social movements' (2001: 188-89).

I warm to this interpretation, partly because Michael Peter Smith uses some of the ideas I developed with my colleagues at Roehampton and brought together in the book I edited called *Living the Global City* (1997)! More generally, however, his approach accords with the work undertaken by other academics on contemporary London who draw on postmodern and postcolonial approaches to uncover social and cultural links between London and Britain's former colonies, the interweaving of global and local processes developed through political struggles over place and the forging of hybrid, transnational identities. For example, *Edge of Empire* by Jacobs (1996), *New Ethnicities and Urban Culture* (1996) by Back, Alexander's *The Asian Gang* (2000) and the work by Cohen (1997), Gardner (2002), Eade, Garbin and Isabelle Fremeaux (2002) in the 'East End'. They ground the grand theories and debates in careful analysis of local processes and the everyday lives of those who live in London outside of the central business district (the City of London and the West End). What is particularly interesting in Gardner's study of the life course and life histories of Bengali elders in East London (2002) is her exploration of the ambiguities and ambivalences involved in peoples' perceptions of identity.

These reminders of the multicultural diversity of global cities such as London also point to the limitations of the second main theme in Sassen's work – the growth of a new spatial order determined by the polarisation between global elites and the poor servicing those elites. Samers notes three weaknesses in the polarisation thesis – (a) the inadequacy of statistical data concerning the numbers of immigrants within global cities, (b) the limitations of data collected on a national basis given the importance of transnational networks within the global economy and (c) 'the lack of specificity about the timing (not to mention the spacing) of these "causal" (supply/demand) relationships as suggested by Sassen's original thesis' (Samers 2002: 394). With regard to the last point, Gordon and Richardson have argued in the context of urban income data that '"[s]ocial mobility is the real news" (1999: 577).' (2002: 394).

If social mobility is the crucial factor then the multicultural diversity of global cities highlights, in its most vivid form, the presence of diverse forms of social status and lifestyle. Western hierarchies of economic class and social status, shaped by secular modes of consumerism, coexist with non-Western systems of stratification where distinctions may be based around caste and religious traditions, for example. Even among Western hierarchies there are significant alternatives to secular consumerism – most clearly in the former Soviet bloc countries of East Europe, where attachments to the lifestyles of the 'old days' may still be influential, especially the post-Second World War generation.

3. Developing the Middle Ground between Political Economy and Culturalist Approaches

The interweaving of global and local, the interstices of liminal space and the multicultural, plurally stratified character of global cities requires us avoid simplistic dualities between local/global, national/global – a point which Sassen makes in her Foreword to Body-Gendrot's book, *The Social Control of Cities* (2000: xii). We need to develop an analytical framework which draws on both structural political-economy and postmodern interpretations of 'the cultural turn'. This framework is beginning to emerge from the explorations of urban inequality and social justice across local, national and supranational boundaries - see *Cities of Difference* edited by Fincher and Jacobs (1998), *Transnationalism and the Politics of Belonging* written by Westwood and Phizacklea (2000), Tajbakhsh's *The Promise of the City* (2001) and the contributors to the volume edited by Eade and Mele, *Understanding the City* (2002). In these publications due attention to the structural constraints of changing economic systems is balanced by a sensitivity to social difference, subjectivities and identities shaped by the discourses and practices of gender, sexuality, ethnicity, race and class.

As yet there are very few applications of this framework to European cities. However, Cindy Cooper and Christopher Mele have produced a very useful example of how the middle ground between political economy and culturalist approaches can be developed through their recent study of Berlin. I will first draw out their key arguments before making a comparison with another European city – London.

a) Analysing the Middle Ground in a Globalising City: The 'Redevelopment' of Berlin 'East End'

According to Hall's hierarchy of world cities, Berlin can be included within the second level, which is comprised of 'sub-global cities' (see his chapter in this volume). These cities include 'all European capitals apart from the global cities, together with "commercial capitals" (Milan, Barcelona) and major provincial cities in large nation states (Glasgow, Manchester, Lyon, Marseille, Hamburg, etc.)' (Hall in the volume). Berlin's pretensions to become a global city rested not just on its elites' ability to attract business and financial services but on its future as a central political magnet within central Europe. Clearly, this was a future bound up with the expansion of the European Union through the entry of the East European accession states. In fourteen years Berlin had moved from being a city where two political and economic regimes confronted each other to a place where global capital, nation-state institutions and metropolitan agencies were dramatically transforming the political and social life of its citizens. In former East Berlin this process not only entailed the destruction of socialist political and economic institutions but also rapid changes in the physical appearance of this part of the city and in the everyday lives of its inhabitants.

Cooper and Mele analyse this process through a study of redevelopment and the contestation of urban space in an area of former East Berlin – Spandauer Vorplatz. They locate Spandauer Vorstadt's 'redevelopment' within the 'larger vision of a new, united global city' and they analyse a process where '[a]t any given time, the types of motifs, the themes emphasized, and the meanings implied in a selective narrative of development are contingent on not only state interests and corporate objectives but the changing qualities of the lived city itself', i.e. a 'complex *middle ground* between selective narratives of development and everyday practices (not one or the other *but the relationships between them)*' (2002: 298-99, italics in the original). They draw on Urry's work on visualisation and the gaze to examine gazing as both discursive, everyday practices 'implicated in the redevelopment agenda' and 'instrumental to an entire range of sociospatial or material processes of urban redevelopment - from producing new places to targeting new forms of place consumption' (2002: 299-300).

Spandauer Vorplatz was 'seen' by the city's political, administrative and business elites as a part of an old socialist world ripe for a modernising redevelopment, which would make use of certain 'positive' images and historical traces. Jewish heritage would be preserved in order to attract tourists and newcomers from abroad and 'upscale, new businesses such as ateliers, galleries, and computing services' were encouraged to attract 'the young entrepreneurs of the New Berlin who were envisioned to populate the "revived" area' (2002: 301). Squatters involved in the alternative artist scene, on the other hand, were threatened with eviction after the expiry of 'the Grosskunsthaus rent-free occupancy agreement with the city' and after several years of struggle they were forced to agree to a corporate-sponsored rent scheme. An elite vision of a young, cosmopolitan artistic world, suffused with a Jewish past and the memory of the Weimar Republic's cabaret nightlife, looked past, co-opted or transformed the survivals of a more recent past – the locality's older residents, their shops (e.g. *Konzumen* and *Tante Emma Laden*) and public spaces. The older residents resisted this vision in their everyday practices but clearly they were fighting a continual rearguard action against the powerful forces, which linked the city's elites to national, transnational and global processes.

Those brought up in the everyday world of former East Berlin and the squatters who had arrived from former West Berlin after the Berlin Wall came down shared a common position – their lives were determined in crucial ways by the power of others, e.g. wealthy cosmopolitan newcomers, city politicians and planners, real estate companies, the police and sanitation departments and - at further remove - the national and global elites who wished to invest in the 'new' Berlin. National and municipal governments 'have become increasingly entrepreneurial in their efforts to promote urban developments' through a process of gazing, which engages with 'ordinary and quotidian practices within the city' (2002: 307).

So what Cooper and Mele are describing is a process of colonisation where capitalist elites encourage the development of a consumerist local society which marginalises those attached to the 'old order' of former East Berlin. Although those brought up in the old order are unable to stop their locality being physically changed, they may well maintain rhythms of everyday life based on pre-1989 differences of lifestyle and status. In other words they resist the total colonisation of their world by the new consumerism, the new entrepreneurs and wealthy settlers. Two systems of stratification co-exist, even if one is more powerful in the public arena than the other. If social mobility is the key issue in the global city debate, then in this globalising city the main substantive issue is the degree to

which the children and the grandchildren of those brought up in the 'old order' adopt the lifestyles and status distinctions of consumer society. What will be the language of social distinction and the everyday markers of status which they will create? Who will be their role models? How will they contribute to the changing landscape of their locality through engaging with and shaping globalising forces?
Structuralist understandings of state and capital fail to grasp this colonisation process adequately – hence the emphasis by Cooper and Mele on a middle ground perspective which:

> contends that the multiple forms of everyday practices and flexible redevelopment strategies exist in dialogic interaction with each other. It is only through an analysis of these interactions that we can say something about both the relevance and meaningfulness of everyday practices to urban redevelopment (2002: 307).

b) Analysing the Middle Ground in a Global City: London's East End
The co-existence of different systems of stratification is even more striking in London. Although this plurality is shaped by the arrival of migrant workers from around the globe, this is not the complete story. As in Berlin older modes of social distinction influence the everyday lives of local residents who trace their ancestry back to migrants from the surrounding English countryside or other areas of the United Kingdom.
The changes in London's socio-economic order have been even more dramatic than in Berlin. London's economy has long been determined by services but industrial production also played a significant role until the 1970s. By the 1950s subtle distinctions between grades of workers were accommodated within a discourse of class cultures, which were etched onto the physical differences between a heavily upper and middle class 'West End' and a predominantly working class 'East End' (see Eade 2000). During the 1970s the socio-economic structures informing this discourse began to collapse. The process was partly driven by London's position as a 'global city'. This position rested on the ability of the City of London's business elite to attract a large share of footloose global capital, building on a structure of international business and finance networks shaped by empire and continuing connections with Commonwealth countries.
However, these historic links were combined with a responsiveness to changes in global capital flows – a responsiveness encouraged by central government. After winning the 1979 general election, Conservative leaders supported the redevelopment of the docks to the east of the City of London as an extension of the City's service industry. A new social and economic order was rapidly built up in 'Docklands', stretching along the Thames across the boroughs of Tower Hamlets,

Newham and Southwark was transformed largely for the benefit of financial and business services competing nationally and transnationally for global flows of capital, personnel, information and ideas (see Budd and Whimster 1992; Butler and Rustin 1996; Church and Frost 1998; Foster 1999). The decline of the white working class was offset by the arrival of new middle class residents, with a resultant modification of long-standing debates concerning inequality and social justice. This modification was also shaped by the growing power of overseas settlers, especially those from Bangladesh who established a major presence in wards to the north of Docklands. The issue of inequality of inequality and justice had to be formulated in ways which more openly acknowledged and engaged with the history of non-class differences and their contemporary influence (see Forman 1989l; Eade 1989, 1997, 2000; Cohen 1996, 1997; Jacobs 1996).

The creation of 'Docklands' resulted in a sharp social and economic division within Tower Hamlets, where Canary Wharf rose up to dominate the local landscape and physically demonstrate the transition from an older industrial society to a new world represented by the new middle class and wealthy elites who were employed in the service sector. In the north of Tower Hamlets remnants of the old industrial order survived and were sustained, ironically, not by the old white working class but by Bangladeshi settlers. At the same time Bangladeshis contributed to the expansion of the service sector (retail and wholesale clothing and food shops, taxis, travel agencies and white collar, private professional services and public sector jobs) but at its more insecure and less well-paid levels.

Bangladeshis were drawn, therefore, into the class system both structurally and culturally. At the same they retained – in varying degrees – attachments to their country of origin where economic class and social status were shaped by different traditions. Anthropologists have long reminded us of the different socio-economic contexts from which migrants have come and their continuing, if weakening, economic and social investment with those contexts. Katy Gardner (1995, 2002), in particular, has shown how migration to Britain and the Middle East has shaped the social and economic strategies of families dependent on rural landholdings in Sylhet, the Bangladeshi district from which most have migrated. Although relatively poor in terms of Britain's urban economic structure, many migrants have been able to improve the social status and economic fortunes of their families within Sylhet. During the late 1980s and 1990s this strategy may have come under strain as Bangladeshis settled permanently in Tower Hamlets and elsewhere. However, recent research on marriage arrangements indicates a continuing social and economic investment through the maintenance of transnational exchange and alliance ties between families in Britain and

Sylhet (Samad and Eade 2002). Since the vast majority of Bangladeshis are Muslims Islamic traditions play a key role in marriage arrangements and the younger second and third generation are sensitive to Islamist critiques of Western secular 'decadence' (see Eade and Garbin 2000). In other words, we are dealing with a transnational context where different notions of inequality and social justice interweave and influence each other. Bangladeshi needs in terms of British welfare discourses and practices have to be understood in this wider context. At the same time this context is itself changing as Bangladeshi families invest socially and economically more and more within British urban localities as this change in response to national, transnational and global processes. Across Tower Hamlets' neighbourhoods of the transnational, global city, therefore, a socially and economically diverse population of Bangladeshi residents encounter a complex world where social mobility cannot be understood solely in Western terms. As in Berlin, secular consumerism and the lifestyles of wealthy people within the service sector have enormous influence over those brought up in different traditions. However, it is clear that older residents in former East Berlin and the first generation of Bangladeshi settlers remain attached to alternative ways of assessing social prestige. Yet, as the urban landscape is altered by the impact of global capital the younger generations are encouraged to abandon the old ways and compete for jobs within the service sector. Empirical research is needed to uncover what is happening, the extent to which the old orders are fading away and what alternatives to consumer society may be emerging.

Conclusion
In this chapter I have argued that discussions of globalisation and globalising cities in the European context should explore the middle ground between the structural and cultural interpretations which dominate the field. Analyses of the flows of people, goods and capital between European cities by urban planners and political economy investigations of the socio-economic structure of urban centres take us only so far. As the critique of Sassen's global city work shows, they fail to reveal the complexity of urban society. We have to go beyond her influential polarisation thesis to investigate the 'real news' – social mobility – but, in so doing, we have to consider the meanings through which people make sense of their everyday worlds. Political economy and cultural interpretations have to be brought together if we are to reveal the plurality of those meaning systems. When we consider the relationship between economic class and social status, we must avoid a western-centric model and explore the co-existence of more than one hierarchy of social differentiation, especially in our globalising cities.

Recent publications show how such a middle ground can be uncovered and analysed and I have drawn on one such example by Cooper and Mele to make a comparison between Berlin and London. The main points emerging from this comparison are as follows:

1. More than one system of social stratification and mobility operates in these European cities, despite the significant differences between the two cities, such as the deeper impact of global flows of finance and people across central London. Consumerism and the service sector are clearly dominant but alternative modes of social distinction are present – in the case of Berlin, a mode shaped by the lifestyles and everyday practices of former East Berlin, while in London settlers from Britain's former empire, for example, maintain attachments to their country of origin which offer other ways of life and social differentiation. Western-centric models of economic class and social status have not allowed for this plurality. An openness to the structural constraints of the expanding service has to be balanced, therefore, with a sensitivity to multicultural diversity, whether this comes from a fading socialist order or a rural society in South Asia.
2. The plurality of social differentiations raises the question – what does social mobility mean to people in their everyday lives? More research is needed to answer this question adequately but the evidence already available suggests that the colonisation of local lives and local space by consumerism and the service sector does not go unchallenged in these two cities' East Ends. At the same time the influence of older lifestyles and social distinctions on the younger generations in both localities may be weakening. Yet, in the case of young Bangladeshi Muslims, Islamist critiques of secular consumerism offer fresh alternatives and shape the everyday lives of at least some of them.
3. Although I have used the term 'global city' to refer to London, the discussion suggests that 'globalising cities' may be a more useful term to explore what is taking place within both cities. 'Global city' is useful because it indicates the greater degree to which Londoners' everyday lives and social distinctions are influenced by global flows of capital, people, goods, information and ideas when compared with Berlin. However, the term suggests that the process of globalisation has been completed in a specific place – the dominant regions of Western Europe, N. America and the Pacific Rim. As I noted at the beginning of this chapter, Marcuse and van Kampen remind us that no particular city becomes simply or totally global and that we must attend to the world-wide character of the process rather than focus on a few 'Alpha cities'. The use of the

'European city' can also result in the reification and essentialisation of place. Berlin and London may territorially share a European space but the discursive constructions of that space and the events taking place within it are multiple and contradictory, reflecting different histories and diverse contemporary engagements with global flows.
4. Finally, the nation-state plays a crucial in shaping these different histories and contemporary engagements. The 'redevelopment' of London's docks was ruthlessly pursued in the 1980s not only by business elites but also by a government determined to encourage the expansion of the service sector. During the 1990s Conservative and Labour leaders shared the view that London must be open to global flows in order to compete with its European rivals such as Frankfurt, Paris and Amsterdam. The role of nation-state in Berlin's redevelopment is not very evident in the analysis by Cooper and Mele. However, since there are significant differences in approach towards globalisation between the British and German governments, these differences may have influenced what happened in Spandauer Vorplatz – if only indirectly.

Clearly, more research needs to be undertaken but, in my view, we have reached an exciting stage where we can frame this research in terms of the middle ground between political-economy and culturalist interpretations.

References:
Alexander, C. (2000) The Asian Gang, Oxford: Berg.
Back, L. (1996) New Ethnicities and Urban Culture, London: UCL Press.
Body-Gendrot, S. (2000) The Social Control of Cities: A Comparative
 Perspective, Oxford and Malden, Mass: Blackwell Publishers.
Budd, L. and Whimster, S. (eds) (1992) Global Finance and Urban Living: A
 Study of Metropolitan Change, London and New York: Routledge.
Butler, T. and Rustin, M. (eds) (1996) Rising in the East? London: Lawrence and
 Wishart.
Church, A. and Frost, M. (1998) 'Trickle down or trickle out: job creation and
 work-travel impacts of Docklands regeneration', Rising East 2 (2) 73-103.
Cohen, P. (1996) 'All white on the night?: Narratives of nativism on the Isle of
 Dogs', in Butler, T. and Rustin, M. (eds) Rising in the East? London:
 Lawrence and Wishart, 170-96.
-, (1997) 'Out of the melting pot into the fire next time: Imagining the East
 End as city, body, text' in S. Westwood and J. Williams (eds), Imagining
 Cities: Scripts, Signs, Memory, London and New York: Routledge.
Cooper, C. and Mele, C. (2002) 'Redevelopment as contingent process:
 Implicating everyday practices in Berlin's renewal', City and Community 1
 (3) 291-311.
Eade, J. (1989) 'The Politics of Community: The Bangladeshi Community in East'
 London, Aldershot: Ashgate.

-, (ed.) (1997) 'Living the Global City: Globalisation as Local Process', London and New York: Routledge.
-, (2000) Placing London: From Imperial Capital to Global City, Oxford and New York: Berghahn Books.
-, and Garbin, D. (2002) 'Changing narratives of violence, struggle and resistance: Bangladeshis and the competition for resources in the global city', Oxford Development Studies 30 (2) 137-50.
-, Fremeaux, I. and Garbin, D. (2002) 'The political construction of diasporic communities in the global city' in P. Gilbert (ed.), Imagined Londons, Albany: State University of New York Press.
-, and Mele, C. (2002) Understanding the City: Contemporary and Future Perspectives, Oxford and Malden, Mass: Blackwell Publishers.
Fincher, R. and Jacobs, J. (1998) Cities of Difference New York: The Guilford Press.
Forman, C. Spitalfields: A Battle for Land, London: H. Shipman.
Foster, J. (1999) Docklands: Cultures in Conflict, Worlds in Collision, London: UCL Press.
Gardner, K. (1995) Global Migrants, Local Lives: Travel and Transformation in Rural Bangladesh, Oxford: Clarendon Press.
-, (2002) Age, Narrative and Migration: The Life Course and Life Histories of Bengali Elders in London, Oxford and New York: Berg.
Giddens, A. (1990) The Consequences of Modernity, Cambridge: Polity Press.
Gordon, P. and Richardson, H. (1999) Review essay: 'Los Angeles, city of angels? No, city of angles', Urban Studies 36 (3) 555-91.
Jacobs, J. Edge of Empire: Postcolonialism and the City, London and New York: Routledge.
Le Galès, P. (2002) European Cities: Social Conflicts and Governance, Oxford: Oxford University Press.
Af Malmborg, M. and Stråth, B. (eds) (2002) The Meaning of Europe, Oxford and New York: Berg.
Marcuse, P. and van Kampen, R. (eds) (2000) Globalizing Cities: A New Spatial Order?, Oxford, UK and Malden, US: Blackwell Publishers
Robertson, R. (1992) Globalization, London: Sage.
Robinson, J. (2002) 'Global and world cities: a view from off the map', International Journal of Urban and Regional Research 26 (3) 531-534.
Samad, Y. and Eade, J. (2003) Community Perceptions of Forced Marriage, London: Foreign and Commonwealth Office Community Liaison Unit.
Samers, M. (2002) 'Immigration and the global city hypothesis: towards an alternative research agenda', International Journal of Urban and Regional Research 26 (2) 389-402.
Sassen, S. (1991) The Global City, Princeton: Princeton University Press.
-, (1998) Globalization and Its Discontents. New York: The New Press.
Robertson, R. Globalization, London: Sage.
Smith, M.P. (2001) Transnational Urbanism: Locating Globalization, Oxford: Blackwell.
Sykes, R., Palier, B. and Prior, P. (eds) (2001) Globalization and European Welfare States, Basingstoke: Palgrave.
Tajbakhsh, K. (2001) The Promise of the City: Space, Identity and Politics in Contemporary Social Thought. University of California Press.
Westwood, S. and Phizacklea, A. (2000) Transnationalism and the Politics of Belonging, London and New York: Routledge.

Globalisation, Eyes and Urban Space: Visual Perception of Globalising Prague

Jana Temelová, Hedvika Hrychová

Prague, the capital of the Czech Republic, has been significantly changed during the transition period. Since 1989 transformation processes have influenced the urban structure of the city. The capital has opened itself to foreign investors, immigrants and tourists as well as to plural life styles and cultural patterns coming from the Western World. In Prague, similarly to other main cities, internationalisation and globalisation shape not only the everyday life of its inhabitants, but also the whole social and functional pattern of the city. Double transition, consisting of transformational and global processes has not affected all parts of the city equally. Thus, the spatially selective manner of these processes contributes to the social, economic and spatial differentiation of Prague.

Globalisation and its impact on cities have been recently a popular topic discussed in literature. Even though many conclusions have been based on statistical analysis we wonder if the given results could be confirmed by pure observation of actors, their activities and physical settings in urban space. Our purpose is to find out whether the impact of globalisation has its visual reflection in urban environment and whether it is possible to spot its spatial inequality.

Globalisation and Cities: the Socio-spatial Dimension

Internationalisation, globalisation, new spatial organisation of production as well as deindustrialisation in advanced economies hangs tightly together with formation of global cities. Geographical decentralisation of production has led to the spatial dispersion of economic activities but at the same time to the need of centralisation of command structures and control functions (Friedmann 1995). Sassen (1991) believes that a new role has been opened for major cities as for the sites where decision-making activities internationalised advanced services and innovations are generated and concentrated. Accordingly, a new hierarchy of urban centres has been created on the global level. The cities occupying the top position in the hierarchy - the global cities - are seen as the centres of power and control over the world economy. While there is a broad consensus that New York, London and Tokyo lead the world city hierarchy the ordering under this top level is unstable and a subject to a fierce competition (Castells 1996, 290).

Nevertheless, the concept of global cities has not been the only one describing the contemporary socio-spatial urban configuration and besides also the notion of globalising cities and networks has appeared to challenge the global city framework (Yeoh 1999). Not just global cities, as Smith (1998, 608) suggested, but "all cities can be viewed in the fullness of their particular linkages with the worlds outside their boundaries". Similarly, Marcuse and van Kempen (2000) assumed that the organisation of urban space differs from city to city nevertheless almost every urban structure has been affected by the same trends. Yet, the extent and the manner of global influence is not identical everywhere. The creation of integrated world system and the production of global cities have created social, economic and spatial inequalities not only among the cities but also within the cities (Hall 1998).

Sassen (1991) regards the impacts of economic restructuralisation on labour market as one of the main sources of social polarisation witnessing in global cities. Highly polarised labour market, which has been created, has resulted in sorely unequal distribution of incomes and opportunities in global cities (Hall 1998). In this regard Sassen (1996, 632) emphasised that beside the highly paid professionals operating in producer services "in day-to-day work of the leading services complex dominated by finance a large share of the jobs involved are low paid and manual, many held by women and immigrants". Thus, whilst a small group of managers and specialists forms a new social elite, a number of manual workers, people with temporary jobs, unstable incomes and unemployed extends the lowest social classes. Moreover, King (1995) accentuated the important role of international migration since transnational professionals, Third World migrants and tourists often choose large cities as their destinations. Accordingly, different cultures weave one another and create a multicultural environment in these sites.

The economic globalisation and the expansion of producer services have significantly effected the spatial organisation of cities and have contributed to the selective development of urban space. Thanks to the capability of internationalised service sector and its ancillary activities (such as top-of-line restaurants and hotels) to generate extremely high profits these sectors dominate the competition for space, resources and investment in the attractive central parts of large cities (Sassen 1996). Consequently, economic activities with moderate and low profit-making capacities (such as manufacturing, low-value added services, trade) have been displaced into the less popular parts of cities, often to the outskirts, or became a part of informal economy (Sassen 1996). Considering Sassen's (1996, 634) remark referring to "replacement of neighbourhood shops tailored to local needs by upscale boutiques and restaurants catering to new high-income urban elite" the local population is the one who might be the most concerned with the new situation. Accordingly, richer employees of producer services have been slowly drawing out the original and often poorer inhabitants. The coexistence of two fundamentally distinct social classes in the cities leads to the creation of quartered city (Marcuse/van Kempen 2000).

Portes and Sassen (1993, 475) pointed out that "high-income residential and commercial gentrification accompanies sharp decay in low-income communities" in global cities. The fact that specific economic activities and certain groups of people prefer the city centre for their operation has its positive impact in revitalisation of some central and inner city neighbourhoods. On the other hand deterioration of certain urban zones, namely abandoned brownfields, has occurred in many particularly former industrial cities. Nevertheless, in the last 20 years some of these declining inner city areas have been successfully redeveloped.

Concerning the physical environment, Sassen (1996) conceived that international firms and business people, those who she called the new city users, have significantly marked the urban landscape (airports, top-level business districts, top-of-the-line hotels and restaurants etc.). But at the same time Knox (1996, 609) emphasised that urban space is not produced purely by global forces and flows but by their interaction with specific cultures and local settings. Similarly, Beauregard and Haila (2000) concluded that contemporary city reflects not only global trends but also processes associated with the past which had shaped the modern (Fordist) city.

What Makes the Impact of Globalisation Visual?

In this paper we will focus on the observation of several localities in Prague which we consider to be significantly influenced by globalisation. Marcuse and van Kempen (2000) would label this type of places as "soft locations". Even though the global forces and flows are present in a number of urban realms, we will consider especially their reflection in social, spatial and physical environment of Prague. Thereby we will omit some other not less important effects of globalisation in for example political, cultural or ecological sphere. Our purpose is to demonstrate that some of the impacts and consequences of global processes witnessed in large urban centres and discussed in literature could be spotted also in Prague just by looking at actors, their actions and physical settings in certain neighbourhoods. Further, based on our observations we want to show that global processes do not effect all the selected localities to the same extent and in the identical way.

Accordingly, we will try to find the answers to the following questions:
- Is the impact of globalisation on urban space visually distinct so that we can spot it by eyes?
- Can we see that globalisation does not influence different localities within the city equally?

Hannerz (1993) identified the most important categories of people who create the transnational manner of world cities. These categories include:
- *Managerial elites*, highly educated and skilled professionals and managers are one of the most conspicuous actors in world cities. Even though the locals form their majority, many of them are foreigners since their occupational career mobility is combined with geographical mobility.
- Third world population consists largely, but not entirely, of people involved in low-skill and low-wage jobs. Thereby they usually occupy the opposite end of scale from transnational managers.
- *Expressive specialists* form a smaller group of people who are concerned with culture and specialise in expressive activities (art, fashion, design, filmmaking, writing, music, cuisine etc). They maintain a high profile in world cities.
- *Tourists* are always present in considerable numbers. They are actively engaged in the transnational flows of culture by being mobile themselves.

We believe that the major part of the above mentioned transnational categories is visually recognisable in Prague, nevertheless the frequency of particular groups varies in different urban areas and thus indicates unequal extent to which different places are globalised.

Social polarisation is frequently mentioned as a product of economic globalisation and expansion of producer services. Two crucial social groups are primarily involved in polarisation: those of highly paid managers and professionals and, on the other end of the income spectrum, those of manual, low-wage workers, unemployed and homeless. We expect that these antithetic social groups are in evidence in selected localities and thereby make the social polarisation visible in Prague.

Multicultural and cosmopolitan environment are other relevant features of global cities, which we believe, have visual implications in social and physical background. As Jencks (1996) emphasised, heterogeneity in terms of ethnic variety, diversity of economic activities and "lifestyle clusters" is typical for global cities. Even though certain signs of cosmopolism, multiculturalism and coexistence of different activities and styles appear in Prague we do not think it has reached the level common in large urban centres.

Linking up to the transnational categories identified by Hannerz (1993), King (1995) tried to point out how these groups represent themselves in spatial and built environment of cities. He brought forward that transnational business class and tourists create cityscape which could be the best described by Zukin's term "landscapes of power". He presumed that institutions of international business class (such as headquarters, banks, hotels, corporate offices) "reproduce transnational symbolic forms and styles" of the same institutions in hegemonic states (King 1995, 225). We suppose that managerial elite is the most conspicuous and distinct class in built and spatial environment of Prague since it has the power and resources to mark the cityscape. We believe that the environment has been visibly adapted to the needs of managerial elite in some of the areas we selected.

Further, King (1995) remarked that Hannerz omitted two groups which are also significant in large cities: the first one of academics and scholars and the second one of practitioners of architecture and urban design. King (1995, 226) sees the architects and urban designers as those who "provide the surface representations" and thus considers them to be "some of the main brokers in the economy of signs in the world city". The global architectural elite, who designs buildings of international institution, helps to reproduce their symbolic forms and styles (King 1995). Although we actually hardly spot international architects by their appearance we can easily distinguish their products - constructions which contribute to create the "landscapes of power".

Sassen (1996) brought forward that it has been increasingly difficult for activities generating low or moderate profits to compete for space and investment. Therefore services and shops aimed to the locals have been replaced by those oriented on the needs of high-income urban elites. We suppose that uneven frequency of particular transnational categories in different neighbourhoods has its outward reflection in built form as well as in functional organisation of space. Therefore we believe that we can visually distinguish the dominance of internationalised companies and appropriated services in some localities while in other rather local firms, shops and services tending vernacular inhabitants prevail. We believe that it is feasible to spot uneven development in various neighbourhoods by observation of social, physical and functional environment, its actors and elements. Even though all the localities we selected could be qualified as „soft spots" (Marcuse/van Kempen 2000) we expect that the global forces do not effect all of them to the same extent.

Double Transition Shaping the Urban Environment of Prague

Prague, the capital of the Czech Republic has roughly 1,2 million inhabitants and its position in the national urban system is undoubtedly dominant. Since the iron curtain fell down the Czech Republic has opened itself to the world trends, foreign actors and capital flows. Compared to the rest of the country, Prague metropolitan area shows an exceptionally high attraction, importance and development potential (relatively high concentration of investment, foreign capital and producer services, fast development of service and construction sector). Therefore, Prague is

regarded as a gateway city. A complex of processes termed as double transition has affected the social, economic and physical structure of the city. Double transition includes (Sýkora 2001):
- Local transition (Central and Eastern European) to market economy and democratic policy-making, the openness to world economy.
- Global transition (common for cities around the World) caused by economic globalisation and its impact on local political, economic, social as well as cultural restructuring.

Although the both components of double transition – the global and the local – have been affecting all the sectors and regions in the country their influence has been neither spatially equal nor of the same intensity. Since the impact of globalisation on cities has been already discussed earlier in the paper now we will shortly draw our attention to the local transition. The local transition consists of a wide range of transformation processes, which has led to the political, economic and social restructuring of the Czech society and space. Democratisation and decentralisation of state administration has brought the self-government to regional and local authorities. The economic restructuring meant a shift to the Western model with the consequent occurrence of deindustrialisation and tertiarisation. The employment in business services, FIRE sector and services oriented on foreign tourists has risen up rapidly especially in Prague. The Czech society became more differentiated (esp. by income) than it had been during the forty-year long period of nivelisation. Together with the coming plurality of life styles these trends led to the socio-spatial differentiation of the Prague metropolitan area.

Sýkora (1996) suggested, that the most visible processes of change in physical, functional and socio-spatial structure of Prague have been:
- commercialisation of the city centre
- revitalisation of some inner city neighbourhoods (commercialisation, gentrification)
- residential and commercial suburbanisation in outer city.

The socio-spatial structure of Prague has been changed fundamentally and we can expect further changes in the future since a considerable share of rents has not been deregulated yet. While the full deregulation of rents (together with continuation of current trends) might bring revitalisation and gentrification to some inner-city neighbourhoods, deterioration and decay might strike another inner-city localities as well as some of the suburban housing estates areas.

Selection of Soft Locations in Prague

Marcuse and van Kempen (2000) identified urban locations, "soft locations", in which globalisation and postfordism seem to have a particular impact. The nine soft locations include:

1. Waterfronts
2. Centrally located manufacturing locations
3. Brownfields
4. Central city office and residential locations
5. Central city amusement and tourist locations
6. Concentrations of social housing
7. Locations on the fringe of CBD
8. Structures of historic meaning
9. Public spaces

Using the concept of soft locations we selected seven spots in Prague which we consider to be appropriate for demonstrating the impacts of globalisation on urban space. The localities are situated in three different city zones - two in the city centre, three in the inner city and two in the outer city.

1. Na Příkopě
The first of the selected places is located on the shopping street Na Příkopě in the Prague's CBD. Therefore we assume it can be described both as a *Central city office and residential location* and a *Central city amusement and tourist location.* Considering the fact that Prague historical core is a part of the UNESCO cultural heritage this locality may be also included to the *Structures of historic meaning.*
2. Národní třída metro station
The central-city soft spot is a traffic junction. It is situated on a noisy street, by the entrance to the underground station, adjacent to a tram stop and a department store. It can be rank as a *Central city office and residential location* as well as a *Central city amusement and tourist location.*
3. Vinohrady
This locality represents a *Location on the fringe of CBD.* It is an inner-city neighbourhood where gentrification has occurred. Although the character of neighbourhood is primarily residential, Vinohrady has undertaken a shift from residential to business use during the transition period.
4. Anděl
Anděl is one of the four inner-city areas, which the strategic plan identified as a new developing centre of polycentric Prague. It is a traffic junction. The area is an example of a large *Brownfields* redevelopment – new polyfunctional buildings have been constructed on the place of abandoned industrial sites.

5. Karlín – Křižíkova metro station
There are many similarities in the character of Anděl (the locality described above) and this soft location. Karlín is also one of the inner-city neighbourhoods where the CBD functions have been expanding to in recent years. Compared to Anděl, the *Brownfields* redevelopment has more often the form of reconstruction than predominantly new construction of commercial space.

6. Letňany housing estate
As the locality represents a housing estate on the fringe of Prague it the best fits to the type *Concentration of social housing*. However, we have to admit that we do not find the term *Concentration of social housing* suitable for any area in Prague notably because the process of socio-spatial differentiation has not fully progressed yet. Unlike Marcuse and van Kempen we suppose that housing estates in double transition cities have not been considerably influenced by globalisation so far.

7. Regional shopping centre Černý Most
We chose this suburban, housing estate location because we are convinced that the area has undertaken a fundamental change during the double transition period. The regional shopping and entertainment centre and many other retail facilities have recently grown up next to the highway and metro station. It is obviously not just a *Concentration of social housing*.

Marcuse and van Kempen (2000) did not identify any suburban areas as soft locations. One of the reasons might be that suburbanisation, originally a process of modernity and Fordism, has been already well developed in Western cities. However, in the cities experiencing double transition the suburban structures are being created now and their character is similar to the contemporary form of Western suburbs. Thus, the trends of modernity are concurrent with global trends in postsocialist cities.

Approach to Observation and Urban Elements under the Lense
We carried out several empirical observations in the seven selected soft locations. For each area two separate observations were accomplished, both during the working days nevertheless varying as to the time of day. We focused especially on the following three matters:
- People (e.g. age, sex, social group, visage, nationality, family status).
- Activities (e.g. social contacts, reason of one's presence in the locality).
- Physical setting (e.g. condition of buildings, public space, communications, structure of shops and companies, quality of cars).

We divided the observed people into fifteen categories for a detailed elaboration (see Table 1). For a broad view we grouped the fifteen categories into three clusters according to people's presumable life styles and occupational and income structure (all based on our visual experience). Thus, we distinguished upper strata (categories 1,2,3), middle strata (categories 4,5,7,12) and lower strata (categories 6,8,9,10,11,13,14,15). We intentionally did not call these clusters "classes" since social classes could be defined primarily in terms of their relation to production (Johnston – Gregory – Smith, 1994). From our point of view yuppies belong to upper strata. Similarly, Hannerz (1993) talked about "managerial elites" who can be hardly included to middle strata.

Table 1: 15 categories of observed people

1	male workers in advanced services - managers and professionals in suits
2	female workers in advanced services, fancy ladies with boutique paper bags
3	tourists, foreigners
4	ordinary and grey looking people
5	mothers with small kids
6	Pensioners
7	school-kids
8	working class and lower class looking people
9	cleaning workers, messengers, taxi drivers, security workers, gate-keepers
10	manual and construction workers
11	Gypsies
12	non-conformists (e.g. unconventional outlook, hippies, dreadlocks hair style)
13	fops, dandies, sparks, street-girl outlook, gay outlook
14	street criminals, black marketers, pickpockets, dealers
15	homeless and underclass

We are fully aware of the fact that classifying of people into the above mentioned categories and strata is a very subjective question which could be a subject to a wild discussion. Moreover, many of the identified groups are overlapping and thus one person could be often easily included in more than one category. Therefore we do not offer any purely statistical conclusions which would be based either on absolute data or relative proportions of particular categories. In this kind of research statistical analysis would be misleading also due to the fact that those people who are distinctive and contrast are more likely to be noticed than the ordinary masses. Thus, we want to stress that our research is primarily qualitative using description, analysis and explanation of the matter we could observe and spot by watching.

Footprints of Managerial Elite in Urban Landscape

According to our expectations transnational managers and professionals operating in advanced service sector represent the most conspicuous and distinct group in social, built and spatial environment in Prague. Among the seven selected localities we observed the highest relative share of high-income strata in the shopping street Na Příkopě, which we earlier classified as a *Central city office and residential location* and a *Central city amusement and tourist location*. Wealthy looking employees of banks and progressive services, yuppies in suits, smart-dressed customers of luxurious shops and, of course, foreign tourists belonged to the most common users of this area (see Photo 1). On the contrary, working-class and old people who both can be regarded as low-income strata in the Czech Republic were rarely seen in the crowds floating in one of the most luxurious shopping streets in Prague.

Since the beginning of 1990s the urban landscape has been influenced by foreign and international actors especially in the city centre. Managerial elite together with tourists has significantly marked the cityscape and have been creating so called "landscapes of power" (King 1995). Obviously, the presence of yuppies and tourists has the most significantly effected the centrally located pedestrian zone Na Příkopě. The urban environment has been visibly adapted to the needs of tourists, managers and professionals who are the relevant users of the space. Alongside with the expansion of producer service companies and managerial workers an appropriate structure of shops and services has appeared in the area. Walking down the street Na Příkopě we would hardly find anything else but doorplates of companies specializing in real estate, law, consulting or banking and luxurious shops, designer's boutiques and expensive restaurants aimed to the well-off clientele.

Photo 1: Shopping street Na Příkopě

A relatively high frequency of upper-strata was visible also *on the fringe of CBD*, namely in the inner-city neighbourhood Vinohrady. The people present there appeared to be a mixture of local gentrifiers, high-income office employees, and vernacular permanent inhabitants. The last mentioned group, the "indigenous" inhabitants, are those who have been living in the neighbourhood for a long time and belong mostly to the middle age group and middle strata. Vinohrady has kept its good-address image even during the egalitarian period of socialism which could explain a limited amount of low-income social groups living in the area today. Just as in the city centre the foreign and international capital have contributed to the physical revitalisation of buildings in Vinohrady. The reconstructed residential houses, clean streets and tidy public spaces describe the quality of physical environment in the neighbourhood (see Photo 2). Furthermore, the shops and services in the area focus rather on high-standard products (e.g. cosmetics, oracle, design) than on the goods of every-day use and thus reflect the presence of high-paid elite. A similar trend shows the structure of local restaurants and pubs. There are many facilities where professionals and managers would come for a lunch or for a drink but also where young people who search for a trendy place would go.

Photo 2: Gentrified inner-city neighbourhood Vinohrady

Although the group of managers and professionals was not as dominant in Anděl and Karlín as in the zones mentioned above this group has considerably influenced the landscape in the two *Brownfield* locations. The both neighbourhoods are situated close to the city centre, which made them attractive for new development projects. The construction of several office and commercial centres initiated the brownfield redevelopment in these former industrial zones and created the conditions for emergence of new secondary city centres. Consequently, the majority of high-income people we observed were yuppies employed in the recently constructed office blocks. As the use of foreign languages suggested some of them came from abroad. Similarly, the company logos on the new buildings suggest the involvement of foreign and international capital in the projects. King (1995) emphasised the role of global architects as of those who help to create the "landscapes of power". In Anděl, a well-known French architect Jean Nouvel designed an office and shopping complex Zlatý Anděl for a multinational developer ING Real Estate (see Photo 3). Likewise, in Karlín, a Spanish architect Ricardo Bofill drew up a regeneration plan of a vast brownfield area for a foreign developer Real Estate Karlín.

Photo 3: Commercial complex Zlatý Anděl in Smíchov

The soft locations in outer city of Prague represent the opposite to rather centrally located areas with high frequency of upper-strata. We hardly spot any managers and professionals in the housing estate Letňany or in the shopping centre Černý Most. Obviously, these people have no reason to come there - they do not live there, they do not work there, they do not use the services there. Although the centrally located Národní třída is certainly a different case we also did not notice many managers and professionals, nevertheless foreign tourists represented the upper strata.

Surfing between Footprints:
The Middles and the Lowers in Urban Landscape
Now we move to the groups of people who visually evoke a middle or a lower social status. It follows from the text above that we registered a relatively high share of these people in the two inner-city brownfield areas, in the outer-city housing estate and on the traffic junction Národní třída in the centre of Prague. On the contrary, people belonging to lower-strata were rarely present in the city-centre shopping street and in the gentrified inner-city location.

We observed a considerable concentration of lower class looking people, pensioners and local gypsies in the two originally industrial city-quarters, now redeveloping Brownfield locations Anděl and Karlín. In Anděl, the low-income groups included working class (local or travelling home or/and shopping) and to smaller extent also low or underclass people hanging around in front of the commercial complex. Besides, many ordinary and middle-strata looking people were doing shopping in one of the several shopping facilities newly built on the brownfield sites. Thanks to its role as an important traffic junction Anděl is a popular meeting point for various groups of people. In Karlín, most of the lower social status population seemed to be local inhabitants including an above-average amount of local gypsies. The members of upper and middle class employed in modern offices usually just passed by heading to work or for a lunch and thus suggesting their non-residential status in this location.

Yet, the coexistence of different social groups, namely of mobile highly paid yuppies and local low-income inhabitants creates two contrast physical environments in Anděl and even more distinctly in Karlín. The modern and shiny commercial buildings create a sharp opposite to rather neglected residential houses and public spaces. While foreign and international companies occupy the new or reconstructed palaces, shops and services for locals have to put up with much less splendid and often second-class quality spaces (e.g. backyards, basements etc.). Thus, the physical environment reflects the existing social polarisation in Anděl and Karlín where two completely different environments have been surviving next to each other (see Photo 4). Accordingly, the structure of services reflects the existence of two different kinds of users. While shops and services aimed to vernacular inhabitants coexist with those for managerial elites in Anděl, the shopping facilities for locals clearly dominate in Karlín (clothing, footwear, electronics, grocery, butcher's shop, toys etc.). Although the high-income employees, the potential consumers of the new facilities operate in the area the appropriate services have not expanded there yet.

Photo 4: Contrasting environments in Karlín

In many ways the socialist urban landscape has survived in housing estate Letňany (soft location *Concentration of social housing*) since not many changes have been happening there under the influence of transformation and globalisation. The neighbourhood represents a monofunctional area of prefab residential houses with almost no public space and services, with unsatisfactory parking opportunities and quite large areas of wasteland (see Photo 5). Even though the technical, architectural as well as urbanistic quality of housing estate is very poor the regeneration has involved only a few buildings so far. In some high-rise houses small shops oriented on local customers were established to enrich the supply of two supermarkets in the area. As the appearance of present people indicated (often fat, shabby-looking, not smartly-dressed) most of the population in the housing estate apparently belonged to lower-middle-strata and working class. We suppose that the observed people were local permanent residents or inhabitants of neighbouring housing estate who came for shopping to adjacent large shopping centre. In Letňany housing estate we could clearly see how a poor physical environment of residential area corresponds to social milieu of local working-class and lower-strata social groups.

Photo 5: Socialist cityscape in housing estate Letňany

Regarding the quality of physical and social environment the observation of cars parked in the neighbourhoods could also indicate the potential prosperity or stagnation of a soft location. Even though it does not mean that the cars parked in a certain neighbourhood belong only to the people living there it certainly shows which kind of users (inhabitants, workers, visitors, etc.) operate in certain areas. We conducted a detailed survey oriented on parked cars in the housing estate Letňany. Lower standard cars, mainly Czech-made and old-type vehicles created 55 % of all the parked cars. On the other hand only 22 % of all cars fell to non-Czech made vehicles younger than 5 years. Expensive and luxurious cars (e.g. Mercedes, BMW, off-roads, etc.) were almost missing in the area. This might indicate rather stagnation and a generally lower social status in housing estate zone in the comparison to the centrally located neighbourhoods where the majority of cars created expensive and rather new vehicles.

We registered a recognizable amount of local lower-strata people in all of the observed locations apart from the CBD shopping street and the gentrified inner-city neighbourhood (presumably due to the expensive housing there). We already indicated earlier, that the soft location Národní třída, even though centrally located and defined as a *Central city office and residential location* and a *Central city amusement and tourist location* showed a completely different scene from the other two central spots. In the surrounding of Národní třída metro station we observed a relatively highly concentration of pathological social groups and underclass (categories 14, 15) likely created by non-locals. Accordingly, the untidy and dirty character of physical surrounding in Národní třída reflects an extensive occurrence of underclass. An interesting structure of retail facilities arises on the one hand from the area's function as a traffic junction (fast foods, takeaways, supermarket etc.) and on the other hand from a considerable concentration of "black activities" in the area (betting shop, non-stop pawnshops, etc.). People embraced into underclass seemed to be unemployed, some of them homeless or fond of alcohol, who used the public space by metro station to gather together and to enjoy chatting and drinking beer (see Photo 6). As the language suggested they were Czech including Czech gypsies (we suppose non-local in the area). The second group included in underclass consisted of people whose appearance and even more acting strongly reminded this of street criminals, pickpockets and dealers. Most of them were youngish and obviously did not have a Czech origin (seemed to be immigrants from the East). They usually came there either for a „business meeting" or to visit a non-stop pawnshop situated nearby. Finally, unskilled employees of tertiary sector, such as shop assistants selling fast food, people offering leaflets and cleaning streets were also active in the area. Again, concluding from the used language and the accents, a particular amount of them might have been immigrants from Ukraine or other East-European countries.

Photo 6: Underclass in traffic junction Národní třída

In the outer-city shopping and entertainment centre Černý Most, the majority of people seemed to belong to middle strata while the share of people with presumably lower or upper social status was relatively small (see Photo 7). The regional shopping centre does not serve just to the inhabitants of neighbouring housing estate but to the users from a much wider district extending far behind the city boarders. It is obvious from the cars parked in front of the mall – between 30 and 40 % did not have a Prague registration number. The project of a suburban shopping and entertainment complex in Černý Most is very similar to the same kind of facilities built in many West-European cities. Thus, the global aspect is represented in the universal international architecture, in standardised supply of products, in organisation of interior space as well as in the creation of multifunctional rather than monofunctional space (combination of shopping and entertainment facilities). The restaurants (e.g. McDonalds, Italian pizza, Chinese and Spanish fast food), fitness centre and Village Cinemas inside the entertainment centre seemed to reproduce the international style especially distinctly.

Photo 7: Shopping centre Černý Most

Conclusion: Polarisation, Eyes and Urban Space

The observations that we carried out in seven selected soft locations in Prague proofed that some impacts of global processes are visually perceptible in urban space. The transnational categories identified by Hannerz (1993) are recognizable in Prague, however, the frequency of certain social groups and categories varies in different urban areas depending on the character of a soft spot and on the intensity at which the global processes win recognition in particular locations (see Figure 1).

Figure 1: Social stratification of people observed in selected localities

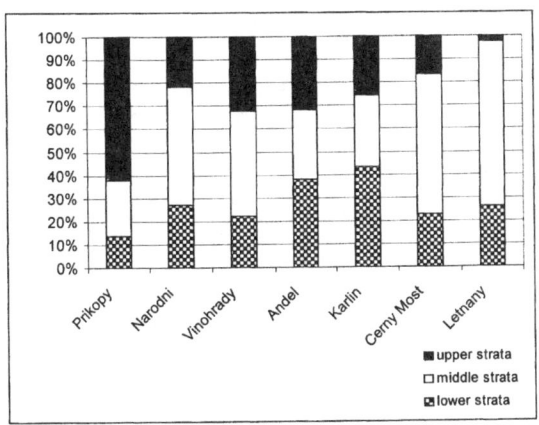

Note 1: Upper strata consists of yuppies, other high-income people and foreign tourists (groups 1,2,3). Middle strata includes middle income people skilled or relatively educated, families with children, students (groups 4,5,7,12). Lower strata is composed of the poor, workers and unskilled low-waged people, unemployed and homeless people, criminals and immigrants from the Third World (groups 6,8,9,10,11,13,14,15).
Note 2: In the chart localities are arranged according to their distance from the city centre – the closer the more left.

Consequently, the polarisation of social and physical environment has been emerging in some areas in Prague. The transnational managers and professionals and low-wage manual workers on the other side of social stratification are considered to be contributing to the socio-spatial polarisation in cities (Sassen 1996). Concerning the employees of low-tertiary sector (e.g. messengers, security workers, porters, cleaners, taxi drivers) we noticed their presence in each of the selected soft locations with the exception of housing estate Letňany (unskilled low-paid employees of tertiary sphere could not have been distinguished). Moreover, only very few upper-strata people were apparent in Letňany.

Thus the outer-city housing estate represents a location where polarisation has not been occurring till now. We suggest it is not appropriate to call the area a soft location at present time. The second district where we did not observe social polarisation was the pedestrian zone Na Příkopě in the centre of Prague. Almost no lower-strata appeared in the luxurious shopping street. On the other hand specifically the city centre attracts non-conform and eccentric looking people. Similarly most of the tourists move only in the historical core of the city. Considering the fact that population of the Czech Republic is quite homogenous a relatively significant presence of people from different countries could be understand as a certain degree of cosmopolism. On the contrary we registered a strong trend towards polarisation especially in the two inner-city brownfield redevelopment areas, Anděl and Karlín. The professionals and managers mixed with the local low-income residents and thus have been creating a contrast in social as well as physical environment. To certain extent social polarisation was visible also in the central-city traffic junction Národní třída. Concluding from our observations we ranked the inner-city gentrified neighbourhood Vinohrady and the outer-city shopping centre Černý Most as the areas with mild polarisation. We have to add that although we did not distinguish polarisation in each of the selected localities at the level of whole city polarisation processes have been obviously recognisable.

The social environment is strongly tied in with the quality and conditions of its physical surrounding. Accordingly, among the selected soft locations considerable differences exist not only in social milieu but also in built environment. It indicates that global processes do not influence particular areas equally. For example the frequency of foreign and international companies and shops varies in different areas and creates inequalities among soft locations. The flow of transnational investment is a visible sign of globalisation and could be interpreted as an indicator of place's "global-ness". Multinational and foreign companies are frequent users of commercial spaces in the city centre (Na Příkopě, Národní, Vinohrady) and of the new buildings in emerging secondary centres (Karlín, Smíchov). On the other hand local companies dominate in Letňany and in second-class quality spaces in Karlín and Smíchov. The competition for space and investment occurs in all selected soft spots excluding Letňany. Thus, revitalisation contributes to the improvement of physical environment the most distinctly in brownfield redevelopment areas Anděl and Karlín and creates contrasts between the old and the new buildings, facilities and social groups. On the other hand resulting from uneven development rather decay has been affecting the housing estate Letňany.

References:

Beauregard, R. A.; Haila, A. (2000) The Unavoidable Continuities of the City. In: Marcuse, P. – van Kempen, R. (eds.) Globalizing Cities. A new spatial order? Oxford: Blackwell.

Friedmann, J. (1995) Where We Stand – A Decade of World City Research. In: Knox, P.L. ; Taylor, P. J. (eds) World Cities in a World-System. Cambridge, Cambridge University Press.

Gregory, D. ;Johnston, R. J. ;Smith, D. M. (1994) The Dictionary of Human Geography. 3rd edition.

Hall, T. (1998) Urban Geography. London: Routledge.

Hannerz, U. (1993) The Cultural Role of World Cities. In: Cohen, A. P.;Fukui, A. (eds) Humanising the City? Social Context of Urban Life at the Turn of the Millennium. Edinburgh University Press.

Jencks, Ch. (1996) The City that never sleeps. New Stateman, Vol. 125, Is. 4288 [sic] – 6/28/96, p. 26 – 28.

King, A. D. (1995) Re-presenting World Cities: Cultural Theory/ Social Practice. In: Knox, P.L.;Taylor, P. J. (eds) World Cities in a World-System. Cambridge, Cambridge University Press.

Marcuse, P.; van Kempen, R. (2000) Conclusion: A Changed Spatial Order. In: Marcuse, P.; van Kempen, R. (eds) Globalizing Cities. A New Spatial Order? Oxford: Blackwell.

Portes, A.; Sassen, S. (1993) Miami: A New Global City?. Contemporary Sociology, Vol. 22, Is. 4, p. 471 – 477.

Rauen, M. (2001) reflection on the Space of Flows: the Guggenheim Museum Bilbao. Journal of Arts Management, Law and Society, Vol. 30, Is. 4, p. 283 – 301.

Sassen, S. (1996) Cities and communities in the global economy. American Behavioral Scientist, vol. 39, Is. 5, p. 629 – 639.

-, (1991) The Global City. Princeton University Press.

Sýkora, L. (2001) Post-communist city. In: XII Konwersatorium Wiedzy o Mieście. Miasto postsocjalistyczne - organizacja przestrzeni miejskiej i jej przemiany, s. 41-45. Łódź, Katedra Geografii Miast i Turyzmu Uniwersytetu Łódzkiego, Komisja Geografii Osadnictwa i Ludności PTG, Łódzkie Towarzystwo Naukowe.

Sýkora, L. (1996) Transformace fyzického a sociálního prostředí Prahy. In: Hampl, M. (ed.) Geografická organizace společnosti a transformační procesy v České republice. Přírodovědecká fakulta Univerzity Karlovy, s. 361-394.

Yeoh, B. S. A. (1999) Global/ globalizing cities. Progress in Human Geography, Vol. 23, Is. 4, p. 607 – 616.

Learning from „CHINA" or Urban Design beyond Modern Time

Carl Fingerhuth

The challenge of urban design is to develop structures and forms for urban areas, which are anchored in the needs, the emotionality and the spirituality of the people concerned. Urban "Gestalt" is in this sense always a reflection of the economic, social and cultural situation of a society. As professionals taking care of the transformation of the "Gestalt" of urban areas, we are primarily "translators", giving the needs, dreams and visions physical shape.
Chinese philosophy – learning from "CHINA" and not from China - gives us a radically different approach to interacting with the world of the „ten thousand things". It talks of the game of polarities instead of absolute truths, of listening instead of proclaiming and of unity with nature and not of the war against it.
Applying this advice to the theory and practice of urban design leads to different principals, methods and instruments. This way of thinking opens a new and wider approach to the phenomena of globalization. Respecting the polarity and interdependence of global – local and collective – individual makes it indispensable to look also at the other side of globalization. The process of transformation is not any more linear but deals with more or less. Monologues have to be replaced by dialogues. Different instruments have to be developed, which do not depend basically on control but on agreement.
Working on urban projects in Western and Eastern Europe, in Africa and China has taught me a way of operating which is connected with the principles of Tao, Yin and Yang, Wu Wei and Feng Shui. This means being attentive to the local, the differences and the individual situation, this means refraining from playing the prophet and salesman of the global world and this means developing different methods of interacting and instruments of design.
I would like to present experiences from my work and discuss the conclusions. The main focus will be on a European, an African and a Chinese Town:

- Basel, a European urban agglomeration encompassing territories of Germany, France and Switzerland
- Owerri, the capital of the in 1976 newly created Imo State of Nigeria
- Kunming, the capital of Junan, the province in southwestern China.
The main emphasis will be on reflecting the "other side" of Globalisation.

Globalisation or the conflict between the New and the Existing

„Que signifient les coutumes indiennes aujourd'hui, si vous dîtes oui à la machine, aux pantalons et à la démocratie?" („How can the Indian traditions still be relevant, when you say yes to the machine, to pants and to democracy ").[1]

That was the answer of Le Corbusier during his work in Chandigarh, when he was asked by the Indian architect Mulkarj Anand about the importance of indian traditions.
The conflict between the existing and the new, between the white tiger and the blue dragon, between male and female energy is the oldest and yet the most current theme in dealing with the transformation of the town.
People and their towns need the New, because new needs, goals and visions are continuously arising; needs which are necessary for survival on the physical level, for being anchored in the sensing and feeling of today, but also in awning of the expansion of the consciousness.
But men and their towns also need the continuity. Infrastructure defines towns for generations. Public spaces define the identity of the town in the memory of men. This is indispensable for the social, economical and cultural quality of towns.
Continuously society has to decide, if the existing is more important then the new or if the new is necessary to maintain or build up again the vitality of the town.
Continuously society has to differenciate between the destructive utopian dreams or the opposition to the new which arises out of fear of change.

Not enough change   too much change

---

[1] Bianca, Stefano; op. cit.

Three Case Studies

Owerri
"Listen Carl. They will talk to you about African identity. Forget about it. Look at me. I wear an English suit and a French necktie. The fashion is the same all over the world. We want a town like Paris or London."
That was the instructions that I got when in 1973 I was commissioned to design the master plan for the Capital for the newly created Imo State in Nigeria. 12 000 civil servants were ready to move to Owerri as soon as possible. This would generate an increase of about 250 000 people for old Owerri, a small market town in the area of the Igbo, who had recently lost the Biafra war against the central government. "A town like Paris or London?"
Opposite our camp there was the billboard of a magic healer and the newspapers talked about juju's, little spirits, which would have to be talked to before you could cut down their tree.
On the other hand the commissioner asked me, which would be the ideal tree for Owerri, and what would be the most beautiful color for houses. I should let him known and he would make a law that only this tree should be planted and only this color used.
And then there was the global world with machines, pants and democracy, which promises clean water in every house, access to schools and mobility.
But what about African identity? Wasn't it also my job to draw the attention of the government to the polarity of any process of transformation?
When the Master Plan for the new Capital was approved by the Government I was asked to supervise the construction of the town during the first four years.

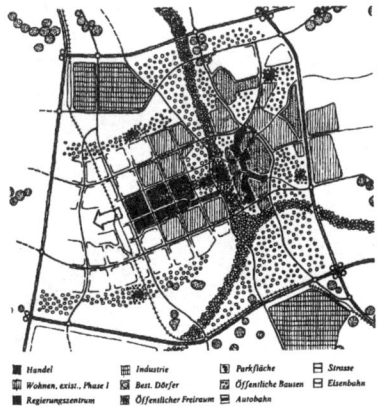

When we built the headquarters for the Owerri Capital Development Authority, we tried to create a building relating to the local needs and potentials: Low rise, with wide roofs, inner courts, careful orientation according to the sun, local materials and techniques. When the headquarter was completed according to these principals, I was blamed that the building was not up to representative standards of a ministry.

At a certain moment I decided to focus all my energy on the global aspect of the project. The people needed a functional and economic infrastructure and a long-term robust and economic urban structure. Only the aspect of this aspect of globalization seemed to be free of cultural ideology, so I set my focus there.

Basel

> "Those old towns, which – at their origin have been small fortified hamlets – and only through time have grown to big cities are, compared to the regular squares which an Engineer has designed on an open plain, most of the time thoroughly out of proportion."[2]

In 1979 I was asked to work for the town of Basel as the head of the building department. I just had turned 42 and I was very much interested to get out of the role of the consultant and be in a position of direct responsibility. The job was on the first sight a technical position, but I soon was aware that it was primarily a cultural assignment. A war of truths was going on.

The army of the Cartesian "Globals" had been beaten. They had developed and had been hailed for 40 years for their global vision of a New Town. They had designed a network of new roads and had planned to tear down most of the historic part of Basel. Now the conservative "Locals" were hailed for a different truth. "Bauen ist Umweltzerstörung" ("Building is a way of destroying the environment") was their new truth.

---

[2] Descartes, René: Von der Methode des richtigen Vernunftgebrauches und der wissenschaftlichen Forschung, Meiner, Hamburg, 1990. S. 17f.

I had started reading Taoist literature, particulary Alan Watts, and it was for me very clear, that it would be disastrous if I would have proclaimed myself to be the general of the one or the other army. As I had the power to interfere I tried acupuncture. With an intensive process of projects for new buildings – starting with very small projects – I tried to create a public platform. Through this a cultural awareness of the interdependency of the need for the new and the respect for the continuity developed. The war disappeared.

Kunming
In the book about his travels to Kublai Khan in the 13th century Marco Polo reports about his stay in Kunming:

> "On the eve of the fifth day one reaches the magnificent capital of Jaci (Kunming). It is inhabited my many merchants and craftsmen. The population consists of many different groups. There are Mohammedens and Heathens and also some nestorian Christians."[3]

1992 I had been "in office" for 14 years, like a bishop responsible for his territory and his flock or a football trainer for his team. As I had turned 56 it seemed time to let go of formal authority. I felt anxious to extend my activities beyond Basel. I got a fascinating teaching job for urban design in Darmstadt and I was asked to go to China. If you do not cling and listen carefully the right things come to you. In Taoist terms, that would correspond to practicing Wu Wei or awareness.
For ten years already the town of Zurich had been engaged in a Town partnership with Kunming, the capital of the Chinese province of Junan. Zurich assisted Kunming in an unprecedented phase of globalization advising them with their infrastructure problems: water, sewage and traffic. In a next phase it was agreed that challenges connected with urban design should be integrated in the collaboration. I should be responsible for giving "assistance" in this area.

---
[3]Polo, Marco; Die Wunder der Welt, Bericht von seiner Reise nach China, geschrieben 1298/99, Manesse Verlag, Zürich, 1983, S. 190f.

From the beginning it was very clear for me, that it was not appropriate for me to give "assistance". It would have to be a completely different approach. Taking the approach of the visiting "expert" was wrong. It had to do with a consciousness of polarity, which meant giving dialogue a much more important place. Dialogue requires awareness of the moment and respect for the partner, his social, economic and cultural position.

We agreed to do all work in joint workshops. Our Chinese Partners named the themes they wanted us to discuss. We would meet for two weeks in Kunming, have an opening and closing meetings with the different bosses and produce joint protocols. These were mainly drawings and plans with Chinese and English handwritten text. In Zurich we only improved the readability, print them and send 100 copies back to Kunming. And I think I may say, that the system proved to be successful.

- Old Kunming

During our first workshop the construction of a new wide urban highway through the center of the historic town had just started. Hundreds of old buildings were torn down. Our friends wanted to discuss possible strategies to deal with the remaining parts, which were fortunately the essential elements.

Basically it seemed clear to them, that they should be torn down. "Wood is not a sustainable building material!" was one of the arguments – even if the buildings had survived for centuries. The Kunming Urban Planning Institute (Kupti) was working on plans to recreate an artificial historic town on top of huge underground parking lots.

Within the workshop we discussed goals, developed alternative scenarios and concepts and showed what the necessary instruments and methods could be to implement the different concepts. When we came back for the next workshop the officials proudly presented the decision of the town government, through which the still existing part of historic Kunming had been protected.

- North Kunming

A similar process took place for the extension of Kunming to the North. The KUPTI had prepared a draft for this huge area, which was supposed to make space for about 500 000 places for working and housing. This plan should be the basis for the next workshop. I asked, which element could be discussed? The answer was that only the existing highway and the clearly defined Feng Shui axis should not be questioned.

After two workshops a quite different urban design concept was approved, which allowed a less risky phasing, created a higher identity, promised more favorable conditions for a sustainable developement, especially for the introduction of public transport.

Learning from „CHINA" or Urban design beyond modern time

I am convinced, that we are at the beginning of a profound change of consciousness. This is not an alternative to the modern time but an expansion of what we know. The Taoist philosophy is for me a fascinating guideline to the practice of urban design beyond modern time.
The following 6 aspects could be considered. They follow the structure of Alan Watts book "The watercourse way".

Symbol: The "Gestalt" of the town – in its shape and its structure - always has a meaning. The more aesthetic the "Gestalt" is, the stronger will be her power.
Tao: Man has to be taken serious in his whole essence und should not be reduced to his rationality.
Yin und Yang: The transformation of the "Gestalt" of the town has to be a continuous game of more or less, of too much or not enough.
Wu Wei: The main job of the urban designer is to play this game with awareness and care.
Feng Shui: The rising consciousness for the unity of man and the universe has to be integrated in to the "Gestalt" of the town.
Te: If the five first point are taking seriously we will experience a much richer culture and politic of urban design.

What we call globalization is, as we all know, very complex phenomena. It has the positive aspect of bringing people together, of transfer of knowledge and of expanding collective consciousness. But it also has a vicious side. Where it becomes dogmatic, imperialistic and destructive. Following the Taoist strategy will enhance its positive side and eliminate as much as possible its negative side.

Practical implications for working in China as a western architect or townplanner

My experiences took place in very specific circumstances.
We did not work in the costal towns or Bejing where the energy of the towns is much more dynamic and in interaction with the western global world. Kunming has an extremely high ratio of growth but the impulse comes from migration in to a provincial capital.
We did not work within a commercial contract. My team was part of a townpartnership between Zürich and Kunming. Our participation was offered to Kunming by the town of Zürich. Therefore we were not in a seller – buyer situation.
These circumstances permitted specific methods.

I was not forced into giving answers to problems I was not sure that they were really problems of the local authorities or problems they wanted to get an answer to.

The method was exclusively the workshop in Kunming. For two weeks we worked on the themes the local government had proposed, together with the staff of the planning office of Kunming. At the end of the workshop the results were presented to the representatives of the government.

Back in Switzerland the approved elements were put into a report in English and Chinese, without any modifications of the plans.

This method opened the dialogue to a wide range of urban aspects; from the dealing with the old town, developing the urban public space to plans for an extension of the town for another 500 000 inhabitants.

If I would be asked what the essential aspects to consider are, I would mention three:
- The most important partner is the translator. He has to be a person who knows the profession and is able to notice, when ideas are not understood – on both sides.
- Follow my advice about learning from CHINA.
- Remember what Sir Patrick Abercrombie said, the Planner of Greater London in the 50ties, when he was asked about the essential qualities for a townplanner:
  "He has to know, that water only flows downward, he should be over 40 years old and he has to be able to listen!"

References:
Fingerhuth, C. and J. (2002) The Kunming Project: Urban Development in China – a Dialogue. Ernst, Edit. Birkhäuser, Basel.
Fingerhuth, C. (1996) Die Gestalt der postmodernen Stadt, VdF Verlag, Zürich
Fingerhuth, C. (2000) Städtebau jenseits der Moderne, in Hassenpflug, Dieter; Die Europäische Stadt – Mythos und Wirklichkeit, Bauhaus Universität, S. 263ff.

Linking the local and the global: transnational architects in a globalizing world

Paul Kennedy

This paper is based on an exploratory study of a small sample of professionals working in the building-design industry. This comprises one of the group of business activities Sassen (2000) has designated as the 'producer service industries'. These knowledge-based industries, including law, finance, banking, management consultancy, and so on, have become increasingly crucial to wealth creation, especially within the advanced economies. At the same time, some of the largest firms within these sectors have spread more and more of their activities overseas as de-regulatory, open-market, neo-liberal policies along with post-Fordist flexible regimes of capitalist accumulation have been introduced across the world thereby accelerating and intensifying the process of economic globalization. My intention in this paper is to examine how architects and related professionals have become increasingly caught up in the processes we associate with globalization and from two overlapping perspectives: first, as influential agents who actively shape the built environment of cities and other locations and therefore influence the ways in which globalizing forces are experienced by society at large and, second, as individuals and companies compelled to respond and adapt to the pressures generated by these same global forces.

1. The Study

The study explored the work and non-work experiences of professionals working in the building-design industry in the UK. Eight enterprises were investigated, seven in London, and one in Manchester. Access to these firms was difficult and was based on previous contacts which were then followed up through a "snowball" effect. These firms were engaged in the design of various kinds of buildings but they often supervised the implementation of such projects, on site, through various sub-contracting arrangements. Thirty two professionals were interviewed. Twenty three had originally trained as architects, though some had since acquired further qualifications, six respondents had trained as building engineers and three were in business management or interior design. It was not possible to select these respondents on a statistically random basis because many employees were on leave, working abroad or otherwise engaged during the research period. However, given that the study focused on individuals with personal experience of working continuously outside their native country at some time during their careers, many employees were excluded from the survey in any case.

Twenty nine respondents fulfilled these criteria while the remaining three had travelled abroad for shorter periods on numerous occasions. Many had worked overseas in two or more different locations. Twenty one respondents had worked abroad for more than two years and fifteen people had done so for more than four years. In addition, made many repeated short visits abroad – perhaps two or three days every week or fortnight - as part of their current UK post. The group included an assortment of nationalities: only twelve were born in the UK and/or had single British nationality status. The remaining twenty individuals hailed from seventeen different countries. Working in Britain exposed the latter to the same transnational experiences as their UK counterparts who had previously worked abroad. Eleven of the non-British nationals had worked overseas prior to repeating this experience in Britain. Most interviews were conducted in the summer and autumn of 2000.

2. Bringing the local and the global into conjunction; re-constituting place

I begin this section by examining professional tasks and skills that are unique to the building-design industry and then consider how the changes generated by globalization are placing new or additional demands on those who work in this area. In so far as they respond to these challenges they help to re-constitute the nature of localities and the roles these play in the lives of citizens under while their actions may help to bring globalizing forces into closer conjunction with local, everyday meanings and lifestyles. In discussing these issues I draw wherever possible upon the perceptions and experiences of the respondents.

The unique character of the building-design industry
It was noticeable that the respondents attached a very high value to their profession and their work and not just as a job but as an entire way of life. Of course, this propensity is not unique to the building-design industry nor to individuals who become transnational employees. However, it is possible that working abroad and therefore the exposure to so many different work and other cultural experiences combined with the encapsulation in an evolving set of transnational relations may deepen this propensity. Thus, their aesthetic, intellectual and indeed emotional investment in their careers was formidable. Although their leisure and lifestyle concerns were obviously important to them, work appeared to be the pivot around which the greater part of their lives were built, at least until and unless they eventually founded a family; the central core of their personal identities. Their accounts of their work experiences suggested that they found much of their work challenging,

innovative and sometimes stressful but in ways that tested their skills and enabled them to build on their capabilities. Most were immensely proud of having been involved in certain previous projects (for example the Pompidou Centre in Paris) – which they discussed in great detail – or of the prestigious companies they had sometimes worked for. They described at length their particular learning curves, perceptions of contemporary architectural practice, their insights about different national and local styles and preferences and much else besides.

Here, the insights of one respondent are especially revealing and they point to one major aspect of this situation, namely, that for people working in the building-design industry it is often difficult to separate clearly the spheres of work and non-work, leisure and relaxation; one is never "off duty". She was of Cypriot-Greek nationality and in her mid forties. After her first overseas job in South Africa she had moved to London in 1984. She made the following comments:

Whatever I do, it involves things which are a continuous tourist experience in the sense that (professionally) I deal .. .. with issues relating to the physical environment ...so when I visit in a museum, for example, for some aspect of my work, I can't distinguish that from pleasure...or if I look at a new town square my company has designed.. it's still a combination of both work and pleasure. If I meet a client and we go out for supper and a drink after work to discuss the project - it's a combination of people that I work with, they are very pleasant, I like them -- nevertheless they are my clients ..... so there's a constant confusion ... between professional life and social life ... Also, if I go into a market or other retail places to do some shopping, I must also get a feel about its character and issues of style. Because of the broadness of what I do.. .. one could see that every aspect of life is linked to what I do, my profession.

Obligations and social relations, centered around work, cross-over constantly into socializing and leisure time. Moreover, work concerns never really go away but instead are taken into weekend and evening life since wherever they go architects cannot avoid making mental notes on every kind of building they see and enter. Meanwhile the aesthetic interest or pleasure in every line and style of the physical environment they encounter merges into intellectual knowledge and thinking about their current or next project.

Second, it appears that the core work of architects and their fellow professionals is situated at a sort of crossroads where two different kinds of skill intersect. Moreover, each of these skills, in turn, sub-divides into a range of possible orientations. Thus architecture involves an artistic-design versus technical - engineering function but also a theoretical versus practical, hands-on activity at the same time. Involved in the first, is the simultaneous need for both a creative - artistic aspect alongside a more technical orientation in terms of knowing how the original design can be realized into a series of practical, material objectives. This requires calculation, planning, detailed understanding of building techniques and materials, sequencing and coordination. Individual architects probably differ in terms of their preferences and aptitudes with respect to these twin skills. Yet, they all need to be aware of the problems posed by both aspects of the work involved. With respect to the second continuum, a capacity for theorization alongside the need for a practical, hands-on orientation, one American sociologist (Powell 1990: 390) has argued that this combination tends to generate knowledge that overlaps between different but necessarily linked activities. As such, it facilitates effective collaboration and team work. He further suggested that these cooperative capacities are not evenly distributed across the professions but are especially likely to be evident among architects and engineers. Certainly, the accounts of their work experiences provided by the respondents supports this argument. Indeed, interpersonal cooperation appears to be even more significant and necessary where professionals are immersed in a transnational work situation for reasons that will be discussed later. Additional evidence for the central importance of collaboration is also shown by the following quotes taken from the publicity manuals of two companies included in the study:

'We assign 'the responsibility for all aspects of a project to a single dedicated team for the duration of a project........This is the collaborative spirit from which our best work emerges, and it sponsors a palpable sense of pride in each individual's contribution and in the collective efforts of the project team...' (KPF 1997: 9).

'Our architectural product comes out of the cooperation of everybody. The architect's role is as much to understand the mechanical and structural side of the building as it is to understand the materials' (Rogers 1995: 160).

Thirdly, what professionals working in the building design industry actually do is to create an idea for a particular project. Then, as often as not, they play a leading role in following through the implementation – involving many elaborate and possibly difficult stages - of this design into a completed construction. What this project involves, in total, is the creation of a grounded set of objects that generate form and that enfold and re-configure space. The end result is an entity that has materiality;

something that is rooted in, and tied to, a particular location or place. Throughout history this has always been the role of architects and building engineers. In addition, however, buildings – and those who work to design and produce them - have always played a central role in expressing cultural meanings. They provide vehicles for representing particular collective identities, including, more often than not, the "colloquialisms" of the surrounding society. Jones (2003) has shown how this cultural role was especially evident in the era of the modern nation-state when government and other buildings were deployed as a means of helping to construct a discourse of the nation and to project the claims being made concerning its allegedly unique character and history. In the contemporary period Delanty and Jones (2003) have explored how the European Union has pursued similar aims by striving to use certain landmark building projects, such as the Jewish Museum in Berlin, as signifiers for representing the idea of a post-national, emergent European identity and unity.

The possible role and impact of the building-design industry under globalizing conditions.
In the light of the previous discussion concerning the unique and special character of this profession, what might its members contribute to the wider social order in a global age? The experiences and perceptions of the respondents included in the study pointed to at least three such possible contributions.

Firstly, the "traditional' role architects and related professionals have always played in creating the space of place perhaps assumes an added significance given that globalization means we increasingly live in a world of endless movement; of diverse mobilities (Urry 2001). We are perpetually engulfed from all directions by the various fragmentary flows of other people's cultures, media images, company brands, celebritry icons, knowledge, information, symbols, images, goods and migrating peoples and individuals. Castells (1996), for example, has argued that globalization, now massively intensified by the revolution in the informational and communication technologies, means that everyone on this planet, albeit to markedly different degrees, now lives not just in the space of place (particular locations) but also the space of flows.

However, it could be argued that the tasks architects and their colleagues undertake in situating their clients and the public in the local, the particular, the material – in the "old-fashioned" space of place – are perhaps assuming an additional significance under globalizing conditions because they provide one of the few "stabilizing" forces capable of providing a degree of embeddedness and familiarity in everyday life capable of partly countering endless global flows. Building projects and sites are stationary and solid entities; they offer relatively still points in an endlessly turning world (although the meanings and identities that buildings possess clearly have never remained constant and are even less likely to do so today). Castells (1996) seems to be saying something similar when he suggests that the 'more societies try to recover their identity' in the face of the loss of meaning brought by postmodernity and globalization, so they increasingly require an architecture and professionals that can root themselves 'into places, thus into culture, and into people' (423), though hopefully this could be achieved without retreating to fake historical styles.

A second contribution that building-design professionals may be able to make to everyday social life in a global age harks back to the point made earlier concerning the cultural and identity meanings embodied in buildings. Such processes were clearly at work in the case of many of the projects implemented by the companies included in the study and whose clients intended that their buildings would function as vehicles for legitimizing their owner's claims to international status. The following two quotes, again taken from the KPF brochure and the remarks of Sir Richard Rogers (the founder of Richard Rogers Partnership), demonstrate this growing awareness of the implications of living under globalizing conditions and the new kinds of cultural meanings and identities that the projects in which they were involved might be required to relay to the public at large.

Thus, speaking about the European Court of Human Rights in Strasbourg, Rogers said; *'I also think that it has a futuristic image not limited by national styles that is appropriate for the EU, an international alliance that points towards the twenty-first century'* (1995: 46). In a wider vein he also suggested the following. *'Not surprisingly we are seeing changes and our own perspective has changed. We are now looking at the earth as a whole. The symbol of space travel has allowed us to look globally'* (Rogers 1995: 123). Similarly, the KPD brochure declared that *'(O)ur exposure to the clients, programs, cultures, and environments we encounter continues to broaden and extend the dimensions of the firm's personality, especially in an ever-shrinking world where cultures increasingly cross-pollinate'* (KPF 1997: 11).

A number of respondents, too, were proud to be working for companies and with fellow professionals they regarded as leading exponents of innovative and exciting design models in international architecture. Moreover, some of these projects had achieved wide public recognition as offering path-breaking styles and working procedures that were clearly relevant to the current world situation. A British architect who had previously studied and worked in the USA made the following comments.

'There is a growing international type of project, quite different from local idiosyncratic ones...a flavour of common themes can be found in such projects that are carried out by big global companies......A building as an expression of open democracy ..... lots of glass...light facades ... transparency and openness. Then there is the theme of environmental sustainability...the more interesting companies are trying to deal with these issues as we are in this office'.

A Dutchman who had worked for a large London company for eight years in addition to spending numerous shorter spells in other countries, offered the following comparison between the kinds of building projects he had been fortunate to work with in Europe compared to the situation in the USA.

'European projects tend to be much more diverse in style and more urban-life-oriented compared to the big sky skyscrapers you see in South East Asia or in America. Also this company has become very green....the importance of this has become built-into all aspects of company practice and the work of all company members. Partly this is linked to our awareness of the wasteful misuse of energy in America'.

A forty year old Manchester-based architect who had made numerous short visits on behalf of his company to Moscow, over a period of years, made the following observation. *'Our company has changed so much since I joined in 1985......then we didn't have any projects outside the UK ...now a substantial part is abroad......we are a European practice now but we couldn't have contemplated this ten or fifteen years ago. Now, I've no doubts about flying off anywhere in the world to operate if required to do so'.*

Thirdly, despite the need and the opportunity for building-design companies to increasingly work on projects capable of providing an orientation appropriate to a more open world of emerging post-national identities, continuous mobility and frequent inter-country comparisons, many respondents remained strongly aware of the continuing importance of locality, roots and local accountability. The following four examples drawn from field notes illustrate some aspects of this continuing need for embeddedness alongside cosmopolitanism.

A forty year old British urban planner and architect who had worked in Germany for over four years on a freelance basis before joining her current London-based employer, argued that compared to the people she had met abroad who worked in the media – who tended to speak several languages and constantly moved from one country to another – professionals in the building-design industry were more grounded. *'A large company can plan the construction and design of a project in London but they still have to work with the local architects of the country concerned...deal with the local detail. The implementation is essentially local......by contrast urban planning remains conceptual and strategic...it comes before the architecture and so flows around much more. Architecture does have global, flow aspects too.....design ideas and knowledge etc ....but further down the line it becomes more concrete. This is where the ability to work in partnership with other nationalities comes in'.*

An American architect who had worked in London for eleven years contrasted those working in the building-design industry with artists and stressed that the former are inevitably accountable to the immediate situation in which they find themselves. Artists, she suggested, *'don't have to be socially responsible in the same way that architects do. We are liable for damage and have to be socially responsible because buildings have a much larger impact on society and on a bigger proportion of the population'.*

The comments of a Japanese professional in his mid thirties, with both architectural and engineering qualifications and who had worked in London on two separate occasions – spending the period in between back in Japan - illustrates well the combination of cultural sophistication, linked partly to his overseas experience, but combined with a cautious awareness of the continuing importance of national culture. On the one hand, after working in one of the most open, democratic London companies for several years he now found it difficult to operate within a Japanese office, with its slowness, constant negotiation and indirect approach to inter-personal elations, though he acknowledged that some changes were now taking place in Japan in these areas. Yet, at the same time, and as a professional architect he knew that *'buildings cannot move and nature and climate make a huge continuing difference to locals styles'.* Moreover, *'local cultural differences won't change or shrink that much'.*

Recounting his experience of living and working in Malaysia, Singapore, Denmark, France and Britain for long periods of time, a sixty year old Danish engineer observed that, *'everywhere globalization is having similar effects ......encouraging a reassertion of local ties and links......also hard-won national identities won't easily die ... they are hard to resist and offer advantages'*. Despite affirming that he was personally committed to a European outlook, he suggested that this was *' even true of the gentle Scandinavians and Danes who fear to lose their national identity and can't cooperate to make the EU work'*. Referring to his involvement in projects spanning several countries he pointed out that experience had taught him that national differences remain profound. As a practicing professional, until you accept this, it is difficult to cope with these. Accordingly, he insisted that even within Europe, which shares so much common history, and in situations where clients are committed to projects with a strongly international flavour, sentiments of national pride along with deeply rooted parochial cultural mentalities and professional traditions often survive and require careful negotiation. On a more personal note, he also suggested that following a life of movement which had left him feeling at ease in most places, with an innate respect for, and interest in other cultures, he nevertheless had never enjoyed a close involvement with any one country. At the end of his career, therefore, he was left wondering to which country or place he felt the most loyalty. As he put it, *'my personal life is more problematic than my professional life'*. He concluded that *'you need strong roots in one country but combine this with an international orientation'*. This final remark could stand as succinct but pointed summary of the argument developed here.

3. A globalizing profession: the company perspective

In the UK, and no doubt elsewhere, some companies in the building-design sector have increasingly sought overseas business; they have "gone global". Companies wishing to attain global reach need to establish close relationships with partner companies in those countries where they wish to bid for tenders or they must set-up their own branches abroad, or both. To facilitate these processes, companies may also find it beneficial to encourage mutual flows of personnel between the home and overseas offices since this is likely to lead to the pooling of cross-national design knowledge. It may also increase the range of linguistic, cultural and technical skills available to the company and it will expose employees to transnational professional experiences. The percentage of companies registered in 2000 with the Royal Institute of British Architects that had either recently undertaken projects abroad and/or which had overseas partners or offices was quite small; around 4.3 per cent or around 185 out of 4,300 enterprises. Moreover, these firms continued to engage with national projects. It was difficult to determine the relative share of their global operations as a proportion of the total because the firms studied had not tried to produce such statistics. Nevertheless, this proportion seems to have increased quite markedly since the 1980s and could be anything between 15 and 30 per cent depending on the firm in question.

Despite their relatively small numbers, most of these "global" firms revealed some interesting characteristics. First, many were much larger than the mainly UK-based companies. Arup Associates, for example, is one of the largest groups of engineering, building and design companies in the world. It currently has 70 offices in 32 countries. Second, these global companies often revealed an extremely diverse employee nationality profile as can be seen from the case study of Kohn Pederson Fox Associates examined below. Thirdly, most of these companies were located either in London (nearly half) or the South East plus small concentrations in Bath and Bristol. Outside London and the South East, these firms were spread thinly except for Manchester, Glasgow and Edinburgh. The role of London as a global city, providing immediate proximity to the kinds of clients who offer overseas contracts but also a ready supply of qualified professionals from diverse backgrounds, helps to explain this tendency towards regional concentration.

The following case study illustrates the combination of factors that have increasingly thrust some building-design firms into the global marketplace and the strategies required in order to make such venture successful.

Kohn, Pederson, Fox Associates, *was founded in New York in 1976 by three American partners. By 2002 the company had seventeen partners and employed around 350 people worldwide. It had offices in London, Tokyo and New York. Since 1976 the company has been involved in projects spanning thirty different countries. In June 2002, the London office – with around one third of the overall worldwide workforce – employed forty nine UK nationals and forty five foreign nationals. The latter hailed from sixteen countries including twenty five individuals from outside the EU. From 1986, and driven more by growing overseas markets than by an internal cosmopolitan impetus, the company began to move in an international direction when it won the contract for a Middle East American embassy. Soon, the firm's reputation, including for quality high-rise projects, enabled it to win European tenders and this prompted the establishment of a London office. This, in turn, helped the company to establish EU contacts from the 1980s onwards and eventually enabled it to gain from growing EU prosperity, economic integration and single market regulations. However, in 1990 the crash in the UK property market meant that several projects were terminated in mid-flow. Nevertheless, accumulated overseas expertise enabled the company to weather the British economic storm by winning contracts in Germany after reunification*

and by following the economic boom across South East Asia which continued until 1997.
Although, this expanding involvement in overseas work from the late 1980s onwards has been partly client-driven it has also involved three additional elements. One is that successful overseas projects bring further contracts as satisfied clients refer the company to other potential entrepreneurs. Also attractive buildings advertise themselves and their designers by winning widespread admiration. Secondly, the company learned from its initially unanticipated success in building-up a global profile and began to deliberately market its skills and reputation. Third, this ability to cope effectively overseas was underpinned early on by the decision to build a multi-national workforce thereby enhancing the capacity to mobilize a range of cultural, linguistic and technical skills. Attracting young, talented and probably unattached professionals from overseas is also essential because as national employees grow older and establish families it becomes more difficult to persuade them to accept long-term spells overseas. As the firm's international reputation has grown so it has received year by year a growing number of CVs from young professionals of all nationalities enabling it to build just such a multi-talented as well as a multi-national team.

This case study suggests some of the reasons why companies increasingly seek overseas work. However, there are further and more generalized factors involved in the globalization of the building-design industry and these are as follows:

- The ease of mobility and collaboration facilitated by the continuing revolution in electronic communications has made it easier for firms in the service industries to manage business activities over vast distances.

- The increased global reach of the transnational corporations (TNCs) has spawned the need for a host of supportive services industries across the globe. Moreover, TNCs are likely to tender their global contracts to service firms that can demonstrate world class attainment in their own right.

- The parallel rise of an integrated system of global cities (Friedman, 1986, Knox and Taylor, 1995, Sassen, 1991 and 2000, and Eade (ed) 1997) - serving as strategic centres for global capital and as sites of economic agglomeration – offers lucrative contracts but also attracts a huge number migrants, some or whom are technically qualified. The latter may also provide overseas social connections and information that help the more sophisticated firms to pursue opportunities for contracts.

- Fourthly, in the case of the European Union, single-market regulations stipulate that enterprises from any member state are eligible to bid on equal terms for the contracts offered within the region while all EU citizens are entitled to seek employment across the countries governed by the union.
- As far as the UK is concerned, Britain's early industrialization, imperial history and leading role in developing technical expertise in a wide range of services, including building construction and design, has meant that the UK's architectural schools have strongly influenced countries in Africa and Asia. This has generated many exchanges of technical personnel between Britain and the rest of the world but also gives UK-based companies important business contacts in many countries.
- Sixthly, some of the most prestigious overseas building-design projects emanate from the national and international "public sector" (museums, art galleries, railway stations, state or intergovernmental buildings etc). Such "public sector" projects are called upon to carry a good deal of political baggage and to make appropriate cultural statements. Building/design companies with an established reputation in a global context are again more likely to be taken seriously for such contracts.
- Lastly, global diversification offers a sensible insurance policy against those difficult times in national economic cycles when local contracts diminish, as during the early and mid-1990s when the falling property market in Britain coincided with a construction boom in the newly unified Germany.

The processes involved in going global appear to vary considerably according to the producer service industry in question though much more research is needed here. Thus in the field of law, Beaverstock et al (1999 and 2000), have demonstrated that firms desiring to establish a network of overseas subsidiaries need to be able to access localized, nationally grounded relevant knowledge given that legal codes are strongly tied to nationhood and history, though they may also rotate home professionals between partner offices. In the building-design industry, and especially in the case of projects that are intended to signify some degree of macro-regional or global identity, the "product" does not necessarily need to reflect or encapsulate local/national cultural codes. On the other hand, as already suggested, and like law firms - though perhaps to a lesser degree - even projects that are strongly intended to reflect globality still need to be embedded into a particular national space and this requires the presence of local experts who can help navigate non-national team members through the inescapable jungle of regulations and codes.

4. Going Global; the individual perspective

This section draws on the experiences and stories provided by the respondents concerning the ways in which their professional and social lives were changed by globalizing influences as a consequence of working overseas. Space does not allow a full examination of all the many ways in which their lives were altered nor in the detail that might be desirable [1]. Here, therefore, I concentrate, first, on the ways in which they benefited professionally and in career terms from working in a diversity of national situations and, second, how in many cases their personal identities and social lives were altered fundamentally by transnational experiences.

Gaining professionally

<u>Enhanced problem-solving abilities.</u> Working overseas, especially for the first time, inevitably creates a number of difficulties both personal and social – perhaps initial loneliness, homesickness and feelings of relative social exclusion from the host society – but also professional. Among the latter are the following: coping with the local language in dealings with colleagues, clients, suppliers, officials and so on; winning the trust of work colleagues and others associated with the project; exceptionally long hours of work in the case of overseas contracts; learning how to deal with the technical rules, regulations, codes of practice, bureaucratic complexities as well as cultural nuances required in that particular country; and working out how to operationalize and ground the project into a finished material object in the face of changing client demands and the requirements of officials, sub-contractors, suppliers and artisans. Moreover, most respondents arrived abroad with little or no social capital; they already knew few, if any, of the other members of the overseas work team. However, they did bring some important cultural capital (Bourdieu 1984) - a bundle of professional skills that could be adapted to meet the requirements of the new work situation and which they shared with colleagues. Accordingly, when asked about their encounters with foreign work situations and cultures and how they dealt with the difficulties they encountered the respondents usually made reference to one or more of the following situations.

---

[1] A more detailed examination of some of these themes can be found in Kennedy (2004 a and b).

Several respondents insisted that while custom and practice varies widely across nations the underlying problems involved in designing a project and then grounding it into an actual material site are fundamentally the same everywhere. As one observed: *'everywhere the real problems are the same as are the objectives; it's just the implementation that changes'*. Alternatively, many respondents observed that the ability to transpose skills to new situations, to constantly learn new skills while topping-up existing ones, to be flexible, to develop the trick of seeing problems as challenges rather than as formidable obstacles, and so on, were intrinsic to the nature of their job and their profession. Part of their training had alerted them to the need for this constant adaptability and had helped to prepare them for such eventualities. Such aptitudes have been noted by sociologists for some time. Both Merton (1957) and Gouldner (1989), for example, distinguished between professionals dependent upon locally-relevant and company-bound attachments and those who relied more on knowledge applicable to many locations and who sought the validation of wider peer groups. Intrinsic, therefore, to certain types of professionalisms is their inherent transferability between sites and projects and the possession of a roughly shared frame of reference despite national differences in culture and practice. It was evident from the accounts provided by the respondents that they had been able to draw upon just such a shared body of orientations and decontextualised skills.

Looked at from another perspective, we can also see that these transnational professionals were engaged in a continuous process of creative problem-solving, something that several social scientists (for example, Reich,1991, and Castells, 1996) have insisted is increasingly important to the symbolic wealth or informational economy. They argue that the symbolic analysts, approximately twenty per cent of the global labour force working in every kind of design activity, research, knowledge dissemination, the media, information technology and so on, have become the main wealth generators in the information society and their central task is to identify and find ways to solve problems. This seems particularly relevant to the individuals included in this study. Thus, and to a greater or lesser extent, problem-solving and trouble-shooting lie at the heart of most kinds of building work and are required everywhere, not just in overseas locations. Nevertheless, the growing awareness of wider horizons, the ability to increase one's professional repertoire of skills and the enhancement of problem-solving capacities were gains from working overseas of which many respondents were keenly aware. Here, are some typical comments made by three respondents on this topic:

'Overseas work means acquiring a diversity of professional experiences and perspectives ......regulations are always there but dealing with them in different situations makes you become more eclectic, confident in seeing that the rules can be overcome – manipulated – so you can still put design considerations first'

'I'm not afraid of challenges ...indeed now I relish change and new languages'

'I've acquired a degree of adaptability. My first period abroad in Cairo changed my life completely, for ever .... I decided that if I could tackle this then I could do anything.

Becoming a more confident professional. Closely tied to the acquisition of greater problem-solving abilities is the likelihood that those exposed to overseas work will also become more confident and certain about their capabilities. This, in turn, seems likely to benefit their career prospects but also any future companies that decide to employ them. Again, the following comments by several different respondents make this point quite strongly. Moreover, they represent widely felt and frequently expressed sentiments.

'Working abroad makes you more self-sufficient ... so you become more confident and you gain professional exposure to a wider range of technical skills. You learn that there are many possible technical solutions – all valid'

'I'm not afraid of challenges ...indeed now I relish change and new languages'

'Working in Germany increased my range of skills......gave me advantages over people who had only worked in the UK. It increased my sense of self-reliance and independence'

'I feel definitely that I've gained from the experience.....more confident and have a sense of achievement. It's an opportunity that not everyone has and I want it to continue for a while longer'.

Transferring skills between different countries. Few respondents commented directly on their ability to transfer acquired or enhanced skills directly from one country to another or the possibility that the increased mobility of certain professional practices might then lead to greater cross-border diversity, versatility and even hybridity. Nevertheless, this was often strongly implied by many of their responses while several individuals made quite explicit reference to such possibilities. In doing so they were clearly indicating that individuals and companies would benefit from the ability to acquire an ever-increasing portfolio of knowledge and skills which could then be switched between sites, offices or countries according to need. The following four comments illustrate this possibility well.

'Being here in Britain has made me stronger ... I can learn and take these skills away with me... it's made things easier for me professionally'.

'My company has developed a set of offices across twelve countries....mostly these are joint ventures but it has also sent some professionals from this London base to remain permanently in these overseas offices. They will stay a while and so learn a lot ....this will strengthen the firm as a whole.....many clients want to be involved with a worldwide company...so they come here first ...then they can utilize our worldwide network of offices and established skills'.

It's become second nature now and easier to adapt to different rules and procedures ... and to acclimatize and re-acclimatize between cultures.... Broadens your skills and outlook ...... You are able to transplant items from one country to another and this is welcomed. If I'd stayed in American I'd have been much narrower'

'If you don't have a wide range of skills and global range you will eventually lose out even in you own national market...(and from the company's perspective).... to be successful it is important to have world wide skills and this means attracting and retaining young people who desire to gain access to other countries'.

Personal identity and non-work social life.

<u>Friendship networks</u> .As we have seen, working overseas creates numerous difficulties. Probably the most important resource which enabled the respondents to cope with both the professional and personal problems they encountered was the support they received from the friendship networks into which they were drawn. For the most part these were constructed around the collaborative activities generated by the work team but sometimes clients, suppliers and others involved in the project and/or other architects and building professionals engaged on similar work in other parts of the locality, but working for different companies, also became part of these networks. Without the

cooperation, patience, assistance, good humour, mutual respect and liking emanating from fellow members of the work team the effectiveness of the respondents and the successful implementation of the project would have been in question. What is most striking about these friendship networks is their national composition. Altogether, and counting all their various combined stints, the respondents had worked overseas semi-permanently on forty nine such occasions. During these episodes, friends from the host society (locals) were much more likely than expatriates (fellow-nationals) to be present in these networks despite the obvious benefits - a common language and cultural background- and therefore the relative ease with which friendships with fellow-nationals might be negotiated. On the other hand, the greater involvement with locals is hardly surprising since they are present everywhere; in streets, shops, bars, public buildings and places of residence. In addition, there is a strong likelihood that several, perhaps most, work colleagues will be locals along with suppliers, clients and sub-contractors. However, despite the obvious presence of host society members everywhere, remarkably few of these friendship networks were *predominantly or entirely* built around relationships with nationals. Thus, in only nine of the forty-nine overseas situations had host society friends been the *sole* source of network companions. Instead, those who provided a large and frequent component of these non-work friendship networks tended to be people of different nationalities.

Thus, in thirty two of the total number of overseas stints friends from several or many nations other than the respondent's own, or the host nation, made up a substantial, the main or the sole component. Thus, these networks were partly, mostly and sometimes completely multinational in composition. Moreover, most had survived the dispersal of those involved far and wide from the locations where these ties were first forged. Nearly two thirds of the sample had maintained contacts with some of their former overseas friends of different nationalities over the years including, in twelve cases, through mutual visiting often connected to holidays or where a business trip offered opportunities to meet. Sometimes these visits involved entire families. Only much more research will reveal whether professionals in the building-design industry represent a very special case. However, for the moment it may be valid to suggest that what we are seeing here is the emergence not just of transnational affiliations that span national borders but, more interestingly, the construction of post-national relations and the foundations off an embryonic and truly global society.

Mixed-nationality marriages. Closely related to the previous point, it emerged that of the twenty five respondents who were involved in long term/permanent marriages or partnerships at the time of the interview or who had been for a long period prior to the study, in sixteen cases this had involved mixed or cross-nationality relationships. In four instances these relationships preceded the main period spent working overseas - and indeed helped to motivate the decision to work abroad in three instances. On the other hand, mixed-nationality marriages/partnerships contracted later seemed to have been one of the major consequences of working overseas and becoming involved in transnational friendship networks. In may also be the case that professional women in mixed nationality relationships who decide to prioritise their career over family life – and who are therefore able to continue to seek overseas work rather than settling down in one country, as must eventually happen where there are children – are especially likely to form a social life that revolve around a constantly circulating pool of transnational friends and couples caught in the same circumstances. If so, and again more research is needed, globalizing influences of a socio-cultural nature could be said to be cumulative and self-generating but also every bit as powerful as economic forces in propelling some individuals along a transnational life trajectory.

New or more complex personal identities. Nearly all the respondents, insisted that working and living abroad had drawn them into experiences which led them to undergo a personal transformation, one which altered the ways in which they thought about their identities and how they experienced the world. They varied a good deal in the extent to which they emphasized these experiences and the number of changes they had perceived. Length of stay abroad was clearly a major factor here. Nevertheless, most recorded at least one and often several of the altered perceptions that I now outline briefly.

First, some respondents argued that their transnational experience had compelled them to view their earlier mostly national experiences from a perspective not so very different from the ways in which 'others' - previously regarded as outsiders or foreigners – saw them. Consequently, they had become more critically aware of the limitations and disadvantages of their own nation and culture but also, perhaps, more convinced of its particular strengths. Contact with the global, in this case through living abroad, brings more clearly into focus what is unique about each national culture. A second likely consequence was that the foreign 'other' came to be seen as less and less different. Moreover, they had become more empathetic towards the host society. Previous prejudices and generalizations concerning the national "character" of the host society were now seen to be unfair, unfounded or simplistic and the visitor discovered that s/he had much more in common with the 'others' than s/he had previously realized.

Third, a number of respondents also suggested that on their return from living and working abroad they had tended to view those who had remained behind through a very different lens. Thus, the returnee may see their fellow citizens as parochial and out of touch; obsessively observing customs, lifestyles and prejudices that now seem at best quaint and at worst as unnecessary, narrow or even dangerous. Now, the local is perceived as another overseas visitor might view it. Of course, just like the sojourner abroad, the local has also changed during the interim period and this partly explains the sense of estrangement that is experienced.

A fourth possibility mentioned by several respondents was that living abroad had helped them to discover who they really were since this experience had deepened their self reliance, intensified the need to engage in constant self questioning and created circumstances where the cultural baggage they had brought with them to a foreign country was repeatedly tested and contrasted against their new experiences. Fifth, quite lengthy stays away from the homeland and perhaps spent in more than one country may mean that these individuals and their partners, if any, increasingly move within a circle of other fellow transnational/multinational professionals and friends who are also coping with life away from home. All may share a sense of estrangement both from the local society and from their respective homelands and this became a crucial common bond. Mixing in a pool of other transnationals just like oneself becomes a way of life. Their experiences and views become a reference group; the source of one's standards, meanings and values. The common experiences shared transcend nationhood. Such friendships are likely to be preserved.

Finally, as we have seen, living overseas tends to alter people in fundamental ways that make it impossible for them to ever return to their homeland on the same terms as they left it or to view it in quite the same way. In a sense, therefore, there is no going back because the person who returns is different and s/he perceives the social landscape quite differently However, a few respondents went much further than this. They observed that they had stayed away from their homeland so long that they neither could return permanently to live in their country of origin nor did they wish to do so. They had become so distanced that their country or origin now seemed more 'other' - when they visited - than the host society or societies in which they had been living for so long. For these respondents, therefore, returning permanently in order to settle down really was no longer a viable option.

References:
Beaverstock, J.V., Smith, R.G. and Taylor, P. J. (1999), 'The long arm of the law: London's law firms in a globalizing world-economy', Environment and Planning A, 31, 10, 1857-1876.
-, (2000) Geographies of globalization: United States law firms in world cities. In: Urban Geography, 21, 2.
Bourdieu, P. (1984) Distinction: A Social Critique of the Judgement of Taste. Cambridge: Harvard University Press.
Castells, M. (1996) The Rise of the Network Society. Oxford: Blackwell.
Delanty, G. and Jones, P.(2003) Europe, post-national identities and architecture. In: Burgess, P. J. (ed) Museum Europe :European Cultural Heritage Between Economics and Politics. Oslo: Norwegian Academic Press.
Eade, J. (1997) (ed) Living the Global City: Globalization as a Local Process. London: Routledge.
Friedman, J. (1986) The world city hypothesis. In: Development and Change, 17.
Gouldner, A. W. (1989) Cosmopolitans and locals: towards an analysis of latent and Social roles. In: Steven, J. (ed) Classic Readings in Organizational Behaviour. Pacific Grove: Brooks/Cole Publishers.
Hadid, Z. M. (1995) Global Architecture Document Extra 02: Richard Rogers, Tokyo. A. D. A. Edita.
Jones, P. (2003), Contested Discourses: National Identities and Architecture, Unpublished. Ph.D awarded by Liverpool University.
Kennedy, P. (2004a) Making global society: friendship networks among transnational professionals in the building design industry. In: Global Networks. 4, 2, 2004.
-, (2004b), 'Informal sociality, cosmopolitanism and gender among transnational professionals: unraveling some of the linkages between the global economy and civil society' in Eade, J. and O'Byrne, D. (eds), Global Ethics and Civil Society, Aldershot: Ashgate.
Knox, P. L. and Taylor, P.J. (1995), (eds), World Cities in a World System. Cambridge: Cambridge University Press.
KPF (1997) The Master Architect Series II: KPF, Selected and Current Works, Mulgrave, Victoria, Australia: The Images Publishing Company.
Merton, R. (1957) Social Theory and Social Structure. Glencoe: Free Press.
Powell, W. W. (1990), 'Neither market nor hierarchy: network forms of organization', Research in Organizational Behaviour, 12, 295- 336.
Reich, R. (1991) The Work of Nations: Preparing Ourselves for Twenty-First Century Capitalism, New York: Simon and Schuster.
Sassen. S. (1991). The Global City. Princeton University Press.
-, (2000) Cities in a World Economy. Thousand Oaks: Pine Forge.
Urry, J. (2000) Sociology Beyond Societies. London: Routledge.

Large-Scale Urban Waterfront Developments as an Integral Part of the Metropolitan Transformation Process: Case Studies from Lyon, Hamburg, and Gdańsk

Alexander Tölle

1. The metropolitan transformation process in «global times»

The development of the Western European metropolises is increasingly determined by socio-economic changes that are linked to the process of globalization. This process is characterized by an ever-increasing internationalization of economic relationships and a growing division of labour on a global scale. These worldwide international and intranational relationships have become feasible by the modern electronic information and communication technologies, and they manifest themselves in what numerous authors have come to refer to as global «flows» (Stratmann 1999; Castells 1989). The process of globalization incorporates a change of production and consumption patterns that leads to - and in turn is also stimulated by - a fundamental transformation of socio-economic structures. This is also referred to as the shift from the Fordist mass production and consumption age to post-Fordist times.

For the metropolises in Western Europe, the impact of the globalization process has notably led to the loss of mass production functions to remote countries mostly in the Asian Pacific region, and has thus resulted in a rather dramatic deindustrialization process. This incorporates nothing less than the loss of the traditional factors that shaped cities in the past and that defined their role and standing in relation to other cities. However, contrary to what had been feared by some, this has not led to the European city falling into insignificance. Rather the intertwined relationship of globalization and localization, deriving from a newly emerging logic of centralization (Sassen 2001), has awarded them new roles such as places of specialized production, as financial nodes, as business command and control centres, as preferred locations for creative activities, and as places for consumption and tourism (Hall/Pfeiffer 2000, 114).

Yet the transformation process from a Fordist metropolis, based on mass production and consumption, to a post-Fordist metropolis, based on producer, financial and consumer services, unfortunately is not just an automatic shift from one state to another. Rather, the emerging worldwide economic competition of cities entails an uncertainty about the future development of each individual city in the new urban network. «No place can be sure of retaining its traditional place in the urban hierarchy, its traditional role, for long.» (113) Hence the metropolitan transformation process is characterized by two factors. Firstly, it is an enduring process requiring constant adaptation and lacking any fixed ending or final state. Secondly, it is an active process requiring from cities the creation of structures and environments suitable for the attraction of firms and institutions related to the new functions, although that is not to deny that there are important development dynamics beyond the influential scope of municipalities, and that some cities may profit from better initial positions than others retain. The various strategies cities employ in order to meet the challenges deriving from the globalization process may be broadly summarized under the four terms of «good governance» structure, public-private partnership, festivalization and city marketing (Stratmann 137). The transformation from Fordist to post-Fordist structures of the cities in the Western world being an ongoing process that has started some two or three decades ago, hierarchies of the European metropolises may be established as indicators of how well or bad cities have mastered their transformation (Cattan 1999, 165; Dematteis 1997, 92)

2. The Central and Eastern European cities - metropolises «in statu nascendi» or global periphery?

However, the metropolises of the post-communist Central and Eastern European countries have still to find their places in these hierarchies, having been shielded from any impacts of the globalization process by the «iron curtain» until the end of the 1980s. Subsequently the transformation process from a command to a market economy determined spatial development, notably characterized by the introduction of private land ownership and the installation of local and democratic self-governance. Yet unfortunately the idea of a fast and swift transition to Western standards, manifested in the early 1990s by the implementation of economic «shock therapies» in nearly all post-communist countries, has been proved too optimistic by the course of history (Bohle 2002, 43).

Instead, this transformation process has become a continuing one, and one that has become more and more influenced by the impact of globalization, a parallelism sometimes referred to as the «double transformation». In recent works, the transformation process and its spatial aspects are in the case of Poland predominantly discussed in the context of the integration into the given international framework. Yet if the analytical «protection shield» of Poland and the other Central and Eastern European «transition» states being «special cases» in the international context and are not as yet allowing for any scientific comparison to western countries has to be lifted, then on the contrary developments in these countries will have increasingly to be explored in relation to international and European events.

From this viewpoint, it becomes evident that the Central and Eastern European metropolises already have to be regarded as participants in the competition of European metropolises for the best possible result of the transformation process into post-Fordist structures. Albeit the post-communist cities are characterized by certain common development features (Hall/Pfeiffer, 136), they are not forming a homogenous category of their own. This entails two difficulties. On the one hand's side, it has to be feared that their «late-comer» status and the lack of long-established political, economic and social structures may result in such serious competitive disadvantages that these cities are destined to form a «new European periphery»(Bohle 2002, 273 instead of swiftly enlarging the urban network of important metropolises eastwards. On the other hand's side, the chronic lack of fixed structures and reliable data in those cities still makes any assessments of their present or future standing difficult.

3. Why waterfront sites do matter in the metropolitan transformation process

The emergence of vast derelict sites in the inner city's cores of Western metropolises has become a familiar occurrence during the last three decades. It is one of the most prominent spatial indicators of the global economic transformation leading to a deindustrialization process in the developed countries (Schelte 1999). Apart from the actual production sites, there are also infrastructure sites affected, notably railway land, and former harbour areas having fallen victim to «containerization» (Schubert 2001, 21).

These now derelict areas having mostly been created in the times of industrialization in the 19th century, they are frequently situated adjacent to what was then the historic city area that in turn usually has become today's city centre, as well as along the city's waterways, water having been a prerequisite for industrial production. Hence there are today extensive derelict sites located next to the inner city's cores and often along potentially attractive waterfronts. Since the collapse of communism, this phenomenon resulting from globalization processes is also occurring in the cities of Central and Eastern Europe, and does so rather in a time lapse.

Western metropolises have been trying for a number of decades now to use such derelict sites on waterfronts to develop on them large-scale urban projects. The general aim may be summarized as to create attractive new urban districts for modern living and working functions, districts that will become internationally-known icons of the city. In the context of increasing competition between cities on a European and global scale, these districts are to represent an environment that is particularly attractive for the new important producer, financial and consumer services, and if possible to serve as an «engine» for the structural transformation of the entire agglomeration (Malone 1996, 13). The common features of these projects include the creation of remarkable urban and architectural design, mix of functions, staging of major city events, or the implantation of big urban objects as so-called «light houses» or «flagships». Among the most famous European examples are of course the London Docklands, the «Kop van Zuid» in Rotterdam, or the redevelopment projects along the riverbanks in Bilbao and the sea banks in Barcelona. These as well as numerous other projects, indeed around the globe, are commonly regarded as models for successful developments by many metropolises and their municipalities.

The key issue here is that waterfront areas have thus become, though not exclusively, a laboratory (e.g. with respect to implementation tools, design quality definition, re-use concepts for derelict industrial buildings, models of public-private cooperation, etc.) for the tasks and policies of the urban renewal process of the post-industrial city at the end of the twentieth century itself. «The waterfront can be seen as paradigmatic of the condition of the post-industrial city and its vicissitudes will make it possible for the fortunes and errors of urban policies to be interpreted» (Brutemesso 2001, 47).

This potential of large-scale urban waterfront projects turns into a particular importance when applied to the conditions of cities in the transformation countries of Central and Eastern Europe, in this case to Poland. For more than a decade now, Polish cities are undergoing rapid economic, social and spatial changes. Yet the question how well prepared these metropolises in constant transformation will eventually become in comparison, and indeed competition, to Western metropolitan regions remains to be answered; and the pessimistic viewpoint, as has been discussed here earlier, would expect the entire region to become a «European periphery». Without any doubt, apart from an anticipated pre-eminent position of the capital city Warsaw, parameters and quantities do not as yet allow for any predictions about which of the metropolitan areas are likely to master their transformation process in the most beneficial way and emerge at a dominant position in the Polish city network (Dutkowski 2000, 65), or indeed will become part of a European metropolitan network (Cattan 1999, 167). So assessing the existing possibilities and restrains to implement the first major urban waterfront project in a Polish city and comparing and relating it to two similar projects in western metropolises may allow for conclusions concerning the capability of the city to master the transformation process towards a metropolis of national or even international standing.

4. The spatial context: the agglomerations of Lyon, Hamburg, and Gdańsk

The three project cities regarded here have in common that they have a century-long legacy as trade cities of international importance that became also production centres during the industrialization process in the 19th century. Therefore the deindustrialization process heavily affected all three cities at the end of the 20th century. However, mainly due to a rather diversified production structure, Lyon has still a powerful industrial basis and is also, as the undisputed first city of the French «province», a centre of services as well as finance and trade (Bonneville 1997). The city has formed an «urban commonwealth» with the municipalities of its agglomeration, called «Grand Lyon» that has started in the 1990s to implement a number of strategies to create a coherent and competitive metropolitan area. Hamburg, though still one of the major port cities in the world, has undergone in recent years in effect a transformation from an industrial and port city to a media and service centre (Möller 1999). As a traditional free Hanseatic city, today still a federal state on its own, strategies to create a coherent metropolitan region together with neighbouring states and municipalities are recently starting to emerge.

The city of Gdańsk underwent rapid transformational change in the early 1990s, with a major negative mark stone having been the bankruptcy of the Gdańsk shipyard company in 1996. However, the economic basis is still rather dominantly focused on the sea and sea-related economy sector (Pankau 2001). Together with the cities of Sopot and Gdynia, Gdańsk is forming a spatial entity called the Trójmiasto, which translates into «Three-City». However, as yet, there is nearly no cooperation between the three municipalities. There rather prevails a sense of rivalry, e.g. concerning the two ports in Gdańsk and in Gdynia. The idea by experts of creating a coherent Trójmiasto metropolitan area in order to foster a sustainable development of the entire agglomeration is so far hardly heeded by officials (Baranowski 2000).

5. The project case studies: Lyon Confluence, Hamburg HafenCity, and Gdańsk Młode Miasto

In all three case study cities, the objects are large derelict areas with a waterfront and adjacent to the existing city centres. In Lyon, it is a site of 150 ha formerly occupied by various infrastructure uses such as a wholesale market, a mail sorting centre, a river port, railway land, and so on. In Hamburg, the chosen project area is on 155 ha of already derelict harbour land in the «Hamburg Freeport» area, adjacent to the outstanding urban storage house ensemble of the «Speicherstadt». In Gdańsk, it is the 73 ha site of the former Gdańsk shipyard, that of course has become world famous in 1980 as the birthplace of the Solidarność movement, but that has ironically fallen victim to the new market economy and has gone bankrupt in 1996. The project name «Młode Miasto» translates into «Young City».

Though obviously being situated within three quite different national and regional contexts, all three projects are remarkable similar in their targets and in their design outline. The concept that in all three cases is based on preliminary studies undertaken in the middle of the 1990s is to build new urban districts on a scale of 1.000.000 to 1.500.000 m^2 in a period of around three decades. All three new districts are conceived to have an urban and green atmosphere, characterized by mixed functions (flats, offices, retail, leisure, and culture) in a perceptible waterfront ambience. All are to be presented as high-quality city centre enlargements, marked by a dominant object as a «lighthouse», notably a museum of science and culture in Lyon, a cruiser terminal in Hamburg, and a «Solidarność» convention centre in Gdańsk. All three projects are designed to become internationally known icons of their respective entire metropolitan area and, in this respect; they are to be become the attractive hearts of their newly producer, financial and consumer services-based metropolitan regions.

6. The key project development parameters

As an examination framework defining the parameters of large-scale inner city projects, a triangle of the factors *Location - Implementation - Integration* will be used (Tölle 2001, 31):

6.1. Location

As has already become evident, the general targets and conceptual determinants are conspicuously identical in all three case studies and may be regarded as referring to the factors generally perceived as essential components for convincing waterfront operations (Brutemesso 1999; Lorens 2001), such as high urban quality, mixed functions, lighthouses, green environment in a perceptible waterfront context, modern living spaces and innovative working sphere. This similarity is not too surprising as these determinants are characteristic for similar advanced major developments in Western metropolises, and as these benchmarks regarded as guarantors of success are spread by internationally renowned urban planning and economic consulting companies. This may actually also be regarded as a feature of globalization.

6.2. Implementation

Here major differences are becoming apparent between the Lyon Confluence and Hamburg HafenCity projects on the one hand's side, and the Gdańsk Młode Miasto project on the other hand's side. The leading force behind both Western projects is the respective city municipality that intend to cooperate with the private sector through public-private partnership. Hence, if massive private capital investment is to be achieved, the public sector, as a potentially commonwealth-oriented protagonist, obviously has to take into account the demands of the private sector, as a potentially profit-oriented protagonist. Though an act of balance may have to be performed, the driving role of the municipality is not questioned, and particularly manifested by development bodies with private-sector working structures but under public control, as well as by a significant municipal financial engagement in the starting phase of the project.

In France, a well-developed and experienced practice and legal framework for implementing urban «Grands Projets» exists for decades now (Rousseau/Vauzeilles 1995) and is directly applied to the structure of the Lyon Confluence project. At its core is the urban instrument of a designated development area «ZAC», in one go a legal basis foremost for building permissions, real estate management including a municipal charge for participation at land price increases, as well as for the creation and activity of a public-private development company «SEM». In Hamburg, the project area is nearly completely owned by the municipality, which created a publicly owned development company that can act like a private company, but under municipal supervision. On the basis of an informal master plan (Bodemann 2001), the legal planning framework will be successively prepared and the lots priced for each sub-area in a negotiation process possibly involving potential investors.

In Gdańsk, however, a private company aiming at developing its real estate initiates the project. The potential of this area to become an attractive enlargement of the city centre is seen as a possibility to market the land and to enhance profitability. Yet this potential is also strongly stressed by urban planners of consultancies and notably of the Technical University of Gdańsk, where the initial studies in this direction were undertaken (Kochanowski/Kochanowska/Lorenz 2001). Unfortunately, the Gdańsk municipality appears to be rather reluctant to be involved in this project, whilst paradoxically it is the private developer that is trying to create a public-private partnership agreement. As an ambitious urban venture like the Młode Miasto project may be regarded as not feasible without strong municipal support, the risk lies in the land being developed in a way well below its potential significance for the city, or even contrary to the commonwealth of the agglomeration.

Particularly with building activities in the inner city of Gdańsk being strongly hampered by a lack of suitable and foremost available land, and therefore with developments such as the building of new housing estates and major hypermarkets taking place rather on «green field sites» around the city leading to an already strong suburbanization process

(Pankau 2001), the former shipyard area would offer a great opportunity in the sense of sustainable development of the agglomeration. Moreover, it offers the potential to create the central business district deemed a necessity for the future prosperity of the city (Kochanowski; Kochanowska; Lorenz 2001, 228), as well as without a doubt to become the engine project for the whole agglomeration when compared to similar sites in Western metropolises.

6.3. Integration

The degree to which a project is oriented towards social objectives strongly influences its outcome (Malone 1996, 5). On this field, again important differences between the two Western projects and the Gdańsk project are to be detected. The definition of a vocation for the respective new district, i.e. its placement on the real estate market, and foremost its position within the urban and social context of the agglomeration, is a major task in the development process of the two projects in Hamburg and Lyon. Appealing information centres and regular public meetings are offering an informal way of continuous public participation, that enables to promote the venture from the city's point of view, as well as to early spot potential points of conflicts and to consider them in the course of the development process. In Gdańsk, this aspect yet unfortunately appears to be a rather neglected issue. The municipality again takes a rather passive attitude. However there are first attempts initiated by the development company to launch their project in the broader public, such as staging small cultural venues on the site and to publish the first official brochure. Yet as there are also no initiatives by the public, the preconditions for positioning the Młode Miasto within a social context appear to be rather slim, which in turn means unfortunately that the process of designing the project all along was so far hardly influenced by regards to the needs of the general public.

Conclusions

The comparison of the Gdańsk project, the first advanced of this kind in Poland, with two similar ventures in Western metropolises demonstrates the areas on which an international exchange of experiences, which should encompass more than common benchmarking, might be beneficial for city developments in the Central and Eastern European transformation countries. The particular problems there do not just derive from well-known «hard factors», i.e. conditions such as still inefficient planning legislation, an unbalanced real estate market, limited public financial means, and so on.

Rather a lack of know-how is apparent on fields such as, e.g., public private partnership, planning culture and transparency, or public participation. Particularly the experience on how to use these methods or instruments in order to influence the implementation process and to enhance the integration into the general urban context is still to be made. This is not to say that the practice in Western metropolises in this respect is necessarily mature; however the skills required to pursue a process-oriented development approach may well become evident and may be exemplary. Acquired competence on these «soft» issues may perhaps even help to solve «hard» problems and may decide on whether projects like the Młode Miasto will contribute to a sustainable development of its agglomeration, or just become an opportunity missed.

In the context of the municipal capacity and capability to organize a development process for prime inner-city waterfront sites as a potential engine for the successful tackling of the task of economic and social transformation, it becomes apparent that, in comparison to Western metropolises, still a long way is to be gone. Without a doubt, the Gdańsk shipyard area offers a chance, like no other potential site in the region could, to develop an attractive new inner-city waterfront district that may well become an icon of the agglomeration, due to all land being in the hand of one owner willing to develop the site, its advantageous location, and foremost its unique and worldwide aura as the birthplace of the Solidarność movement, and therefore in a figurative sense the graveyard of communist dictatorship. The identified problems for implementing the project on the «soft» issues are also strong restraints for the general spatial, social and economic development of the whole agglomeration. Even though the outcome still remains to be seen and predictions are obviously difficult to make, the Młode Miasto «waterfront» project may in this respect in either way well become a «watershed» project for the future development and standing of the entire metropolitan area.

References:
Baranowski, A. (2000) Plan strategiczno-operacyjny równoważenia struktury
    Aglomeracji Trójmiasta. Gdańsk. Unpublished script.
Bodemann, U. (2001) HafenCity Hamburg - Anlaß, Masterplan, Chancen, in:
    Schubert, D. (ed.) Hafen- und Uferzonen im Wandel. Analysen und
    Planungen zur Revitalisierung der Waterfront in Hafenstädten. Berlin: Leue.
Bohle, D. (2002) Europas neue Peripherie. Polens Transformation und
    transnationale Integration, Münster: Westfälisches Dampfboot.
Bonneville, M. (1997) Lyon. Métropole régionale ou euro-cité?, Paris: Anthropos.
Bruttomesso, R. (2001) Complexity on the urban waterfront, In: Marshall, R.
    (ed.) Waterfronts in Post-Industrial Cities. London/New York: Spoon.
Castells, M. (1989) The Informational City. Information Technology, Economic
    Restructuring and the urban-regional process, Oxford: Blackwell.
Cattan, N. (1999) Le système des villes européennes. Paris:Anthropos.
Dematteis, G. (1997) Représentations spatiales de l'urbanisation européenne. In:
    Bagnasco, A.; Le Galès, P. (ed.) Villes en Europe, Paris: La Découverte.
Domański, R. (1998) The Spatial Transformation of the Economy. Studia regionalia

KPZK PAN, 7.
Dutkowski, M. (2000) The changing post-socialist metropolitan areas in Poland. In: Chojnicki, Z.; Parysek, J. J. (ed.) Polish Geographie. Problems, Researches, Applications. Poznań.
Hall, P.; Pfeiffer, U. (2000) Urban Future 21. London/New York: Spoon.
Kochanowski, M.; Kochanowska, D.; Lorens, P.(2001) Land Use Structure Determinants for the Gdańsk Shipyard Area. In: Lorens, P. (ed.) Large Scale Urban Developments. Gdańsk: p. 227-239.
Lorens, P. (2001) Rewitalizacja frontów wodnych nadmorskich miast portowych. Doctoral thesis (unpublished). Politechnika Gdańska.
Malone, P. (1996) Introduction. In: Malone, P. (ed.) City, Capital and Water, London/New York, p. 1-14.
Möller, I. (1999) Hamburg. Stuttgart/Gotha: Perthes Länderprofile.
Newman, P.; Thornley, A. (1996) Urban Planning in Europe. International competition, national systems and planning projects, London/New York.
Pankau, F. (2001) Transformacja struktury funkcjonalno-przestrzennej Trójmiasta. In: Kołodziejski, J.; Parteka, T. (red.) Kształtowanie ładu przestrzennego polskich metropolii w procesie transformacji ustrojowej III RP. Biuletyn KPZK PAN 193..
Rousseau, D.; Vauzeilles, G. (1995) L'aménagement urbain. Paris: Presses Universitaires de France.
Sassen, S. (2001) The Impact of the New Technologies and Globalization on Cities, in: Graafland, A. (ed.) Cities in Transition. Rotterdam: 010 Publishers.
Schubert, D. (2001) Revitalisierung von (brachgefallenen) Hafen- und Uferzonen in Seehafenstädten, in: Schubert, D. (ed.) Hafen- und Uferzonen im Wandel. Analysen und Planungen zur Revitalisierung der Waterfront in Hafenstädten. Berlin: Leue..
Schelte, J. (1999) Räumlich-struktureller Wandel in Innenstädten. Moderne Entwicklungsansätze für ehemalige Gewerbe- und Verkehrsflächen. Dortmunder Beiträge zur Raumplanung Nr. 97.
Stratmann, B. (1999) Stadtentwicklung in globalen Zeiten. Lokale Strategien, städtische Lebensqualität und Globalisierung. Basel: Birkenhäuser.
Tölle, A. (2001) Entwicklung innerstädtischer Brachflächen. Parameter der Umsetzung großer innerstädtischer Quartiersentwicklungen am Beispiel der Projekte Lyon Confluence und Hamburg HafenCity. Master Thesis European Urban Studies (unpublished). Bauhaus-Universität Weimar.

The 'new' Berlin: multiple spatial conceptions of the capital city in the 'Palast der Republik'/ 'Stadtschloss' debate

Monika de Frantz

Analyzing globalization in the European context means to take into account European integration as another related - though not equivalent - spatial phenomenon relevant for cities and their relations with states. While the future role of cities and states remains unclear in the context of political and economic integration of the EU, capital cities represent the central places of nation states as well as just being 'normal' cities. They are diverse places characterized not only by local, but also by national and increasingly supra-national processes, past and present. Within this complex urban spectrum, the role of politics ensuring the city as a place of cultural and political cohesion becomes increasingly difficult. In addition to the economic pressures, urban politics also faces conflicts associated with the past and future of the nation state in the context of European integration and globalisation. The political debates about the 'new' Berlin therefore illustrate how the conflicts and tensions among different spatial aspects of European multi-level governance are perceived from a specific local perspective and thus contribute to change that place.

Capitalist globalization processes turn global cities into the economic centers of a globalized corporate world with decreasing regulation capacities of nation states and local governments (Sassen 1991; 1994). But European integration contributes to a transfer of political power from nation states to the supra-national and the sub-national level resulting in a system of multi-level governance (Marks et. al. 1996; Hooghe and Marks 2001). Within a context of increasing economic competition, Europe's important urban heritage gives rise to the assumption that urban elites not only challenge the economic primacy of nation states but also make cities the future political centers of European integration (Le Gales 2002). But differences of central-local relations in the European context show the continued relevance of nation state systems for the political steering of the local (Keating 1991; 1993; Harding 1999). The contradictory assumptions about the spatial tendencies of political power relations in Europe propose the need for further research into the dynamics of identification with place in the context of multi-level institutional reterritorialization (Shields 1999).

This paper presents a case study of how urban decision-makers are challenged by the multi-level restructuring of their spatial context, a process that in return challenges and changes these spatial structures themselves. Focusing on urban culture the question is posed how spatial concepts such as globalization and European integration are conceived through the cultural lens of place. Regarding the ambiguous theoretical positions on the hollowing-out of nation states versus their continued importance for European cities, the research enquires how local, meaning national and/or urban, identities change through multi-level restructuring processes. The fact that this case study is situated in Berlin, the new capital city of reunified Germany, therefore offers an interesting example of how local-global conceptions interact with national identities.

By conceptualizing the city as a field of struggle over specific symbolic places, it will be shown how different spatial identifications of the city transform urban culture. An operationalization of the cultural and symbolic dimension of such struggles is attempted here by approaching the concept (1) in terms of a politically symbolic site such as an architecture and museum project planned at a strategic place in the city center; (2) in terms of the diverse meanings of the city represented and associated with the conceptualization of this project; (3) in terms of discourse and public communication through which urban decision makers from within and outside the representative institutions renegotiate the identifications with place and thus change the legitimate basis of politics. A discourse analysis of the media debates (Wodak 1999) about a particularly conflictive project such as the 'Palast der Republik'/'Stadtschloss' in the center of Berlin gives an indication of the symbolic struggles associated with urban politics in the context of restructuring space.

1. Berlin: divided city, capital city, and 'normal' European city

Berlin has been selected here as a case study because it is a city that continuously struggles with its different spatial conceptions in the context of internal and external restructurings. It therefore serves as an interesting example to illustrate the problem how spatial challenges like globalization and European integration are conceived through the cultural lens of place. In particular the decision to make Berlin the new capital of reunified Germany has given rise to discussions about what these spatial conceptualizations mean for local identity.

Due to a comparatively quick pace of innovation and change in the early twentieth century Europe, Berlin was associated with the myth of modernization and industrial metropolization, the anti-type of a European city and the proto-type of everything that was admired or disliked about American cities (Thies and Jazbinsek 1999; Biber 2002; Kramer 2001). But today, giving up the hopes of the early Nineties to become once again a so-called 'global city', Berlin's urban leaders struggle to make the city what they consider a 'normal European city' (Strieder 2000). Berlin's changing history from the Prussian empire, to the national socialist regime, to the working class movements, through the GDR, and the cold war until European unification, has on one side made it the central place of European history. On the other side, this very problematic historic heritage has contributed to a high conflict potential in present day urban politics.

Due to its past partition and only recent reunification as well as high immigration rates, Berlin is characterized more than most other European metropolises by spatial divisions, cultural diversity, social segregation and differing political and economic interests (Häußermann and Kapphan 2000). Moreover, the recent decision to make Berlin the new national capital city of reunified Germany offers the opportunity to research the multiple values and interests involved in the political process of reconstructing national identity (Welch Guerra 1999). Berlin's urban planners also experience an increasingly competitive market environment in the context of globalization and the economy's recent integration into the European market (Strom 1996; 2001; Heeg 1998; Lenhart 1998; Seiler 1998; Kraetke 1999; Kraetke and Borst 2000). Due to the exposed geographic position to the political changes in Eastern Europe and envisaged EU enlargement, Berlin's leaders struggle to combine its new function as a national capital with that of an emerging local center of relevance beyond the national boarders (Seitz 1998).

Under this impression, the perceived need for a repositioning within the enlarged European space has provoked intense public debates on the visions and objectives of urban development. These debates reflect the tensions among the multiple spatial identifications with the city as local society and polity, as national capital, European center or even a global city (Habermas 1995; Marcuse 1998; Cochrane and Thomas 1999).

2. The 'Palast der Republik'/'Stadtschloss' in Berlin

Like no other city Berlin's cityscape characteristically reflects its changing history and continues to be formed and transformed by the complex restructuring processes affecting the city. Among the construction projects that have received most public attention since the beginning of the Nineties are the new tourism and entertainment quarter around 'Potsdamerplatz', the commercial district around 'Friedrichstrasse', the government headquarters at 'Spreebogen', the planned office buildings at 'Alexanderplatz' and finally the Palace of the Republic ('Palast der Republik') on the 'Schlossplatz', the site of the former Berlin castle ('Stadtschloss'). Most of these new construction development have been planned as part of the economic restructuring processes (Strom 2001) or, in the case of the capital city buildings, for mostly political-administrational functions. But the 'Schlossplatz' debate represents the focal point of a highly emotional and politically sensitive controversy about Berlin's identity transformation from a divided city to the capital city of reunified Germany, looking for its place within an integrating Europe and a globalizing world.

Constructed by the GDR regime in 1973 at the site of the former Berlin castle of the Prussian kings Hohenzollern ('Stadtschloss'), the Palace of the Republic ('Palast der Republik') serves as the contested site of this symbolic struggle. The castle, partly in ruins after World War II, was demolished in 1951 to make place for a parade area. As part of the GDR regime's redesign of East Berlin's center the former representational building contained the plenary room of the people assembly ('Volkskammer'), the powerless GDR parliament. For a short period after the fall of the Communist regime in 1990, the East German transitionary parliament used it for its few sessions. But more than these political functions, the Palace of the Republic constituted to many East Berliners mainly a memory of their everyday lives, the official cultural center and one of the few public social meeting-places offering concerts, theaters, restaurants, a discotheque and other recreational facilities. Since its closure in 1990 for reasons of asbestos contamination, the GDR building stands as an empty ruin. Situated both at the border between former East and West Berlin and in the area of the former historic city center, it has turned into a politically sensitive place loaded with symbolic meanings.

The political debate ranges over wide possibilites: whether to pull down the Palace of the Republic or rather to conserve, renovate and adapt it; whether to reconstruct the old castle in its place or rather to construct a modern building; whether to construct a building in that place at all, or whether to leave it empty until an appropriate use concept is found. The conflict has been going on now for more than ten years. In this time it has turned from a local issue constituting one of many urban planning problems confronting the urban authorities in the formerly partitioned city into one of the most symbolic problems of Berlin's reunification and capital-city planning. With high media attention and mobilization from mainly interest lobbies and experts, the issue still waits to be solved jointly by the urban and national governments. The parliamentary measure passed in June 2002 finally resulted in a slight majority for a historicist design, a new construction with form and facade of the former baroque castle combined with some of the remaining parts of the GDR palace. However, due to the present economic crisis as well as to the resistance of Berlin's recently leftist government, the destiny of the project remains more unclear than ever.

The discourse analysis of the political debate has covered the twelve-year period from the closure of the Palace of the Republic in 1990 until the decision of the federal parliament to reconstruct the historic form and façade of the former 'Stadtschloss' in July 2002. The arguments disclosing different conceptions of Berlin's urbanity have been divided according to respectively different positions about the demolition of the 'Palast der Republik', the reconstruction of the 'Stadtschloss', or in general into those pushing for the realization of the project against those aiming to postpone the decision in an attempt to slow down urban development. While the arguments chosen for analysis have been repeated so often in the course of the twelve years of debate that they have turned into so-called 'topoi', the actors employing them have changed and switched arguments several times. The following will give an analysis of the spatial conceptions used as arguments and frames in the public debate about the 'Palast der Republik'/'Stadtschloss'.

3. Spatial conceptions in the 'Palast der Republik'/'Stadtschloss' discourse

References to space have served since the beginning of the discourse on the 'Palast der Republik'/'Stadtschloss' to support different argumentations by defining the framework for Berlin's diverse images and functions as a social, cultural, political or economic center. The political transformations in the beginning of the Nineties implied a vast range of spatial changes affecting Berlin from its small neighborhoods and districts to its global image. The recent political and economic changes characterizing the spatial context of the political identification debate include: city's spatial context the fall of the Wall and the need for urban integration of the partitioned city; the reunification of Germany and therefore the sudden integration with the surrounding region Brandenburg; the decision to make Berlin the new capital of reunified Germany and the consequent establishment of federal institutions in the city; the sudden absorbtion of Eastern Germany into Germany and the European Union; the political and economic transformations across the border in Central Eastern Europe and the preparations there for EU enlargement; the deepening of European integration among the existing EU member states; the sudden world-wide expectation that Berlin would possibly regain its former status as a metropolis of global importance and the recent economic crisis affecting Berlin more heavily than Germany and the rest of Europe. Within this divers spatial framework the 'Schlossplatz' represented an important symbolic issue for discussions about about different conceptions of the city and the construction of spatial identification processes...

> "Freiheit und Einheit, Hauptstadt und Kulturstadt, oder einfach Metropole, Urbs, mit Berlin kann man vieles verbinden so viel, daß sich immer wieder Nichtberliner gern wenigstens ideell als Bewohner dieser Stadt fühlen ob es den Berlinern nun paßt oder nicht paßt."
> (Renzo Piano, international architect, Beze 18.12.1998)

As a free and reunified city, a national capital, a metropolis and European city, Berlin incorporated a diversity of meanings that was reflected through and created by the different spatial conceptions of its inhabitants. But also far beyond the city's local borders people in Germany, Europe and all over the world associated diverse images with Berlin. The Palace of the Republic/'Stadtschloss' served to renegotiate these spatial conceptions under participation of mostly urban actors, partly also national players and a few globally engaged architects or real estate enterprises with interest in the location. The spatial conceptions employed in the argumentations were often not equivalent to the speakers' spatial origins. They mostly aimed at changing the dominant meanings associated with the city in line with the specific interests, political functions as well as personal attitudes, tastes and values of the speakers.

Originally most East Berliners attributed little symbolic importance to the Palace of the Republic as a location of cultural recreation. But its contestation by the Western governing elites as a political symbol of past Communist power and neglect of local – Prussian - history caused the building to emerge as a central place of struggles over urban identifications. Already in the beginning of the Nineties, immediately after the fall of the Wall, the closure of the Palace of the Republic emerged as a spatial confrontation between East and West German identities over the cultural occupation of Berlin's center. East Berliners' stood up for their rights to separate historic identities which were built, if not on the political appreciation of the old regime, then at least on personal memories of everyday life during the GDR period. West Berliners fought to regain what they considered their historic identities, or what was left of them after the destructions of two world wars, the politically imposed demolitions of historic heritage by the GDR regime, and the German partition during the cold war.

While initially the debate about the Palace of the Republic and the reconstruction of the castle had been interpreted as a fight between Eastern and Western Berliners for the occupation of the new center, the need to construct a new, shared identity around this site became a common objective.

> "Nötig aber ist eine essenzielle Entscheidung. Gemeint ist die rigorose Abwendung von der Alternative Palast der Republik oder Stadtschloss und die Hinwendung zur politisch-nationalen Bedeutung des öffentlichen Stadtraums. (...) Denn der Stadtraum trägt hier die politische Symbolik, an seiner Gestaltung und Verwendung wird gemessen werden, wie die Generation nach dem Mauerfall mit dem Geschenk und Erbe der Deutschen Frage umgegangen ist, ob sie fähig war, die politisch-historische Botschaft des Mauerfalls in Architektur zu manifestieren und als geschichtliches Sediment abzulagern." (Zohlen, cultural historian, Beze 12.2.2000)

The desire to overcome the political partition of the past and the socio-cultural division of the present by constructing a new symbol of the urban unity found expression in many statements about the 'Palast der Republik' /'Stadtschloss'. Then the capital city decision added another issue: the need to create a symbol that would represent not only the reunified city but that would also symbolize the capital city the political center of the reunified Germany. The many references to the term 'new Berlin' expressed the aim to define a new national identity around the new status of its capital.

'An diesem Ort, der die Mitte Berlins und damit die Mitte der Haupstadt und damit wiederum die Mitte Deutschlands markiert, muß unsere Zeit etwas zustande bringen, das Sinnbild dessen ist, was diese Stadt, dieser Staat darstellen will.' (Monika Zimmermann, journalist, Tsp 6.1.1997)

Since the capital city treaty had settled the conflicts among the municipal and the federal government over the establishment of federal political institutions away from the 'Schlossplatz', the general consensus was that the place would symbolize the new cultural unity of city and nation. The discussion about the palace/castle'Stadtschloss as city center ('Stadtmitte') and state centre ('Staatsmitte') served to negotiate this new identity of the capital city.

While anything belonging to the national and the urban sphere was considered necessarily politically opinionated and biased, references to space outside the national borders tended to add a general impression of objectivity. Be it a political body such as the 'international expert commission'; the prestige of 'international culture institutions'; an 'international real estate fair' with 'international audience'; the 'international world of experts' such as that of the 'international protection of historic monuments', an international organization such as UNESCO, or such abstract terms as 'world cultural heritage', 'international image' ("internationale Ausstrahlung") and an 'idea' or 'utopia of international dimension' (Schuster, museum manager, Beze 19.4.2000) - the references to abroad generally served as a positive frame of reference for the local debate. Similarly comparisons to other European culture or architecture projects such as the Paris Louvre (Volker Mueller, journalist, Beze 21.6.1995; Boddien, Beze 9.5.2000), the Vienna Castle (Boddien, castle lobbyist, Beze 16.12.1998), the Paris Centre Pompidou (Eichstaedt-Bohlig, Federal Green MP, Beze14.1.2000), or even the Mostar bridge (Boddien, 18.1.2000) appeared as objective measures for different local orientations. Also the option to use the building as a seat of 'European institutions' was proposed several times by different opponents in the conflict (Gruene Tsp 23.3.2000, PDS, Boddien et.al.). But such spatial references were neutral only at first sight, as a closer analysis of spatial conceptions of the city, the state, Europe and the international or rather global sphere disclosed diverse meanings competing for representation in the symbolic construction of the 'new Berlin'.

The castle supporters went so far in their cross-European comparisons that they introduced a specific type of 'European city' as a general measure of urbanity. A historic center, a grown cityscape, public life in the urban squares, a mostly bourgeois citizenship engaged economically and politically for their city, and above all an architectural landmark were the main characteristics estimated in other European cities and desired for Berlin (Beze 16.10.1999, Beze 27.8.1997, Beze 25.4.1994). The former castle which stood for all these features had been demolished and should now be reconstructed in order to readjust Berlin to the perceived 'normality' of other European cities.

"Dadurch würde Berlin ein Zentrum bewahren, das neben den großen historischen Erinnerungsstätten und repräsentativen Monumenten anderer Orte wie dem Zwinger in Dresden, dem Louvre in Paris, dem Dogenpalast und Markusplatz in Venedig, dem Hradschin in Prag und dem Kreml in Moskau würdig bestehen könnte." (Hamann, arts historian, statement against castle demolition already in 1950, and requoted by Paul, journalist, Beze 7.9.2000)

The reconstruction of 'one of the biggest and most artful castles in Europe' (Moenninger, journalist, Beze 20.12.1996) would stress Berlin's former role as 'an old centre in Europe' (Ruehle, cultural expert, Tsp 20.6.1993) and in addition make it the place of 'the most interesting construction project in Europe' (Grosse, real estate investor, Tsp 9.3.2000). The historicist reconstruction would enhance the city's specific local character. It would thus increase residents' positive identifications with their city at the same time as it would constitute a locational advantage in competition with other European cities. It was a way out of Berlin's exceptional historical status, to 'normalize' its historic heritage by reconstructing its architectural landmarks as other European cities had done already after the war. The castle should be reconstructed in order to create an urban specificity that was different but still similar to other European cities. Normalizing Berlin without adjusting it, the castle would enforce Berlin's specific identity among other European cities against the 'homogenizing' forces of globalization.

"Der Augenblick und das Nichts. Das ist das Schicksal der jungen Mega-Städte Asiens und Südamerikas, für die die europäische Stadt als Modell längst ausgedient hat, und nicht nur, weil städtische Zivilisation erst anfängt, wenn die Not ein Ende hat." (Kollhoff, architect, Tsp 3.1.1997)

The skyscrapers of Asia's global cities created by profit-oriented global investors were posed as a threatening vision against the European model. 'Civilization' and welfare should be realized through the reconstruction of the castle as a symbol of local identity. For 'the more global the architecture, the more exchangeable our cityscapes, the more important become urban symbols such as the castle' (Peter Neumann, journalist, Beze 19.4.2001). While the architects of the 'European city' generally preferred small and gradual urban development rather than reaching ever new 'personal height records', the big project of the castle was appreciated because it would enable 'social events' and a 'point of identification' (Klaus-Dieter Weiss, journalist, Beze 16.10.1999). Against globalization as a threatening tendency towards chaos, disintegration and poverty enhanced by the partisan interests of profit-oriented global investors and architects, the image of the European city stood for a civilized community characterized by welfare, social integration and local identity through the positive symbols of a common past.

"Der Schlossplatz steht fuer das Geschichtsbewusstsein der Deutschen. Dabei geht es nur vordergruendig um Architektur." (Schaeuble, CDU federal parliament party leader, Beze 19.9.1997)

The 'Schlossplatz' represented the historic consciousness of Germany. Despite all previous architectural considerations about aesthetics, the reconstruction lobbyists surpassed their concentration on the castle's spatial function for the immediate urban environment. Instead many reconstruction supporters stressed the symbolic function of the castle as a symbol of the state in the centre of the new national capital. As the new place in the center of Berlin constituted the center of city and state equally, the project to rebuild the castle turned from an urban planning issue into a matter of national importance. It would become the center and symbol of the reunified Germany that had overcome the post-war partition and could now build a new national self-consciousness. Following the 1998 nomination of a federal minister of culture despite of a federalist constitution that attributed cultural legislation as a regional competence of the 'Laender', the reconstruction of the castle was claimed as a task of national culture. As Berlin was now the capital of Germany, its center design was not considered a local problem to be solved amongst 'the neighboring districts' anymore butrather the responsibility of the federal state. Against the resistance of the West and Southern German 'Keine Mark fuer Hohenzollern Fraktion' and Berlin's local left, all federal provinces were asked to participate in the reconstruction of Berlin for the sake of the symbolic representation of the reunified German state. (Moenninger, journalist, Beze 19.1.2000). While the Federal Republic of Germany had been characterized during the Cold War period by a basic fear of Prussian centralism as the cause of two World Wars, the 'Berlin republic' posed the question of a renewed tendency towards a more centralist state. The reconstruction of the castle stood for the wish to restore the historic importance of the capital city Berlin by reestablishing the Prussian heritage as a positive or at least neutral part of German culture.

"Das Ensemble Unter den Linden ... sagt inhaltlich folgendes aus: In der Mitte der Ort fuer die politische Macht (...) Darum herum – eingebunden – war die Museumsinsel, waren die Universitaeten, waren die Opern, war die Neue Wache – sie stand damals fuer Militaerreform und nicht fuer Militarismus – und waren die Kirchen als Ort der Toleranz. Das heisst, dieses Ensemble war eine politische Landschaft, es war Ausdruck einer grossen europaeischen Kultur der Toleranz, der Aufklaerung und Humanitaet. (...)
Ich glaube, dass es erlaubt ist, sich zu dieser Tradition zu bekennen. Ich glaube sogar, dass es vor dem Hintergrund des Europa, das wir bauen werden, wichtig ist[.] (...)
Die Menschen unserer und wohl auch der folgenden Generationen suchen Identitaet in ihrer Geschichte. Zumindest in ihrer grossen Mehrheit brauchen sie diese Identitaet auf dem Weg in ein neues, groesseres Gemeinwesen, in das Gemeinwesen Europa. Dass dieser Weg beschritten wird, wollen und befuerworten auch wir. Diesen Weg kann man aber nur gehen, wenn man weiss, wer man ist.
Im Uebrigen tun sich andere Voelker sehr viel leichter und gehen sehr viel selbstverstaendlicher damit um, wenn es solche Entscheidungen zu treffen gibt. Wir wissen warum; wir sollten aber auch ein Stueck von diesem ganz natuerlichem Geschichtsverstaendnis uebernehmen." (Antje Vollmer, Federal Green MP, 248. Sitzung Deutscher Bundestag, 4.7.2002)

Not Prussian militarism, but rather military reforms, tolerance, enlightenment and humanism were the values to be reconstructed with the historicist center and the rebuilt castle. These traditions were acceptable as a historic basis necessary for the construction of a German identity 'on the way into a new, larger community, the European community'. Similar to other nations' 'natural historic awareness', Germans were to normalize their attitude towards history, especially the Prussian heritage, in order to participate successfully in the European integration process. Local animosities among the federal provinces were a consequence of Germany's post-war political culture but they would now undermine the constitution of a new national self-confidence symbolized by the capital city Berlin. The normalization of national identity implied an appreciation of its historic art treasures including those of Prussia as the former center of a European empire (Stefan Speicher, Beze 31.1.2001). In order to realize European integration successfully, the different nations needed to rely with equal confidence on their historic traditions and identities. And European integration served as the framework to enable and embed the development of a national culture free of the dangers and restrictions of Germany's historic leverage.

„Wenn die Stadt seit Jahren in der Schlossplatzfrage nicht recht weiter kommt, dann weil sie wie erstarrt ist vor der Angst vor sich selbst. Ein Schloss wiederzuerrichten, das dahin ist, das ist die verrückteste aller Ideen. Das macht sie so gewinnend. Und was das Preußische anlangt, so reicht der Hinweis, dass es ein Schloss des Barock war, jenes Stils, den man den letzten gesamteuropäischen nennt." (Stephan Speicher, Beze 31.1.2001)

The fears of a strong national identity with re-centralization tendencies symbolized and enhanced by a reconstructed Prussian castle were countered by the argument that what was reconstructed was not so much a nationalist manifestation but rather an artistic work of European importance. Reconstructing a Baroque castle meant to enhance the awareness of a common European heritage that predated the emergence of nationalist movements, the original cause of the twentieth century wars resulting in Berlin's and Germany's ambiguous identities. European integration offered an opportunity to overcome this problematic heritage and to establish positive and self-confident identifications with the concept of nation, the 'reestablishment of that old European state when the Vienna Congress made Russia a part of the comprehensive European order' (Wolf-Jobst Siedler, cultural publisher, 1999). With reference to Germany's older historic roots in the Prussian monarchy its status as a normal European state was embedded in a European Community linked by a shared heritage of nineteenth century European empires. Berlin's status as a national capital of the 'Berlin republic' became possible only through this 'historicist' Europeanization of the nation state and would be enhanced by the reconstruction of the former 'Stadtschloss'.

On the other side, skeptical commentators discarded the European idea symbolized by the castle as a 'regressive desire for a pre-modern harmony' that negated major parts of Germany's history, namely those that had caused the development from a nationalist to a federal state (Buddensieg, cultural journalist, Beze 21.11.1998). Although Berlin had become the capital of Germany, this should not pave the way for sentimental longings for a renewed nationalist centralism. Germany's improved self-confidence in international relations as well as in European integration should be possible only under strict observance of the federalist constitution. The design of the former 'Schlossplatz' was therefore regarded as a local matter to be decided by the municipal authorities. If the site took on national importance this could not be as a symbol for a new harmonious national and Prussian identity represented by the castle.

"In keinem Fall kann ein Schloss das bauliche Symbol der dritten deutschen Republik sein. Die Debatte sei vor allem eine Angelegenheit der Stadt, die in Berlin entschieden werden müsse." (Nida Ruemelin, SPD Federal Minister of Culture, Die Zeit in Beze 8.3.2001)

Berlin's national role was to symbolize a 'republican center' of the reunified Germany' (Eckehadt Barthel, federal SPD MP and head of parliamentary committee of culture, 248th session of German federal parliament, 4.7.2002) so that it necessarily attracted all kinds of cultural struggles fought out in a pluralist society. The new building in its center should therefore represent 'Germany's federal diversity in an integrating, cosmopolitan Europe' (Bodewig, SPD federal minister of construction, Tsp 17.1.2001). A modernized center design thus aimed to symbolize the opening up of national identity towards a federal state based on a pluralist interplay among multiple cultures inside Germany and, through its embedding within Europe, within the international world. Instead of posing a threat to local traditions, globalization thus offered an opportunity to challenge the self by confrontation and exchange with the other.

"Damit würde der Ort des Schlosses in die Spannweite einer Idee von Universalität auf der einen und der nationalen Geschichte auf der anderen Seite hineingestellt. Diese Spannung nicht als Konflikt, sondern als ohnehin zu bewältigende Aufgabe der Gegenwart zu verstehen und ihr sinnfälligen Ausdruck zu verleihen - das wäre die eigentliche Herausforderung der Wiederaufbaudebatte." (Helmut Engel, historic protection specialist, Beze 3.6.2000).

In the castle opponents' view, Europe constituted not the protectionist umbrella against globalization but the bridge to the global world. European integration was the first step towards this interaction with the world. It enabled a self-confident national culture as the basis for the equal participation of Germans and their state in the global realm. The new capital Berlin, some castle opponents argued, presented the ideal place for the purpose of redefining Germany's identity along a pluralist process of renegotiating the national 'self' in confrontation with the European and global 'other'. With its cultural diversity Berlin constituted the only globally important city of Germany. Instead of reconstructing a castle, Berlin's existing cultural qualities should be maintained and promoted (Norbert Lychatz, reader, Beze 19.11.1997). The right response to the unsuccessful global city boom of the beginning of the Nineties was not to long sentimentally for an apparently glorious past but to build on Berlin's present cultural diversity. Through its new status as the national capital, Berlin would automatically challenge and transform

Germany's otherwise more homogeneous cultural identity towards a globally open European society. However, in face of the budgetary crisis of the city, such continuous cultural development needed financial support from the federal state. To fill the 'intellectual vacuum' in the country, the federal state should take on political responsibility for national culture. It should financially ensure and promote Berlin's existing cultural diversity as the symbol of the reunified Germany (Conradi, SPD Federal Mp and architects association, Beze 27.7.1998).

However, following the general negative feeling about modern architecture aesthetics, urban design ultimately could not be used to create a cosmopolitan touch around local culture. This symbolic function was attributed instead to the use concept. The so-called 'Humboldt Forum', named after the 19th century German humanists Wilhelm and Alexander von Humboldt, was planned as a national museum of extra-European cultures complementing the focus on European arts represented by the neighboring 'Museumsinsel'. This increase in the city's symbolic importance and global reach was accompanied by a dramatic loss of political power for the city. In addition to the cultural conflicts following Berlin's reunification, the political coordination problems following its sudden national capital status and the restructuring problems of an economy in transition, Berlin's bankrupt budget was to be submitted fully to the control of the federal government. The leadership problems within the urban government caused a practical competence transfer of the 'Schlossplatz' issueto the federal parliament which discarded the political will of the urban leaders and chose a historicist design. Moreover, due to the city's deep budgetary crisis, decisions about any major urban investments were to be submitted to a strictly constitutional procedure involving the federal government and the rest of the German provinces. In lack of the necessary financial resources from the federal state and minor political interest from the part of the federalist oriented regional leaders in the construction of any symbol of state centralism, more public engagement was improbable. By the early year 2003, the cultural conflicts over Berlin's center planning were about to be left to the profit orientation of private investors. If anything would be constructed on the 'Schlossplatz', this building will be far from symbolizing a political consensus or even expected symbol of unity. Most probably the project would be realized as a historicist reconstruction with mostly commercial use and a very reduced public part representing an official image of high culture. At best, such a project can be expected to cover the cultural divisions that emerged in the course of the planning debate. Still, most importantly, the process of public discussion by itself has constituted an important step towards representing and communicating different urban identities. Although it has opened up and deepened political conflicts across the established party lines, it might have also contributed to a greater sensitvity of the political elite towards the problems of cultural integration and reunification.

4. The 'new' Berlin: outline and limits of a dominant image

Berlin's former partition into an Eastern and a Western part of the city continues after reunification through a competitive struggle among the two parts of the city over the symbolic occupation of the urban center. The conflict stands symbolically for the new political identity of the whole state and the former GDR citizens' rights, participation and contribution of their political heritage therein. But the continued domination struggle soon resolved in the shared insight of the need to create a new, common identity that must symbolize a new beginning as well as building a synthesis of the two existing halves. The 'Schlossplatz' becomes this new symbol of the reunified city.

Since Berlin is now the capital also of reunified Germany and it is the place where the two parts of Germany confront each other most immediately, the city considers itself the 'Werkstatt der Einheit' ('workshop of unity'). The debate about the 'Schlossplatz' therefore not only concerns the center of the reunified city but also the center of the reunified nation. Out of a struggle between national and urban interests and symbolisms over the center of the new capital city emerges the shared identity of the 'Berlin republic', a new reunified Germany symbolized by the integration processes in its new capital city. Because of the important political symbolism of the city for the reunification of the nation, the municipal interests in urban planning for an integrated urban society are given priority over the federal use interests in Berlin's center. But on the other hand the urban institutions lose their political and financial independence to the control of the federal government in the course of the capital city building process.

The symbolic importance of the capital city Berlin for the new reunified nation also causes severe tensions between these recent centralization tendencies and the established federal constitution of the German state. The conflict is fought between Berlin and the state government on one side and the other federal provinces fearing to lose competences especially in the cultural field on the other side. But it concerns not only political competences but also an essential cultural fear of the authoritarian Prussian heritage associated in the past with a German great power centralized under Berlin's leadership. Attempts to neutralize the historic meaning of Prussia focus on the arts-historic heritage of Prussian architecture, e.g. the 'Stadtschloss', and its meaning for European culture. But the struggle over the role of Prussia in the history of the German nation cannot be solved. The compromise is finally a merely symbolic recentralization focusing on Berlin as the central symbol of German federalism but subordinating it politically and economically to federal state control. The 'new Berlin' integrates and also needs to subordinate its local identity into its status as the national capital of the reunified Germany. Aiming to overcome the problematic heritage of its national history, the new capital city symbolizes more than the German reunification project. Embedded in a Europe preparing for deeper integration and enlargement the 'Berlin republic' stands for Germany's new self-confident attitude towards the international world. In face of Germany's negative historic experiences, this reevaluation, and to a certain extent re-centralization, of national identity is made possible and fostered only by the pioneering role of German reunification in the European integration process. Europe therefore constitutes a generally positive frame countering the nationalist tendencies within Germany and enhancing a new international self-confidence. Europe thus serves as an opportunity if not to forget but to overcome the negative national associations from the First to the Second World War, from the National Socialist atrocities to the foreign occupation, from its Cold war partition to the authoritarian regime of the GDR. Although these periods still belong and need to be accepted as part of national history, Germany's Europeanized national identity and the political conflicts within the German state should and can now be directed more towards its future contribution to Europe and international politics. But as the process of national emancipation is still very recent, the international scale is still considered more a positive authority for domestic conflicts than an arena object to creation by the nation in equal cooperation with others. The many references to international experts or international organizations as well as comparisons to other European cities illustrate this generally shared tendency to accept international benchmarks as apparently neutral and objective arguments for either side in the conflict.

But the actual meanings associated with European integration or globalization diverge strongly between the respective attitudes towards national identity and relate to the cultural cleavage among modernization and traditional visions. For those finding the new identity of the capital city in the historic culture of place, namely in the cultural heritage of Prussia as a former European big power, globalization means a negative threat for local identity. Europe represents in this perspective the protection against destructive cultural homogenization pressures from the capitalist global economy through European cities' shared historic consciousness of their respectively different local traditions. Against this the modernization vision views globalization as a positive challenge for local identity through the cultural influences balancing and liberalizing the negatively perceived implications of local tradition. European integration thus represents the bridge that opens up a closed local identity to the world and thus builds an important basis of Germany's modernization and equal participation in the international world.

The general perception therefore defines Europe as a positive new opportunity to overcome a negatively perceived national history and turn the hopes of the nation towards a positively defined self-confident and cooperative international future. But the question how this should be realized opens up a conflict reflected in the debate about the center of the capital city between traditional and modernization visions of national society, between reconstructing and confronting history, between harmonizing social conflict and discussing democratic decisions in a pluralist society. The existing urban and federal institutions turn out to be inappropriate to solve this conflict over national identity, which emerges from the construction of the new capital city. The resulting institutional vacuum gives rise to institutional restructuring processes transferring power to the federal state institutions and emerging private actors.

5. Conclusion

The 'new Berlin' needs to subordinate many aspects of its urban center planning to its status as the national capital of the reunified Germany. Local identification processes therefore merge urban and national elements in the new capital city. Europe serves here as a positive framework for any changes in the cultural orientations and legitimacy bases of political decision-making. Aiming to overcome the problematic heritage of its national history, the new capital city symbolizes more than only the German reunification project. Embedded in a Europe preparing for deeper integration and enlargement, the 'Berlin republic' stands for Germany's new self-confident attitude towards the international world. In face of Germany's negative historic experiences, this reevaluation and, to a certain extent, re-centralization of national identity is made possible and fostered only by the pioneering role of German reunification in European integration. Berlin, the new reunified capital city, represents the central place of these multi-level identification processes in which the 'Schlossplatz' has emerged as a contested symbol.

But underneath this dominant image of the 'new' Berlin the struggle over the 'Schlossplatz' discloses a diversity of partly conflicting spatial interpretations. These multiple conceptions indicate the direction defended by structural theories, namely the tendency towards an increasing importance of the supranational and global scale. But within the analytical field of Berlin's urban politics, the concepts of Europe and the global world are used with reference to different meanings according to the respective political context. The present analysis of identification processes shows how local identities are indeed challenged by spatial changes in the structural context. But the case of the capital city Berlin also proposes that globalization and European integration can serve as arguments for the construction of a new national self-confidence. The fact that these national identification processes take place in the capital city inhibit or at least weaken the urban potential of the 'Schlossplatz' to serve as a symbolic site of integration processes within the city. Berlin's political elites, due to the symbolic quality of the city's new political capital status, find it more difficult than those of other German cities to reconstruct their city center around their specifically urban interests. Instead the city gains a new important role through its capital status that weakens the urban elites while showing a renewed symbolic importance of the city as a place.

The global cities literature's predictions about the weakening of the local through capitalist globalization need to be qualified in view of the capital city's growing importance in national perception and ensuing engagements of some parts of the national elites within the capital city. Moreover, the example of the capital city Berlin demands modification of the multi-level governance literature with regard to the renewed importance of the national scale within the local realm. From the point of view of identification processes, the present study therefore proposes a flexible view of multi-level governance with differing spatial relations in different places and contexts.

References:
Begg, I. (1999) Cities and Competitiveness. in: Urban Studies, 35 (5-6), 795-809.
Bourdieu, P. /Wacquant, L. (1992) An Invitation to Reflexive Sociology. Chicago: Polity Press.
Cheshire, P. (1999) Cities in competition: Articulating the Gains from Integration. In: Urban Studies, 36 (5-6), 843-864.
Cochrane, A. / Jonas, A. (1999) Reimagining Berlin: World city, national capital or ordinary place? In: European Urban and Regional Studies, 6 (2), 145-164.
Delanty, G. / Jones, P. (2002) European Identity and Architecture. In: European Journal of Social Theory, 5 (4) 453-466
Habermas, J. (1995) Die Normalität einer Berliner Republik. Frankfurt: Suhrkamp.
Häußermann, H./Kapphan, A. (2000) Berlin: von der geteilten zur gespaltenen Stadt? Sozialräumlicher Wandel seit 1990. Opladen: Leske+Budrich.
Harding, A. (1999) Review Article: North American urban political economy in urban theory and British research', British Journal of Political Science, 29, 673-98.
Heeg, S. (1998) Vom Ende der Stadt als staatlicher Veranstaltung'. Reformulierung städtischer Politikformen am Beispiel Berlins. In: PROKLA, 110 (28), 5-23.
Hooghe, L./Marks, G. (2001) Multi-level governance and European integration. Lanham: Rowmam and Littlefield.
John, P. (2000) The Europeanisation of sub-national Governance. in: Urban Studies, 37 (5-6), 877-894.
Keating, M. (1991) Comparative urban politics: power and the city in the United States, Canada, Britain, and France. Aldershot: Elgar.
-, (1993) The Politics of Economic Development. Political Change and Local Development Policies in the United States, Britain, and France. In: Urban Affairs Quarterly, 28 (3), 373-396.
-, (1995) Size, efficiency and democracy: consolidation, fragmentation and public choice. In: Judge et.al. (eds) Theories of urban politics, 117-135.

Krätke, S. (1999) Berlin's regional economy in the 1990s: Structural adjustment or ‚open-ended' structural break? In: European Urban and Regional Studies, 6(4), 323-338.
Krätke, S./ Borst, R. (2000) Berlin: Metropole zwischen Boom und Krise. Opladen: Leske+Burdrich.
Le Gales, P. (2002) European cities: social conflicts and governance. Oxford University Press.
Lenhardt, K. (1998) „Bubble-politics" in Berlin. Das Beispiel Koordinierungsausschuß für innerstädtische Investitionen: eine „black box" als Macht- und Entscheidungszentrale" – in: PROKLA, 110 (28), 41-66.
Marcuse, P. (1998) Reflections on Berlin: The Meaning of Construction and the Construction of Meaning. In: International Journal of Urban and Regional Research, 22 (2), 331-337.
Marks, G. et. al. (1996) Competencies, cracks and conflicts: regional mobilization in the European Union. In: Marks, G. et. al. (eds) Governance in the European Union. London: Sage.
Sassen, S. (1991) The Global City. Princeton University Press.
-, (1994) Cities in a world economy. Thousand Oaks: Sage.
Seiler, G. (1998) Von Subventionsmentalitäten und Metropolenträumen. Wirtschaftspolitik in Berlin. In: PROKLA, 1998, 110 (28), 25-39.
Seitz, H. (1998) Die Hauptstadt Berlin in der Nachwendezeit. In: Eglen, J./Seitz, H. (eds) Städte vor neuen Herausforderungen. Baden-Baden: Nomos.
Shields, R. (1999) Culture and the economy of cities. In: European Urban and Regional Studies, 6 (4), 303-311.
Siedler, W. (1998) Phoenix im Sand. Glanz und Elend der Hauptstadt. Berlin: Propyläen.
Strom, E. (1996) In search of the growth coalition. American urban theories and the redevelopment of Berlin. In: Urban Affairs Review, 31 (4), 455-481.
-, (2001) Building the New Berlin. The Politics of Urban Development in Germany's Capital City. Lanham: Lexington.
Strieder, P. (2000) Principal Berlin. In: Senatsverwaltung für Stadtentwicklung (ed) z.B. Berlin. Zehn Jahre Transformation und Modernisierung. Berlin.
Thies, R./Jazbinsek, D. (1999) Embleme der Moderne. Berlin und Chicago in Stadttexten der Jahrhundertwende, WZB Working Paper FS II 99-501. Berlin.
Welch Guerra, M.(1999) Hauptstadt Einig Vaterland. Berlin: Bauwesen.
Wodak, R. (1999) The discursive construction of national identity. Edinburgh Universtiy. Press.

Towards a sustainable post-suburbia?
The sustainability of new economic centres in European metropolitan regions

Marco Bontje

Deconcentration has been the major trend in most metropolitan areas in Northwest Europe since the 1960s, and most other parts of Europe followed that example towards the end of the 20th century. With regard to policy goals of sustainable regional development, deconcentration has so far mainly been seen as a counterproductive tendency. Initially, the deconcentration process mainly resulted in mono-functional housing, employment and consumption areas in low densities, generating increasing car traffic and huge losses of open space. The negative consequences for regional sustainability of these developments are obvious. However, in recent years we can increasingly witness a tendency towards new multifunctional concentrations in the area around the cities formerly known as 'suburbia'. The central question of this paper is how this shift from 'suburbia' to 'post-suburbia' might contribute to a more sustainable regional development of metropolitan areas.
Instead of condemning and generalising further deconcentration tendencies with negatively laden terms such as 'urban sprawl', we might want to consider the possible positive effects of some forms of deconcentration as well. Employment deconcentration might contribute to a more sustainable regional development by 'bringing jobs to the people', especially when it leads to new concentrations close to, or even in, suburban housing areas. In addition, combinations of production and consumption could produce areas that are used more intensively than the traditional mono-functional industry or office areas. The possibilities to produce such mixed-use areas have improved considerably since most present-day employment concentrations produce much less noise and pollution than the industrial complexes of the past. However, a really constructive contribution to sustainable regional development is only reached when the new job concentrations meet various other sustainability criteria like promoting the use of public transport, applying forms of intensive and multiple land use, or decreasing transport distances to suppliers and customers.
Sustainable regional development might be defined as:

- A development in which human activities are balanced with their environmental resource base. This involves a balancing of economic, social and environmental dynamics, which is generally summarised in policy and strategy documents with either the key words 'people-

planet-profit' or the 'standard elements' environment, futurity, participation and equity;
- A development with a long-term perspective, encouraging an improved health, wealth and welfare for current generations without jeopardising the chances of future generations;
- A development with a regional rather than a local perspective, based on integrative planning for a region as a functional entity. Regional co-ordination on the scale level suited for the activity that is planned for might prevent 'not in my backyard'-tendencies at the local level

(Wheeler 1998; Ewing 1997; Ravetz 2000; Palmer et al. 1997; Roberts 1995)

Sustainable (regional) development should not seen as a fixed goal or a desired 'end state', because such an ideal situation is probably impossible to reach given the continuously changing social, economic and environmental circumstances. What we consider 'sustainable' today might very well not be seen as sustainable by future generations. In addition, the dynamic character of the concept should be stressed: it includes an aim for development and change instead of being a synonym for conservation (as it is often misunderstood). If the concept of sustainable development is applied in a too conservative way, it might result in sustaining or even strengthening unjust status quo situations (Marcuse 1998). An equally important consideration is that sustainability is not the same in different parts of the world: "What may be accepted as normal or acceptable at one place may be unacceptable elsewhere" (Roberts 1995, 212). Instead, the search is rather for developments that contribute to a 'more sustainable' situation. The move towards more sustainable metropolitan regions could be summarised as a "(...) move toward greater resource efficiency, environmental quality, social equity, and community vitality, while moving away from automobile dependency, non-renewable resource consumption, hazardous waste generation, and inequity" (Wheeler 1998, 439).

Employment deconcentration in Northwest-European metropolitan regions
Initially, the deconcentration process of Northwest-European metropolitan regions mainly consisted of population deconcentration, while employment remained concentrated in the cities. Under the circumstances of rapidly increasing wealth, increasing car possession and improvements in road and rail transport infrastructure since the 1960s, ever larger parts of the population managed to realise their move to what they considered as the ideal living environment: the detached or semi-detached home with private garden in a rural or suburban living environment. Even though the force of this suburbanisation process in the developed countries lessened somewhat since the 1980s, as a result

of the dropping share of family households and the rising share of singles and childless couples with generally a more urban-oriented household preference, non-urban population growth remained at a higher level than urban population growth (Champion 2001; Bontje 2001). Meanwhile, employment deconcentration started more hesitantly, with only a few branches in search for expansion space and better accessibility moving to the city edges or beyond. However, especially since the manufacturing crisis of the 1970s and 1980s and the shift from a manufacturing-oriented towards a service-oriented economy, employment growth outside of the cities accelerated while urban economic growth lagged behind. While most central cities of Northwest-European metropolitan regions managed to recover from their economic crisis in the 1990s and created new employment opportunities in the service sector, their once dominant position in the metropolitan economy was increasingly challenged by the surrounding suburbs and smaller cities. A new geographic division of labour came about, in which the hierarchy with multifunctional city centres on top was gradually replaced by a polycentric metropolitan economy with various specialised employment concentrations (Kloosterman and Musterd 2001; Van de Ven 2000; Lambooy 1998). The new divisions of labour in metropolitan regions are certainly also linked to the new international division of labour produced by the globalisation process. As Graham and Marvin (2001) argue, the international integration of metropolitan economies often led to a disintegration of geographic and economic elements of those metropolitan economies. 'Archipelagos' of largely disconnected economic activities, with stronger interregional and international connections than intra-regional ones, have replaced the traditional 'vertical integration' of industrial production complexes.

Frequently, the deconcentration of population and employment in Northwest Europe has been compared to earlier North American experiences. The metropolitan region of Los Angeles was most often taken as the point of reference. The extreme form of deconcentration in regions like Los Angeles was often generalised as 'urban sprawl', which was generally considered as a negative development. Opponents of urban sprawl claimed that it would encourage the segregation of residential areas of other land uses. The negative image of urban sprawl was strengthened through the upsurge of environmental awareness in the late 1980s. Urban sprawl would produce a considerable growth of mobility and it would make the metropolitan regions highly dependent on the private car. It would also mean a huge loss of open space to new housing areas, office parks, shopping malls and the infrastructure needed to connect all these developments. Moreover, it was feared that urban sprawl would lead to a loss of social cohesion, identity and 'sense of place' for the people that lived, worked and recreated in them

(Anderson et al. 1996; Sudjic 1993). These developments were (on both sides of the Atlantic) contrasted with the idealised image of the 'traditional European city': a compact settlement in which all locations could be reached with public transport, by bicycle or even on foot. This compact city was seen as a much more 'sustainable' development model. It was no coincidence that so many European countries followed a compact-city planning strategy in the late 1980s and the 1990s, a period in which the debate on sustainable development claimed a prominent position on the national and international policy agenda. In the US, academic and political initiatives promoting 'new urbanism' and 'smart growth' were rapidly gaining ground.

Meanwhile, the academic and political debate seems to have moved away from opposing the two extremes urban sprawl and compact city and their supposed advantages and disadvantages. The simple dichotomy of American and European cities has also been departed, as both American and European cities are obviously highly diversified groups (Hassenpflug 2002). It has increasingly been acknowledged that the processes of population and employment deconcentration cannot be generalised as 'urban sprawl', because deconcentration has come in various shapes in different metropolitan regions, including relatively compact versions with concentrations along highway corridors or in new activity centres (Ewing 1997), and that deconcentration does not need to have negative consequences for a sustainable regional development (Headicar 2000; Breheny 1996). At the same time, the positive contribution of compact city growth to sustainable regional development was not beyond dispute either. Especially the supposed effects of compact city development on travel behaviour are increasingly doubted (Ravetz 2000; Dieleman et al. 1999; Headicar 2000). Moreover, compact city development can lead to negative effects on sustainability too, creating a living environment in which the impact of air, water and noise pollution is more acute and risk hazards of potentially dangerous facilities affect larger parts of the urban population (De Roo and Miller 2000).

In various recent studies of metropolitan regions, it is claimed that the traditional image of suburbia is no longer valid. Suburbia is gradually becoming a highly fragmented place, where low-density housing areas are increasingly mixed with higher-density housing areas, but also to an increasing extent with employment, shopping and recreational facilities. The city seems to have been turned 'inside-out', with the new urban centres emerging on the metropolitan fringe (Keil and Ronneberger 1994). This emergence of new centres in the former metropolitan periphery seems to harm the development of the traditional core city much less than was initially feared by many. Parallel to the emergence of new growth poles, also these central cities have recently enjoyed a revitalisation in most European metropolitan regions (Burdack and

Herfert 1998). Therefore, instead of 'the end of the city', a polycentric structure has developed in many European metropolitan regions, in which concentrations of people and employment can be found both in the cities and in their suburbs. Furthermore, due to scale enlargement of daily private and commercial traffic, new polycentric structures are developing when several formerly monocentric urban regions start to overlap each other. These emerging metropolitan structures have been described in academic literature and policy reports as 'network cities', 'urban networks', polycentric urban regions' or polynucleated urban regions' (Batten 1995; Dieleman and Faludi 1998; Kloosterman and Musterd 2001; Ministerie VROM 2001). In the following, the Randstad in the Netherlands is discussed as an example of such polynucleated structures, where recent tendencies of deconcentration have led to new threats, but also new potentials for sustainable regional development.

The Randstad towards increasing polycentricity: consequences for sustainable development
The Randstad is the area in the West of the Netherlands where the four largest cities and several medium-sized centres are concentrated. To the extent that it can be considered as one functionally integrated whole, a claim which is still fiercely debated among Dutch as well as foreign geographers, one of its most characteristic features is its polycentric structure. This polycentric nature of the Randstad was even increased further through the spatial dynamics of the last decades. Since the 1960s, a combination of planning policies and market forces has led to the emergence of new centres of population and job concentration at the city edges and in suburban locations within the Randstad. Population deconcentration, which will not be discussed in more detail here, took place across quite large distances, partly stimulated by the development of large-scale housing areas in new and extended towns (Bontje 2001). Employment deconcentration was generally directed towards the city edges and to suburban locations directly outside the large cities. Planned new cities such as Almere, Capelle aan den IJssel, Nieuwegein and the municipality of Haarlemmermeer were among the fastest growers in terms of employment in the late 1990s. In the case of Haarlemmermeer, a large share of this growth is directly or indirectly linked to the expansion of Schiphol airport, located in this municipality. However, also other suburban municipalities that were not planned to have population and job growth at all have developed into economic sub-centres of some importance. The recent job growth and job distribution dynamics seem to indicate that companies are aiming for locations that combine the advantages of a suburban environment and nearness to a larger city. They are leaving the (centres of the) large cities, or prefer to locate in suburban areas from the very start, because of space, accessibility and

maybe also safety considerations, but at the same time they are reluctant to locate far from the agglomeration advantages that large cities still have to offer.

Contrary to what was feared by many politicians and researchers, the emergence of new centres hardly damaged the employment base of the large cities. Even though the employment growth of the largest cities in the 1990s was only 'average' in the Dutch context, this was already a spectacular recovery after decades of growth stagnation or even large-scale job loss. This urban recovery took place in the favourable context of an economic recovery of the Netherlands as a whole. Moreover, especially Amsterdam and to a lesser extent also Rotterdam and The Hague seem to a have claimed a rather prominent position in the network of world cities (Taylor 2002). Amsterdam specialises as a location of global or European headquarters, even though neighbouring municipalities (most notably Haarlemmermeer, with Schiphol airport) sometimes beat Amsterdam in the headquarter competition. Rotterdam still is one of the main seaports of the world, and The Hague recently attracted quite some international diplomatic functions. In addition, due to the increasing importance of 'cultural industries', it can be expected that the large cities as the most favourable environment for these industries will enjoy further economic growth in the near future (Kloosterman and Lambregts 2001). Nevertheless, also within the large cities a strong tendency towards further deconcentration of jobs from city centre to city edge took place. Several new employment concentrations, often adjacent to railway stations and/or ring roads, have already been established since the 1970s, but this development accelerated considerably in the late 1990s. If these developments will continue on the longer term is not yet clear. Since 2001, economic growth and job growth in the Netherlands have stagnated due to the worldwide recession. As the length of this stagnation period is hard to predict, so are the longer-term effects on the spatial dynamics of job distribution in the Randstad. The political chaos in the Netherlands in 2002 adds another factor to the uncertainty about the Randstad's future, as the future course in Dutch spatial policy as well as economic policy is undetermined.

What could be said about the possible consequences of employment deconcentration for the possibilities on a sustainable development of the Randstad region? The most important positive effect that job deconcentration might have is that it might decrease problems of 'job mismatch' that resulted from the massive suburbanisation movement in the 1960s and 1970s. A large share of the people that moved out of the large cities kept working in or near the large cities and often also kept using the large city's shopping and cultural facilities. This led to a strong increase of traffic between the suburbs and new towns on the one hand and the large cities on the other. As highway connections were generally available earlier and to a larger extent than public transport connections, the vast majority of this suburban-to-urban traffic took place by car. The rather modest share of people that uses public transport to get to the large cities is still enough to produce crowded trains in the rush hours. Both the highway and the rail network seem to have reached their maximum capacity. An increase in employment in these suburban locations might reverse these problematic mobility trends. It increases the chances of suburbanites to find a job in their place of residence, or at least close to it. Unfortunately, however, the above argumentation is only valid for high-skilled workers that are over-represented in suburban living environments. A continuing job deconcentration might work out negatively for low-skilled workers that are over-represented in the central areas of the large cities. In this way, employment deconcentration produces a movement of jobs towards the high-skilled workers and away from the low-skilled workers (Van Ham et al. 2001). Therefore, the process of employment deconcentration has at best mixed consequences for sustainable development: it might 'bring jobs to the people', but only to those people that can afford to live in the suburbs. Keil and Ronneberger (1994) as well as Graham and Marvin (2001) expressed similar concerns about areas around the traditional and new nodes that become subordinate or even 'bypassed' in the process of globalised economic development.

Another unsustainable aspect of recent office park development in the Dutch Randstad is the increase of automobile dependency. Most new office parks developed in the last few years are situated very close to highways. Even though many of these sites are also quite easy to reach with public transport, the infrastructure facilities often tend to be much more suited for car traffic than for public transport or 'slow traffic' (cycling and walking). Additional question marks with respect to the sustainability of many new office parks concern their inefficient use of space, their energy use, their relations with the neighbouring housing, recreation and nature areas (integral parts of a city / region or 'business islands'?) and their mono-functional character. Several office parks could have been planned with a much higher density and still function very well. Adding the 'time' dimension, most of the new office parks are now only used during office hours, which means they are totally deserted and unused during most of the day.

Various initiatives from governmental and non-profit organisations as well as from business representatives have in recent years been undertaken to improve the contribution of new business sites to sustainable local and regional development. These initiatives were either directly aiming at a more sustainable design of business sites, or included this goal in a local or regional sustainable development strategy. Until recently, judging from the vast amount of sustainable development initiatives, sustainability claimed a prominent place on the policy agenda and in business strategies in the Netherlands. These initiatives included attempts to create more sustainable business sites both in traditional central cities and in the new economic centres. Unfortunately, in 2003, it looks like the heyday of sustainability policies in the Netherlands is over. The conservative government gaining power in 2002 shifted its policy priorities away from sustainability and the environment. It remains to be seen if the new elections of early 2003 can result in a more sustainability-oriented government.

The case studies: Hoofddorp-Beukenhorst and Almere-Poort

To get more insight in the role that sustainability considerations play in the design and use of office parks, two case study locations have been selected. These case study locations are Hoofddorp-Beukenhorst, an office park already largely developed, and Almere-Poort, a mixed-use site where construction still had to start when the research took place (2002). At these two case study locations, a group of 'stakeholders' has been interviewed. These stakeholders are either directly or indirectly involved in the development of the new office locations. Acting from their principal interests, the actions of these individuals or groups might either encourage or discourage a sustainable design and/or sustainable use of the business site. The central focus of the interviews was to what extent these groups and individuals see sustainable development principles as important and what measures (if any) these persons or groups took to promote a more sustainable development of the business site. In addition, as much documents as possible were collected and studied on the importance of 'sustainability' that is expressed in them. These documents include policy statements, land use plans, designs of architects or urban designers, statements of lobby groups and strategic documents of the businesses (or their representatives) located in, or planning to locate at the new business sites.

Both Hoofddorp and Almere can be considered as part of the 'North Wing' of the Randstad, consisting of the metropolitan regions of Amsterdam and Utrecht. While Hoofddorp has a very central position within the Randstad area, Almere is at the north-eastern edge of the region (see Figure 1). This is to some extent reflected in the local economic structure: while Hoofddorp managed to attract several headquarters or important branch offices of transnational corporations, Almere (so far) rather is the location of 'back offices' of national firms. Both Hoofddorp and Almere started out as satellites to Amsterdam, but are trying to develop into more 'independent cities'. It is questionable to what extent this ambition can be combined with the integration of Hoofddorp and Almere as new sub-centres of the Randstad or the Amsterdam region. Both Hoofddorp and Almere are among the very few places in the Randstad where there is still some space to expand. Especially national politicians seem to be quite keen on large-scale developments at both sites and consider them as places where are large part of the future space demand of the Randstad can be provided for. Their relatively generous space supply might contribute to unsustainable developments in which unnecessarily large amounts of space are used for new expansion areas.

Figure 1. Location of the two case study locations within the northern part of the Randstad.

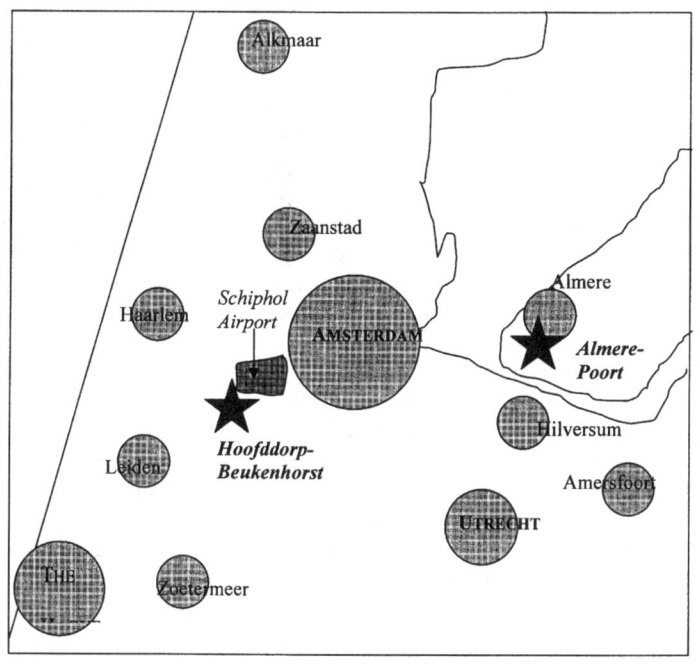

Hoofddorp-Beukenhorst: gradually growing towards sustainability?

The office park Beukenhorst in Hoofddorp started to develop in the 1980s and has expanded ever since. Each of the phases of the office park reflects the quality standards at the time of construction and the attention to sustainability aspects as a part of these quality standards. The earliest phase (Beukenhorst-West), built in the late 1980s, consists almost exclusively of low-rise offices and infrastructure, while little attention was paid to architecture and public space. The next development phase of the 1990s (Beukenhorst-East) is still predominantly low-rise, but demonstrates considerable variation in the architecture of the individual buildings and increased attention for the office surroundings through measures like 'landscaping' and public art. Both early expansion schemes are entirely mono-functional office sites and at the time of their construction, sustainability considerations were not yet important planning and design principles. This is reflected in the generous amounts of space reserved for ground-level parking, the absence of substantial green spaces and the rather poor integration in their wider surroundings (the settlement structure of Hoofddorp). The newest expansion phase now under construction, the station area and Beukenhorst-South, is supposed to reach a considerably higher design standard. The land use plan promises spectacular architecture as well as a high priority for sustainable development: the development is described as a 'sustainable office park' (Gemeente Haarlemmermeer 2002).

Beukenhorst-South was one of the exemplary projects in the 'sustainable business parks programme' of the Department of Economic Affairs. This programme was part of the broader package of measures towards a more sustainable economy in the Netherlands in which various national departments participated (Ministerie VROM et al. 1997). The municipality of Haarlemmermeer included various criteria for sustainability in its 'programme of demands' for the new office site, like energy- and water-saving measures, intensive and/or multiple space use and sustainable construction materials. For Dutch standards, the office complexes at Beukenhorst-South will be rather space-intensive. While so far, office blocks up to about 20 m height were common in Hoofddorp, the new development will include some towers of 80 m. It should be kept in mind that high-rise building is still a rather exceptional feature in Dutch cities and even more so in the region of Amsterdam. Also, a so-called 'double ground level' will be created. Most of the parking facilities as well as the access roads for cars will be realised at a lowered ground level. Above this level, the offices and surrounding public space are built at a slightly raised second ground level. Further sustainability considerations include attempts to create a functionally mixed area, like a hotel, conference centre, child care and research facilities, and the integration of the cultural monument Geniedijk in the plan (Gemeente Haarlemmermeer 2002). This Geniedijk is part of the UNESCO World Heritage site 'Stelling van Amsterdam', a series of defense works around Amsterdam built in the late 19th century. More in general, attempts are made to optimise the integration of the office park in its surrounding landscape, with a prominent role for water currents. The function mix as well as the improved use of multiple levels of construction were proposed by the architect Wiel Arets, who in his recent work demonstrated a strong commitment to high-density, high-rise building and a more intensive use of the scarce space left in the Netherlands (Beunderman and Bontje

2001). Public transport connections could hardly be better: a railway station is right next-door and a high-frequency bus service crosses the office park. The rail and bus facilities provide direct connections with Schiphol airport and the cities of Haarlem and Amsterdam. Finally, Beukenhorst-South will probably make use of park management to stimulate the shared use of facilities by companies settling in the office park. These facilities might include surveillance, maintenance, waste collection, traffic management, childcare and parking facilities.

Hoofddorp's strong connection to the growth of nearby Schiphol Airport dominates the development strategy for new office locations: the developers are trying to attract especially 'Schiphol-related' companies. Several multinational and large national companies have already settled at Beukenhorst with their European, Dutch or regional headquarters. This has several consequences for the extent to which the realisation of Beukenhorst South and the station area might be called 'sustainable'. In general, one might question the degree of sustainability of an office area that is highly dependent on being close to an airport. The international companies at Beukenhorst will encourage further air traffic growth between Schiphol and sites of branch offices and global headquarters. The nearness of Schiphol sometimes poses limits to Hoofddorp's building plans. Building heights are limited due to fears of disturbing the airport's radar and radio traffic, and there is a 'noise contour' around the airport where building houses or employment sites is not allowed. This is the main reason why, as mentioned above, the new office development at Beukenhorst will only contain a few high-rise buildings. The air traffic authorities of Schiphol and the national government only allowed for these buildings as scarce exceptions to their strict safety rules. These safety regulations and the 'noise contours' also limit the possibilities for adding functions to the office park considerably. It is impossible to build houses in the office park, for example, because the Schiphol-related noise criteria for housing are much stricter than for employment complexes.

Other presumed sustainability aspects of the Beukenhorst-South development might be questioned as well. For many companies locating in Beukenhorst, the importance of the nearness to the highway A4 was probably of more importance than the rail and bus connection. A recent study of mobility behaviour of employees working at Beukenhorst indicated that the relatively good public transport connections do have a positive effect on the modal split. About 25% of people working at Beukenhorst travel by public transport, while the average for all business sites in Haarlemmermeer is only 20%. Still, the vast majority of Beukenhorst employees (65%) travel by car (Onderzoek and Statistiek, 2001a). The share of public transport might improve, though, because three national administrative institutions will settle in one of the largest office complexes on the new site. The Dutch national administration has a relatively high share of public transport users due to favourable collective public transport contracts. Park management might contribute to sustainable development when it provides collective provision of services that would have to be arranged by the individual companies otherwise. However, this is only true when this includes services that contribute to better environmental and social circumstances. The danger is that companies choose only the minimum (obligatory) package, mainly aimed at safety measures, and refuse to pay extra for (voluntary) social and environmental items. Finally, the relation of the office park with the housing areas of Hoofddorp has not very intensive so far. In 2000, only 12% of the employees working at Beukenhorst were living in Hoofddorp and an additional 5% elsewhere in the municipality of Haarlemmermeer. Actually, more Beukenhorst employees were living in the adjacent large city Amsterdam (18%) than in Haarlemmermeer itself! (Onderzoek and Statistiek, 2001b) This indicates that the provision of a large employment complex close to suburban housing areas does not automatically mean that many inhabitants of these areas will work there. While the area so far hardly has other functions than offices, this probably also means that the vast majority of inhabitants of Hoofddorp never visits Beukenhorst. The inclusion of functions like shopping or entertainment might have intensified the relations between the Hoofddorp housing areas and office park Beukenhorst; now they will probably remain 'worlds apart'.

An additional problem emerged as a result of the economic stagnation: at the end of 2002, the office park faced a vacancy rate of 15%. Large amounts of office space were planned when economy was still going strong; unfortunately, they only became available when the office market had already gone into crisis. This is rather a problem of the Amsterdam region in general, but it was increased in Hoofddorp due to the breakdown of the ICT sector, of which the Beukenhorst office park was one of the major concentration sites.

Almere-Poort: high sustainability ambitions threatened by many uncertainties

Almere wants to create additional jobs to improve possibilities for the local labour force to work in their home municipality and decrease the need for commuting. The problem to be solved is huge: in 2000, two-thirds of Almere's working population was commuting to work in another municipality. About half of these commuters were working in Amsterdam (Teunissen et al. 2001), resulting in traffic jams and crowded trains in rush hours. The city also wants to improve its offer of cultural and recreational facilities. One of the most ambitious projects to change Almere into a more complete city is Almere-Poort. This project actually involves building an entire new city, as a further extension of the polynucleated structure of Almere. Almere-Poort should include a number of employment concentrations, each with its own specialisation: office parks, a logistics and Distribution Park, a site for small-scale manufacturing and a retail and consumer services site (MVRDV and KCAP 2001). These employment sites should all to some extent be mixed with housing, cultural and recreational functions. In the centre of Almere-Poort, a new multifunctional sports complex was planned as well as health care and educational facilities, with apartment blocks and office towers directly adjacent to it. Construction activities at the first part of Almere-Poort were supposed to start in early 2003. At the moment of writing this paper, however, it was still highly uncertain to what extent the Almere-Poort project would actually be realised. The local elections of March 2002 resulted in a huge victory of the party 'Leefbaar Almere' ('Liveable Almere') that is particularly opposed to the high costs of the multifunctional sports complex. This complex has such a key position in the Almere-Poort plans that the opposition to this sports stadium might endanger the entire development. In addition, as mentioned above in the Hoofddorp case, a currently growing over-supply of office space in the Amsterdam region, resulting from a collapsed office market under the influence of economic recession, makes the realisation of yet another large-scale office development near Amsterdam questionable. Several stakeholders in the development of the employment locations of Almere-Poort, including the project manager and the director of the local business society, expressed their doubts about the development policy of the municipality of Almere. Many new employment locations are realised almost at the same time, and some of them are direct competitors of each other. The office locations in the centre of Almere-Poort will be very expensive due to the high standards of architecture, design of public space and various sustainability criteria. Therefore, the centre locations of Almere-Poort should aim for the highest segments of the office market. Almere-Poort might be developed too late for that, though, since another ambitious development project aiming at the same upper market segments is already in its building phase: the restructuring of the city centre of Almere Stad. The other employment locations of Almere-Poort aim at other business activities like back offices and light industry, but they also have to deal with various competing sites being developed in the same municipality. Because these sites should also meet rather high sustainability standards, they might lose the competition with other more 'traditional' business parks if companies consider short-term costs (rent prices) more important than potential long-term gains (savings in resource use etc.). Several interviewed stakeholders argued that the municipality is not selective enough in its search for new employment opportunities. In a recent survey, the most mentioned reason for commuters for not working in their own municipality was that they could not find suitable employment opportunities in Almere (Teunissen et al. 2001). Instead of trying to attract those types of employment that Almere is still missing, the municipality seems to welcome all companies that wish to move to Almere, which will not solve the commuting problem. Not only Almere is to blame for its growth-oriented strategy, though. The Dutch national government has seen Almere as the preferred site to solve many of the space pressure problems of the Randstad since the 1970s and wants Almere to double its population in the next twenty years. The amount of money required for such a fast growth and the problems to realise matching job opportunities, services and infrastructure, however, have been underestimated by the national planners so far.

The design of the employment locations of Almere-Poort contains various sustainability-enhancing concepts that might be called revolutionary in the context of Almere. So far, Almere was constructed in a predominantly suburban setting, with low densities, low building heights and a strict separation of functions and traffic flows. It is above all a residential town, much more than a place to work or recreate (Brouwer 1999; Deben and Schuyt 2001). The high densities and high degree of function mix planned in Almere-Poort might give this part of Almere a more urban atmosphere. The most daring proposition of the designers is probably the creation of an 'artificial space scarcity'. The designers of MVRDV and KCAP proposed to claim a large part of the available land for the creation of a nature and recreation area, which would serve as a green entrance to Almere-Poort. The loss of building land resulting from this choice should be compensated through higher densities and an increased use of the spaces above and below ground level (MVRDV and KCAP 2001). The municipality of Almere initially agreed to these design principles. However, in a later stage, the municipality council decided to give the land destined to become a park a new functional description: 'strategic reserve location'. This means that the area might be partly or completely built on after all. The municipality council feared that office sites being located too far from the highway would not be 'marketable' enough. Moreover, comparable concerns of 'marketability' apply to the rather extreme degree of function mixing, both at the business sites and within the individual buildings. Especially the designer's proposal to combine several functions within individual buildings might not be realised. This is partly because of inflexibility of government regulations, still largely based on traditional zoning principles, but also because planners estimate that interest in these buildings (both on the office and on the housing market) would be very limited. The main problem, however, might lie with the project developers planning to build in Almere-Poort and not with the eventual users who might be much more interested than the planners and developers tend to think. The green setting and mixed character of Almere-Poort might also be seen as assets making the site different from the highway locations surrounding it. The designers and project managers of Almere-Poort are organising meetings with project developers to convince them of the possible advantages of their designs and plans. If the planners give in too much to perceived (or imagined?) market pressures, Almere-Poort runs the risk of becoming a rather traditional extension of Almere instead of a showpiece example of sustainable urban development.

Final remarks
The point of departure of this analysis was that new employment concentrations outside of the traditional city centres are not necessarily counterproductive for a more sustainable regional development. The move from monofunctional 'suburban' housing areas to multifunctional 'post-suburban' complexes might be a 'blessing in disguise' for sustainable regional development. The criteria for a positive contribution to sustainable regional development are largely the same for central city sites as for city-edge or more peripheral locations. The only real difference is probably that much more space is available at suburban locations than at central city locations, which could decrease the sense of urgency for optimal space use at suburban locations considerably. The two case studies in the Netherlands have shown that even in such circumstances, there are chances to develop new business sites in a more or less sustainable way. This requires first of all the will (maybe even courage) of the stakeholders to choose for a sustainable rather than unsustainable design, even though the sustainable design is almost always much more costly and complicated to realise. Both in Hoofddorp-Beukenhorst and in Almere-Poort, most of the parties involved showed enough of such good intentions. However, good intentions are not sufficient for good results: in both cases, but most of all in Almere-Poort, old-fashioned planning and building regulations and a fear of the 'new' and the 'unknown' block the choice for a more sustainable design. The Dutch national and local government might want to reconsider their land use planning laws and principles to facilitate intensive land use and mixing of functions to a larger extent. On the other hand, project developers and companies apparently need some encouragement to overcome their initial fear of intensive and multifunctional land use. Once such a sustainable design has been realised after all, this still does not mean that the business site is also used in a sustainable way. The example of Hoofddorp-Beukenhorst indicates that even with optimal public transport connections right next door, the private car remains the most attractive means of transport for most employees. Furthermore, the relationship between the office park and its surroundings might be seriously questioned in both cases. Especially Hoofddorp-Beukenhorst

seems to develop as a 'business island' with hardly any relations with the housing areas of Hoofddorp, even though they are just around the corner. If the planners of Almere-Poort manage to overcome this problem remains to be seen. In the next step of this research, a comparison with sustainable development initiatives in suburban locations of other European metropolitan areas should demonstrate to what extent these findings are 'typically Dutch' or valid for larger parts of Europe.

References:
Anderson, W.P.; Kanaroglou, P.S. ; Miller, E.J. (1996) Urban form, energy and the environment: a review of issues, evidence and policy. In: Urban Studies, 33 (1), 7-35.
Batten, D. (1995) Network cities, creative agglomerations for the twenty-first century. In: Urban Studies, 32 (2), 313-327.
Beunderman, J.; Bontje M. (2001) De kaart van Nederland opnieuw tekenen met 40 miljoen mensen. De visie van Wiel Arets op ruimtegebruik in Nederland. In: AGORA, 17 (4), 4-7.
Bontje, M. (2001) The challenge of planned urbanisation. Urbanisation and national urbanisation policy in the Netherlands in a Northwest-European perspective. Amsterdam (PhD thesis).
Breheny, M. (1996) Centrists, decentrists, and compromisers: views on the future of urban form. In: M. Jenks, E. Burton and K. Williams (eds.), The compact city, a sustainable urban form? London: Spoon.
Brouwer, P. (1999) Boomtown Almere: form follows lifestyle. In: Archis, 1999 (11), 10-19.
Burdack, J.; Herfert, G. (1998) Neue Entwicklungen an der Peripherie europäischer Großstädte: ein Überblick. In: Europa Regional 6 (2), 26-44.
Champion, A.G. (2001) A changing demographic regime and evolving polycentric urban regions; consequences for the size, composition and distribution of city populations. In: Urban Studies, 38 (4), 657-677.
Deben, L.; Schuyt, K. (2001) Social cohesion in Almere. Social relationships in a young city. Amsterdam.
Dieleman, F. M.; Dijst, M.J.; Spit, T. (1999) Planning the compact city, the Randstad Holland experience. In: European Planning Studies, 7 (5), 605-621.
Dieleman, F.M.; Faludi, A. (1998) Polynucleated metropolitan regions in Northwest Europe; theme of the special issue. In: European Planning Studies, 6 (4), 365-378.
Ewing, R. (1997) Is Los Angeles-style sprawl desirable? In: APA Journal, winter 1997, 107-126.
Gemeente Haarlemmermeer (2002) Bestemmingsplan Hoofddorp station en Beukenhorst Zuid (voorontwerp). Hoofddorp.
Graham, S.; Marvin, S. (2001) Splintering urbanism. Networked infrastructures, technological mobilities and the urban condition. London: Routledge.
Ham, M. van; Hooimeijer, P.; Mulder, C. (2001) Urban form and job access; disparate realities in the Randstad. In: Tijdschrift voor Economische en Sociale Geografie, 92 (2), 231-246.
Hassenpflug, D. (2002) Die europäische Stadt als Erinnerung, Leitbild und Fiktion. In: D. Hassenpflug (Hrsg.), Die europäische Stadt - Mythos und Wirklichkeit,

11-48. Münster: LIT.
Headicar, P. (2000) The exploding city region: should it, can it be reversed? In: K. Williams, E. Burton and M. Jenks (eds.), Achieving sustainable urban form, 161-173. London: Spoon.
Keil, R.; Ronneberger, K. (1994) Going up the country; internationalization and urbanization on Frankfurt's northern fringe. In: Environment and Planning D: Society and Space, 12, p. 137-166.
Kloosterman, R.C.; Lambregts, B. (2001) Clustering of economic activities in polycentric urban regions; the case of the Randstad. In: Urban Studies, 38 (4), 717-732.
Kloosterman, R.C.; Musterd, S. (2001) The polycentric urban region: towards a research agenda. In: Urban Studies, 38 (4), 623-633.
Lambooy, J.G. (1998) Polynucleation and economic development: the Randstad. In: European Planning Studies, 6 (4), 457-466.
Marcuse, P. (1998) Sustainability is not enough. In: Environment and Urbanization, 10 (2), 103-111.
Ministerie VROM (2001) Ruimte maken, ruimte delen. Vijfde nota over de ruimtelijke ordening 2000/2020. Den Haag.
Ministerie VROM, EZ, V and W and LNV (1997) Nota Milieu en Economie. Den Haag.
MVRDV and KCAP (2001) Ontwikkelingsplan werklocaties Almere-Poort. Rotterdam.
Onderzoek and Statistiek (2001a) Omnibusonderzoek bedrijven en instellingen 2000/2001. Hoofddorp
Onderzoek and Statistiek (2001b) Autoratiometing Beukenhorst. Hoofddorp.
Palmer, J.; I. Cooper; Vorst, R. van der (1997) Mapping out fuzzy buzzwords – who sits where on sustainability and sustainable development. In: Sustainable Development, 5, 87-93.
Ravetz, J. (2000) Urban form and the sustainability of urban systems; theory and practice in a Northern conurbation. In: K. Williams, E. Burton and M. Jenks (eds) (2000), Achieving sustainable urban form. London: Spon.
Roberts, P. (1995) Environmentally sustainable business; a local and regional perspective. London.
Roo, G. de; Miller, D. (2000) Introduction – compact cities and sustainable development. In: G. de Roo and D. Miller (eds.), Compact cities and sustainable urban development.. Aldershot: Elgar.
Sudjic, D. (1993) The 100 mile city. San Diego: Harcourt Brace.
Taylor, P. (2002) Amsterdam in a world city network. Loughborough.
Teunissen, K.S.; De Groen, M.; Stijnenbosch, M.H. (2001) Beroepsbevolking en pendel provincie Flevoland 2000. Utrecht.
Ven, J. van de (2000) Van monocentrisch stadsgewest naar polycentrische netwerkstad. Den Haag.
Wheeler, S. (1998) Planning sustainable and livable cities. Reprinted in: LeGates, R.. and Stout, F. (eds.), The city reader. London: Routledge..

A society to match the scenery: ordering the spaces of the Veneto *città diffusa*

Luiza Bialasiewicz

The Veneto, an administrative region of 4,5 million people, lies at the heart of the Italian *Nordest* (North East)[1], one of the most successful – and wealthy - productive areas in Europe. It is a region that exports over 80% of its production and where single industrial districts boast earnings that exceed the GDPs of many small nation-states. There exists a wide literature in economic geography on the "Veneto model", along with numerous studies that have attempted to locate the region's post-war economic success within a series of distinct territorial and social structures that have allowed for the development of industrial districts based on "local trust" and informal networks of association, mediated in large part through the extended family and the institutions of the local Church.

It is not my aim here, however, to discuss the organisation of Veneto production networks. I would like to focus, rather, on the *geographies* of the "Veneto miracle" and, especially, their social and political implications. Indeed, the Veneto has come to popular attention recently as the site of some of the most reactionary regionalist/localist rhetoric in present-day Italy. The region is currently governed by the Forza Italia/Lega Nord coalition and has been a key player in recent debates over regional devolution. It was the first to call for regional autonomy in policing and the regulation of immigration flows, as well as the first region in Italy to specify its own curriculum for primary and secondary education, overseen by a regional commission for "Regional Identity and Culture". In this paper, I would like to explore the links between the transformations in the Veneto economy over the past decades and the emergence of increasingly reactionary regionalisms, particularly worrisome in the context of an Italian national politics that is, at present, strongly tinged with anti-democratic and xenophobic tendencies. I will

---

[1] I will adopt this term in the Italian throughout the piece as it is not simply a locational descriptor referring to the North-Eastern Italian regions of Veneto and Friuli-Venezia Giulia but, rather, a metaphor that evokes a number of other geographies, political as well as economic. Economic geographers speak of the *Nordest* model when referring to the diffuse, family-based networks of firms that have characterized industrialization in this region; similarly, political geographic analyses of Italian electoral behaviour have focused on the *Nordest* as a distinct context for the articulation of regionalist/autonomist aspirations (for political geographic readings see Agnew 1995, 2002 and Diamanti 1993, 1996, 1998; for an understanding of the *Nordest* as an economic actor see Anastasia and Coro 1996, as well as the essays in Coppola 1997).

argue that it is only through an understanding of the new geographies of production and consumption that structure the Veneto space – a space that is increasingly de-territorialized and de-centred, suspended between its rural past and an unaccomplished urbanisation – that we can begin to fully understand the increasingly reactionary identity politics of actors such as Giancarlo Gentilini, the Lega Nord Mayor and self-styled "Sheriff" of Treviso, who in recent years has proposed, among other things, "organized hunts" on African immigrants who don't make themselves "useful" on the factory floor. I will suggest that it is only through a "cognitive mapping" of the new Veneto spaces that we can begin to understand such reactionary attempts at fixing identity; it is only through an understanding of its pre-/post-modern geographies that we can begin to understand the ways in which the globalised Veneto *città diffusa* that has made its fortunes on the global market and on global migrants is increasingly reacting against both; a contradiction that, I will note, is firmly emplaced in the geographies of today's Veneto.

1. The history of the boom: from a "piccolo mondo antico" to a "Los Angeles che nasce"[2]

Since the years of the Serenissima (the Venetian Republic), the Veneto had been a rural hinterland, its "noble" cities (Venezia itself[3], Padova, Vicenza, Verona, Treviso and many other smaller centres) surrounded by a sea of semi-feudal rural poderi (see Lanaro 1984). Between 1876 and 1915, a full third of all Italian immigration to North America, Latin America and Australia departed from this region. The land reform that followed the Second World War created a highly fragmented pattern of land ownership and did little to alleviate the persistence of pockets of rural poverty that paralleled many in the Italian South. In the early post-war years, the Veneto's inhabitants were, in the words of one of its pre-eminent popular historians, still either "migranti o braccianti" (Franzina 1976) working the land as paid labourers, or leaving to seek fortune elsewhere. The last wave of significant out-migration came as late as the 1950s, following the disastrous floods in the Polesine, with Veneti scattering across the four continents (for a thorough account of Veneto

---

[2] "A dying rural world – or a Los Angeles being born?" (Paolini, 1999).

[3] Venezia stands, in many ways, worlds apart from its region: politically, economically, culturally. The transformations described in this paper have not touched it, although it has undergone its own set of transitions and changes (for an excellent description of the challenges facing the city today, see De Rita and Galdo, 2001), and while some of the regional(ist) ideologies may adopt myths of belonging that appeal to an idealized past under the *Serenissima* Venetian Republic, present-day regional ideologies are fundamentally anti-urban and reject/resent the city and its "messy difference" (Rumiz 1997; 33-34).

emigration see Bevilacqua et al., 2001; Lanaro, 1984). Between 1950 and 1970, the Bassa (the area around Rovigo - see Map 1 below) lost half of its population, with young men abandoning the land for the rapidly industrialising cities of the North-West, or emigrating abroad (principally to Germany and Switzerland).

Map 1.

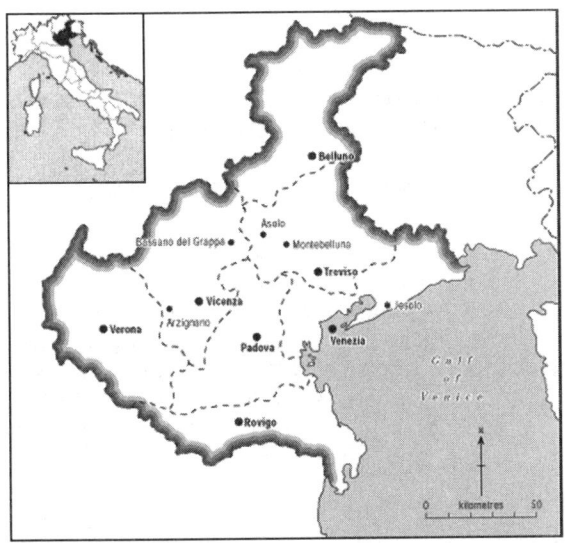

Today, the Veneto is Italy's economic powerhouse. In 2002, 450,000 firms were registered in the region, 98% with fewer than 15 workers. Regional per capita GDP: 23,000 Euro (over a third higher than the national average); 3,000 bank branches, with over 41,000,000 Euro in deposits. If the regional data are impressive, the economic weight of individual provinces is even more astounding. Just the three provinces of Venezia, Padova and Treviso (see Map 1) accounted for 23% of *all* national exports and over 40% of Italian "luxury" goods sold abroad (for a total exceeding 951 million Euro) (all data from CENSIS, 2002). The export earnings of the province of Vicenza alone were equal to those of Greece (Tomasoni 2002).[4]

The geographies of production in the Veneto have been cited as the archetype of post-Fordist flexible accumulation: a system of firms and associated sub-contractors concentrated within highly specialized

---

[4] The province's most studied municipality, Rossano Veneto, has 6,000 inhabitants and 2,000 firms (practically a factory every two families) and produces 60% of the world's bicycle saddles.

industrial districts (see, among others, Bagnasco 1999; Becattini and Rullani 1993; Conti and Sforzi 1997; Scott 1988, 1998; Storper 1997; Storper and Scott 1993). Over the years, the region has attracted legions of scholars and analysts, all eager to understand the "Veneto miracle". Along with its high degree of specialization and aggressive export strategies, the success of the "Veneto model" has been traced, above all, to what many observers have termed "distinctive territorial and social structures", based upon "local trust" and informal networks of association, consolidated around the key nodes of Veneto society: the family, the Church (the *campanile*), and the spaces of local socialization (the *osteria*). It is these informal networks that have allowed for the emergence of the "un-structured competition and co-operation" (Becattini and Rullani, 1993) that so many economic geographers have identified as key to the Veneto boom – and to the flexibility and innovation that characterise its firms.

Already in the late 1970s, economists studying the region began to speak of a localized "economic thickness" (*ispessimento localizzato*), observing the growing concentration of small industries in particular localities. This new "thickening" of economic activity was not simply a new form of economic agglomeration, however. It was, rather, a new "*entità socio-territoriale*", a new socio-territorial entity, "characterized by the active co-presence, in a territorially circumscribed area [...] of a community of people and industries [...] forming an interpenetrating whole" (Becattini 1991; 52), the one defining the other (see also Conti 1996; Conti and Sforzi 1997; Sforzi 1991, 1995). The pre-eminent scholars of the "Veneto model" over the years have insisted, indeed, that the mere concentration of industries in a single locality did not suffice to constitute an industrial *district*, but simply an industrial zone/area. Districts arose only there "where the community of individuals and the community of firms create a single system and share a collective identity [...], which becomes both means of communication and the basis for reciprocal trust" (Rullani 1995, 29-33; see also Bagnasco 1982, 1999; and Becattini 1991, 1997).

The existence of a common "communicative code" as well as of the above mentioned networks of "local trust" has been key to the Veneto miracle (see, above all, the work of Vagaggini, 1991 and Rullani, 1995). Such "networks of trust" were fundamental to a rural social-territorial structure, centred upon the family and the parish, with local solidarity forming the backbone of all interaction with the "outside world", and the parish priest entrusted as the mediator with external authority (see the descriptions in Galletto 1982; Meneghello 1986; Turri 1995). The function of the "organizing sites" of the Veneto space - the family (and the family house), the local *campanile*, and the town *osteria* – was also economic, however. It was the family that constituted the primary economic unit and site of capital accumulation. Farm plots here had always been small – for most, not enough to sustain a family. From the 1950s on, many families decided to "do a little something on the side", starting up businesses in the home, or at most in the shed (*capannone*) out back. In capillary fashion, little industries grew: all family based, with father and sons, brothers and cousins in the "factory" out back, the wife handling "home duties" and later, the firm's accounts. The family-based organization had a number of advantages: practically negligible overhead costs, no need to pay taxes or contributions on the work of family members to the state. The growth of such family firms was not entirely spontaneous or new, however. The emergence of particular industries in particular locations built upon long-standing traditions of local craftsmanship – whether in textiles, boot-making or metal work. It is only with the progressive abandonment of the land in the 1950s and 1960s, however, that what previously were side-occupations became the primary sources of income (for an account of this period of transformation in the Vicentino see Turri 1995).

The parishes were also important economic actors in the Veneto miracle. "Ever since before the war, the parish priest would collect one *soldo* a week from every family, held "*in caso de mal*" – for any misfortune that might befall any town inhabitant" (Lando, personal interview, 2001). These so-called "*Casse Peote*" (also called *Casse Rurali*) were to serve as an "insurance" for town dwellers – as well as a source of money for those needing a short term loan: a sort of latter-day micro-credit association. Over time, these parish "purses" became a fundamental pivot in the start-up capital for new factories. These informal rural *Casse* still exist, but their economic weight has grown with the Veneto "boom": in the 1980s in Feltre, the local *Cassa* was gathering 50,000 million lire a month in voluntary contributions. In the past two decades, some of the *Casse Rurali* became institutionalized as banks and savings associations – many, nevertheless, still retain the informal status they had since their inception. They are, in many ways, symbolic of the networks of local trust and co-operation highlighted by scholars of the Veneto model – and markers of the intricate interpenetration and "co-presence" of local community and industry.

The "un-structured competition and co-operation" theorized by external observers of the region's economic development was laughingly called the "*mi-ti*" ("me and you") strategy by Veneto entrepreneurs (as a tongue-in-cheek spoof of the powerful Japanese Ministry for Trade and Industry, MITI). The principle was simple: "*quel che te fa ti – fazo anca mi*"[5], "what

---

[5] Most of the citations that appear in the text are in Veneto dialect, not in Italian. The use of dialect is pervasive in the region, not only amongst family and friends but also in business dealings: very much part of the local "communicative code" described above.

you do – I'll do", only better. Gian Antonio Stella (2000) recounts many stories of such start-ups in his *Schei* – with conversations overheard in the local *osteria* leading to innovations that would create new *global* market niches. "It was a very simple process", explains Fabio Lando, economic geographer at the University of Venice who has written extensively on the transformations in the region's industrial structure. "Once a worker got good at doing what he was doing, he would leave the firm and, with the help of relatives, set up his own business making the very same product as his previous employer, just with a slight variation. And his original employer – who was quite often a relative - would usually guarantee him a share of the market". As markets continued to grow, this was never a problem: "and anyway, it all stayed in the family" (Lando, personal interview, 2001).

As important as this unique socio-territorial fabric was, two other factors have been vital to the "Veneto miracle": the local *political* and the global *economic* contexts. The social-territorial fabric that allowed for the development of these industries may have been pre-modern, based upon allegiances to family, Church and the local community – but the fortunes could not have been made without the global market and its hyper-modern thirst for innovation. A thirst that Veneto entrepreneurs have been masterful in exploiting.

The mythology of the "Veneto miracle" quite often tends to conceal, indeed, the political economy of the "boom", with leading regional entrepreneurs themselves (like Renzo Rosso, founder of *Diesel* clothing) asserting that all there was to the "Veneto model" was "hard work and creativity": the region was a "self-organising system", its success due to "spontaneous organization" (see interviews in Stella, 2000 and Tomasoni, 2001, as well as Rosso's (1999) self-published book *FoRty*). Such discourses of self-sufficiency and self-organisation mask, however, a distinctive regional (and *national*) political context in the 1970s and 80s that, although it did not directly shape the Veneto boom, certainly allowed it to occur. Prime here was the unquestioned local hegemony of the *Democrazia Cristiana* (Christian Democrats) that held power in Italy throughout the whole post-war period (for a thorough discussion, see Agnew 2002, Ginsborg 1990, 2002). The party and its territorial structures (mediated by the local parishes, acting as its de facto representatives) assured both political stability as well as sufficient opportunities for economic graft for regional entrepreneurs to go about their strategies largely un-interrupted. "The local DC shut both eyes – the tacit agreement was you don't ask, we don't look" (Rumiz 1997; 38, also Diamanti 1996; Stella 2000)

It was international markets, however, that played a central role in assuring the region's stellar economic fortunes. The devaluation of the lira in the 1980s allowed regional products to become highly competitive in export markets (see Lando and Tallone 2001). Even more crucial, however, were shifts in post-Fordist consumption and, especially, the emergence of a global service class with a growing desire for Italian luxury goods. As Lash and Urry (1994), Urry (1990, 1995) and many others have argued, this new global elite calibrates its status - defines *its very existence as a class* - precisely by means of its consumption patterns and predilections. Consuming Italian goods, whether *cappuccino* and *biscotti* or clothing, kitchenware and furniture, has become a marker of the service class' *habitus (*Bourdieu 1984), with consumption choices marking identity and conveying belonging (for a humorous look at the buying preferences of this new professional "caste", including their Italophilia, see Brooks 2000).

A great many of the icons of service class consumption come from the Veneto's "urbanized countryside". From luxury eyewear made in the foothills of Agordo and Belluno by Safilo or Luxottica (which between them control almost 80% of the global eyeglass market – including the recently bought out Ray Ban and Bausch and Lomb), to the "boot district" of Montebelluna where 75% of all ski boots and 50% of all technical hiking and climbing apparel is made, to the "total look clothing" of companies such as Benetton, Diesel, Replay, Sisley, Stefanel or Gas, Veneto firms have come to dominate an infinite number of micro-niches in the global market for up-scale, highly specialized consumption.

2. Narrating the new Veneto spaces

Describing the spaces of this boom is a challenging task. Morphological accounts of urban development cannot capture a growth that has not only been super-imposed upon a still-existing rural territorial structure, but that has proceeded largely without any regulatory or planning controls. Here, one *comune* (municipality) seamlessly flows into another: a multiplicity of centres, yet without centre.

Marco Paolini is a playwright and actor, and perhaps the best known contemporary bard of the region. His 1998 theatrical piece *Bestiario Veneto* is an attempt to narrate the changing landscape of the region, to trace its geographies:

Once, all you could spot along the Piave was an occasional
osteria
Now, there are the strongest industrial districts in Europe
On a starry night, looking down from the Montello, you can see light up
the *Galassia Pedemontana* – the lowlands galaxy
coagulating in diverse   nebulosae, following
mysterious pathways
There, under mount Pasubio, there are

textiles, and
machine tools
Under the Montello, between the Piave and Montebelluna
the boot zone   Around Bassano
                            del Grappa, ceramic workshops
Up there, under the Alps, the multimillion vineyards of Cartizze
    Down by Treviso, the reign of Benetton and his ten thousand
    subcontractors
Over the bridge to Priula towards Conegliano
the "Inox Valley" of the global restaurant trade... (Paolini 1999; 25-26)

Both foreign as well as Italian observers have compared the Veneto space to the Los Angeles "exopolis" (the term comes from Soja 1996, 2000). Paolini's (1999) own characterization of the region as suspended between a dying rural world and a Los Angeles being born ("*Un piccolo mondo antico che muore – o una Los Angeles che nasce*") has been picked up by numerous Italian commentators and journalists (see, for e.g., Rumiz 1997) as the most apt description of this still indeterminate spatial "creature". If exopolis has been the term coined to characterize "the new category of city being invented", the "discontinuous constellation of spatial fragments, functional pieces, and social segments" that is today's Los Angeleno "postmetropolis" (Soja 2000; 237), the spatial metaphor *par excellence* for today's Veneto is that coined already a decade ago by Francesco Indovina, urbanist at the Institute of Architecture at the University of Venice (IUAV) the "*città diffusa*" (diffuse city), "an amorphous mass of construction, filling all available space [...] like molten metal" (Indovina 1990).

The metaphor is apt, for it is the metal of the industrial warehouses or *capannoni* that is perhaps the single most characteristic architectural form on the present-day Veneto landscape. Over the past decade, the Veneto has had the highest rate of building construction in Italy: construction that follows a set pattern – detached family house (or *villetta*) and small (though subsequently larger) *capannone*. According to Indovina and others (1990), it is a paradoxical process of concurrent *hyper-* and *de-*urbanisation, producing a "contiguous collage of fragments of urbanity". The *città diffusa* has no centre, no piazza. It has developed along a series of straight lines: the *statali*, the state roads that provide the only visible skeleton giving form to this new socio-territorial "organism". The *città diffusa* fills the spaces between one town and another, with a "dis-continuous continuum" (Indovina 1990) of *villette* and *capannoni*.

In the paragraphs that follow, I will attempt to capture the "dis-continuous continuum" that is today's Veneto in a number of scenes, a number of fragments from this "diffuse" landscape.

Scene I. The *capannone*
The *capannone* (literally: the shed, warehouse) is the icon of the Veneto model – and of its anthropology of production. Based upon family labour, built on family land, this "little place out back" is, nonetheless, the key building block of production complexes that are planetary leaders in highly specialized goods.
The *capannone* is built where it is most convenient: on land already owned, and as close to the road as possible to minimize transport costs. Aesthetics are secondary: the "factory" is often in sheet metal; a square "box" perched in the field behind the house, with a wide driveway to facilitate deliveries If the Veneto can best be mapped as a "galaxy" (to use Paolini's (1999) metaphor yet again), its industrial districts "solar systems" of sub-contracting planets, the individual *capannoni* are the myriad of moons that rotate around them - the sub-contractors of the sub-contractors. Sub-contractors that are, in many ways, invisible; in the Veneto *città diffusa*, the spaces of production are entirely anonymous, blending into the urbanized countryside.
This is true, however, not only for the small *capannone* attached to the individual *villetta*, but also the "factories" of global brands such as the Diesel "central" in Molvena or the Replay factory in the foothills of Asolo. This "hidden" nature of the Veneto production networks has been popularly interpreted as part of a "rural humility" and the preoccupation "*di non apparire*". The latter expression holds a duplicitous meaning in Italian: it is at once the preoccupation not to appear, to be visible - but also not to be conspicuous, ostentatious. Diverse readings of this phenomenon have been advanced: whether as the expression of traditional rural values (see Petrovich 2000, Tomasoni 2000), or of an anti-urban essentialism, the ideology of "*abitare per produrre*" (living to produce) (Turri 1995; 2000). It is also the expression, however, of an iron-clad faith on the part of local entrepreneurs in "spontaneous development" and what urban planner Franco Migliorini, head of Transport Planning at the Regione Veneto characterizes as a "pervasive allergy to any form of spatial planning or regulatory frameworks" (Migliorini, personal interview, 2001).
Apart from the extreme flexibility and high specialization offered by this type of production model, however, such a de-centred, only partially "formal" mode of production has an additional advantage: "small firms prefer to keep production "diffuse" because it is to their advantage to remain hidden", comments Indovina (in Erbani 2002; 36). As I noted in the opening paragraphs, tax and regulatory evasion have facilitated the Veneto miracle since its early days: "family" factories where a bulk of the employees (as family members) were not covered by pension plans, and

where de-centred production also often meant de-centred accounting (Stella 2000).
The invisibility and "humility" of the *capannone* is, indeed, part and parcel of the Veneto myth. It is an integral part of the stories that Veneto entrepreneurs like to tell about themselves and of the "rags to riches" miracle discovered by economists and journalists writing about the region over the past decades. The stories recounted are remarkably similar: "a young man with an idea", begins making (insert: sweaters, jeans, motorcycles, eyeglasses,) "on the side" in his parents' home (after working an eight hour day in someone else's "factory"). A couple years later, he opens a makeshift workshop, delivers his first samples (by bike) to local stores. Two decades later, the firm opens a flagship store in Manhattan. It may sound like an improbable Cinderella story, but it is that of the Benetton siblings, Renzo Rosso's *Diesel*, Ivano Beggio's *Aprilia*, and Leonardo del Vecchio's *Luxottica*. And countless others.

From the capannone to global brand. The above four may be several of the best known Veneto success stories, but there are countless others. Take the Montebelluna "boot district" in the province of Treviso (see Map 1). 75% of all ski boots in the world are made here; 50% of all hiking boots, 65% of all après-ski footwear, 25% of all in-line skates, 60% of all cycling shoes, and 80% of all motorcycle boots. In 2000, just four hundred "factories", most with fewer than 15 workers, exported 30 million specialized sports shoes. Specialised hiking boots and climbing shoes, ice climbing crampons, moto-cross boots, hunting and fishing footwear, even professional ice skates – in every style and material imaginable. Most of the brands dominating today's global hiking, climbing and skiing market were born here: the Zanatta brothers' Tecnica, the Danieli brothers' Diadora, the Caberlotto brothers' Lotto and Caber, Franco Vaccari's Dolomite and Nordica. Every brand, a family name; a start-up story very similar to the one recounted above.

The district's dominance in the boot and sports shoe market is such that not only do local firms exert control over particular niches: when the big global brands hope to enter a highly specialized market, they too come to "learn from Montebelluna". The world's two biggest ski-equipment manufacturers Rossignol and Salomon have, in recent years, bought out two local competitors - Caber and San Giorgio, respectively – and moved half their production to the province of Treviso. What was the "sell"? A highly specialized labour force, along with an already consolidated network of suppliers and sub-contractors, all within the range of a few kilometres. Even Nike has come to learn from the locals: although the company may rely on low-skilled and under-paid labour in East Asia for its sports shoes, when it wanted to enter into the professional ice-skating market, it acquired the Treviso-based Cansar – and remained in the district. So too did the sports colossus Head Tyrolia Mares (SportSystem Montebelluna 2002).

Over the past two decades, the family-run "place out back" has thus become the building block of a production system not only firmly emplaced within global markets – but also often driving the trends that make those very markets. Companies such as Diesel, Replay, or Gas all pride themselves on selling a "total look for a global lifestyle" (as Diesel's owner, Renzo Rosso, likes to boast – see Rosso, 1999: Polhemos, 1998). Diesel's 1400 square metre mega-store on New York's Lexington Avenue (purposefully located right across from the Levi's flagship store), or its concept shop in London's Covent Garden have become nodes in the production of a global style. The company's ironic ads have also gathered international kudos: advertising that, tongue-in-cheek, admits that it no longer sells a product but simply a brand life(style). Naomi Klein (2000, 298), among others, has commented on Diesel's masterful attempt to incorporate anti-corporate rhetoric into its own (corporate) marketing strategies as the ultimate "anti-advertising advertisements" and the latest stage in the evolution of branding in today's global markets.

Scene II. The *villetta*

If the *capannone* is the emblem of the "*Veneto che lavora*" (the "working region", literally, "the Veneto that produces", a slogan favoured by regional industrialists and politicians alike), the detached family house or *villetta* is the other face of the region's economic boom. Over the past two decades, it has undergone the evolution from poor country home to an iconic space of representation, a site for the manifestation of acquired wealth – and new "urban" status.

Though the *villette* are, increasingly, the symbols of new wealth, here too practical considerations prevail over aesthetic ones. The *villette* are very often built right alongside the main road. This is partly to facilitate ease of transport for the goods produced in the *capannone* out back – but also for reasons of representation, of social visibility. "What is the point of building a house that no one can admire?" jokes University of Venice geographer Stefano Soriani (Soriani, personal interview, 2001). "And if you have an old house, an old country house, you'll just build the new one right in front of it – to make it perfectly clear to everyone that you are no longer the old fashioned farmer" (Soriani, personal interview, 2001).

Some observers have tried to trace a continuity between the contemporary *villetta/capannone* model and the Palladian Villas, emblem of Venetian aristocratic power. The argument is, in part, functional to the rhetoric of regionalist ideologues who see the Villas as architectural icons of the Veneto's glorious past, and their present day heirs as testimony to the continuity of the (regional) past in the present (see the essays in De Michelis 1999; Bernardi 1990, as well as the proceedings of the conference on the contemporary Veneto landscape organized by the Fondazione Benetton, September 2001). The parallel is problematic, however, for although the Palladian estates were, similarly, both economic *and* representative spaces; sites of (at that time, agricultural) production *as well as* of symbolic capital, their idealized landscapes were the expression of a broader cosmology. As Denis Cosgrove has argued, the Palladian landscapes embodied the way in which the propertied class of the day "signified themselves and their world through their imagined relationship with Nature and through which they underlined and communicated their own social role and that of others" (Cosgrove 1984; 15; 1993). As representative spaces, the Palladian cultural landscapes acted to support certain dominant sets of ideas and values, as well as certain unquestioned assumptions about the existing social order: that of the rural *poderi*, governed by a small landowning class.

Recent theorization in geography (most notably Barnes and Duncan 1992; Cosgrove 1984, 1993; Cosgrove and Daniels 1988; Daniels 1993; Duncan 1990; Duncan and Duncan 1988) has stressed the role of landscapes as central elements in the production of meaning, suggesting that landscapes are best understood as social "texts [...] through which a social system is communicated, reproduced, experienced and explored" (Duncan 1990; 17). Representative landscapes thus act to legitimate given sets of power relations and are intimately implicated with the articulation of hegemonic "spatial ideologies" (Harvey 1973; Lefebvre 1990). This "regulatory" function of landscapes and landscape ideals proceeds both through material interventions into the built environment (which concretize dominant ideas and values in places), but also through associated processes of "spatial socialization" (Shields 1991) through which individuals become members of distinct territorial entities and through which they (more or less actively) internalize collective spatial ideologies.

What is the spatial ideology of the present-day Veneto "*villetopoli*" (to use architect Pier Luigi Cervellati's term)? What sorts of assumptions about the existing social and economic order does it embody – and communicate? Despite attempts by regionalist ideologues to stress their role in "assuring historical continuity in the Veneto landscape" (see, for example, the arguments made in popular anthropologist Ulderico Bernardi's 1990 book *Paese Veneto*), today's *villette* lack the strong relationship to the land (in both material as well as symbolic terms) that characterized their Palladian predecessors. Their iconic referents are elsewhere: in globalised consumption models and styles. The progressive transformation of simple farmhouses (*case coloniche*) into the fortified luxurious villas of today mirrors the region's momentous socio-economic transformations of the past decades and, indeed, provides an interesting lens through which to examine the ways in which these shifts have been interpreted by the Veneti themselves and, literally, "built into space".

The breaking point came with the first years of the Veneto miracle, the 1960s and early 1970s. As was noted previously, industrialization in the region was, at the outset, *a complement to* farming employment: a "little something on the side" to augment the family's earnings. Production was integrated into what remained, fundamentally, a rural lifestyle. The family and the family house thus remained a focal point of economic life. With new wealth, however, came a new preoccupation: that of "*apparire*" – and especially to appear like the "*siori*" (Ital. *signori* - gentlemen) of old (Turri 1995), to "live well", following the dictates of the models proposed by the mass media in the great Italian economic boom of the 1960s.

This conflictual relationship between a rural past and a rapidly changing present was materialized within the spaces of the home. As Girotto (2000: 141) notes, "things that one would once do in the front yard - whether raising chickens or cultivating a small vegetable garden, were now things to keep hidden, out of sight: "dirty" activities, "*non da siori*" (not for gentlemen)". The chickens – but also the new workshops – were thus relegated to the back of the house, while the façade took on an entirely new function: that of representing the newly conquered economic well-being.

In the new *villette* springing up in the 1970s, the vegetable garden outside the front door was transformed into a landscaped garden: a site for the display of the new wealth. The newly rich attempted to mimic the gardens and parks of the villas of the land-owning elites of the past – the *padroni*, the *siori*. "This was done with complete ingenuity, and the results are still visible today: neo-classical columns, elaborate fountains, perfectly manicured flowerbeds" (Girotto 2000; 142), along with a variety of mythical and mythological beasts populating the immaculate lawn, from the seven dwarves to statues of Venus in Ferrara marble. The late 1970s and 1980s witnessed a further modification: the new villette were built on artificial hills, made to dominate the surrounding landscape, and even better visible from the road. The raised terrain also allowed for the construction of a key new space in the transforming social and economic order: the home *taverna*. At first no more than a glorified wine cellar, over the past two decades, the taverna has become an important space of socialization, a simulacrum of the town *osteria*. Increasingly, this is where evenings are spent – and where deals are made.[6]

---

[6] Alluding to the increasing enclosure and privatization of the region's social spaces, playwright Marco Paolini has characterized the latter-day Veneti as a "*popolo di tavernicoli*" – a word-play on the *taverna* and the Italian word for "cavemen" – *cavernicoli*.

The past decade and a half brought a further shift in building styles. Paradoxically enough, as rural spaces are transformed at break-neck speed into a contiguous "*villetopoli*", there has been a growing concern for "recovering the rural past" (Indovina in Erbani 2002; 37). The new *villette* thus appeal to styles recalling the farmhouses of old: gone are the marble staircases and statues of Venus, replaced by "rustic" building materials like bare brick and wood. "The only problem is that the idealized rural heritage is from elsewhere", comments Girotto (2000; 145). The "country house style" adopted borrows heavily from a mediatic geographical imaginary of *other* Italian regions: most notably, the *casale toscano* – the archetypical Tuscan farmhouse, surrounded by olive trees, and bordered by rock walls. "These are today's markers of distinction, of a certain social status", notes Girotto (2000, 146), "and they are reproduced within the territory, acting also to create an "imitation effect" – this is the way a certain type of house *should* appear" (emphasis added).[7]

In a society that underwent such rapid transformation over the past three decades as the Veneto one, distinctions matter. Since the spaces of production that created the boom are, to a large extent, hidden (and certainly not the monumental spaces of Fordist capitalism), distinction and prestige are communicated within and through the private spaces of the home:

"with the loss of all social distinctions, the only mode of distinction became money: *i schei, la pila* [...] the new legions of *miracolati*[8] could only distinguish themselves through visible consumption [...] There was something feverish in the building boom, an attempt at all costs – and in the shortest time possible – to subvert the existing order to create a new landscape, a new world, a new way of life, refusing the past, submerging it in concrete" (Turri 1995, 217-225)

Scene III. The historical centre

"[...] cities that are doubles of themselves, cities that only exist as nostalgic references to the idea of the city, and to the ideas of communication and social intercourse. These simulated cities are placed

---

[7] The Tuscan inspiration is not accidental. Although Agnew (1998, 217) and others (see, for e.g. Turri, 1998) have noted that as a "late-unifying state with much internal [physical geographical] heterogeneity", Italy lacks a single "representative landscape" that would encapsulate its national identity, nonetheless, if there has been one landscape ideal that *has* exerted an important influence on the articulation of Italian national identity, it has certainly been the Tuscan one.

[8] Literally, "the blessed", drawing on the idea of the Veneto (economic) "miracle".

around the globe more or less exactly where the old cities were, but they no longer fulfil the function of the old cities. They are no longer centres; they only serve to simulate the phenomenon of the centre." (Halley in Soja, 1996; 194)

In the rush to forget and "submerge" the rural past, what has happened to the historical city centres that once served as the organizing nodes of the Venetian hinterland – Treviso, Asolo, Bassano del Grappa, to name but a few? No longer isolated medieval burgs, the historical city cores are, in fact, submerged within the "molten concrete of the urbanized countryside", part and parcel of that "contiguous collage of fragments of urbanity" that Indovina (1990) has termed the *città diffusa*.

"These cities may still imitate the traditional city, its morphologies and symbolic sites. But they have ceased to be cities", comments Indovina (in Erbani 2002, 37), "over the past decades, the historical centres have become de-urbanized, while the surrounding countryside has become increasingly urbanized". The centres, in other words, have been hollowed out. To cite playwright Marco Paolini (1999), they have become "zoo-cities", where to "perform belonging on a Saturday afternoon".

As all productive and, increasingly, also service functions have been moved out to the surrounding "urbanized countryside", the Veneto's historical city centres have become simply spaces of representation. They have become iconic centres of identity: historical, as well as economic. The luxurious store fronts (increasingly of international brands) testify to the growing wealth of the surrounding area but they are not the exhibition of the wealth of the urban merchant class of old. The "revitalised" and "redeveloped" monumental spaces of the past have been transformed into sites of "heritage": sites of spectacle, rather than the spaces of public interaction and dialogue that they once were. Treviso's Piazza dei Signori, the centres of Asolo and Bassano del Grappa, have become no more than ideal stage-sets for consumption: *both the visual consumption of an idealized urban past, as well as that of other products and experiences* (see Graham et al., 2000; Urry, 1995; Zukin, 1995). They have become sites where the *distinction* that Turri (1995) notes is a guiding preoccupation of the Veneto entrepreneurs is communicated. Paolini's characterization of the entrepreneur who comes to town with his family to "perform belonging on a Saturday afternoon" is apt: the city centres come alive on evenings and weekends, the streets and squares becoming products to be consumed. Presence in the spaces of the urban thus marks status, distinction (on this point see Urry, 1995): it affirms this new class as "urbane", as the "new *siori*" (Rumiz 1997; Turri 1995).

Scene IV. On the road

What joins these "fragments of urbanity"? Verona geographer Eugenio Turri (1995, 2000) in his many writings on the Padanian "megalopolis" has stressed the role of the roads as the only visible thread holding together this new spatial "creature".

The roads are not only the organizing structure for the new de-centred spaces of production, however. They are also important symbolic sites within the spatial order of contemporary Veneto. The roads are the object of complaints and the pre-eminent site for political action; they are the symbol of the insouciance of the central state and of the inability of the Veneti to "take care of themselves". Alongside complaints over unjust taxation ("*Roma ladrona*" (thieving Rome) siphoning-off the fruits of Veneto entrepreneurs' "hard work" to the "lazy" South), the other principal grievance of regional (and regionalist) politicians over the years has been the under-funding of regional transport infrastructure by the central government. Early Liga Veneta (the Veneto's ante-litteram regionalist party, prior to amalgamation into the current Lega Nord) posters, along with inducements to a tax revolt against the central state, featured the differential amounts allotted to regional transport infrastructure across Italy, highlighting the Northern regions' under-funding with respect to their Southern counterparts (Editoriale Nord 1996).

The situation has been getting progressively worse from year to year. Everyday, along the *statali*, the small "state roads" that criss-cross the region, a solid block of cars and trucks grinds to a standstill. Shining new SUVs and luxury sedans, interspersed by trucks big and small. "Go on the road if you want to see "*il Veneto che lavora*" (the Veneto that "works")", jokes urban planner Franco Migliorini. "Pity only that a significant percentage of the just-in-time profit margin is lost as soon as the goods leave the warehouse and get stuck on the road" (Migliorini, personal interview, 2001).

Over the past decade, there have been numerous manifestations, led first by the Liga, later by the Lega, that have occupied minor roads as well as the motorways of the region, blocking toll-booths: all to no avail. Repeated proposals by industrialists' associations and Chambers of Commerce volunteering to take on the task of building additional transport networks or augmenting the carrying capacity of existing infrastructure have been rejected by the (national) state administration.

The roads also reveal the geo-economic clues to the on-going transformation of Veneto industry. The A4 motorway has by now become a continuous line of TIR trucks, from the Mestre-Venice interchange to the Slovenian and Austrian borders. Anonymous trucks bearing the names of Hungarian, Romanian, Slovenian and Croatian towns, but carrying inside the icons of global style: Benetton, Diesel, Gas, Geox,

Replay, Stefanel, Sisley. Timisoara may not come to mind to most fashion junkies but this is where a great bulk of the assembly for such brands is now located, benefiting from generous trade and re-export agreements of recent years. In the area around Timisoara (re-baptized of late "Trevisoara"), Veneto entrepreneurs have established, to date, over 4,000 new firms, with over 200,000 jobs. The relocation of certain parts of the production process "East" is the new vogue: so much so that the Treviso Industrialists Association held its 2000 annual meeting in Romania (Possamai 2001; Tropea 2001).

The roads are also, however, the new spaces of consumption. Outside of the de-urbanised historical centres, spring up countless multiplexes and hypermarkets. Italy may be seen as the place where artisanal production and the small shopkeeper still resist the vagaries of globalised production and consumption, but the Veneto has one of the highest concentrations of out-of-town commercial centres and malls in continental Europe, and the highest presence of such centres in Italy: the Auchan complex in Mestre, Cittamercato in Padova, the Piramidi complex outside of Vicenza, the Giardini del Sole in Treviso, and many others.

Scene V. The spaces "between"

The *capannone*, the *villetta*, and the historical centre are the fragments that make up the Veneto *città diffusa* – fragments that are increasingly privatized and segregated; increasingly urbanized but lacking the urbanity of a city. What lies in the spaces between the fragments, however? Or, better yet, *what and who* do the "invisible" landscapes of production conceal?

The regional boom, built first on the exploitation of family labour, has increasingly grown dependent on the exploitation of immigrant labour. For example, the leather districts of Arzignano and Chiampo, in the valleys north of Vicenza (see Map 1), are staffed predominantly by Serbians and Moroccans. The Arzignano-Chiampo-Montebello "leather triangle" is one of the most important tanning and leather processing zones in the world: some six hundred companies, with over 6,000 employees. Companies that, today, rely almost exclusively on an immigrant workforce. The growth of the local industries over the past two decades has thus been coupled with an astonishing demographic transformation. Up the Chiampo valley lays a little town called San Pietro Mussolino which holds the dubious distinction of having the highest percentage of extra-EU immigrant residents in Italy: 17% of the local population (Tomasoni 2001). For the most part Moroccans, Ghanaians, Serbians and Macedonians, all employed by the tanning industry.

The economic figures, as elsewhere in the region, are flattering. Arzignano is one of the ten municipalities with the highest per capita

GDP in Italy; the other towns in the area trail closely behind. But the acrid smell in the valleys is overwhelming. Most of the tanneries that generate such stellar earnings – and that furnish some of the best known apparel and furniture brands in the world - are no larger than any of the other *capannoni* that dot the Veneto landscape; rusting, run-down warehouses belching smoke into the air. What also becomes immediately apparent is the absence of houses. My guide to the district, architect Lucio Coltri who is Director of Urban Planning for the Vicenza Municipality points up: "everyone lives on the hills – away from the toxic smells. Everyone who can, that is" (Coltri, personal interview, 2001). The green hills are, indeed, scattered with *villette*. "You will find only the immigrants down here in the *concia* [tannery]". "Down here" on the road, in fact, the only people visible within what appears an endless stretch of warehouses are young, dark-skinned men, walking, or hanging out in small groups in front of small apartment blocks that, as Coltri informs me, have been bought up by the tannery owners to rent to their foreign employees "since no one here wanted to rent to these people". [9]

In the valleys of Arzignano and Chiampo, but also elsewhere in the region, young male immigrants are, indeed, often the only people visible on the roads "between": once out of the *capannone* at the end of the working day, they have no private/privatized spaces of their own:
"Once night falls, and the *capannoni* are progressively abandoned, the roads fill with cars and trucks, trucks and cars. The only living things on the roads are the immigrants – blacker than the night, so visible in their invisibility. Walking, pedalling along the road, they vanish somewhere into the urbanised countryside" (Rumiz 2003b, 13)

At dusk, they are joined by another "homeless" community, a new "mobile" component on the landscape of the Veneto *città diffusa*: hundreds of Nigerian, Ukrainian and Albanian prostitutes, beckoning clients from the curb-side. "This is the other face of the boom", notes urban planner Franco Migliorini. "On the one hand, it's just part of the new consumption of the newly rich. But it is also a symptom of the changing social fabric. The excuse is: 'when you work like this, you don't have time for normal relationships'. And with immigrants, the prices are

---

[9] Rather than "importing" immigration and its associated problems, some clothing and footwear conglomerates such as Benetton, Sisley and even Diesel have chosen to export parts of the production process: first to Turkey and, in recent years, to the East (Romania above all). Smaller companies, eager to boost profits, find other spatial "fixes". In the year 2001, police in the region raided three separate immigration rings that held illegal Chinese labourers – entire families, in fact – locked into sweatshop- farmhouses in the middle of the Padanian plain. In September 2001, 30 people were found locked in a windowless barn, sewing garments for the subcontractor of the sub-contractor of "a global brand" (Il Gazzettino 2001; see also the account of the diffusion of this phenomenon in Stella 2001).

low." (Migliorini, personal interview, 2001). Road-side prostitution is the Veneto's new flexible consumption, the region's much touted "local values" in this case, literally left by the wayside. But the social sanction of the "dying rural world" (to use Paolini's (1999) characterization) still claims its occasional victims. Last year, a young man from Musile di Piave (20 km south of Treviso) hanged himself after being caught with a Nigerian prostitute.

3. Dis-location

"One enormous, single city   many comuni
                                many peripheries
                                many mayors
But really   no centre, no periphery
        Everything spinning, spinning, spinning
Few roads, they say, and all blocked with traffic [...]

Every once in a while, two ragged fields of corn
or soy along the road fool you into thinking
that you've left the centre...
                      No!
                   the line of *capannoni/villette* runs alongside
You can't see it   but it is right around the corner
And so you find yourself back in the same industrial
                        crafts
                            residential
zone that you have just left
          WHERE ARE WE HERE?
          WHERE DO YOU COME FROM?
          OK, BUT WHERE ARE WE HERE?
          WHERE DO YOU COME FROM?
The signs at the intersections are insane,
     instead of names of municipalities the names of companies
     every crossing 60 companies and a municipality with
     a name written
                       ... in miniscule" (Paolini, 1999; 27-28)

"Ten kilometres, approaching Treviso: 19 sets of lights, average speed: 25 km/hour, over 100 Mercedes and various other megahorse powered speed-machines, 180 trucks, 15 tractors, 15 foreign prostitutes, 160 *capannoni*, a few corn fields scattered here and there. [...] In ten kilometres, there is nothing that tells me: this is the Veneto. Neither the architecture, nor the names on the signposts (that now mark plant names, not place names), nor the faces on the street" (Rumiz 1997; 43) "an urban psychastenia [...] defined as a disturbance between self and surrounding territory" (Olalquiaga 1992:1)

What has rushed into this semantic and spatial confusion? In his theatrical pieces Marco Paolini (1999; 2000) evokes not only the dislocation that characterises the Veneto *città diffusa* but also new landscapes of fear: the region as "carceral archipelago", mimicking also in this the Los Angeles described by Soja (1996; 2000), Davis (1998) and Flusty (1994). The *villette* built today are heavily fortified: encircled by walls, and guarded by ready-response alarm systems and "120 decibel dogs"[10]. The increasing fortification of the houses is, in part, a response to a surge in burglaries over the past decade, many quite violent. The region's diffuse industrialization has created a diffuse wealth that has, indeed, attracted the attentions of petty and not-so-petty criminals. Over the past three years, the situation reached crisis proportions: in 2001, there were 150,000 burglaries and 2,000 hold-ups, an average of 630 crimes per day (Jori, 2001). Fear of crime is now regularly cited in polls as the major problem facing the region: the frustration expressed by the Liga Veneta and Lega Nord in years past against "unjust taxation", and an oppressive state bureaucracy has given way to calls for security and safety (see the report published by the Istituto Poster 2001).[11] In September 2001, after a week which witnessed 7 violent burglaries in 5 days in *villette* in the provinces of Padova, Vicenza and Treviso (the work of the same "*banda di slavi*" (Slavic gang) as the local papers pronounced (Pennisi, 2001; 3), Renato Martin, the Lega Nord mayor of Jesolo[12], decided that the only response to this latest crime wave was to arm himself and the entire City Council, encouraging his townsfolk to do the same: "the State is not able to give us certainties. The citizens want facts, not talk. If not, they try to defend

---

[10] "*abitano in blisters full-optional, con cani oltre i 120 decibels e nani manco fosse Disneyland...*" ("they live in all-option capsules, with 120 decibel dogs and garden gnomes as though they were in Disneyland..." (Frankie Hi-n-rg MC, "Quelli che Benpensano", 1999).

[11] Riding the media frenzy over the "criminal emergency", the Forza Italia coalition (of which the Lega is a part) organized a national "Security Day" to "highlight the legitimate fears of citizens over the inability to feel safe in their homes and places of work".

[12] Italy's second largest beach-resort, see Map 1.

themselves in whatever way they can – and with weapons, they feel safer" (Martin, interviewed in Bianchin, 2001; 25; see also Coen 2001)[13]. But, as local commentators have noted, the Veneto's "ecology of fear" (Davis 1998) is also the expression of "a deeper, almost primeval anxiety" (Rumiz 2000; 27; also 2003). It is a fear of returning to the origins. "*No gavevo, no gavevo, go paura de no gaver*" (I didn't have, I didn't have, I am afraid of not having), an endless incantation on the part of region's "blessed" – the *miracolati* (to use Eugenio Turri's (1995) expressive term). The fear of not having, of returning to the misery of the fathers. A fear that, as many observers have noted, had been the motivation, the "push" behind the iron-clad work ethic that fuelled the Veneto machine (see Stella 2000; Turri 1995) – but that now has become "the crucible of all postmodern anxieties: fear of the market, of Europe, of immigrants, globalisation" (Rumiz, 2003; 180).

The figure of the stranger is increasingly becoming the target of all these anxieties. Although the Veneto production machine would grind to a halt without immigrant labour, this "urbanized countryside" still has not reconciled itself with the presence of difference. "We may have the export figures of California – but we still don't realize that we have *become* California", comments Ilvo Diamanti, one of the pre-eminent scholars of the Italian *Nordest* (in Tomasoni 2000; 6). The growing immigrant presence has been blamed for everything from increasing crime to urban decay to a "loss of family values" (building on the stereotypes of immigrant men as drug-pushers and immigrant women as prostitutes): fears masterfully exploited by local – as well as national - political leaders.

But while the immigration issue has become the winning rhetorical tool in political contests, the "*Veneto che lavora*", the "working region", has altogether different concerns. The Federation of Veneto Manufacturers, the regional branch of the national industrial conglomerate Unindustria, as well as countless provincial and municipal chambers of commerce and industrial associations have been raising an alarm call for the past five years that without further immigration, the Veneto miracle may well soon be over. The most often cited estimate is that by 2020, the region will have to rely on immigrants for 40% of its labour force (Favaro 2001; 2, see also *Il Gazzettino*, 2000, and the report of the Fondazione Nordest 2000).

The 2002 Bossi-Fini law regimenting immigration flows (pushed through the national parliament by the Berlusconi coalition) has found strong opposition from Veneto entrepreneurs – often the very same people who voted the Lega and the Forza Italia coalition into office. "With a stop to

---

[13] Martin had already made the national news some months earlier after the City Council decided to confer an honorary citizenship to FPOE leader Joerg Haider.

new immigration, our firms will be forced to close" (Gavaz 2001; 4) pronounced Veneto manufacturers' associations in chorus. The 2001 figures published by Unioncamere (the association of regional chambers of commerce) are revealing: only 149,000 foreign workers were granted visas, a small percentage of the 714,000 requests forwarded to national immigration authorities by Veneto firms (cited in Jori, 2002; 8)

The figure of the foreigner lays bare the contradictions between political convenience and economic necessity. It reveals the semantic and spatial confusion over what the Veneto *città diffusa* has become. Immigrants are necessary to make the "miracle" continue. But "*guai se si li vede fuori*" ("God forbid you see them outside"). "Outside" what, one might ask. This (by now rhetorical) phrase, re-evoked by regional politicians and journalists alike says it all. The notion of an outside alludes to a hidden space of production (where the immigrant, as a factor of production, is necessary) and a world outside, a world of charming *villette* and gentrified historical centres: spaces of representation of the region's wealth, testimony to the miracle, where the presence of the immigrant is dissonant with the image that the new *siori* – the new lords of the urbanised countryside - try to project. "For a world that moved in one generation from the plough to trading on global markets, from the pre-modern to the post-modern", writes Paolo Rumiz, "the only way to survive is to keep the local and the global rigorously apart" (2003; 158, 176). The necessity to keep "the right people in the right places" thus becomes paramount.

Someone who knows quite a bit about keeping "the right people in the right places" (the phrasing is his) is Giancarlo Gentilini, currently in his second mandate as the Lega Nord mayor of Treviso. Known affectionately as "the Sheriff" (a self-ascribed moniker), Gentilini walks around the city every morning, "checking up on work in progress", and stopping to drink coffee with the Trevigiani. "The people love me", he says, "because I roll up my sleeves and do the work – rather than jabbering all day in political-speak (*politichese*)" (Gentilini, personal interview, 2001). The Trevigiani seem to agree: in national polls, Gentilini regularly appears as one of the top three "best loved" local politicians.

"The Sheriff" is also known nationally, however, for his incendiary pronouncements against immigrant workers. During his two terms in office, Gentilini has come up with a variety of strategies to "assure order and discipline within the city, [...] and to put everyone in their proper place" (Gentilini, personal interview, 2001). One of these was the removal, in 1997, of all benches from city parks in order to "dissuade those good-for-nothing drug-peddlers and prostitutes from laying about in public spaces that are for the people" (on similar tactics implemented in North American cities see Davis 1998; also Katz 2001; Smith 1996). Some local businesspeople, inspired by the Mayor's suggestions, have put into place their own strategies for controlling access to the spaces of the city centre. Just recently, one bar owner decided to double the price of coffee for *extracomunitari* (the commonly used term for extra-EU immigrants), to prevent them "from hanging out in the garden in front of his bar" (Genga 2003). The initiative brought a storm of protests from local Catholic and immigrants' rights associations and, again, Treviso made the national news.

Beyond regimenting the proper use of public spaces, the Mayor also has strong ideas about what immigrants' "purpose" in Treviso society should be: "I want people that can stand on an assembly line, not those who are used to running away from lions.[14] These people that come here to sell counterfeit goods in the street or to wash windshields at traffic lights – I don't need these people" (Gentilini, personal interview, 2001).[15] The right place of the immigrant is, therefore, on the factory floor. The urban centre - now the space of representation, not production – is not the place for them. They have no citizenship here. They are, in Gentilini's own words, "out of place", "not needed".

Gentilini may be the loudest face of the Lega Nord in the Veneto – but he reflects a much broader discourse within regional politics that counter poses the dis-placed/out-of-place immigrant against the strongly "placed" family values of the Veneto. The varieties of proposals that have come up for a vote in the regional assembly over the past two years reflect, indeed, a strong preoccupation with "grounding" immigrant workers. Lega politicians have repeatedly called for all foreign workers (whether legal or illegal) to be finger-printed, and a series of new laws will now regiment work permits to be granted only to single men for a prescribed period of time, with no possibility of renewal or migration of family members (much like the German and Swiss *Gastarbeiter* systems of the 1960s and 1970s), and monitor closely immigrants' residence. The 2002 Bossi-Fini law on immigration has, indeed, put many of these requirements into practice, creating (in Umberto Bossi's own words) "finally a logical link between immigrants and work" (Bossi in Colaprico, 2001; 8), while the newly introduced requirement of taking digital finger-prints from all extra-EU immigrants "will make sure that the foreigners who come here pursue legitimate work rather than turning to crime" (Canetti 2002; 13; Casadio 2002a, 2002b).[16]

---

[14] A veiled allusion to the predominantly Senegalese street vendors that are, by now, a common sight in all major Italian cities.

[15] In 2000, the Mayor famously suggested that unemployed immigrants could be "made useful – we could dress them up like rabbits and let the hunters have some target practice: bam, bam" (Adamoli 2001; 11)

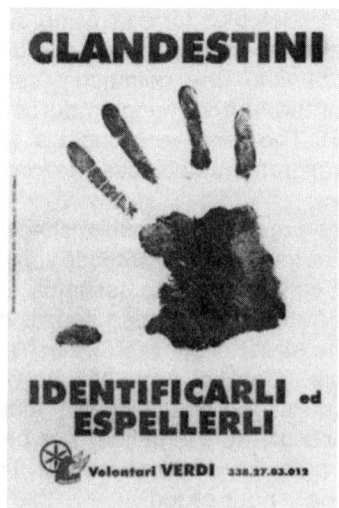

In the dis-placed, diffuse landscape of the Veneto miracle, the preoccupation of "putting everyone in their place" is becoming increasingly violent, as the popular imaginaries of the figure of the immigrant become increasingly racialized and criminalized. The figure of the "black man" – or "black woman" - on the corner (whether they are dark-skinned or not is a small matter) has become a popular trope, a symptom of – but also explanation for – all the ills that assail the region. "Drug peddlers, robbers and prostitutes", all those that inhabit the "spaces between" of the *città diffusa*: the roads, the abandoned city centres, the stretches of countryside between the fortified *villette*. During the 2001 "Padania Day" (celebrated by the Lega Nord in Venezia each September since 1996), a variety of pamphlets incited the *"Popolo Padano"*[17] gathered around the Laguna to "push back the immigrant threat" (Edizioni Ghenos 2001). The two images reproduced below, offer disturbing caricatures of immigrants, and implicitly deny these individuals citizenship within the spaces of the *città diffusa*: in both posters, the immigrant "Other" is confronted by the Padanian vanguard, affirming family values and ownership of the local.

---

[16] This new provision of the Italian immigration law caused an uproar not only in Italy but also abroad: a long list of foreign artists and intellectuals signed a declaration penned by Steven Spielberg condemning the practice as xenophobic and branding immigrants as criminals (Spielberg 2002;2)

[17] "The Padanian people"

Conclusions

Scholars of regionalist mobilisation, both those studying Northern Italy as well as other contexts, have focused their attentions largely on the ideal and idealised landscapes that are an integral part of regional mythmaking, noting the ways in which such "representative landscapes" (Duncan, 1990) are deployed by regional ideologues to convey belonging and emplace identity. I would like to argue, however, that to understand regionalist mobilisation it is equally important to consider the lived, everyday spaces of the region – spaces within which such regionalist politics are born.

Slavoj Zizek (1998) contends that to understand Europe's "new fundamentalisms", we cannot separate politics from political economy. I would suggest that an examination of the geographies of production and consumption of the Veneto *città diffusa* can be an important aid in better understanding the region's increasingly reactionary politics for it is here, in the *capannoni*, in the *villette*, and on the roads "between" that such politics of exclusion emerge.

There is a second reason why it is important to pay attention to the spaces of the *città diffusa*. Italian sociologists including Carlo Trigilia (1981, 1986) and Arnaldo Bagnasco (1977, 1982, 1999; see also Bagnasco and Trigilia 1984) have long argued for the role of local political subcultures in creating the conditions necessary for successful "diffuse industrialisation" and, in particular, for the emergence of the dynamic industrial districts that characterise the Italian *Nordest*. It might be intriguing to reverse the above argument and ask *what sort of politics is emerging in the spaces of diffuse industrialisation?*

Finally, looking at the geographies of the Veneto *città diffusa* can also help us to examine with a critical eye the much-mythologised "Veneto model" and the "local networks of trust" that make it work. As I have tried to argue within this paper, in the "discontinuous continuum of fragments of urbanity" (Indovina 1990) that is today's Veneto, those who lie *outside* of such networks of association and trust - the foreigners, the strangers – these individuals become a "disturbance in the landscape", forced into the spaces between the fragments and thus immediately visible, immediately Other.

Acknowledgements
Research for this paper was carried out as part of an Economic and Social Research Council-funded project on "Regional Identity and European Citizenship" (ref. no. L21325 2031), part of the *One Europe or Several?* Programme.

References:
Adamoli, G. (2001) Gentilini, lo "sceriffo" dalle maniere forti. La Repubblica June 4: 11.
Agnew, J. (1995) The rhetoric of regionalism: the Northern League in Italian politics, 1983-1994. Transactions of the Institute of British Geographers NS 20:156-172.
-, (1998) European landscape and identity. In Modern Europe. Place, Culture, Identity. (B. Graham, ed.) London: Arnold.
-, (2002) Place and Politics in Modern Italy. Chicago: University of Chicago Press.
Anastasia, B. and G. Coro (1993) I distretti industriali in Veneto. Portogruaro: Ediciclo.
-, (1996) Evoluzione di una economia regionale. Il Nordest dopo il successo. Portogruaro: Ediciclo.
Bagnasco, A. (1977) Le Tre Italie. La Problematica Territoriale dello Sviluppo Economico Italiano. Bologna: Il Mulino.
-, (1982) Economia e società della piccola impresa. In Italia: centri e periferie. (S. Goglio, ed.) Milano: Franco Angeli.
-, (1999) Tracce di comunità. Temi derivati da un concetto ingombrante. Bologna: Il Mulino.
Bagnasco, A. and C. Trigilia (1984) Società e politica nelle aree di piccola impresa. Il caso di Bassano. Venezia: Arsenale.
Becattini, G. (1991) Il distretto industriale Marshalliano come concetto socio economico. Distretti industriali e cooperazione fra imprese in Italia. Studi e Informazioni. Quaderni 34:51-65.
-, (1997) Dal distretto industriale alla distrettualizzazione: alcune considerazioni. In Le vie dell'industralizzazione europea. Sistemi a confronto. Bologna: Il Mulino.
Becattini, G and E. Rullani (1993) Sistema locale e mercato globale. Economia e Politica Industriale 80:25-48.
Becattini, G. and S. Vaccà, eds. (1993) Prospettive di economia e politica industriale in Italia. Milano: Franco Angeli.
Bernardi, U. (1990) Paese Veneto. Dalla Cultura Contadina al Capitalismo Popolare. Edizioni del Riccio: Firenze.
Bevilacqua, P., A. De Clementi and E. Franzina, eds. (2001) Storia dell'emigrazione italiana. Vol. 1 Partenze, Vol. 2 Arrivi. Roma: Donzelli Editore.
Bianchin, R. (2001) Tutta la giunta con la pistola e a Jesolo è subito Far West. La Repubblica September 11:25.

Bourdieu, P. (1984) Distinction: a social critique of the judgement of taste. London: Routledge and Kegan Paul.
Brooks, D. (2000) Bobos in Paradise: The New Upper Class and How They Got There. New York: Simon and Schuster.
Canetti, N. (2002) Immigrati, ecco la legge xenofoba. L'Unità March 1:13.
Casadio, G. (2002a) Immigrati, impronte schedate. La Repubblica May 30:2.
-, (2002b) Passa la legge delle impronte. La Repubblica June 5:2.
Casellato, A. (2001) Venetismi. Diario di un gruppo di studio sul Veneto contemporaneo. Verona: Cierre Edizioni.
Castells, M. (2000) The Rise of the Network Society. 2nd. ed. Oxford: Blackwell.
Coen, L. (2001) Il popolo delle villette assediate. "Pronti a difenderci da soli". La Repubblica September 7:13.
Colaprico, P. (2001) Immigrati, patto Bossi-Fini. "Resta solo chi ha un lavoro". La Repubblica August 7:8.
Conti, S. (1996) Geografia economica. Teorie e metodi. Torino: UTET.
Conti, S. and F. Sforzi (1997) Il sistema produttivo italiano. In Geografia politica delle regioni italiane. (P. Coppola, ed.) Torino: Einaudi.
Coppola, P., ed. (1997) Geografia politica delle regioni italiane. Torino: Einaudi.
Cosgrove, D. (1984) Social formation and symbolic landscape. Totowa, N.J.: Barnes and Noble.
-, (1993) The Palladian Landscape. Leicester: Leicester University Press.
Cosgrove, D. and S. Daniels, eds. (1988) The Iconography of Landscape. Cambridge: Cambridge University Press.
Daniels, S. (1993) Fields of Vision: Landscape Imagery and National Identity in England and the United States. Princeton: Princeton University Press.
Davis, M. (1998) Ecology of Fear: Los Angeles and the Imagination of Disaster. New York: Henry Holt.
De Michelis, C., ed. (1999) Identità veneta. Venezia: Marsilio and Consiglio Regionale del Veneto.
De Rita, G. and A. Galdo (2001) Capolinea a Nordest. Venezia: Marsilio.
Diamanti, I. (1993) La Lega. Geografia, storia e sociologia di un nuovo soggetto politico. Roma: Donzelli.
-, (1996) Il Male del Nord. Lega, localismo, secessione. Roma: Donzelli.
-, (1998) Idee del Nordest. Torino: Fondazione Giovanni Agnelli.
Duncan, J. (1990) The City as Text: the Politics of Landscape Interpretation in the Kandyan Kingdom. Cambridge: Cambridge University Press.
Duncan, J. and N. Duncan (1988) (Re)reading the landscape. Environment and Planning D: Society and Space 6:117-126.
Editoriale Nord (1996) La Lega Nord attraverso i manifesti. Milano: Editoriale Nord.
Edizioni Ghenos (2001) Etnonazionalismo: L'Unica Speranza per l'Europa.
Erbani, F. (2002) La citta diffusa: cosi villette e capannoni diventano una megalopoli. La Repubblica July 24:36-37.
Favaro, A. (2001) Carraro: manodopera, fine di un'epoca. Il Gazzettino January 12:2.
Flusty, S. (1994) Building Paranoia: The Proliferation of Interdictory Space and the Erosion of Spatial Justice. West Hollywood: Los Angeles Forum for Architecture and Urban Design.
Fondazione Benetton Studi Ricerche (2001) Nei luoghi della citta diffusa veneta. Che fare? Idee e strumenti per conoscere e per governare le modificazioni. Conference proceedings. Treviso, August 28 – September 6.
Fondazione Nordest (2000) Demografia, mercato del lavoro e immigrazione.

Venezia: Osservatorio Permanente sull'Economia dell'Nordest, Fondazione Nordest.
Franzina, E. (1976) La grande emigrazione. Venezia: Marsilio.
Galletto, P. (1982) La firma: una famiglia Veneta tra due secoli. Roma: Borla.
Gavaz, E. (2001) Con il blocco degli ingressi, aziende del Nordest costrette a chiudere. Il Gazzettino August 7:4.
Genga, L. (2003) Prezzi maggiorati a immigrati e tossicodipendenti. Il manifesto April 24:5.
Ginsborg, P. (1990) A History of Contemporary Italy. London: Penguin.
-, (2002) Italy and its Discontents: Family, Civil Society, State. London: Penguin.
Girotto, C. (2000) La casa del Nordest: dalla casa colonica alla villetta dei giorni nostri. In Venetismi. Diario di un gruppo di studio sul Veneto contemporaneo. (A. Cesellato, ed.) Verona: Cierre Edizioni.
Graham, B., G. Ashworth and J. Tunbridge (2000) A Geography of Heritage. London: Arnold.
Halley, P. (1987) Peter Halley: Collected Essays. Zurich: Bischofsberger Gallery.
Harvey, D. (1973) Social justice and the city. Baltimore: Johns Hopkins University Press.
Il Gazzettino (2000) Imprese a caccia di operai stranieri. November 2:3.
Indovina, F. (1990) La città diffusa. In La città diffusa. (F. Indovina, F. Matassoni, M. Savino, M. Sernini, M. Torres and L. Vettoretto, eds.) Venezia: IUAV.
Istituto Poster (2001) Crimalità a Nordest. Fondazione Nordest.
Jori, F. (2001) Assalti alle ville, ormai è incubo. Il Gazzettino September 5:1-2.
., (2002) Immigrati, bocciata la linea veneta. Il Gazzettino February 21:8.
Katz, C. (2001) Hiding the target: social reproduction in the privatised urban environment. In Postmodern Geography: Theory and Praxis. (C. Minca, ed.) Oxford: Blackwell.
Klein, N. (2000) No Logo. London: Flamingo.
Lando, F. and O. Tallone (2001) Industrializzazione e terziarizzazione diffusa. Il caso del nord-est (1971-1991) Nota di lavoro. Venezia: Università Ca'Foscari di Venezia.
Lanaro, S., ed. (1984) Storia d'Italia. Torino: Einaudi.
Lash, S. and J. Urry (1994) Economies of Signs and Spaces. Cambridge: Polity Press.
Lefebvre, H. (1990) The Production of Space. Oxford: Blackwell.
Meneghello, L. (1986) Libera nos a malo. Milano: Mondadori.
Olalquiaga, C. (1992) Megalopolis: Contemporary Cultural Sensibilities. Minneapolis: University of Minnesota Press.
Pacini, S. (2001) Dagli industriali case per extracomunitari. Il Gazzettino (insert: Il Veneto) June 29; 1)
Paolini, M. (1999) Bestiario Veneto. Parole mate. Pordenone: Edizioni Biblioteca dell'Immagine (book and video)
-, (2000) L'Anno Passato. Pordenone: Edizioni Biblioteca dell'Immagine.
Pennini, F (2001) Assalto nella villa d'un imprenditore vicentino: ennesima irruzione notturna di una banda di slavi. Il Gazzettino September 5:3.
Petrovich, G., ed. (2000) Cultura e società nel Veneto. Venezia: Marsilio.
Polhemos, T. (1998) Diesel: World Wide Wear. London: Thames and Hudson.
Possamai, P. (2001) NordEst, i distretti arrivano fino in Romania. La Repubblica Affari and Finanza. July 7:47.
Rosso, R. (1999) FoRty. Molvena: Diesel.
Rullani, E. (1995) Distretti industriali ed economia globale. Oltre il Ponte 50:5-61.

Rumiz, P. (1997) La secessione leggera. Roma: Editori Riuniti.
-, (2000) L'angoscia di tornare poveri nella terra del grande boom. La Repubblica July 18:27.
Rumiz, P. (2003a) È Oriente. Milano: Feltrinelli.
-, (2003b) Mestre, quei Tir bloccati dal traffico, un fiume di "schei" a passo d'uomo. La Repubblica February 25:13.
Scott, A. (1998) Regions and the World Economy: Oxford University Press.
-, (1988) New Industrial Spaces: Flexible Production, Organisation and Regional Development in North America and Western Europe. London: Pion.
Sforzi, F. (1991) Il distretto industriale marshalliano: elementi costitutivi e riscontro empirico nella realtà italiana. In Miti e realtà del modello italiano. Letture sull'economia periferica. (S. Conti and P.A. Julien, eds.) Bologna: Patron.
-, (1995) Sistemi locali di impresa e cambiamento industriale in Italia. Geotema 1(2)43-72.
Shields, R. (1991) Social Science and Postmodern Spatialisations: Jameson's Aesthetic of Cognitive Mapping. In Postmodernism and the Social Sciences. (J. Doherty, E. Graham and M. Malek, eds.) New York: St. Martin's Press.
Smith, N. (1996) The New Urban Frontier: Gentrification and the Revanchist City. London: Routledge.
Soja, E. (1996) Thirdspace. Journeys to Los Angeles and Other Real-and-Imagined Places. Oxford: Blackwell.
-, (2000) Postmetropolis. Critical Studies of Cities and Regions. Oxford: Blackwell.
Spielberg, S. (2002) Se lo straniero è un nemico. La Repubblica June 5:1-2.
SportSystem Montebelluna (2002) http://www.museoscarpone.it
Stella, G. A. (2000) Schei. Dal Boom alla Rivolta: Il Mitico Nordest. Milano: Mondadori.
-, (2001) Altivole, un abitante su sette è immigrato. Nel Trevigiano i cinesi insidiano i piccoli imprenditori tessili. Corriere della Sera March 19:17.
Storper, M. (1997) The Regional World: Territorial Development in a Global Economy. London: Guilford.
Storper, M. and A. Scott, eds. (1993) Pathways to Industrialisation and Regional Development. London: Routledge.
Tomasoni, S. (2001) Cuore di Nordest: Viaggio nel Vicentino. Schio: Edizioni Menin.
Trigilia, C. (1981) Le subculture politiche territoriali. Milano: Feltrinelli.
-, (1986a) Grandi partiti e piccole imprese. Comunisti e Democristiani nelle regioni a economia diffusa. Bologna: Il Mulino.
Tropea, S. (2001) Timisoara, nuova provincia del Nord-est industriale. La Repubblica Affari and Finanza. March 5:15.
Turri, E. (1995) Miracolo economico: dalla villa Veneta al capannone industriale. Verona: Cierre Edizioni.
-, (1998) Il Paesaggio Come Teatro. Venezia: Marsilio.
-, (2000) La megalopoli padana. Venezia: Marsilio.
Urry, J. (1990) The tourist gaze: leisure and travel in contemporary societies. London: Sage.
-, (1995) Consuming Places. London: Routledge.
Vagaggini, V. (1991) Quatro paradigmi per un distretto. In Miti e realtà del modello italiano. Letture sull'economia periferica. (S. Conti and P.A. Julien, eds.) Bologna: Patron.
Zizek, S. (1998) Ein Pladoyer fur die Intoleranz. Wien: Passagen.
Zukin, S. (1995) The Cultures of Cities. Oxford: Blackwell.

City of Angels? Lives and Struggles of Migrants in Bangkok

Alexander Horstmann[1]

Bangkok is by far the largest concentration of people in Thailand. The population reckons seven to eight million people and the tendency is increasing. The next biggest urban conglomeration, Chiang Mai in the north, counts one million people. Thus, Bangkok also is a main form of living for most of the Thai. Bangkok is a symbol of cultural representation and state cosmology. In this ideology, Bangkok is imagined as the centre of Thai civilisation and thus in a hierarchical relationship with other civilisations in the periphery. Bangkok is also a primate city of Southeast Asia. Hardly mentioned in the literature on global cities, Bangkok has been affected by globalisation since the fourteenth century as a centre of maritime trade. In the global markets, Bangkok is falling apart. Bangkok is characterised by harsh polarisation- into specialised spending service classes and low-paid temporary workers on their whims (Sassen 1991). Because Thailand was understood as a predominantly agrarian society, Bangkok was largely bypassed by sociologists and anthropologists. One of the first comprehensive ethnographies on Bangkok focused on the social organisation of the slum (Akin 1978). Since then, the slum was a major motif in the sociological and anthropological imagination of Bangkok. Two scholars did much to enhance our understanding of Bangkok- Rüdiger Korff and Marc Askew. Korff worked extensively on social relations of the slum, the social organisation of the city, the informal sector, everyday life and modernity in Bangkok and urban symbolism (Korff 1989, Evers and Korff 2000). Askew on the other hand was interested in thick description of well-grounded case studies, doing fieldwork with sex workers in red-light districts, small gardeners, middle-class townhouse settlements, slums and urban politics and representation (Askew 2002). Less known is the work of Thai scholars, because it is largely published in Thai-language journals and monographs. Here, the work of Akin Rabibhadana, Nithi Aeusriwongse and Paritta Chalermpow Koanantakool is singled out.[2]

---

[1] The paper draws on personal fieldwork in Bangkok 1993/1994 and on the work carried out by Askew (2002), Mills (1999) and Korff (1989). I also acknowledge communication with Jim Taylor who is editing his forthcoming book on Buddhist spaces in Bangkok. My fieldwork resulted in a study group on 'urban consumption and everyday life' and a homepage on Bangkok urban popular culture: http://www.watanasala.net.

[2] For a excellent introduction, see Paritta Chalermpow Koanantakool/Askew, Marc (1993)

In this essay, I want to highlight the role of migrants in the constitution of Bangkok as a living form, by shedding light on the lives and struggles of migrant workers. Further, I will also take a look at the migrant workers' negotiation with Bangkok, with the working conditions in which they are part and with their forms of organisation. While Bangkok is imagined as a "Thai" city, I want to highlight the fact that migrant workers come from outside, from China, Lao-speaking North-Eastern Thailand and Burma. The imagination of Bangkok as a homogenous Thai entity is a myth.

Migrants/difference from China, from Java, from India, from Northeast Thailand (Isan) and more recently, from the neighbouring countries- Burma, again China, Laos and Cambodia have been incorporated, conscripted, swallowed or rejected. It is the migrants/the outsiders who have literally *built* Bangkok and who are found in all the work that link Bangkok with the world and make huge contributions to its economy.

While migrants from Burma are concentrated in the border province of Ranong, migrants continue their careers into the centre- Bangkok- as students, construction workers, prostitutes, modern helots, etc. In Bangkok, they join a vast pool of cheap and flexible labour from Northeast Thailand (Isan). The young women and men from Isan work as pedicab drivers, factory labour, in the informal sector and in construction- increasingly competing with even cheaper labour from Burma.

Very little research has been carried out on the lives and struggles of migrants/the other in Bangkok.[3] The numbers of street children, beggars, cleaners are not known. What is sure is that this pool of urban labour is crucial to the maintenance and growth of the urban conglomerate. The migrants have given shape to the making of a cultural bricolage, in which differences and play are the norm. The others within Thai-Buddhist national culture are everywhere in the urban space of Bangkok's central business district, the hotels, the shops, the parking lots, the sweepers, the bus-drivers, the receptionists and the watchmen.

Here, we are concerned with people that are integral to urban life and to the role of Bangkok in the global economy. We like to show that immigration laid at the roots of Bangkok, of society, culture, economy, and of the state. The history of Southeast Asia is one of the ritual integration of the stranger into local society. Multi-culturalism, hardly discussed in Bangkok- is nothing new to the city. Today, Indian, Chinese, Vietnamese, Burmese, Khmer, Tamil and Indonesian culture is part and parcel of Bangkok.

---

[3] For a notable exception, see the series edited by Charnvit Kasetsiri: Thailand's neighbours in Southeast Asia funded and distributed by the Thailand Research Fund, in Thai language. For a comparative study in a different Asian setting, John Clammer shows in his recent book "Japan and its Other" how much the engagement with the other contributes to ethnic self-identity of modern Japan (Clammer 2001).

Immigration provided the pool of labour that enabled industrialization, the expansion of services and the integration of sweat shops into the world economy. The most recent wave of immigration brings a new urban lumpenproletariat of refugees and dissidents from Burma. To the disarray of the Thai state, Burmese students are organising in Bangkok or try to survive in low-profile jobs.

The outsiders/foreigners are not liked, but fairly needed. As the prices for land and housing climbed up, the labourers moved to illegal squatter areas, so-called slums.[4] The slums are in the central business area, like Klong Toey. Illegal squatter settlements grew in parallel to urbanisation, centralisation and rural poverty and are spread all over the city.

People from China, Java, India, Pakistan, and the Cham from Vietnam and Cambodia migrated to Bangkok in search of a better life or have been enslaved as war captives and brought to Bangkok by the Siamese army. All this outsiders are giving shape to the many localities in the City. Slowly, they are looking for their ecological ethnic niche in the City, are an integral part of it and shape its culture (e.g. Cohen 1997). Large-scale immigration occurred in great leaps. In this essay, I like to sketch three stories of immigration to Bangkok: Immigration of Chinese labour in the nineteenth and mid-twentieth century, rural-urban migration of hundreds of thousands of young rural women who migrate to Bangkok to fill the factories and sweatshops of the metropolis and the most recent wave of forced migration and refugees from Burma to Thailand and to Bangkok. All these stories, while filling books for each, illustrate the role of Bangkok in absorbing labour and relating to the world. The essay thus wants to shed light on the role of migrants in shaping Bangkok. On the way I want to question some of our "romantic" use and understanding of key words such as "community" or "locality" in the context of city and the production of its globality and cultural identity.

First, in the nineteenth century, Chinese migrant labourers arrived in the thousands in junks to work on the port of Bangkok. They constituted the first urban proletariat. When Chinese workers stopped working, Bangkok's economy came to a standstill. So the control over Chinese workers was vital to the Thai state. Second, Northeast Thailand provided the hinterland of Bangkok and supplied the metropolis with a vast pool of cheap and flexible labour. In the period from 1970 until today, people from Northeast Thailand migrate to Bangkok in the one hundred thousands. Northeast Thailand is the poorhouse of Thailand, with very arid land, poor harvests and low education. Seasonal labour is arriving during the dry season as there is nothing to do in the village. Especially young people are moving to the city, leaving old people and babies behind. Migration has a crucial gender aspect. The remittances sent from the city, especially from

---

[4] Further studies on slums in Bangkok include

daughters, are vital to the reproduction of the rural economy. On the global map of travel and fantasy, Bangkok stands out as a space of sexual pleasure and consumption. The commodification of sex work began to flourish in relation to the Vietnam war and developed in a very dynamic business. Sex work was one way to lure tourists from Europe, Japan and Taiwan to Bangkok. Finally, Bangkok provided a vast attraction for migrants from poor neighbouring countries in the latest process of regionalisation and the opening of borders. Refugees and migrants from Cambodia, Laos and war-torn Burma are to be found in the construction-sites of Bangkok, on the rubber plantations and on the ships, sometimes competing with North-eastern labour.
The concept of the borderland and global ethnic spaces (Cohen 1997, Donnan and Wilson 1999, Horstmann 2002, Horstmann and Wadley, forthcoming) shows, I argue, that the bounded concept of community in the city is not a concept that somehow faded away with globalisation- it was problematic from the beginning. John Eade, Martin Albrow, Jörg Dürrschmidt and Neil Washbourne show that the locals- far from living in traditional communities- reconstitute their ties in extended milieus, which transcend time and space (e.g. Dürrschmidt 2000 and 2002, Eade 1997). Outsiders/foreigners/migrants at the bottom of urban society not only played a crucial role in the constitution of Bangkok, but also in the constitution of globalism. Thus, the milieus of Chinese, Isan and Burmese migrants extend far beyond the boundaries of the City. The transnationalisation of labour and sexualities characterise the globality of Bangkok itself- namely the webs and relationships that the urban poor nurture with kin, acquaintances and friends- or, in the case of sex-workers, tourists- over great geographical distances. Chinese migrants were transported over the Chinese sea and many did not survive the journey. In Bangkok, Chinese males communicated with their families through letters. Many sex-workers have begun their careers in the low-paid sweat-shops, domestic service, or factories before entering the sex business. Many of them end up marrying one of their clients/lovers and move to Germany after exchanging love-letters for years. Burmese students seek political exile in Australia or Japan through Bangkok.
The steady influx of foreigners/outsiders into Bangkok sensitises us for the fact that the city of angels from the start was far from being a homogenous, pure city of the Thais, but always engaged foreign cultures. The foreigners/migrants/forced labour reproduced their ethnic identity and flavour in the imagined localities, which make the term 'indigenous urbanisation' in Southeast Asia problematic. The Chinese customs in a foreign land are nicely illustrated in the novel "Bhotan-Letters from Thailand", in which the traditional world of a Chinese migrant slowly dissolves. Numerous Isan vendors and cookeries attest to the fact that hundreds of thousands of factory workers move between

Bangkok and their home villages in Northeast Thailand. The tasty food also appeals to the sex-workers who meet in the cookeries of the inner-city to gossip about their pimps and clients. Indeed, the foreigners not only provided the labour for the construction of the monuments and palaces, they also contributed to the material culture of the City, including its inner-city slums, red-light districts and factory outlets.
Being illegal, Burmese migrants are vulnerable to harassment, arrest and super-exploitation. Chinese, Isan and Burmese migrants have in common that they are all crying for a re-conceptualisation of forms of belonging that belie academic inventions of traditional communities in the city. Rather, we should focus on the ways and tensions in which 'localities' are constituted, destroyed, policed, reconstituted and how diasporic cultures form their extended milieus against the pressure of assimilation. Until today, the Chinese stick to their advantageous ecological niche and to their Chinese temples and rituals and the Isan labourers stick to their food and to their dialect, as well as to their animistic practices.[5]

Urban Chinese Labour

In the early nineteenth century, supplies of labour were very scarce. To meet the enormous demand, the court increased labour supplies by capturing war captives and by attracting immigrants. The court put considerable effort into registering *phrai*, tattooing wrists, and chasing down runaways in order to secure enough labour to man the army, maintain the administration, build the palaces and temples of the new capital, and dig the canals required for trade and warfare.

The court imported Chinese to overcome the labour shortage. Six to eight thousand migrants arrived each year on the junks from the ports of Southern China. Around half of them returned to China after a few years, but the net annual inflow to Siam was around 3000. The rulers encouraged this migration. The Chinese were granted entry, allowed to travel freely, and excused corvée. Once in three years, they owed a poll-tax. By mid century they were around 40000-60000 Chinese in Bangkok (ibid.: 174).

By most accounts of the period, the Chinese in Bangkok outnumbered the Siamese, possibly by around two to one. As Pasuk and Baker argue, the court developed a dual policy on labour supplies, and maintained the policy until the end of the century. For state works in the city, the Chinese were preferable. The Court helped develop urban Siam as a Chinese preserve. In the 1860's, steamships increased the capacity and cheapened the price of passage from China. Recruiting and shipping

---

[5] More in-depth research needs to be done on the extended milieus of global diasporic cultures in the city.

labour became big business, both for Chinese labour agents and for the European shippers, who took over the routes. From the 1870's onwards, the demand for urban labour increased rapidly as the paddy, tin and timber trades grew. The increased demand was met almost wholly by Chinese immigration on the new steamships. From 1882 to 1917, Chinese immigration added around 450,000 to the population. The first census in 1904 showed that there were 200,000 Chinese in Bangkok, and around 400,000 in Siam as a whole. Skinner (1957: 74) argues that this may be a heavy underestimate, and the total was probably around 600,000. The Chinese also worked the sugar plantations in Prachinburi, Nakhorn Chaisi, and the tin-mining of Phuket. The government employed Chinese in large numbers to build the railways. The port became virtually a Chinese preserve. Much of the new urban businesses and shops were run by Chinese entrepreneurs who again favoured Chinese labour. By the turn of the century, Bangkok had some fifty rice-mills and around some fifty sawmills and again the labour force was primarily Chinese. During rapid urban growth from the 1880s to the 1910s, even the plentiful flow of immigrants could not keep up with demand. Foreign merchants joked that the Chinese worker had become "master of port" through awareness of his scarcity value (Skinner 1957: 116). To recruit labour for the Siam Cement factory opened in 1913, labour agents travelled to southern China and marched armies of recruits down to Bangkok overland. Among the immigrant Chinese, the main form of organisation was the *angyi*, which combined the functions of clan association labour exchange, protection racket, welfare society, and political club in ways similar to organisations among immigrant labour communities elsewhere. To the rulers, these "secret societies" were alien and by implication dangerous. From mid-century, the court grew nervous about the growing power of the Chinese and their organisations. The nature of government mechanisms of urban control and its combined fear of Chinese organisations ensured that the confrontations in the labour struggle was bloody and violent. In 1910, the government raised the poll-tax on the Chinese, and in reaction the Chinese associations organised a general strike which closed down the shops, ports, rice mills, construction sites, and rail ways for five days. The government attempted to control these outbreaks by negotiating with the *angyi*, by sending in the troops, and by putting troublemakers on the boat back home. After riots among rice mill workers in 1889, 900 were put on trial and punished with fines, prison, and flogging. Note that the local population sometimes used the legitimisation of the rulers to turn against the Chinese. When poor working conditions and wages touched off a riot in Chachoengsao, the government sent its troops and provoked the local population to turn on the Chinese and massacre several thousands.

Most migrants had a short-term working horizon. Employers and rulers treated them as renewable resource. The rulers attempted to manage the rebellious labour force through registration, deportation, and riot control. The Chinese brought with them a cultural system of shared values, of kinship, marriage, and business ethics, they were the architects of urban space, symbolised by the Chinese shop-house which precedents the townhouse settlements of the urban middle class- the *mubaarn jatsan*. In sum, the Chinese have been crucial to the expansion of markets and to its global integration, while the local population *phrais* and freed *that* left Bangkok for the agrarian frontier.[6]

Urban Isan Labour
In the late twentieth century, the Isan youth replaced the Chinese as main pool of urban labour. Hundreds of thousands of young rural women migrate to Bangkok to fill the factories and sweatshops of the metropolis. Local arenas of social and cultural production increasingly intersect with global processes of capitalist expansion and mass-market commodification. In her study *'Consuming Desires, Contested Selves'*, Mary Beth Mills (1999) goes beyond the abstract female global assembly line and explores the dynamics of self-estimation and respect which are involved in the decision of young women to accept low wages, harsh working conditions, and to resist sexualized discourses on prostitution and pre-marital sex in the city to which they are subjected in the media and in the home village.

In Baan Naa Sakae, Northeast Thailand, young women's responsibilities as members of households coupled with aspirations for desire and consuming selves to propel their movement into Bangkok jobs. There, they joined the thousands of other rural migrants as members of the cheap, flexible labour force that fueled Thailand's urban economic boom throughout the 1980s and 1990s. The young women are prepared to fill positions of domestic service, sweatshops, factories and construction which keep the urban giant moving. Migrants' urban experiences were most immediately affected by the kinds of jobs they entered. Baan Naa Sakae youth found work primarily in domestic service and in manufacturing. Mary Beth Mills succeeds in her study in illustrating the women migrants' negotiation of the self with the limiting and opening of options. While both forms of employment sharply limited avenues for agency and autonomy in the city, they did so in very different ways.

Domestic Service
"Lan went to Bangkok as a domestic servant. She was hired to cook and clean in the household of a distant relative. Land wages were

---

[6] This section relies on Pasuk/Baker (1995: 174-207) and on Skinner (1975).

embarrassingly low when she compared her monthly earnings of 1,000 baht to the nearly 3000 baht that she knew other women from Baan Naa Sakae were making at factory jobs. Still, Lan could ask for favours that would never be possible in a different situation. If she had a particular need, an illness or other emergency at home, Lan could ask for extra money. Her employer even participated in a merit-making ceremony for the temple of Baan Naa Sakae, the donations for which Lan helped to organise."

Domestic servants develop kinship relations with they employers, calling their employers naa (maternal aunt/uncle). This bun khun relationship offers the advantages of a secure source of income and assistance as well as the promise of extra cash or gifts of illness, debt, or other troubles arise back in the village. In the isolation of private households, migrants were aware of their vulnerability to abuse, including physical and sexual assault, withheld wages, inadequate food, or inhumane living conditions. The general dissatisfaction with which women viewed domestic service was reflected in the discourse of Bangkok middle class households that "good help" was hard to find. Most women judged their situation according in terms of the wages they earned (Ibid.: 114) and were ready to reject employer's claim on their personal loyalty if the wages were not good enough.

"Wan is from Khon Kaen province in the Northeast, and has worked in a large textile factory for the last twelve years. She described her experience while working as a domestic servant just after her arrival in the city. Her employer was a soldier, the friend of a cousin-by marriage who had helped Wan when she first got to Bangkok. The man treated her "like a family member, but the money just was not enough. "When friends told her of the chance for factory work, she decided to go."

Small Sweatshops

Migrants preferred small factories to domestic service because of the better wages and because they saw it as more independent during their leisure hours. Some of the people of Baan Naa Sakae found jobs in small family enterprises, where paternalistic relations continued to shape the labour process.

Maem worked in a small garment-manufacturing shop that was run by a couple with kinship ties to Baan Naa Sakae. In a small, three story row house in one of Bangkok's main garment districts, Maem worked with more than a dozen young women, including several from Baan Naa Sakae. On the ground level, the main workshop was occupied by long tables with industrial sewing machines. Maem and the other seamstresses sat on small wooden stools in front of their machines for eight or twelve hours at a time.

Maem was twenty-five and had come to Bangkok after an early marriage broke up. When Maem heard through the shop owners' cousins in Baan Naa Sakae that they needed more help, Maem left her son in her mother's care and headed to the city.
The restrictions in small factories are similar to those found in domestic service. The linkage of employee and employer through kinship and patronage connections in the village usually strengthens the owner's authority over new workers. The erratic pay of piece-rate work and the stresses of working as many as twenty hours a day during peak periods pose real economic and health problems. Finally the close quarters of sweatshop production subjects workers to the same round-the-clock surveillance with which domestic servants also must contend.

Factories
Despite strict regulations (no fans were allowed in the heat of the concrete rooms), labour control and sexual harassment of supervisors, and health complains (disrupted menstruation, frequent headaches, etc) factory work was best valued by most women migrants from Mahasarakham, because the work was better paid (including better-paid overtime shifts) and there was more freedom in leisure time. Finding and keeping such a job was not a simple task, since the limitless pool of migrants and potential migrants meant that few companies had problems recruiting employees. Listen to Noi, another woman from Ban Naa Sakae:

Sex Work
Bangkok's world of prostitution was established from the mid-nineteenth century and its growth was directly related to the demand for sexual services generated by the Chinese male immigrant workforce of the city. The Chinese quarter of Samphaeng was the centre of the city's brothels and the prostitutes were indentured Chinese and Japanese women trafficked into Siam. The involvement of Thai women was minimal at that time. So established was Sampheng as the city's red-light district that well into the twentieth century the term *Sao Sampheng* (*Sampheng Girl*) was widely used as a euphemism for prostitutes. In 1928, there were 203 licensed brothels with 974 prostitutes in Bangkok, although there were at least a further 2000 non-registred prostitutes working in the city (Askew 2002). Bangkok's foreign-orientated sex trade was stimulated from the mid-1960's by the surge in demand accompanying the US military Rest and Recreation (R and R) programme, which brought thousands of servicemen to the metropolis. It was Vietnam-related money flows that laid the basis for Bangkok's best known red-light district, *Patpong*. This foreign-orientated prostitution quickly became a gigantic business which

attracted male tourists with foreign currency and brought Bangkok an entry into a dictionary as a city with 'many prostitutes'.
Marc Askew argues that women sex workers should be perceived as agents, not as victims. The dominant form of prostitution engaged in by Thai women should be described as "open-ended" (Cohen 1996).

> "Understanding such pattern as practiced strategies of self-recovery is important. Such self-recovery requires transgression of normative cultural sanctions and necessitates movements between specialised sites of the sex-industry and public areas of the city. The women's encounters with the city can be interpreted from a life-course perspective as an experiment in life style changes stemming from personal crises. Open-ended prostitution is a conscious choice to defy normative constraints, in pursuit of cultural capital." (Askew 2002: 281)

The women engage their foreign partners in webs of sexual dependence, financial responsibilities and eventually, marriage and migration and use their body as a tool to escape from poverty and to support their children. Many of them were engaged in urban work, in hairdressings salons, factories and sweat-shops before entering prostitution. Like their sisters in the factory, they help to transform the city and are integrated in the international division of labour or international division of commercial sex. Recently, Thai women have become replaced by a vast pool of prostitutes from Burma, China, Laos and Vietnam. Recently, many of these women have been trafficked into prostitution and are the most vulnerable to HIV/AIDS infection.

Burmese Migrant Workers/Refugees
In constant fear of arrest, migrants from Burma have to hide in the dark corners of the metropolis or to use the support of sympathetic NGO's. People from Burma have migrated to every part of Thailand: to the eastern borders with Laos and Cambodia, and to the southern border with Malaysia. It is said that they will take any job that the Thais refuse to do, working on fishing trawlers, carrying timber in the jungle, selecting fish, peeling shrimp, doing labour in a rice mill. In fishing piers, forest plantations, fishery-related factories, all the workers are migrants. As a result of state persecution, Mon, Karen and Shan refugees/migrant workers are not able to organise effectively. Without any security and belonging, their sweat has replaced the hard and dangerous labour of Chinese and Isan workers.[7]

---

[7] For a moving portrait of Burmese migrant workers in Thailand, see Pim Koetsowang (2001) and Lang Hazel J. (2002) for Burmese refugees in Thailand.

Sticking together: Life-worlds of Migrants, Labourers, Sex-Workers
Connections with people from home are also a shield against the dangers and uncertainties of life alone in a hostile city. Young women migrants in Bangkok have to juggle growing *thansamay* (modern) autonomies with growing experiences of marginalisation. Migrants' urban sojourn begins as an encounter with a chaotic, sprawling giant. The uninitiated is overwhelmed by the noise and the traffic. Migrants help themselves by relying on kinship ties and friends in the city. This continuity of familiar relationships assists migrants in finding jobs, accommodation and to deal with the stress of urban pace. Like most young migrants, Tiw, remembers her first days in the capital as a period of difficult adjustment. "But", she said, "I was with my sister and there were others from *our* village working nearby, so it wasn't so bad." (ibid. 1999: 111). Almost none of the women Mills met made their first move without the assistance of friends and kin (112). It is not at all uncommon for young women to have a job waiting for them in the city before they left the village. Migrants go to Bangkok to 'visit' relatives, but find a job and stay on. People from Baan Naa Sakae relied on friends and kin to find city jobs. Migrants prefer work in factories to domestic service, because it is better paid and seen as more 'independent'. In Bangkok, young migrant women are subject of surveillance as maid or worker. However, the migrants develop strategies to deal with the pressure of their employers. The most important is sticking together with kin and friends in the locality. The dense networks provide security, a place to stay, job information and solidarity in hard times. Their outings (*thiaw*) in apartments of friends or Non-Governmental Organisations provide fun and relief from the stress of daily labour.

In the 1970s, some illegal squatter settlements like Klong Toey have already developed a system of committees to fight eviction. Events from the mid-1980's, set in motion changes in the tactics of the urban poor that involved more concerted efforts of lobbying, public demonstrations, the use of media, and the organisation of umbrella networks covering slum settlements. James Ockey has argued that it represents the birth of new forms of resistance, involving a transition in the mode of slum leadership, from traditional forms, relying on local gangsters, and patronage networks within slums, to modern forms, centering on more educated leaders who facilitate access to basic needs through formal NGO networks, lobbying and the media (Ockey 1996, 1997).

Conclusions
O'Connor's indigenous theory of urbanisation in Southeast Asia argues that urbanisation is organised around community and hierarchy. 'Community' is the personal relations among people in the city, while

'hierarchy' stands for the urban design of the elite in which everybody and every community has its ranks (O'Connor 1983).

In search of a better analytical tool, Hans-Dieter Evers, Rüdiger Korff and Erhard Berner developed the concept of locality (Evers/Korff 2000, Berner 1997, Berner/Korff 1995). Berner (1997: 57-8) proposes locality as a key framework to understand socio-spatial relationships underlying group identity of the urban poor. Locality, he argues, are 'socially defined and created spatial identities'. A key dimension of localities is that they are products of collective agency in the guise of locally-based organisations (Berner 1997).

Focusing on the mechanisms of control and discipline and on the forms of social organisation of migrant workers, I attempted to develop a framework for further research on Bangkok. This project deals with a basic tension of Bangkok. Bangkok is a vast magnet for desperate and poor migrants who seek a better life. Thus, migrant workers continue to flood the city and to provide the labour on which Bangkok depends for its survival. Shedding light on the social organisation of migrant workers, I show, how migrants are carving their cultural spaces in difficult circumstances.

It is no exaggeration to state that the presence of migrants in Bangkok questions traditional concepts of "community" and forces us to radically rethink the relation of the local and the global in the city. The concept of social agency allows, I suggest, for a more dynamic analysis of the tension between the local and the global in the city in terms of cultural location in the city (see Korff 1996). More research has to be done into the spatial practices of migrant workers in Bangkok from the perspective of the migrant workers.

References:
Akin, R. (1969) Rise and Fall of a Bangkok Slum. Bangkok: Thai Khadi
    Research Institute.
Askew, M. (1994) Bangkok: transformation of the Thai city, in Askew, M./Logan,
    W.S. (eds.) Cultural Identity and Urban Change in Southeast Asia.
    Interpretative Essays. Geelong: Deakin University Press.
-,   (1999) Labor, Love and Entanglement: Bangkok bar workers and the
    negotiation of selfhood, Crossroads: an interdisciplinary Journal of Southeast
    Asian Studies 13, 2, 1-28.
-,   (2002) Bangkok. Place, Practice and Representation. London/New York:
    Routledge.
Berner, E. (1997) Defending a Place in the City: Localities and the Struggle for
    Urban Land in Metro Manila, Quezon City: Ateneo de Manila University Press.
Berner, E.; Korff, R. (1995) Globalisation and local resistance: the creation
    of localities in Manila and Bangkok. In: International Journal of Urban and
    Regional Research 19, 2: 208-22.
Clammer, J. (2001) Japan and its Others. Globalisation, Difference and the
    Critique of Modernity. Melbourne: Transpacific Press.

Cohen, E. (1996) Thai Tourism: Hill Tribes, Islands and Open-Ended Prostitution. Bangkok: White Lotus.
Cohen, R. (1997) Global Diasporas. An introduction. Seattle: University of Washington Press.
Dürrschmidt, J. (2000) Everyday Lives in the Global City: The Delinking of Local and Milieu. London: Routledge
-, (2002) Globalisierung. Bielefeld: Transcript.
Eade, J. (ed.) Living the Global City. Globalisation as local process. London/New York: Routledge.
Evers, H. /Korff, R. (2000) Southeast Asian Urbanism. The Meaning and Power of Social Space. Hamburg: Lit.
Horstmann, A. (2002) Incorporation and Resistance: Border-Crossings and Social Transformation in Southeast Asia (Review Article). In: Antropologi Indonesia, 67, 12-29.
Korff, R. (1989) Bangkok and Modernity. Bangkok: Chulalongkorn University Social Research Institute.
-, (1993) Bangkok as a symbol? Ideology and everyday life constructions of Bangkok, in: Nas, P. J. M.. (ed.) Urban Symbolism: Leiden: Brill.
-, (1996) Global and Local Spheres: the diversity of Southeast Asian Urbanism, SOJOURN 11, 2, 288-313.
Mills, M. (1999) Thai women in the Global Labor Force. Consuming Desires, Contested Selves. New Jersey: Rutgers University Press.
Pasuk, P.; Baker, C. (1995) Thailand. Economy and Politics. Oxford University Press.
O'Connor, R. (1983) A theory of indigenous Southeast Asian Urbanism. Singapore: Institute of Southeast Asian Studies.
Ockey, J. (1996) Eviction and Changing Patterns of Leadership in Bangkok Slum Communities. Bulletin of Concerned Asian Scholars 20, 2, 46-61.
-, (1997) Weapons of the Urban Weak: Democracy and Resistance to Eviction in Bangkok Slum Communities. SOJOURN 12, No. 1, 1-25.
Paritta Chalermpow K. /Askew, M. (1993) Urban Life and Urban People in Transition: Synthesis Reports Vol. II, for the 1993 Year-End Conference: Who gets What and How? Challenges for the Future. Bangkok: Thai Development Research Institute.
Pim, K. (2001) In Search of Sunlight. Burmese Migrant Workers in Thailand. Bangkok: Orchid Press.
Skinner, W. (1957) Chinese society in Thailand: An Analytical History. Ithaca: Cornell University Press.

Globalisation and Urbanism: the case of a European peripheral region, Guadeloupe.

Karine Dupré

Globalisation is a process involving several dimensions at the same time, such as economic, politic, culture and communication. Nonetheless, the difficulty to find a proper definition to it also reveals its complexity. It is not an omnipotent, unidirectional machine levelling everything in its path but rather a phenomenon including one characteristic and its opposite. As the sociologist Tehranian Majid (2000) puts it "from a humanist perspective, globalisation entails both negative and positive consequences: it is both narrowing and widening the income gaps among and within nations, intensifying and diminishing political domination, and homogenising and pluralizing cultural identities".

Thus it seems relevant to use carefully this concept and even more so when talking about parts of the world, which are not "master pieces" on the checkerboard of globalisation.

Urbanism is certainly one particular aspect of life that is affected by the globalising process. The collapse of time and space, the standardisation of experience, needs and values are contributing to reshaping the city of today and its urban forms. Through various institutions and regulations the city has been and is conceived, while, simultaneously, urban realities are offering a landscape and practices not always in accord with the initial urban thinking. Besides, the city is not to be considered as a mere visible element, but rather as an active participant.

Guadeloupe, as such, is a very interesting study case. Part of the globalisation process by its historical attachment to France; and today a European extra peripheral region; it contains all types of apparent contradictions concerning the urbanism of its territory.

Our goal is to question the meaning of globalisation, when confronting urban thinking and urban realities. Thus, we will open this paper by presenting the actors of the urban process (thinkers and makers) for in Guadeloupe they are not always the expected ones, before continuing with the discussion.

Urban thinking in Guadeloupe

Urbanism is quite a recent concept but it does not mean that urban thinking did not exist before it. Cities' history reveals several examples of such thinking, like in the Greek civilisation or in the Chinese ones. In Guadeloupe, mainly one factor (altered by local specificities) has been shaping -and still is shaping- the urban thinking: the influence of France. The idea is to present this situation in its historical context.

To start with, Guadeloupe has experienced a past of colonisation. By the mid- seventieth century natives had almost all disappeared (by one way or another) and since they did not have any type of elaborated urban culture, everything had to be built and thought from the beginning.
French colons were ruling on an island whose population was largely composed of African slaves, who had not a say. But, unlike other colonies in the Caribbean, there never was any earnest wish to deal with urban planning from those in power.
Indeed, if we compare Cuba (Spanish colony), Jamaica (English colony) and Guadeloupe (French colony) on the same period (17th-18th century), we can quickly notice how Guadeloupe presented an undeveloped urban territory compared with the other islands. On a more qualitative approach, the comparison between the main cities of the three previously quoted islands, also shows the absence of systematic planning in the Guadeloupean case, even though some traditional colonial pattern, e.g. checkerboard, can be found (but in a small extent anyway).
This fact can be explained by the reasons, which had grounded the colonisation and by the importance given to the colony by its mainland.
Basically, Guadeloupe was a soil of benefits, satisfying the mere interests of traders and producers, as well as the kingdom's expansion. The island has never been considered as a possible terrain of mainland extension or as land for settling, unlike e.g. Cuba as the "little Spain" in the Spanish case. Thus urban thinking was not a priority for those in power who rather and -almost solely- needed plantations and harbours.[1]
By opposition, cities were important in Spanish colonies for they were conceived as the place where "civilisation" could be carried on (Yacou, 2002); in other words, they were considered as part of the scheme to succeed colonisation.
With humour, in the case of Guadeloupe, one could even thank the traditional rivalry between the French and the English, for it was under the short English domination (1759-1763) that the actual main city of the island (Pointe-à-Pitre) faced its first real urban development...
Nevertheless, in the 18th century, the colony being settled and wealth coming from the sugar-based economy, the first true attempts to plan the city, to embellish it, to regulate it, in other words to *think* it, were made.
Military engineers were the main thinkers. Primarily concerned by defence, they also were in charge of roads, fortifications and town planning. They had to come to Guadeloupe and as they had been educated in France, the reading of their works shows the influence of the Enlightenment period and other French trends. The 19th century was to

---

[1] The lack of a specialised office or administrative service in charge of the cities' development of the island is another evidence of the little interest in urban thinking.

comfort this phenomenon, replacing engineers of the King by engineers of the State. Concerning the territorial development of the island, it would be foolish to believe that urban thinking was commonly practised. Actually it was rather used for localised different entities, not automatically at the same time, hence inducing competition within Guadeloupean cities.[2]

In parallel, the lack of Architects or of other corpus to think over the urban besides engineers, demonstrates the persisting lack of interest towards the island on this subject. The reading of the Colony's Archives, on a modern period (1900-1946)[3], illustrates this fact in terms of reports from the Civil Engineering and Public Works' Office: small amount of workers, restricted budget, lack of educated technicians, lack of planning and projects, provide evidence of the little value given to the urban development of the island. Even though the cyclone of 1928, which entirely destroyed Guadeloupe, has had great effects on urban planning and architecture for there was an urgent need of reconstruction, the same archives picture a motionless situation. Truly, numerous institutional buildings were achieved under the supervision of the architect Ali Tur, commissioned by the French State (1929-1933); truly again numerous projects were designed to embellish, to equip, to drain and reorganize cities and towns of Guadeloupe. Yet, one could wonder whether it was not due to the incredible work talent and force of one particular man, the architect Ali Tur, rather than to the influence of a larger body. The fact that lot of projects or programs were rarely fully completed after his departure, such as the embellishment plan for the city of Pointe-à-Pitre (designed in 1929 by A. Tur and the urban planner R. Danger, Giordani 1996) or for the city of Basse-Terre, etc, seems to confirm this

However, in the mid-20th century, the concept of urban thinking started gaining status.

If the French State remained the principal urban thinker, sending technocrats, engineers, urban planners, architects, etc; political situation created before and after the assimilation law (1946) was to modify the general context. Indeed, by gaining the status of a French Department (instead that of a colony's), the Guadeloupean population was aspiring to French equality. This meant to share the same values *and* the same benefits or advantages. As such, urbanism was not necessarily considered as a domination process, since people wanted to live in the same way as the French mainland inhabitants, but rather as a levelling

---

[2] See the rivalry between the cities of Pointe-à-Pitre and Basse-Terre expressed in the book of Pérotin-Dumont A. (2000) La ville aux îles, la ville dans l'île

[3] Source: French Overseas Archives, collection TP, in Aix-en-Provence (France).

process to fulfil the equality contract. The fact that France had such a central role -through the State- was guaranteeing the adhesion to such conditions and could also be seen as part of this equalitarian process (for it was done in the same way as in other parts of France).

At this point, there was a major shift because urban development became an *active* concept and was not considered anymore as a "passive" activity.

The consequences were radical. As in the past, conceptions, models and thinkers were imported from France but this time, parameters had changed. Time-delay, which so far had influenced urban production and thinking, was not anymore to play such an important role. Indeed, when time-delay had induced the use of styles or urban patterns behind their accurate period (e.g. Renaissance style into the 19th century, etc)[4], the minimising of it, brought -almost simultaneously with France- large-scale programs but without any distance. This is how, for example, in the 1960-70's, the city of Pointe-à-Pitre went under a vast renovation program, utilising "modern" architectural vocabulary (hygiene, tower or bar-like shape, concrete and prefabricated buildings, etc.), while the Parisian suburbs were being erected. In the same way, as before ideas had to cross the sea, they nowadays could reach you the very next day...At the same time, where the intrinsic difference of sites could not allow similar buildings (regarding the material or even the form of the building), the increased system of transportation and the evolution of technologies would allow it.

It resulted into an inappropriate urbanism, faithfully imported from France.

Lately, another important shift has taken place. The decentralisation process, initiated under Mitterrand's presidency (1981), has, for the first time, insured power to local instances.

However, the situation remained quite similar to the past one, for in its general comprehension, urban planning is mostly considered as a French institutional activity (from the law making to the building permit process), supported by officials and a small amount of private firms, more or less well informed and educated on the local particularities. Nowadays, the importation of mainland French workers for both the public and certain private domains still is common practice. Most important, Guadeloupeans have to go to mainland to receive higher education in architecture or urban planning. Indeed, despite the creation of the University Antilles-Guyane in the 1970's, that offers today a certain variety of educations (from business or law studies to experimental sciences or literature studies), there is still no School of Architecture, nor graduate course on Urban Planning in Guadeloupe or other French

---

[4] "archaism of thinking" says D. Bégot, in « Architectures créoles », 269-275

Overseas Department: you need to be educated in France, where, of course, there is no special program on earthquake building, cyclone's management, etc...

Through both processes, it is then a French savoir-faire, practically not adapted to local needs, that is exported. Besides, in terms of local experts, there is little concurrence: in fact, how many of those who have been educated in France, are effectively coming back to Guadeloupe? Like Lucien Parize, civil servant in charge of the urban planning office of Pointe-à-Pitre, comments it: "if the Architects Tessier and Crevaux have been chosen in the sixties (for the renovation program of Pointe-à-Pitre), the simple reason is because there was no one else!"

Finally, it is easy to understand that such a continuing French influence has been lately supported by the globalisation process. Indeed urban thinking has been using the homogenisation of experiences and needs to transfer spatial models on the Guadeloupean territory. At the same time, the desire for common values and the undoubtedly attraction to reach "modern" standards by the insular population, have strongly helped this type of urban thinking.[5]

However, urban realities and mechanisms soften this situation for schemes and realisations do not always tend towards the expected result. This is what we propose to look at in a second phase.

Urban realities

There is no doubt about it, the actual general framework of urban realities is institutional. Laws are made in France and special arrangement is made to fit them to the local case of Guadeloupe.[6] Institutions are the same as in France. That is to say that the "equality" goal has been achieved. To build in France or in Guadeloupe, you have basically to accomplish the same steps.

Besides, the institutionalisation of the status of Guadeloupe within Europe, as an ultraperipheral region, has induced convergence towards European assets e.g. in territorial development.

---

[5] See again what happened to some quarters of Pointe-à-Pitre (main economic city of Guadeloupe) in the 1960-70's: under the name of "great renovation" full districts were demolished and replaced by large-scale concrete programs. It was considered as a big step towards modernity. In 2000, an act has been signed to demolish part of these programs (rue du Pape) for they don't fit anymore the modern criteria... Source: Urban Planning Office of Pointe-à-Pitre, 2002.

[6] Clause 73 of the 1946's Constitution: overseas departments are subject to ordinary laws and decrees but "can also be subject to adapted schemes needed by their particular situation", quoted in Michalon T.(2002) Sur les spécificités de l'Outre-mer: enquête et propositions, in: La France et les Outre-Mers, CNRS Edition, 424

However, three elements need to be considered closely, regarding the urban realities of the island: they are the geoclimatical surrounding, the weight of individual force and a certain longing for modernity.
Even if the change of status has attenuated differences between French and Guadeloupean citizens, there is one thing it had no influence on: this is the natural factors. As such, Guadeloupe is particularly "gifted" for it is regularly subject to earthquake, volcano's eruption or cyclones. In this context, urban realities are heavily dependent on "Mother Nature". Actually, it goes as far as the frequency of natural events influence the urban development of towns (Dupré 2002)[7]. Moreover, this situation is reinforced by the financing system working, which will most likely give loans to State's buildings (e.g. schools, infrastructure, social housing) when technical exigencies are fulfilled prior to comfort.
Besides, the articulation between urban thinking and urban realities seems to be quite weak under this aspect. Indeed, urban planning can be done to develop a district, to embellish a city, etc; but as soon as a natural disaster will hit the island, the initial focus will be displaced. Priority will be given to reconstruction, to prevention, pushing behind initial priorities...
Even if the depicted situation is slightly caricatured; one has to acknowledge that it is not far from the reality for there is obviously a gap between urban thinking and urban realities. The main thing actually to be understood is that it is not possible to develop a proper urban thinking in Guadeloupe as long as local particularities are not taken into account at a global level.[8]
This becomes even more accurate when talking about the commitment of individuals in urban development.Indeed, if we have seen the central role of institutions in urban planning (from macro- to micro-level), actions of individuals, regarding urban realities, are not to be neglected.
Actually, we are not talking merely of one re-arranging his/her lot, but rather of full districts being born out of private will. One just needs to go in some districts of Pointe-à-Pitre (the main economic city of Guadeloupe) or in the countryside to realise how the urban process has developed far from any institutional regulations. People have settled on a piece of land which, in the best case, is their own (they can be renting or just squatting the lot); they have then erected houses but not necessarily

---

[7] Thus, it sounds misplaced to maintain French models as an absolute reference for France does not present at all the same geoclimatic characteristics, but this is another discussion.

[8] Of course, we can try and this has been done for decades, but then we enter in a vicious circle: copied urban production, repairs-adaptation, natural disaster, repairs or new copied production, etc (instead of acknowledgment of local specificities- urban production)

according to the zoning regulation nor to the land qualities (thus enhancing sometimes the risk of land sliding). Most of the time, their wallet has been the final decision-maker concerning the material they have used. This does not always mean material respecting construction standards in terms of earthquake or cyclone safety. The result is an uncontrolled urban development, made of wood, concrete, metal-sheets, etc, in a general form lacking basic elements of infrastructure such as road, water, and electricity network.

This fact is primordial to understanding the urban phenomenon in Guadeloupe for it reveals a *quasi-freedom* of building. More precise studies (Dupré 2002) have even demonstrated the lack of urban planning or urban strategy for the urban development of two towns of Guadeloupe on a contemporary time-span period, and, at the same time, evidence that urban practice is clearly dissociated from urban regulation and planning (at the level of individual or companies): it is relatively easy to build where and when you want without any building permit or following urban regulations.

In addition, institutions are thwarted by a building force which is fast. Interviews with local planners reveal that when a new road has been built, township prefers "to let people appropriate themselves the land besides this new road rather than to plan something that will take too long to be built"![9]

At last, even if literature might dream of an existing urban reflection[10] in these individual actions, it would be honest to admit that there rarely is an idea of conceiving the urban process as a whole by individuals. The urban thinking is rather narrowed to a short-seeing area, restricted to the house or nearby plots, which are anyway often familial.

Two principal factors could explain this situation, totally different from France. Namely they are the failure of the assimilation law, to some extent, and the fact that anyway Guadeloupe remains far from mainland.

Indeed, even if institutions and laws have been implemented in Guadeloupe, it does not mean that, broadly and in its smallest details, the way of thinking became totally French. According to Michalon (2002), such dichotomy is possible because there was not a common cultural background in both places. He argues, where the city in Europe has been conceived on reason and rationality, in Guadeloupe it was conceived on affectivity. The idea of merit by the work and competition extremely prised in Europe was not of equal impact in colonies where slavery was the ruling system. In the latter, the domination of few was reigning on the majority of the population, which had to survive one way

---

[9] Interviews with P. Guyon, urban planner for the town of Gosier, January- May 2002, and quotation from the mayor of Gosier, May 2002.

[10] Read Chamoiseau P. Texaco, Ed. Gallimard, 1992

or the other. Work was not prised as such, for it meant being enslaved. Thus, the family bond and relationships became crucial. Today, this way of thinking is persisting, for there is difficulty to understand the institutions beyond the physical persons who are working for them. Michalon even adds that the notion of State, of law, of citizenship remain hence an abstract concept. In this sense, the institutional "marronnage"[11] is seen as a way to escape the constraints of the Republic, in the same way as before some slaves would run away from their masters. If the statement of Michalon could easily be contested for Guadeloupean *wanted* to be part of the Republic and e.g. give their tribute to military service (Bégot, 2003), one cannot deny that today it remains a certain romanticism of the "marronnage", visible in Rastafarian communities or slum-like districts: freedom of not paying taxes, nor rent, freedom to do without any bond to the society (Yerro, 2002)

To anchor this statement more into real life, we could describe the situation when a township decides to renovate one of its districts. Renovation in Guadeloupe is mostly done at the poorest or less developed districts.[12] One has to understand that such renovation programs touch usually people, who do not necessarily have access to running water, private facilities or legal electricity. But, what is particular is that the same people would in majority prefer to stay in their district, rather than to move into social housing, because of the way of life they wish to maintain (Dupré, 2002). However, honesty should also add that the same people would be queuing to live in the new social housing, as soon as it has been built. We can then understand quickly how this conflicting relation to the built space can offer some type of resistance against institutional planning.

As such, we can see that the law of assimilation has failed to reach every component of the Guadeloupean society, and most important, its cultural marrow (Michalon 2002).

Besides, individual forces are somehow helped by what in the law has once been recognised as the singularity of the island. In some cases, the law has even been adapted to the local context. We could mention two examples, which are illustrating it. One is the indivisible co-ownership law, which is heavily restraining the institutional power, for there is a need of agreement between *all* the owners of a plot before any action concerning it. The other is the particularity of Guadeloupe to pay indemnities for houses which will be demolished. Those two examples are important, because, in both cases, institutions do not have the key-role. In the first example the right of every individual is taken into account

---

[11] from the word describing an escaped slave, "marron"

[12] Whether we agree or not to the name "slum" given to some districts of some cities, is not our point here.

before the common right, while in the second example, it makes it really expensive for the township to build on already constructed plots.[13]

But, on top of those statements, it becomes really interesting to observe more precisely the results of such phenomena. If an individual building has to be taken seriously into consideration in the shaping of urban realities, one could be even more surprised by the architectural language commonly used by individuals or institutions. Actually, concrete and its combined vocabulary (such as surface, function, form, etc.), is the dominant common point. In less than 50 years, it has reached almost every existing building, made by institutions or private builders. Little by little, traditional environment is disappearing to the benefit of a modern one. The cube-like shape has been spread at every corner of the territory, and even if today a certain revival for traditional building type can be acknowledged, it is not conceived without concrete nor functional modern elements. Actually, this revival can be also considered as a westernisation of traditional particularities for there is an adjustment of the latest to the international requirement of buildings.

At the same time, it is true that the wooden cabin remains in the urban landscape but our point here is to explain how modernity is conceived at every level of the society as a goal to reach and to be entitled of. Simply, in these exotic regions, it is easy to understand such a desire for modernity to bypass the restrictive and - alas – long - lasting discourse of "exotic-indigenous-undeveloped". Four-lane motorways, kilometre-long façade building (directly inherited from Le Corbusier principles), minimalist windows or glass wall, and poetry of air conditioning have been used in this purpose against wooden cabins, clusters and galleries... In this sense, globalisation is just comforting the process, accentuating the eternal dilemma tradition/modern.

In conclusion, despite similarities for the last fifty years between French (to be understood as mainland) and Guadeloupean urban processes and products, which show a strong impact of western models as well as "modern" patterns, there is undeniably a gap between urban realities and urban thinking. Moreover, it seems that the acknowledged tendency is mainly for them to adjust to each other, but, one could question whether it is really a proper solution and whether there is not instead a need to reformulate both entities into the context of globalisation.

In fact, since mass culture brought TV, hamburgers and cars in every home, to resume it quite simply and ironically, while technologies such as mobile phone, internet and development of means of transportation have tremendously increased, we could then wonder what the meaning of globalisation is, when confronting urban thinking and realities.

---

[13] Unless they find other ways such as expulsion

Meaning of globalisation as it concerns urbanism in Guadeloupe
Even though western patterns and urban forms reveal an influence of the global urban thinking, born from the Modern movement and the international thinking of the last decades, one has to remember two important things when talking about Guadeloupe. The first is that urban realities expressed rather a two-fold process in Guadeloupe, defined by institutions *and* individuals. The second is that globalisation is a process affecting Guadeloupe mainly *through* France, and this is even more accurate when talking about urban phenomena.

Therefore, we could wonder whether globalisation should essentially mean *French-isation* and by extension, at the image of Russian dolls, westernisation; while, in a second time, we could wonder whether other alternatives could not be considered.

To the light of the brief historical reminder that has previously been proposed, we could state that the urban thinking in Guadeloupe has more or less been the fact of those politically and economically in power: which is to say, France, and made according to mostly one way of thinking, which is to say the French way. "French-isation", and thus westernisation, has undoubtedly dominated.

Considering globalisation, one could say that two specific factors have largely contributed to the urban landscape of the 20th century. One is the *simultaneity* of information which, with combined technologies, has allowed the spread of information to almost every corner of the globe at the same time. The second factor is the introduction of *new building materials* (e.g. metal, reinforced concrete), which, associated with new techniques (e.g. prefabrication), delivers a new formulation of ideologies and aesthetics. Both factors together have undoubtedly helped to drastically transform the designing and building processes, and thus to transform the urban landscape.

In the case of Guadeloupe, those factors surely introduced a new vocabulary into the research for functionality and hygiene, but this lacked necessary qualities: comfort too often became an accessory; integration with the natural environment was neglected, as was the local way of life; and interest in the traditional architecture, with its care for detail for example, was totally neglected (Baptistide, 1980) or became too expensive. Basically, both factors have favoured policies copied from France. The results are visible today in their physical expression, but also in the mode of living that has been implanted by it.

They show the failure of such a system, because globalisation has just increased the gap between urban thinking and urban realities (e.g. how European regulation can fit Guadeloupe?), instead of tightening urban processes together.

Moreover, present situation underlines how the debate on globalisation's meaning should change its targets, for globalisation is not anymore restricted to institutional level (as the reconstruction of Guadeloupe after 1928 could symbolise it) but touches every layer of the society and hence affects the general thinking. There has been a change from institutional globalisation into general globalisation, if such pleonasm can be used.

To illustrate our saying, one just needs to drive along the main roads of Guadeloupe and to read and observe the surrounding.

In fact, the late trend concerning indifferently private or public housing is to propose a so-called "local" architecture. Through advertisements like "live in a Caribbean allotment" or "build your real Creole villa", the idea is to attract people by presenting them a product appealing by its traditional qualities. However, the meticulous observation and analysis of such buildings and urban forms expose that their traditional characteristics are more concentrated in details of façade, on the exterior image, (like decoration, the use of wood here and there or the designing of a sloping roof), rather than the use of real traditional structural elements or forms (such as outside kitchen, natural ventilation, etc.) Furthermore, within the small array of chosen elements for reflecting a traditional vocabulary, we could even assert there has been a process of westernising. Indeed, those "traditional" qualities have been adjusted so as to fit the international (or at least the transnational) requirements of buildings. For example, the width of the wooden panels is set to the industrial criteria (far from the traditional one); gingerbread decorations are manufactured, whereas they were supposed to show the individual skills of the house's owner; the space below a sloping roof can be inhabited while its initial purpose was to offer natural ventilation...

Nevertheless, beyond the simple statement, we need to regard this phenomenon at another level. Actually, it reflects the use of culture for identity purposes, which in itself is not new: it could be also called regionalism in other parts of the world.

Therefore, it is easy to understand that globalisation of *thinking* is playing its part in this process, since the claim of one's culture is a global trend. Here localism is invoked, but without realising it is done in conformity with the global process.

As such, to our initial question of whether globalisation unavoidably means westernisation, we can affirm, in the particular case of Guadeloupe, it has been the main implementing factor and still is. Three main reasons could explain it, which are namely the sequels of History, the continuum between globalisation of practices and globalisation of thinking, and the lack of proper identity of the island.

Indeed, the context in Guadeloupe clearly reveals a strong dependency towards France, which is not merely economic, but also societal. As said before, globalisation is made through France as a direct consequence of colonial past, and it has hence induced a certain type of globalisation of thinking and practices.

Besides, this type of globalisation has been developed on the fact that there has been continuous moves from globalisation of practices to globalisation of thinking, by opposition to other parts of the world where globalisation of practices are totally in rupture with thinking. In fact, as we have explained it earlier, even if local practices in Guadeloupe demonstrate a strong weight of the individual forces, the same practices are bond to a global way of building and conceiving the building. Therefore, all layers of society have been hit by globalisation, even if admittedly at different degrees.

At last, westernisation has been made possible by the question of identity in the island. Indeed what is really Guadeloupe? A European Region, a French department, a Caribbean island..? The multitude of answers is actually revealing that none of them can really fit Guadeloupe, or, considering it the other way around, it also can reveal that all of them could fit Guadeloupe. Then, the "in-between position" of Guadeloupe becomes evident and can partly explain the persisting conflicts (social, economical, political, etc) within the island. For, at the moment, there is no true identity that could be spelled aloud, we can asset that westernisation has been used as a levelling instrument, to reach French identity.

If we ask then, *should* globalisation necessarily mean westernisation, to the light of the Guadeloupean case, we can only say no. Indeed, we hope to have proved enough that such a system has failed because it misses attachment to the local context.

We could then wonder whether there could not be other alternatives.

According to some radical scholars, there is no possibility to understand really the meaning of globalisation if one does not reconsider the whole concept. According to Grosfoguel (2002), globalisation is just a continuum of Eurocentrism, and it could bypass the western strong ideology, only the day when thinking globalisation would be made on totally new foundations.

If, more modestly, we come back to globalisation from the urbanism point of view, we could consider it as a tool rather than something to be subject to. In this sense, to quote Benjamin (1978) who says "urban meaning is the interface between personal memories and experiences, and the historical construction of dominant meaning and values" could enlighten the present Guadeloupean urban context for it seems that only part of its definition has been taken into account. Following Benjamin's lines, globalisation could find a new meaning in helping to restore what is missing ("personal memories and experiences") and to valorise the local particularities. Broadly globalisation could serve localism and for Guadeloupe remains today at the periphery of a centre, it becomes out of date to maintain a single-focused north-south relationship when a south-south relation is obviously lacking.

Furthermore, globalisation could be considered as a theorising tool to be used for the urban process. Theory is helpful in the sense it gives instruments of analysis, tools of understanding, means to go somehow quicker towards the final goals. However, for each city has its own history, own patterns, we propose that globalisation could help by refining properties of each, instead of equalising them.

Conclusion

Even though this presentation has to be understood as rather restricted and drastically simplified, the conclusion is definitely that the meaning of globalisation cannot continue to be westernisation, while confronting urban realities and urban thinking. Too many various criteria intervene in the urban process, which cannot be restricted to one unique moulding type.

Urban realities are one of these criteria and we expect this paper has made clear enough that urban realities are not necessarily the exact reflect of the thinking, but/and could be also modified reflect, inheritance reflect from previous time or sometimes, even something totally unexpected, for a city does not only depend of its thinkers and builders but also from its natural environmental process.

Besides, we hope the concept of city has been understood here in its widest meaning, and that the question of *the point of view* became a crucial one to the reader. Indeed, if for some, the city is a territory, delimited by cadastral boundaries; for others, it is a question of inhabitants' number (200 inhabitants in Denmark, 2000 inhabitants in France, 50 000 in Japan...). In the same way, the city cannot really be defined by its forms for there are a multitude of them: state-city, harbour-city, belt-city, insular-city... Thus, "what is the city?" remains an open debate.

Nevertheless, we could agree the city is a place which gathers humans as well as exchanges processes; a place that transforms the products, and definitely a place of representation (Flagie, 1999). Since "the city of all is not the city of everyone" to quote Body-Gendrot (2001), and, under the context of globalisation, we then believe there is a need of epistemological rupture and of re-conceptualisation to think anew the representation of the space, if one wants to find "solutions" to the problematic of the city.

At last, for there is a diversity of regions within Europe, we modestly hope that this paper has contributed to understanding urbanism within globalisation, as a phenomenon that needs to be based on the recognition and respect of local influences and qualities. Furthermore, could we not emphasise what those regions –like Guadeloupe- could

bring to Europe, as suggested by Azzi (2002), rather than the other way around; and stop thinking about a European identity but rather about European identification, which, as a less fixed and rigid notion, would allow a variety at different times?
Because, after all, one has to remember, that in terms of globalisation, Guadeloupe –as many other places- has a long-term experience: indeed, with the colonial system based on the international trade triangle (goods, slaves, money), was it not already an existing type of global form of economy, politics and society?

References:
Azzi, G.C. (2002) L'Union Européenne et l'Outre-Mer in : La France et les Outre-Mers, l'enjeu multiculturel, 559-568, Hermès 32-33, CNRS Editions.
Baptistide, J. (1982) L'habitat en Guadeloupe. In : Atlas de la Guadeloupe, CEGET-CNRS, Bordeaux.
Bégot, D. (1990) directed by, La Grande Encyclopédie de la Caraïbe, Ed. Sanoli.
(2002-2003) interviews with, unpublished
Benjamin, W. (1978) One way street and other writings, Verso.
Berthelot, J. and Gaume, M. (1982) Kaz antiyé, l'Habitat populaire aux Antilles, Ed. Perspectives Créoles.
Body-Gendrot, S. (2001) Multiculturalism and cities, Seminar in Helsinki.
Chamoiseau, P. (1992) Texaco, Ed.Gallimard.
Dupré K. (2002) Permanencies and ruptures of the urban forms of Guadeloupean boroughs: the case of Gosier and Trois-Rivières, from 1928 until today, licentiate thesis, non published
Flagie, A. (2000) Living in the French Tropics in: Europandom.
Giordani, J.P. (1996) La Guadeloupe face à son patrimoine, Karthala,.
Gorsfoguel, R. (2002) The Modern/Colonial/Capitalist World-System in the Twentieth Century, Greenwood Press,
Michalon, T. (2002) Sur les « spécificités » de l'Outre-mer : enquête et propositions in : La France et les Outre-Mers, l'enjeu multiculturel, 423-433, Hermès 32-33, CNRS Editions.
Miles, W. (2001) Fifty years off Assimilation: Assessing France's Experience of Caribbean Decolonisation Through Administrative Reform", in Islands at the Crossroads directed by Ramos, A. G. Ian Randle Publishers
Pérotin-Dumont A. (2000) La ville aux îles, la ville dans l'île, Basse-Terre et Pointe-à-Pitre, Guadeloupe 1650-1820, Ed. Karthala
Savage, M. and Warde, A. (eds) (1993) Urban sociology, capitalism and modernity, Macmillan.
Tehranian, M. (2000) in "Conference on globalisation", http://www.britannica.com/7b/article
Tribillon, J.F. (1990) L'urbanisme, Ed. La Découverte.
Yerro P.H. (2002) Transferts, emprunts, résurgence: horizon d'une recherché sur le mouvement rastafari, Euroseminar in Martinique

The European City in Transition

Edited by Dieter Hassenpflug und Frank Eckardt

Vol. 1 Frank Eckardt / Dieter Hassenpflug (eds.): Consumption and the Post-Industrial City. 2003.
Vol. 2 Frank Eckard / Dieter Hassenpflug (eds.): Urbanism and Globalization. 2004.

Karin Feiler (ed.)
European Forum on Sustainability of the Club of Rome

Sustainability Creates New Prosperity

**Basis for a New World Order, New Economics and Environmental Protection. Review by Members of The Club of Rome and International Experts. Preface by Klaus Töpfer.
With Contributions by Martin Bartenstein, Orio Giarini, Hans Küng, Uwe Möller, Patrick M. Liedtke, Mahendra Shah, Franz Josef Radermacher, Walter R. Stahel, Ernst Ulrich von Weizsäcker**

Frankfurt am Main, Berlin, Bern, Bruxelles, New York, Oxford, Wien, 2004. 239 pp.
ISBN 3-631-51973-7 / US-ISBN 0-8204-6549-6 · pb. € 19.80*

Since the report to The Club of Rome *Limits of Growth* was published some 30 years ago, the question is still open which approach we must take with our planet. Three factors will have the most influence on the global development of the environment: demographic and climate development and the potential for innovation. The concept of sustainability requires long-term thinking in order to use natural resources in such a way that future generations have the same opportunities we do. This message is confirmed in this review by the members of the Club of Rome's European Forum on Sustainability, which was founded in autumn 2002 in Vienna by the European Support Centre of the Club of Rome in co-operation with the Austrian Federal Ministry for Economic Affairs and Labour and in partnership with the United Nations Information Service (UNIS) Vienna, together with high-level experts and scientists. An immediate and extensive global course correction across the board would, however, be required. Thus far in fact, the price paid for the success of globalisation has been very high – environmental degradation and a global social split. This review presents as potential solutions a new economic model, an international treaty between the North and the South, a fundamental right to food and the principles of a sustainable retirement reform.

Contents: The Significance of Sustainability – Sustainability of Prosperity · Sustainability: Expectations and Reality · Sustainable Development: A Contradiction in Terms or an Economic Necessity · World History from the Viewpoint of Sustainable Development · The Climate Change: Mitigation and Adoption

Frankfurt am Main · Berlin · Bern · Bruxelles · New York · Oxford · Wien
Distribution: Verlag Peter Lang AG
Moosstr. 1, CH-2542 Pieterlen
Telefax 00 41 (0) 32 / 376 17 27

*The €-price includes German tax rate
Prices are subject to change without notice
Homepage http://www.peterlang.de